HERITAGE
KEYWORDS

Rhetoric and Redescription in Cultural Heritage

EDITED BY *Kathryn Lafrenz Samuels and Trinidad Rico*

UNIVERSITY PRESS OF COLORADO

Boulder

Published by University Press of Colorado
5589 Arapahoe Avenue, Suite 206C
Boulder, Colorado 80303
All rights reserved
Printed in the United States of America

The University Press of Colorado is a proud member of
Association of American University Presses.

The University Press of Colorado is a cooperative publishing enterprise supported, in part, by Adams State University, Colorado State University, Fort Lewis College, Metropolitan State University of Denver, Regis University, University of Colorado, University of Northern Colorado, Utah State University, and Western State Colorado University.

∞ This paper meets the requirements of the ANSI/NISO Z39.48-1992 (Permanence of Paper).

Cover Art "Typographic Wall Calendar 2014" by Harald Geisler (haraldgeisler.com)
"Stunning reinterpretation of a calendar is a masterful example of how a designer can completely flip a genre signifier on its head. Geisler reimagines calendars in order to change the way we visualize time, and in turn, redefines what it means to save the date."
—Mike McGregor, Kickstarter

The Typographic Wall Calendar is made of exactly the number of used keyboard keys (i.e., 2000 and 15) that represent the year.

Since 2009 it is printed in original size. Prints can be ordered at www.haraldgeisler.com.

The University Press of Colorado gratefully acknowledges the generous support of the University College London Qatar toward the publication of this book.

Library of Congress Cataloging-in-Publication Data

Heritage keywords : rhetoric and redescription in cultural heritage / [edited by] Kathryn Lafrenz Samuels and Trinidad Rico.
   pages cm
 Includes bibliographical references.
  ISBN 978-1-60732-383-9 (paper) — ISBN 978-1-60732-384-6 (ebook)
  1. Cultural property—Protection—Study and teaching. 2. Cultural property—Protection—Terminology. 3. Historic preservation—Study and teaching. 4. Historic preservation—Terminology. 5. Rhetoric—Social aspects. 6. Rhetoric—Political aspects. 7. Description (Rhetoric)—Social aspects. 8. Description (Rhetoric)—Political aspects. I. Lafrenz Samuels, Kathryn. II. Rico, Trinidad.
  CC135.H462 2015
  363.6'907—dc23
                              2014046104

24   23   22   21   20   19   18   17   16   15   10   9   8   7   6   5   4   3   2   1

To Lynn

Contents

Figures

AHD	Authorized Heritage Discourse
CBD	Convention on Biological Diversity
CHwB	Cultural Heritage without Borders
CoE	Council of Europe
CRM	Cultural resource management
EUROMED	Euro-Mediterranean Partnership
GCI	Getty Conservation Institute
ICBS	International Committee of the Blue Shield
ICCROM	International Centre for the Study of the Conservation and Restoration of Cultural Property
ICH	Intangible cultural heritage
ICMM	International Council on Mining and Metals
ICOM	International Council of Museums
ICOMOS	International Council on Monuments and Sites
IHM	International heritage management
IK	Indigenous knowledge

IMF	International Monetary Fund
IUCN	International Union for Conservation of Nature
IWGIA	International Work Group for Indigenous Affairs
NAGPRA	Native American Graves Protection and Repatriation Act
NGO	Non-governmental organization
SPAB	Society for the Protection of Ancient Buildings
UN	United Nations
UNESCO	United Nations Educational, Scientific and Cultural Organization
UNIDROIT	International Institute for the Unification of Private Law
UNWTO	United Nations World Tourism Organization
WCED	World Commission on Environment and Development
WCPA	World Commission on Protected Areas
WHS	World Heritage Site
WMF	World Monuments Fund

Heritage Conventions, Guidelines, and
Legal Instruments Cited

Art Institute of Chicago et al. *Declaration on the Importance and Value of Universal Museums* (2004)
http://icom.museum/fileadmin/user_upload/pdf/ICOM_News/2004-1/ENG/p4_2004-1.pdf

Australia, *Native Title Act* (Cth) (1993)
http://www.comlaw.gov.au/Details/C2013C00415

Council of Europe, *Declaration on the Role of Voluntary Organisations in the Field of Cultural Heritage* (2001)
https://wcd.coe.int/ViewDoc.jsp?id=204231&Site=CM

Council of Europe, *Framework Convention on the Value of Cultural Heritage for Society* (2005)
http://conventions.coe.int/Treaty/en/Treaties/Html/199.htm

Hague Conference on Private and International Law, *Convention for the Protection of Cultural Property in the Event of Armed Conflict* (1954)
http://www.icrc.org/ihl/INTRO/400

ICOM, *Code of Ethics* (1986, revised 2004)
http://icom.museum/the-vision/code-of-ethics/

ICOMOS, *The Nara Document on Authenticity* (1994)
http://www.icomos.org/charters/nara-e.pdf

ICOMOS, *International Cultural Tourism Charter* (1999)
http://www.international.icomos.org/charters/tourism_e.pdf

Italy v. Marion True and Robert E. Hecht Trib. Roma, sez. VI pen., 13 ottobre 2010,
n. 19360/10

Lao People's Democratic Republic, *National Heritage Law* (2005)

Metropolitan Museum of Art and Republic of Italy, *Agreement* (2006)

New Zealand, *National Parks Act* (1980)
http://www.legislation.govt.nz/act/public/1980/0066/latest/DLM36963.html

Rio Earth Summit, *Convention on Biological Diversity* (1992)
https://www.cbd.int/convention/text/

Second International Congress of Architects and Specialists of Historic Buildings,
Venice Charter for the Conservation and Restoration of Monuments and Sites (1964)
http://www.international.icomos.org/charters/venice_e.pdf

Society for American Archaeology, *Principles of Archaeological Ethics* (1996)
http://www.saa.org/AbouttheSociety/PrinciplesofArchaeologicalEthics/tabid/203
/Default.aspx

UNESCO, *Convention on the Means of Prohibiting and Preventing the Illicit Import,
Export and Transfer of Ownership of Cultural Property* (1970)
http://portal.unesco.org/en/ev.php-URL_ID=13039&URL_DO=DO_
TOPIC&URL_SECTION=201.html

UNESCO, *Convention Concerning the Protection of the World Cultural and Natural
Heritage* (1972)
http://portal.unesco.org/en/ev.php-URL_ID=13055&URL_DO=DO_
TOPIC&URL_SECTION=201.html

UNESCO, *Recommendation on the Safeguarding of Traditional Culture and Folklore*
(1989)
http://portal.unesco.org/en/ev.php-URL_ID=13141&URL_DO=DO_
TOPIC&URL_SECTION=201.html

UNESCO, *Second Protocol to the Hague Convention of 1954 for the Protection of Cultural Property in the Event of Armed Conflict* (1999)
http://www.icrc.org/ihl.nsf/INTRO/590

UNESCO, *Proclamation of the Masterpieces of the Oral and Intangible Heritage of Humanity* (2001–2005)
http://www.unesco.org/culture/ich/?pg=00103

UNESCO, *Convention for the Safeguarding of the Intangible Cultural Heritage* (2003)
http://www.unesco.org/culture/ich/index.php?lg=en&pg=00006

UNESCO, *Convention on the Protection and Promotion of the Diversity of Cultural Expressions* (2005)
http://portal.unesco.org/en/ev.php-URL_ID=31038&URL_DO=DO_TOPIC&URL_SECTION=201.html

UNESCO, *World Heritage Sustainable Tourism Program Charter* (2008)

UNESCO, *Expert Meeting on Community Involvement in Safeguarding Intangible Cultural Heritage: Towards the Implementation of the 2003 Convention* (2006)
http://unesdoc.unesco.org/images/0014/001459/145919e.pdf

UNESCO, *Operational Guidelines for the Implementation of the World Heritage Convention* (updated periodically)
http://whc.unesco.org/en/guidelines/

UNIDROIT, *Convention on Stolen or Illegally Exported Cultural Objects* (1995)
http://www.unidroit.org/instruments/cultural-property/1995-convention

United Kingdom of Great Britain and Ireland, *Ancient Monuments Protection Act* (1882)
http://heritagelaw.org/AMA-1882-

United States of America, *Convention on Cultural Property Implementation Act.* 19 U.S.C. §2601 et seq. (1983)
http://eca.state.gov/files/bureau/97-446.pdf

United States of America, *Native American Graves Protection and Repatriation Act.* 25 U.S.C. §3001 et seq. (1990)
http://www.nps.gov/nagpra/MANDATES/INDEX.HTM

United States of America, *Visual Artists Rights Act.* 17 U.S.C. §106A. (1990)
http://www.law.cornell.edu/uscode/text/17/106A

United States of America v. Frederick Schultz 333 F.3d 393 (2nd Cir. 2003)

UNWTO, *Hue Declaration on Cultural Tourism and Poverty Alleviation*, UN World
   Tourism Organization (2004)
http://sdt.unwto.org/sites/all/files/pdf/vietnam_finrep.pdf

HERITAGE KEYWORDS

Introduction 1

Heritage as Persuasion

KATHRYN LAFRENZ SAMUELS

Against the backdrop of increasing social change, an urgency courses through contemporary life for weaving the past into the present. The process of folding past conditions into present ones is selective; it has to be, given the richly textured inheritance bestowed on each passing generation (Trouillot 1995). The result over the past century plus has been a gradual refining of practices and ways of talking about what came before, encompassed by the concept of 'cultural heritage.' Cultural heritage is variously invoked as something (some object, site, building, landscape, traditional practice) with historic connections that must be properly tended to, as well as the field of expertise that has developed around this care.

Over time, or at critical moments provoked by shifting events, these practices and languages of heritage became incorporated into political and legal institutions with jurisdiction over local, regional (e.g., state), national, or international bodies of governance. National standards have traditionally been the most influential in institutionalizing how heritage is dealt with, but increasingly so too are international norms codified within an expanding oeuvre of global conventions, recommendations, lists, safeguards, management guidelines, and reports picked up as 'best practices.' This expansion at the national and international level

DOI: 10.5876/9781607323846.c001

3

follows broader social trends within which cultural heritage bears increasing relevance. Concomitant with increasing relevance, heritage must be made to work within these systems whose thrust is to norm and generalize. In this volume we offer one particular intervention into these joined processes of expansion and codification within the field of heritage.

We explore the *rhetoric* of cultural heritage, and we do so in two respects.[1] First, we ask how heritage acts as a kind of rhetoric ('heritage as persuasion'), being mobilized creatively within a wide array of social, political, economic, and moral contexts where it gives persuasive force to particular standpoints, perspectives, and claims. This kind of heritage rhetoric can be witnessed especially within appeals to social justice, public sentiment, and the international community, as well as within struggles over cultural resources, where the object or site takes on significance well beyond its more mundane historical value. 'Heritage as persuasion' foregrounds the innovative reworking of cultural heritage and its expansive propensities flowing from its will to relevance. Yet, second, to have greatest efficacy such arguments must be made through existing institutional mechanisms and discourses, an existing 'rhetoric of heritage' that maps out the strength and range of possible uses and meanings within which cultural heritage can be mobilized. For the 'rhetoric of heritage,' one example would be the "Authorized Heritage Discourse" (AHD) outlined by Laurajane Smith (2006). However, accounts of AHD run the risk of painting a fairly bleak picture, of a consistent and hegemonic system immune to external challenges and change. Focusing on the 'rhetoric of heritage' will tend to emphasize codification and institutionalization. The point is that both sides of rhetoric—heritage as persuasion, and rhetoric of heritage; expansion and codification—are required in order to better account for change and development in heritage and foreground the creative work of heritage today.

Certain words give resonance to the tasks of heritage. As Raymond Williams (1976; revised and updated by Bennett, Grossberg, and Morris 2005) undertook in *Keywords: A Vocabulary of Culture and Society*, there are "significant, binding words in certain activities and their interpretation" where "certain uses bound together certain ways of seeing culture and society" (Williams 1976: 15; quoted in Aldenderfer 2011: 487). We argue that heritage is an important lens for seeing culture and society in the present-day, and this volume addresses certain binding words for heritage, e.g., cultural property, intangible heritage, authenticity. However, the collection here is not exhaustive, nor would it attempt to be. We resist codification insofar as this volume highlights heritage as dynamic and resourceful, and we do so through a focus on rhetoric. Communities or practitioners may actively push back against such attempts at codification, and even succeed in changing the field of heritage practice. Such changes may in turn become the subject of codification. For example, the concept of intangible heritage coalesced as a critique of the material-based focus on built heritage and cultural property, and intangible heritage has since seen elaboration across a suite of international conventions, lists, and sites.

In other words, the process is iterative and open-ended, so any collection on heritage key concepts is necessarily provisional. At the same time, individual keywords gain important advantages from having coherent definitions, when the aim is to work through institutional mechanisms for change. Again, though, we place emphasis on mechanisms of change, and not definitional coherence endstop. Contributors to the volume showcase the creative possibilities of heritage unbound from codifying gestures, rather than attempt a synoptic 'authoritative' account of the particular heritage keyword under discussion.

We argue that through rhetoric we can begin to theorize and put into practice mechanisms for transforming prevailing heritage vocabularies, encouraging alternate meanings, and innovating new terminologies. Some terms face rhetorical culs-de-sac of sorts, whereby their narrow and increasingly empty usage circumscribes their potential for inspiring a diversity of meanings and perspectives. Other terms bear a rich history of legal and extra-legal uses, and might be characterized by specific institutional mechanisms for altering their legitimate meaning. In these cases extra attention must be paid to such mechanisms, to work from within institutions for transformation. Further, no term or concept exists in isolation, but together form persuasive assemblages, where each is contingent on the shifting relationships between other components embedded within a given context. The concept of 'cultural heritage' itself could be outlined via such assemblages of terms and their mobilizations, some of which I trace in the following discussion.

CULTURAL HERITAGE

First, it is also helpful to consider briefly how cultural heritage has been defined within the primary heritage conventions and literature on the subject. The UNESCO 1972 *Convention Concerning the Protection of the World Cultural and Natural Heritage* specifically takes cultural heritage to mean monuments, groups of buildings, and sites (of outstanding universal value). The 1972 *Convention* addressed these categories of 'immovable cultural heritage,' in distinction to the moveable cultural heritage (e.g., paintings, sculptures, coins, manuscripts, etc.), called 'cultural property' at the time, covered by the

UNESCO 1970 *Convention on the Means of Prohibiting and Preventing the Illicit Import, Export and Transfer of Ownership of Cultural Property.*

The idea of 'intangible heritage' introduced in the UNESCO 2003 *Convention for the Safeguarding of the Intangible Cultural Heritage* effectively extended the concept of cultural heritage to include "practices, representations, expressions, knowledge, skills," e.g., spiritual practices, folklore, song, dance, cuisine, etc., "as well as the instruments, objects, artifacts and cultural spaces associated therewith" (Article II.1). The Council of Europe's 2005 *Framework Convention on the Value of Cultural Heritage for Society* (known as the Faro Convention) defined cultural heritage in relation to communities as "a group of resources inherited from the past which people identify, independently of ownership, as a reflection and expression of their constantly evolving values, beliefs, knowledge and traditions. It includes all aspects of the environment resulting from the interaction between people and place through time" (Article 2a). The definition provided by the Faro Convention situates cultural heritage within its broader social and political contexts, emphasizing the active role of individuals and communities in sustaining cultural heritage and transmitting it to future generations.

Such is the way cultural heritage has been codified within the international system, and national approaches are so numerous that it makes little sense to catalog them here. However, other conceptions of cultural heritage can be found within the growing literature on the subject. Cultural heritage is rarely explicitly defined by scholars, but one of the earliest interlocutors, David Lowenthal (1997: 4), quipped heritage to be "antiquities, roots, identity, belonging." He likened the new focus on heritage to the semantic shift seen in French *patrimoine* (patrimony) from "goods inherited from parents," to "bequests from remote forebears and cultural legacies in general." Sharing sensibilities with 'history' and 'tradition,' Lowenthal noted that heritage nevertheless enjoyed a much more extensive social relevance and reach (Lowenthal 1997: 3). Blake (2000: 68) reminds us that this social relevance is central to conceptions of heritage, comprising the 'cultural' half of the term 'cultural heritage.' In a similar vein, "heritage is that part of the past which we select in the present for contemporary purposes, whether they be economic or cultural (including political and social factors), and choose to bequeath to the future," the worth of which "rests less in their intrinsic merit than in a complex array of contemporary values, demands and even moralities" (Ashworth and Graham 2005: 7). This societal relevance, moreover, is tightly interwoven with instigating change: "the major use of heritage is to mobilize people and resources, to reform discourses, and to transform practices . . . Don't be fooled by the talk of preservation: all heritage is change" (Hafstein 2012: 502).

THE RHETORICAL EDGE OF CULTURAL HERITAGE

Why rhetoric? We frame the volume around rhetoric to emphasize the creative capacities of heritage. In the following I explain in further detail why attention to the rhetorical nature of heritage is worthwhile for giving firmer grip to the present relevance of heritage. Recent work in anthropology has pursued the rhetorical nature of culture, where culture is understood not as a set of defining practices and beliefs, but rather a spectrum of possible actions and responses, a range of strategic practices acceptable in a given society (e.g., Coombe and Herman 2004; Meyer and Girke 2011; Strecker and Tyler 2009). Michael Carrithers (2005a, 2005b, 2009) has given the most penetrating vision on culture as rhetoric, arguing that it provides more direct access to the historicity and creativity of social life. He positions anthropology as a "knowledge of possibilities and not just of certainties" (Carrithers 2005a: 434), in which rhetoric can raise in sharp relief the historicity of social life, because "the schemas of culture are not in themselves determining, but are tools used by people to determine themselves and others . . . to persuade and convince, and so to move the social situation from one state to another" (Carrithers 2005b: 581). The only constant is creativity.

Further, a number of previous works in archaeology and heritage studies can be pointed to that are of kindred spirit to a rhetoric approach, such as attention to narrative (Habu, Fawcett, and Matsunaga 2008; Joyce 2002; Pluciennik 1999), language (Colwell-Chanthaphonh 2009), semiotics (Preucel and Bauer 2001; Bauer 2013), dialogue (Harrison 2013), and discourse (Smith 2006; Waterton, Smith, and Campbell 2006). Rhetoric depends on narrative forms, language, semiotics, dialogue, and discourses, but we suggest rhetoric is more.

Rhetoric specifically *mobilizes* and *motivates*, giving reasons and courses for action. We are interested in the rhetoric of heritage because of the increasingly strategic role that heritage plays in a wide range of social, political, and economic struggles in our contemporary world. The past is mobilized in the present: it becomes a standpoint, a performance, a metaphor, an ironic juxtaposition, an alternative vision, or a competing narrative for making strategic moves in broader struggles. The will to relevance that distinguishes cultural heritage as a social phenomenon means that heritage must constantly adapt to changing social and political exigencies. We use rhetoric as a focusing device that illustrates transformative action and future-oriented possibilities, drawing on the past to suggest new social formations. For these reasons, we focus on heritage as a kind of strategy ('heritage as persuasion'), examined in this volume across the wide spectrum of contexts and agendas in which the past is implicated.

Therefore, investigating the rhetorical edge of cultural heritage might draw on elements of communication like narrative, discourse, and semiotics, but does so specifically with an eye toward its persuasive capacity to mobilize and motivate specific actions, especially actions that effect social and political change. Contributions to this volume do so by positioning heritage as a social practice, redefining conceptions of community, foregrounding the central role played by expertise, highlighting democratic practice, and above all underscoring mechanisms of change in cultural heritage.

For example, several chapters present daily practices and material culture as rhetorical strategies that break beyond discourse. A call for more research on heritage practices, alongside discourse, is highlighted by Malcolm A. Cooper (Chapter 10) based on his experience in cultural resource management in Great Britain. Cooper argues that discourse takes on a more determining character than actually exists because of the tendency to focus on discursive evidence like policy and legislation, without also taking into account associated heritage *practices*. Legislation and policies become translated through processes of decision-making that are influenced by, among other things, political pressure, media, public opinion, legal interpretation, and the specific perspectives brought by different disciplines, professions, departments, even individuals.

Robert Preucel and Regis Pecos (Chapter 14) also foreground practice, noting the practice-oriented nature of placemaking, which proceeds through both discursive and material practices including social institutions and technical practices. Placemaking is "a technology of reordering reality, and its success depends upon the degree to which this refashioning generates habitual action." Concepts like 'place,' 'heritage,' and 'cultural resource' have no separate meaning for the Cochiti Pueblo in the American Southwest, and "fail to express the core values of what it means to be *of Cochiti*." However, such terms are used strategically by combining them with Cochiti traditional core values, and provide an example of alternative heritage discourses being placed alongside dominant discourses, without being reduced to them.

Embodied ritual practice and performance are meanwhile the focus of Anna Karlström's (Chapter 2) reworking of the well-established term 'authenticity' in heritage research and management. Like Preucel and Pecos, her account makes room for alternate worldviews to coexist with prevailing heritage practices. Specifically she advocates for the acknowledgment and toleration of multiple frames of reference, in this case "alternative perceptions of materiality and preservation" where authenticity arises through embodied practice in local popular religion in Southeast Asia. Moreover, Karlström argues that for concepts deeply embedded in heritage management, like authenticity, they can not and should not be rejected outright, but rather worked through internally to pull out the fluid and dynamic strands of the concept.

Images are also a powerful rhetorical medium, especially for showcasing material culture. Paul Lane (Chapter 16) analyzes both images and texts circulating within the tourism industry to promote East Africa. Drawing on the five canons of rhetorical argument—invention, arrangement, style, memory, and delivery—developed from the works of Aristotle and Cicero, Lane demonstrates how indigenous knowledge is presented as the "epitome of sustainable practice," even though heritage tourism obliges pastoralists into a long-term sedentism that threatens the ecological fabric of a landscape. As raised by several contributors to the volume, it is the temporal character of heritage that gives it especial purchase in some rhetorical concepts (like sustainability) more than others. Orthogonal to the temporal dynamism that cultural heritage supports, sustainability rhetoric instead has an ossifying effect for East African pastoralists and their way of life, freezing seasonal movements and adaptive capacities.

RHETORIC AND REDESCRIPTION

It is necessary to note, too, what rhetoric is *not*, at least within the purposes of this volume. This is because rhetoric bears a deep history within the western classical tradition and has animated such a number of interlocutors that its meanings are varied. Rhetoric is not pursued here as empty talk that twists in any manipulation to win an argument, being unconcerned with moral consequences or social facts. Nor does it take heritage today as 'mere rhetoric,' another form of empty talk that assumes no purpose or responsibility for connecting with practical matters. It would be wrong to presume that individuals or communities are simply 'using' cultural heritage, unscrupulously, as some kind of realpolitik, except insofar as "the form of rule shape[s] the form of revolt against it" (Mamdani 1996: 147). As Mahmood Mamdani described ethnicity in colonial contexts, ethnicity "was never just about identity. Its two contradictory moments involved both social control and social emancipation. This is why it makes sense neither just to embrace ethnicity uncritically nor simply to reject it one-sidedly" (1996: 147). We make the same case for heritage, except the conditions of power have changed, so that whereas ethnicity 'made sense' in the particular racializing rubric of colonialism, now heritage is both "social control and social emancipation" within present-day conditions of post-colonialism and globalization.

In what Richard Rorty coined 'the rhetorical turn' (cf. Simons 1990; Palonen 1997) and Bryan Garsten (2011) called the 'rhetoric revival,' political philosophers have lifted rhetoric from ill regard to a new positive reception. In particular, the renewed interest in rhetoric has been driven by work on deliberative democracy, which we draw on to suggest deliberative approaches to heritage. This volume seeks to demonstrate how the transformation of rhetorical language and the innovation of new vocabularies—a process that Rorty (1989) has called 'redescription'—can provide an incisive tool for the work of heritage in our world today. Redescription shares affinities with the conceptual and intellectual history of Reinhart Koselleck (2004), who speaks of the 'carrying capacity of a word,' and Quentin Skinner (1988: 282), who emphasized what he called the 'anthropological justification' for studying conceptual change. We aim to investigate how, as Wittgenstein (1984: 46) put it, 'words are deeds,' motivating forces for change.

Rorty (1989) provides an account of redescription in *Contingency, Irony, and Solidarity*, where he agues that "the chief instrument for cultural change" is "a talent for speaking differently" (1989: 7). The idea is to radically transform a vocabulary that has become calcified, "an entrenched vocabulary which has become a nuisance" (1989: 9). The main trouble is that discussion and analysis inevitably meet a dead-end of intractable problems of inquiry. Rorty gives as an example dualisms inherited from the Platonic tradition that now compose Western thinking: e.g., appearance-reality, matter-mind, subject-object, and the related subjectivism-objectivism. The issue of dualisms in heritage is picked up by a number of contributors, and discussed in further depth in Trinidad Rico's conclusion to this volume (Chapter 17). Attempts to resolve such intractable issues are invariably "inconclusive or question-begging" (Rorty 1989: 9), because arguments against a vocabulary must be phrased in terms of that vocabulary, which has already set the parameters and standards of justification of what makes for coherent, consistent, and meaningful argument. Therefore, the goal of redescription is to rearrange and show matters in a different light:

> to redescribe lots and lots of things in new ways, until you have created a pattern of linguistic behavior . . . it says things like 'try thinking of it this way' . . . It does not try to pretend to have a better candidate for doing the same things which we did when we spoke in the old way. Rather, it suggests that we

might want to stop doing those things and do something else. But it does not argue for this suggestion on the basis of antecedent criteria common to the old and new language games. For just insofar as the new language really is new, there will be no such criteria. (Rorty 1989: 9)

The goal then is not to argue against current ways of describing the world, but to offer more attractive vocabularies, metaphors, and modes of speech, which over time will become more literalized (Rorty 1989: 44).

The study of heritage and daily practices that surround its care similarly face challenges of description. Such challenges in describing the condition of heritage in our contemporary world limit the capacities for what can be said about heritage and therefore how it is understood and how it is mobilized. Some may argue that the language of heritage at our disposal is sufficient, and that redescription is therefore an obfuscation or waste of time. However, the will to relevance that characterizes cultural heritage argues against status quo contentment (as the conditions of contemporary life change so too must heritage), especially within pursuits of social and global justice. Another argument for redescription is the central role of designation in heritage management. That is, much of the work surrounding cultural heritage is definitional in nature, concerned with recognizing what is, and is not, heritage. With so much riding on defining heritage, questioning the meaning of heritage keywords is part of a healthy system of checks-and-balances vis-à-vis the designation process. Further, the codification of heritage keywords that takes place at the international level is bound up with an ineffectual institutional system of governance in danger of becoming moribund. The significant challenges confronting the international system (e.g., UNESCO, see Meskell 2013a, 2013b), coupled with its lowest common denominator political aspirations as a result of slow negotiations, weak enforcement, and power imbalances between states (Hale and Held 2011) means that heritage terms composed to work within this system will be similarly outmoded.

Rorty's interpretive method of redescription has been picked up by political philosophers interested in reviving rhetoric along Aristotelian lines (e.g., Abizadeh 2002; Fontana, Nederman, and Remer 2004; Garsten 2006; O'Neill 2002; Yack 2006). It was the dualism between rhetoric and reality that was reinforced by the sophistic tradition, critiqued by Plato, and is responsible for the pejorative connotations associated with rhetoric today. However, this dualism dissolves in Aristotle's account of rhetoric, which saw rhetoric as "the faculty of observing in a given case the available means of persuasion" (*On Rhetoric* 1355b25–27). Aristotle's account offers rhetoric as a form of reasoning, designed not "to unmask the pretensions of reason but instead to analyze how reasoning works in public" (Garsten 2011: 169). In addition to logical argument (*logos*), other forms of public reasoning include appeals to emotions (*pathos*) and building the audience's trust in a speaker, i.e., in the character of the speaker (*ethos*).

In the realm of political theory, rhetoric has been of particular importance to deliberative democracy, which is a theoretical orientation meant to supplement and enrich the quality of existing democratic practices (Chambers 2012: 53). In everyday language, deliberation is typically understood as careful consideration before a decision. Like rhetoric it is inherently practical in orientation, asking "what is to be done?" and seeks reasons for or against following particular courses of action. The opposite of reason-giving is manipulation and coercion (2012: 58–59). Further, reason-giving can come in many forms, which is where rhetoric entered into scholarly discussion on deliberative democracy. Rhetoric offered a more capacious account of deliberation, for example in drawing out affective registers of public reasoning and directing attention to audience. The turn to rhetoric was in response to the narrow terms of deliberation developed by Jürgen Habermas (1996) and others (Cohen 1989; Benhabib 1996; Gutmann and Thompson 1996), who were concerned with producing democratically legitimate outcomes and therefore excluded some forms of discourse and speech because they were seen as potentially coercive, threatening the listeners' autonomy by moving them in some respect (Garsten 2011: 167).

Importantly, rhetoric in deliberative situations regularly draws on cultural heritage. This is especially the case once deliberation is reconceptualized from the idealized Habermasian approach to a systemic approach, which link together the many nodes of deliberative activity that takes place in society, from venues like news media and town hall meetings to chats with friends over coffee (Parkinson and Mansbridge 2012; Dryzek 2010a, 2010b; Bohman 2007). Scott Welsh (2002: 680) notes that effective rhetoric:

> constantly aims to modify prevailing cultural terminologies that constitute the common points of reference and governing meanings of a political collectivity. Inasmuch as such common meanings make cooperation and productive communication possible, they are equally understood as sites of intense struggle. We would be better served by thinking of public deliberation as a common struggle over cultural resources marshaled in day-to-day politics.

More than being a kind of background material from which arguments are constructed, Welsh argues that cultural resources are the "'source' and 'goal' of effective political speech" (Welsh 2002: 690), producing new vocabularies and meanings, alternative metaphors, narratives, ironic juxtapositions, and reinterpreted historical events (2002: 691). Therefore the goal is not necessarily to change the minds of individuals as much as "to effect a shift in prevailing relationships between the meanings of key cultural-political terms, events, or narratives" (2002: 690). This is an important distinction, and positions heritage as itself composing a unique and integral rhetorical strategy, providing agonistic sites of struggle and conflict over broader social and material vocabularies.

RETHINKING COMMUNITY AND SCALE

Welsh's (2002) argument also highlights the symbiotic relationship between participatory democracy and deliberative democracy, with participatory approaches being focused on cooperation and dialogue, and deliberative approaches on difference and plurality. Attention to struggle, strategy, and difference can therefore complement the aims of participatory and collaborative approaches to heritage and archaeology, so that rhetoric has the potential to be a powerful tool for more equitable and inclusive research programs. Within political theory, the relationships between participatory and deliberative democracy have been variously imagined (Hauptmann 2001; Fung 2004; Mutz 2006; Wojcieszak, Baek, and Delli Carpini 2010). For the purposes of cultural heritage, one productive intersection between deliberative and participatory approaches would be to focus on how rhetoric shapes a sense of community, for example "by accommodating itself to the particular, substantive, beliefs and desires of the listeners it addresses" (Beiner 1983: 101), or by 'bridging' together the concerns of disparate groups (Dryzek 2010b).

In part, the purpose of this volume is to offer deliberative heritage as a complement to participatory methods for the purposes of strengthening heritage engagement. For example, participatory methodologies work well for small-scale or face-to-face collaborations. Deliberative models meanwhile articulate with a broader scale of relations that are necessary to enter into given the conditions—globalization, mobility, mass communications, mass democracy—of our present era. These broad-scale dynamics are not independent of, or antithetical to, local ones (which is why analyses that pit local vs. global are simplistic at best), but instead arise from and share mutual constitution with situated cultural processes at the local level (Labadi and Long 2010; Meskell 2009). Nevertheless, matters of heritage that reach beyond small-scales require additional tools in order to foster broad engagement representing diverse perspectives.

Participatory approaches to heritage and archaeology are well established and place outreach and community engagement at their core. The stakes of communities living near or otherwise connected to sites of heritage has been a focal point for efforts to better distribute access to heritage and associated resources that accrue from this access (e.g., economic or educational). In recent years, scholars have worked with collaborative approaches to archaeological practice (Atalay 2007, 2010; Colwell-Chanthaphonh and Ferguson 2008; Hodder 2003; Nicholas et al. 2011; Silliman 2008), introduced a politics of engagement (Mullins 2011), and employed participatory action research (PAR) methods (Hollowell and Nicholas 2009; Pyburn 2009). An especially burgeoning field is 'community archaeology,' in which archaeologists position communities as the primary participants and target beneficiaries of archaeological research programs (Agbe-Davies 2010; Moser et al. 2002; Moshenska 2008; Smith and Waterton 2009; Watson and Waterton 2010). Other new directions in participatory heritage employ social media (Giaccardi 2012) and theorize new forms of sociality (Simon and Ashley 2010).

The concept of community continues to be problematized and reworked through the course of such activities. A number of chapters in this volume deal with such questions that arise around community in contexts extending beyond the local or small-scale. Benedict Anderson's (1983) work on 'imagined communities' and nationalism has been particularly influential in archaeology and heritage studies for theorizing community where face-to-face interaction is not possible. Since Anderson's landmark analysis, the effects of globalization have brought new formations of 'imagined' communities, which is why his work continues to bear special purchase even as the power of the state wanes. As in Anderson's account, heritage continues to be a key ingredient.

Alexander Bauer (Chapter 5) proposes that 'metaphysical communities' (cf. Urban 1996) have developed around the international circulation of heritage objects, replacing tired debates over cultural nationalism versus cultural internationalism within which cultural property has been caught for at least the past three decades. Truer to the UNESCO 1970 *Convention*, the newfound sense of collaboration, reciprocity, and shared stewardship is what Bauer calls "a kind of *kula* ring of important antiquities moving among previously competing parties," recalling the gift economy first outlined by Bronislaw Malinowski for an exchange system in the Trobriand Islands of Papua New Guinea. This sea change moreover has tracked alongside a shift in emphasis from 'cultural property' to 'cultural heritage' in international policy, as well as the rise of 'intangible heritage.'

Klaus Zehbe (Chapter 11) offers a rich account of intangible heritage as a kind of 'thought style' (after Fleck 1981) that undergoes observation and stylization, and is transmitted through a community of experts—a 'thought collective' (Fleck's term) or an 'epistemic community' (after Haas 1992)—to its eventual institutionalization. To render strange a familiar topic like intangible heritage, Zehbe discusses the concept of 'brain death' as an instructive metaphor for intangible heritage. Citing the work of philosopher Masahiro Morioka (2000), brain death is found not in the person whose brain has ceased functioning, but rather in the human relationships surrounding this person. So too Zehbe emphasizes that intangible heritage exists not with individuals but as a nexus of relations between humans, being maintained and transmitted through communities both expert and traditional.

Policymaking and management practices for cultural heritage have also followed broader trends in global democratic governance, which adapt the notion of 'community' within specific socio-political roles: civil society and citizenship being the two most prominent. Sigrid Van der Auwera (Chapter 3) addresses the growing importance of 'civil society' within heritage work, focusing in particular on efforts to protect cultural property during armed conflict, where civil society is seen to bear primary responsibility. Though such rhetorical deployment of civil society is seen to promote 'bottom-up' grassroots engagement from society, Van der Auwera argues that projects remain principally 'top-down,' lacking in the inclusive, pluralistic, multilayered communities that effective protection would require. As she notes, mobilizing 'civil society' in and of itself is no game-changer, as civil society can be equally apt to destroy cultural heritage as it is to protect it. Overall, her chapter offers a thorough and welcome analysis of how 'civil society' is envisioned within heritage policy and practice.

Turning to the role of citizenship, Alicia McGill (Chapter 4) shows in the case of education programs in Belize how an appreciation of cultural heritage is seen to aid the development of productive citizens. Belizean children are brought into the global market logics of their national economy and foreign tourism, where knowledge of their country's cultural diversity and rich past will position them as good tour guides and ambassadors for Belize. McGill's chapter is a valuable contribution to the study of education as both transmitter of state and cultural values and as a field of cultural production as these values are reinterpreted and contested. Her work usefully lays plain that education is an active arena for institutionalization and change in heritage rhetoric.

The preceding discussion on participatory and deliberative democracy raises important issues. Why draw on democratic approaches at all, whether participatory or deliberative, for cultural heritage? What can heritage experts hope to achieve? Is there the potential of doing more harm than good? Of intervening with an ill-fitting framework to social contexts governed by principles other than democratic ones? These kinds of questions increasingly confront heritage scholars and practitioners, especially as the scope of heritage work extends beyond well-known and politically unambiguous national frameworks to face a diverse range of social and political contexts both locally and globally. Such questions are also of growing importance as heritage and archaeology have variously been redescribed as social action (Byrne 2008), activism (Atalay et al. 2014; Pyburn 2007; Starzmann 2008), and political action (McGuire 2008).

As a starting point, it is important to underline that democracy itself bears a great diversity of meanings across the globe. Some of the greatest injustices done in the name of democracy have been due to forcing a one-size-fits-all model. Cultural anthropologists have provided some of the most compelling accounts of 'actually existing democracies,' demonstrating the need for contextual studies of democracy that understand the specific configurations and challenges of democratic practice (Caldeira and Holston 1999; Greenhouse 1998; Holston 2008; Paley 2002, 2008). Focusing on the connections between heritage and democracy in specific contexts can achieve similar and complementary ends.

For example, Albro (2006) details how cultural heritage came to define alternative conceptions of democracy in Bolivia. The passage of the Public Participation Law in 1994 granted full recognition to indigenous political groups via legal recognition of 'customary law' (*usos y costumbres*), "establishing legal precedent based on continuity with the past" (Albro 2006: 393). It was through appeals to customary law that indigenous groups gained traction for remaking democratic practice and participation, arguing that democracy needed to be 'reclaimed' (*reivindicar* or *recuperar*) "as a collective political birthright, a birthright they actively 'remember' and rhetorically relocate as a cultural heritage upon which to build for the future" (2006: 402). Here groups looked to the Andean institution of *ayllu*, which is defined by its principles of service, rotating leadership, substantive consultation, communal consensus, and equitable distribution of resources.

However, in some heritage contexts a democratic state or democratic practices may not exist, in which case the political environment of heritage and working conceptions of social justice must be ascertained. In more cases the articulation between cultural heritage and democracy may be poorly understood, and would profit from further inquiry. Several contributions to the volume examine the relationship between democratic practice and cultural heritage. My own contribution (Chapter 15) looks at the construction of heritage rights in the context of heritage development projects seeking to 'build capacity' in pre-Revolution Tunisia. I suggest that under the repressive conditions of now-deposed President Zine El Abidine Ben Ali's administration, heritage rights could be redescribed as the capacity for heritage and its management to support or constrain social imaginaries.

Cecilia Rodéhn (Chapter 6) gives an insightful survey of the deliberative productions of academics on democratic practice in museums. She asks how, in the course of writing about democratization processes, scholars become part of the process they are writing about. The effect, she argues, is to create a temporal map of museum democratization, whereby the past is viewed negatively, the present (the time of the writing) is considered a time of transformation, and the future a state of democratic practice. The quest for fair and equal representation, improved access, participation, and social inclusivity often masks an unequal distribution of political power of greater importance, and democracy is wielded as the sole arbiter of political legitimacy and correctness. Based on her extensive analysis of scholarly deliberations, Rodéhn suggests that "democratization should be understood as a long process of open-ended social constructions" and "eclectic negotiations of power, ideas, and interests."

Like Rodéhn, Jeff Adams (Chapter 8) undertakes a broad comparative analysis, here to provide a perceptive account of 'equity' in sustainable tourism projects and their outcomes in international development contexts. Adams points to the alarming and pervasive disjuncture between project ideals and outcomes. Whereas projects assume that tourism revenues can improve social equity, instead tourism exacerbates already existing social inequalities. Given this state of affairs, he argues that equity talk serves as a "normative signpost" and "justificatory index of program legitimacy," circulating across international heritage policy as "both a conscious strategy to promote the lasting self-adoption of best practices and a practical necessity in the absence of alternatives." Taking the above into account, he asks several provocative questions: "to what extent should heritage managers aspire to be in the social justice business? . . . Can heritage preservation in and of itself . . . nonetheless have the power to promote lasting, endogenous, positive social and economic change?"

With this Adams raises the issue of expertise in cultural heritage, a topic that is picked up in several other chapters as well. Trinidad Rico (Chapter

9) argues that the concept of risk is a tool—"an established instrument of rationalization"—used by heritage experts to police the boundaries of acceptable and unacceptable discourse for identifying and constructing what is 'heritage.' This is in counterpoint to the need for flexibility within terms commonly deployed in heritage work, in order to create discursive space for contextual, embedded meanings. Likewise, the baseline against which risk is assessed should be composed of articulated values and, ideally, shared ones. Taking these points together, the regime of risk presently in place tells us more about expert mentalities than it does the state of a given heritage property, which is why we should give care to the production of heritage constructs, discourse being a central technology in this production.

Similar sentiments are expressed by Melissa Baird (Chapter 13) with respect to the deployment of 'nature' to erase histories: "what seems natural or organic is in fact imagined and constructed." This tendency becomes more dangerous when enshrined in legislation and codes of practice. At the same time, what is referred to as 'heritage' continues to grow, and expertise lags behind even as heritage experts cite authority and obligation, colored with possession, in rationalizing their involvement. As Baird notes, heritage is being called upon for environmental conservation, and with the many environmental challenges facing our world today, this gives greater urgency to understanding how concepts like 'heritage' and 'nature' gain relevance and traction vis-à-vis one another. Overall, the contributions from Adams, Rico, and Baird underscore expertise as the locus for setting the frames and limits of deliberation, for 'setting the agenda' around which talking points become articulated and echoed.

This leaves us with the unsettling sense that changing the conversation is not an option, unless from concerted expert action. Certainly we can point to this as a particularly direct means for redescription, but other routes exist, and indeed one purpose of this volume is to raise that possibility. For example, fostering participation encourages more inclusive, democratic engagement with heritage. However, participatory approaches work best at the small-scale or local level, and increasingly heritage matters extend beyond this to encompass national, international, and diasporic interests and audiences. What is needed are democratic approaches capable of engaging these audiences too. Turning the analytical gaze to deliberative practices helps delineate productive areas or mechanisms for greatest impact on the day-to-day affairs of heritage and its management. Moreover, such approaches move focus 'up river' in the stream of influence, 'studying up' (Nader 1972) in order to target the makers of messaging and policy.

Mechanisms of Change

The strategic redescription and transformation of heritage rhetoric provides one productive avenue for moving global heritage agendas and recontextualizing heritage work within its strengths: the specific historical contingencies, traditions, and contemporary community uses that characterize heritage itself. This volume challenges and takes apart the reified character and foundational assumptions of key heritage categories and terms by demonstrating their alternative and open-ended possibilities. To craft new vocabularies and descriptions of heritage requires a detailed and oftentimes creative understanding of legal and institutional mechanisms, so as to strategically pursue those paths with the most productive results or possibilities for change. Working within such institutional frameworks also allows groups to capture national and international attention and support for pushing forward redescriptions of key terms in heritage, effectively shifting the terms of debate itself.

For instance, chapters in this volume deal with terms of heritage vocabularies and rhetoric derived and drawing force from national legislation, international law and conventions, and professional codes of ethics. The chapters contribute directly or indirectly to ongoing research on law and society, on the mutual constitution and interconnections between the two. In this respect, institutional change might be seen as one end-goal among many, rather than the means and end. Meanwhile, heritage vocabularies developed or redescribed from the grassroots level may penetrate legal and institutional vocabularies of heritage. In such contexts, what rhetoric loses from a lack of institutional backing, it gains in more radical revisioning of how we conceive and talk about heritage.

A number of contributors to this volume highlight specific mechanisms for change in heritage. For example, Cooper (Chapter 10) underscores the translation of policy into practice as a key mechanism for change, where even if the policy or legal wording remains the same, the 'spirit' of the law has changed in line with changing social conditions. He also suggests the importance of public opinion in swaying management and policy decisions, which opens up an important avenue for grassroots efforts in redescription. In the case of setting the global agenda for heritage, Adams (Chapter 8) raises the need for closing the gap between inspirational or delusional talk, to more closely fit agenda-setting rhetoric to what is feasible and doable. Rodéhn (Chapter 6) highlights the key role played by the scholarly literature in setting the terms of debate, and she warns against pursuing constant transformation without concomitant pauses to review and take stock of achievements.

The chapter by Bauer (Chapter 5) gives us a clear account of redescription already taking place, in the shift from cultural property to cultural heritage in the international discourse of law. As he notes, this shift was prompted by a confluence of changing social perspectives and several key court cases. McGill (Chapter 4) foregrounds the negotiations of meaning that take place in educational contexts: between teaching plans, the degree to which these plans are interpreted by teachers, and how lessons are understood and received within the existing worldviews of students. Karlström (Chapter 2) and Preucel and Pecos (Chapter 14) demonstrate the possibility of parallel co-existing discourses, for example Preucel and Pecos show how Cochiti conceptions of heritage/place are set alongside dominant heritage vocabularies without being diminished by them. Images can also be a powerful tool for communication, as related by Lane (Chapter 16), and therefore represent a material mechanism for shifting conceptions of heritage.

Another mechanism for redescription is breaking down a keyword into parts, as suggested by Gabriel Moshenska (Chapter 12) for 'memory.' Moshenska argues that the term 'memory' elides a range of different and specific concepts, thereby confusing and obscuring the work of powerful actors and processes that shape popular conceptions of the past. He suggests instead the use of terms such as 'remember' and 'commemorate' that bring back agency and context to analysis by foregrounding the processual nature of memory, as actions. In breaking apart 'memory,' Moshenska identifies three generative processes composing the term: (1) the creation of narratives within small groups, (2) the promotion and amplification of specific narratives through various media, and (3) disagreement in the public sphere over opposing narratives. In thinking through mechanisms for redescription, Moshenska's chapter offers a straightforward approach: dismantling a keyword into component parts to highlight the agency and contexts of heritage work. More importantly, he raises the issues of scale, audience, and disagreement that are so central to deliberative concerns, as discussed in this introduction.

Rather than breaking apart a term into more useful constituent parts, some terms compose a constellation of related concepts. The case of difficult heritage addressed by Joshua Samuels (Chapter 7) demonstrates how key terms in heritage come into being through scholarly deliberation on finding the 'right' word. As Samuels points out, terms like 'negative heritage' and 'undesirable heritage' were discarded for unintended valences the words carried. The literature seems to have settled on 'difficult heritage' as the best word for describing painful, contested, or awkward heritage. At the same time, Samuels suggests that something is lost in the process of arriving at 'difficult heritage,' watering down the force that other terms carried, and being not entirely satisfactory in its own right. Samuels' chapter raises the important point that scholarly discussions and management strategies require some baseline understanding of key concepts in order to ensure communication and mutual intelligibility. However, we cannot forget the process by which terms came into being and acquired consensus, and that key terms—like 'difficult heritage'—are never wholly satisfactory. The search for 'right' words must still continue.

CONCLUSION

In this volume we are interested in the mechanisms by which redescriptions of the past into present-day purposes take hold and spread, gaining collective currency. These mechanisms might be material, discursive, legal, institutional, or unconventional. More specifically, this volume explores how such mechanisms might be channeled in the pursuit of visionary change. How does the translation of past into present proceed, and how does this translation garner broad acceptance and legitimacy? Further, how does a social focus on heritage enable strategic engagement in contemporary issues? Taking all of these questions together, how might communities, organizations, and individuals mobilize heritage to challenge and reshape the status quo of established norms and relations?

Heritage is particularly well suited to this task of social change. In looking to the deep reserve of times past, heritage draws on a wide diversity of experiences and what, in hindsight, we might call 'social experiments,' demonstrating the limitless possibilities of the human condition. History gives the world today important perspective: that present conditions have not always existed, life is not everywhere the same, alternatives exist, and in fact diversity and creative strategies are the norm and catalyze social transformation. The recent interest in heritage rights, social justice, and participatory models of heritage research signal the utopic potential redescribed from the many pasts of our world. These strengths and successes in heritage research inspired us to put together the present volume.

One of the most fascinating aspects of cultural heritage is its 'living' quality, wherein the past is constantly recreated, remade, and redescribed to align with present conditions and sensibilities. The past is made anew; even efforts to halt the passage of time and preserve its moments requires a great deal of work and reworking. Indeed, this will to relevance defines cultural heritage concerns.

NOTE

1. The contributions to this volume were developed from papers given in two sessions titled "The Rhetoric of Heritage" held at the American Anthropological

Association annual meeting in Montreal, November 2011, and at the Theoretical Archaeology Group in Birmingham, December 2011. Several invited papers were also included.

REFERENCES

Abizadeh, Arash. 2002. "The Passions of the Wise: Phronesis, Rhetoric, and Aristotle's Passionate Practical Deliberation." *Review of Metaphysics* 56: 267–97.

Agbe-Davies, Anna S. 2010. "Concepts of Community in the Pursuit of an Inclusive Archaeology." *International Journal of Heritage Studies* 16 (6): 373–89. http://dx.doi .org/10.1080/13527258.2010.510923.

Albro, Robert. 2006. "The Culture of Democracy and Bolivia's Indigenous Movements." *Critique of Anthropology* 26 (4): 387–410. http://dx.doi.org/10.1177/03 08275X06070122.

Aldenderfer, Mark. 2011. "Editorial: Keywords." *Current Anthropology* 52 (4): 487. http://dx.doi.org/10.1086/661743.

Anderson, Benedict. 1983. *Imagined Communities: Reflections on the Origin and Spread of Nationalism*. London: Verso.

Aristotle. 2007. *On Rhetoric: A Theory of Civic Discourse*. Trans. George A. Kennedy. New York, NY: Oxford University Press.

Ashworth, G. J., and Brian Graham. 2005. "Senses of Place, Senses of Time and Heritage." In *Senses of Place: Senses of Time*, ed. G. J. Ashworth and Brian Graham, 3–12. Farnham, UK: Ashgate Publishing.

Atalay, Sonya L. 2007. "Global Application of Indigenous Archaeology: Community Based Participatory Research in Turkey." *Archaeologies* 3 (3): 249–70. http://dx.doi .org/10.1007/s11759-007-9026-8.

Atalay, Sonya. 2010. "'We Don't Talk about Çatalhöyük, We Live It': Sustainable Archaeological Practice through Community-based Participatory Research." *World Archaeology* 42 (3): 418–29. http://dx.doi.org/10.1080/00438243.2010 .497394.

Atalay, Sonya, Lee Rains, Randall H. McGuire, and John R. Welch, eds. 2014. *Transforming Archaeology: Activist Practices and Prospects*. Walnut Creek, CA: Left Coast Press.

Bauer, Alexander A. 2013. "Multivocality and 'Wikiality': The Epistemology and Ethics of a Pragmatic Archaeology." In *Appropriating the Past: Philosophical Perspectives on the Practice of Archaeology II*, ed. Chris Scarre and Robin Coningham, 176–94. Cambridge: Cambridge University Press.

Beiner, Ronald. 1983. *Political Judgment*. Chicago, IL: University of Chicago Press.

Benhabib, Seyla. 1996. "Toward a Deliberative Model of Democratic Legitimacy." In *Democracy and Difference: Contesting the Boundaries of the Political*, ed. Seyla Benhabib, 67–94. Princeton, NJ: Princeton University Press.

Bennett, Tony, Lawrence Grossberg, and Meaghan Morris. 2005. *New Keywords: A Revised Vocabulary of Culture and Society*. Oxford: Blackwell.

Blake, Janet. 2000. "On Defining the Cultural Heritage." *International and Comparative Law Quarterly* 49 (1): 61–85. http://dx.doi.org/10.1017/S002058930 006396X.

Bohman, James. 2007. *Democracy across Borders: From Dêmos to Dêmoi*. Cambridge, MA: MIT Press.

Byrne, Denis. 2008. "Heritage as Social Action." In *The Heritage Reader*, ed. Graham Fairclough, Rodney Harrison, John H. Jameson, Jr., and John Schofield, 149–73. New York, NY: Routledge.

Caldeira, Teresa P. R., and James Holston. 1999. "Democracy and Violence in Brazil." *Comparative Studies in Society and History* 41 (4): 691–729. http://dx.doi.org/10.1017 /S0010417599003102.

Carrithers, Michael. 2005a. "Anthropology as a Moral Science of Possibilities." *Current Anthropology* 46 (3): 433–56. http://dx.doi.org/10.1086/428801.

Carrithers, Michael. 2005b. "Why Anthropologists Should Study Rhetoric." *Journal of the Royal Anthropological Institute* 11 (3): 577–83. http://dx.doi.org/10.1111/j.1467 -9655.2005.00251.x.

Carrithers, Michael, ed. 2009. *Culture, Rhetoric, and the Vicissitudes of Life*. New York, NY: Berghahn Books.

Chambers, Simone. 2012. "Deliberation and Mass Democracy." In *Deliberative Systems: Deliberative Democracy at the Large Scale*, ed. John Parkinson and Jane Mansbridge, 52–71. Cambridge: Cambridge University Press. http://dx.doi.org /10.1017/CBO9781139178914.004.

Cohen, Joshua. 1989. "Deliberation and Democratic Legitimacy." In *The Good Polity: Normative Analysis of the State*, ed. Alan Hamlin and Philip Pettit, 17–34. Oxford: Blackwell.

Colwell-Chanthaphonh, Chip. 2009. "Myth of the Anasazi: Archaeological Language, Collaborative Communities, and the Contested Past." *Public Archaeology* 8 (2/3): 191–207. http://dx.doi.org/10.1179/175355309X457222.

Colwell-Chanthaphonh, Chip, and T. J. Ferguson, eds. 2008. *Collaboration in Archaeological Practice: Engaging Descendant Communities*. Lanham, MD: AltaMira.

Coombe, Rosemary, and Andrew Herman. 2004. "Rhetorical Virtues: Property, Speech, and the Commons on the World-Wide Web." *Anthropological Quarterly* 77 (3): 559–74.

Dryzek, John S. 2010a. *Foundations and Frontiers of Deliberative Governance*. Oxford: Oxford University Press. http://dx.doi.org/10.1093/acprof:oso/9780199562947 .001.0001.

Dryzek, John S. 2010b. "Rhetoric in Democracy: A Systemic Appreciation." *Political Theory* 38 (3): 319–39. http://dx.doi.org/10.1177/0090591709359596.

Fleck, Ludwik. 1981. *Genesis and Development of a Scientific Fact*. Trans. Fred Bradley and Thaddeus J. Trenn. Chicago, IL: University of Chicago Press.

Fontana, Benedetto, Cary J. Nederman, and Gary Remer, eds. 2004. *Talking Democracy: Historical Perspectives on Rhetoric and Democracy*. University Park: Pennsylvania State University Press.

Fung, Archon. 2004. *Empowered Participation: Reinventing Urban Democracy*. Princeton, NJ: Princeton University Press.

Garsten, Bryan. 2006. *Saving Persuasion: A Defense of Rhetoric and Judgment*. Cambridge, MA: Harvard University Press.

Garsten, Bryan. 2011. "The Rhetoric Revival in Political Theory." *Annual Review of Political Science* 14 (1): 159–80. http://dx.doi.org/10.1146/annurev.polisci.040108 .104834.

Giaccardi, Elisa, ed. 2012. *Heritage and Social Media: Understanding Heritage in a Participatory Culture*. New York, NY: Routledge.

Greenhouse, Carol J., ed. 1998. *Democracy and Ethnography: Constructing Identities in Multicultural Liberal States*. Albany: State University of New York.

Gutmann, Amy, and Dennis F. Thompson. 1996. *Democracy and Disagreement*. Cambridge, MA: Harvard University Press.

Haas, Peter M. 1992. "Epistemic Communities and International Policy Coordination." *International Organization* 46 (1): 1–35. http://dx.doi.org/10.1017 /S0020818300001442.

Habermas, Jürgen. 1996. *Between Facts and Norms: Contributions to a Discourse Theory of Law and Democracy*. Cambridge, MA: MIT Press.

Habu, Junko, Clare Fawcett, and John M. Matsunaga, eds. 2008. *Evaluating Multiple Narratives: Beyond Nationalist, Colonialist, Imperialist Archaeologies*. New York, NY: Springer. http://dx.doi.org/10.1007/978-0-387-71825-5.

Hafstein, Valdimar. 2012. "Cultural Heritage." In *A Companion to Folklore*, ed. Regina F. Bendix and Galit Hasan-Rokem, 500–19. Malden, MA: Blackwell. http:// dx.doi.org/10.1002/9781118379936.ch26.

Hale, Thomas, and David Held, eds. 2011. *Handbook of Transnational Governance: Institutions and Innovations*. Cambridge, UK: Polity Press.

Harrison, Rodney. 2013. *Heritage: Critical Approaches*. Abingdon / New York, NY: Routledge. http://dx.doi.org/10.1093/oxfordhb/9780199602001.013.021.

Hauptmann, Emily. 2001. "Can Less Be More? Leftist Deliberative Democrats' Critique of Participatory Democracy." *Polity* 33 (3): 397–421. http://dx.doi.org/10.2307/3235441.

Hodder, Ian. 2003. *Archaeology Beyond Dialogue*. Salt Lake City: University of Utah Press.

Hollowell, Julie. J., and George Nicholas. 2009. "Using Ethnographic Methods to Articulate Community-Based Conceptions of Cultural Heritage Management." *Public Archaeology* 8 (2/3): 141–60. http://dx.doi.org/10.1179/175355309X457196.

Holston, James. 2008. *Insurgent Citizenship: Disjunctions of Democracy and Modernity in Brazil*. Princeton, NJ: Princeton University Press.

Joyce, Rosemary, ed. 2002. *The Languages of Archaeology: Dialogue, Narrative, and Writing*. Malden, MA: Blackwell. http://dx.doi.org/10.1002/9780470693520.

Koselleck, Reinhart. 2004. *Futures Past: On the Semantics of Historical Time*. Trans. K. Tribe. New York, NY: Columbia University Press.

Labadi, Sophia, and Colin Long, eds. 2010. *Heritage and Globalisation*. London: Routledge.

Lowenthal, David. 1997. *The Heritage Crusade and the Spoils of History*. Cambridge: Cambridge University Press.

Mamdani, Mahmood. 1996. "Indirect Rule, Civil Society, and Ethnicity: The African Dilemma." *Social Justice* 23 (1/2): 145–50.

McGuire, Randall H. 2008. *Archaeology as Political Action*. Berkeley: University of California Press.

Meskell, Lynn, ed. 2009. *Cosmopolitan Archaeologies*. Durham, NC: Duke University Press. http://dx.doi.org/10.1215/9780822392422.

Meskell, Lynn. 2013a. "UNESCO and the Fate of the World Heritage Indigenous Peoples Council of Experts (WHIPCOE)." *International Journal of Cultural Property* 20 (2): 155–74. http://dx.doi.org/10.1017/S0940739113000039.

Meskell, Lynn. 2013b. "UNESCO's World Heritage Convention at 40: Challenging the Economic and Political Order of International Heritage Conservation." *Current Anthropology* 54 (4): 483–94. http://dx.doi.org/10.1086/671136.

Meyer, Christian, and Felix Girke, eds. 2011. *The Rhetorical Emergence of Culture*. New York, NY: Berghahn Books.

Morioka, Masahiro. 2000. *Nōshi no Hito*. [Brain Dead Person]. Tokyo: Hozokan. Available in English online at http://www.lifestudies.org/braindeadperson00.html.

Moser, Stephanie, Darren Glazier, James E. Phillips, Lamya Nasser el Nemr, Mohammed Saleh Mousa, Rascha Nasr Alesh, Susan Richardson, Andrew Conner, and Michael Seymour. 2002. "Transforming Archaeology Through

Practice: Strategies for Collaborative Archaeology and the Community Archaeology Project at Quseir, Egypt." *World Archaeology* 34 (2): 220–48. http://dx.doi.org/10.1080/0043824022000007071.

Moshenska, Gabriel. 2008. "Community Archaeology from Below: A Response to Tully." *Public Archaeology* 7 (1): 51–52. http://dx.doi.org/10.1179/175355308X306004.

Mullins, Paul R. 2011. "Practicing Anthropology and the Politics of Engagement: 2010 Year in Review." *American Anthropologist* 113 (2): 235–45. http://dx.doi.org/10.1111/j.1548-1433.2011.01327.x.

Mutz, Diana C. 2006. *Hearing the Other Side: Deliberative versus Participatory Democracy*. Cambridge: Cambridge University Press. http://dx.doi.org/10.1017/CBO9780511617201.

Nader, Laura. 1972. "Up the Anthropologist—Perspectives Gained from Studying Up." In *Re-inventing Anthropology*, ed. Dell Hymes, 284–311. New York, NY: Pantheon Books.

Nicholas, George P., Amy Roberts, David M. Schaepe, Joe Watkins, Lyn Leader-Elliot, and Susan Rowley. 2011. "A Consideration of Theory, Principles, and Practice in Collaborative Archaeology." *Archaeological Review from Cambridge* 26 (2): 11–30.

O'Neill, John. 2002. "The Rhetoric of Deliberation: Some Problems in Kantian Theories of Deliberative Democracy." *Res Publica* 8 (3): 249–68. http://dx.doi.org/10.1023/A:1020899224058.

Paley, Julia. 2002. "Toward an Anthropology of Democracy." *Annual Review of Anthropology* 31 (1): 469–96. http://dx.doi.org/10.1146/annurev.anthro.31.040402.085453.

Paley, Julia, ed. 2008. *Democracy: Anthropological Approaches*. Santa Fe, NM: School for Advanced Research Press.

Palonen, Kari. 1997. "Quentin Skinner's Rhetoric of Conceptual Change." *History of the Human Sciences* 10 (2): 61–80. http://dx.doi.org/10.1177/095269519701000204.

Parkinson, John, and Jane Mansbridge, eds. 2012. *Deliberative Systems: Deliberative Democracy at the Large Scale*. Cambridge: Cambridge University Press. http://dx.doi.org/10.1017/CBO9781139178914.

Pluciennik, Mark. 1999. "Archaeological Narratives and Other Ways of Telling." *Current Anthropology* 40 (5): 653–78. http://dx.doi.org/10.1086/300085.

Preucel, Robert, and Alexander Bauer. 2001. "Archaeological Pragmatics." *Norwegian Archaeological Review* 34 (2): 85–96. http://dx.doi.org/10.1080/00293650127469.

Pyburn, K. Anne. 2007. "Archaeology as Activism." In *Cultural Heritage and Human Rights*, edited by Helaine Silverman and D. Fairchild Ruggles, 172–83. New York, NY: Springer. http://dx.doi.org/10.1007/978-0-387-71313-7_10.

Pyburn, K. Anne. 2009. "Practicing Archaeology—As if It Really Matters." *Public Archaeology* 8 (2/3): 161–75. http://dx.doi.org/10.1179/175355309X457204.

Rorty, Richard. 1989. *Contingency, Irony, and Solidarity*. Cambridge: Cambridge University Press. http://dx.doi.org/10.1017/CBO9780511804397.

Silliman, Stephen W., ed. 2008. *Collaborating at the Trowel's Edge: Teaching and Learning in Indigenous Archaeology*. Tucson: University of Arizona Press.

Simon, Roger I., and Susan L. T. Ashley. 2010. "Heritage and Practices of Public Formation." *International Journal of Heritage Studies* 16 (4–5): 247–54. http://dx.doi.org/10.1080/13527251003775471.

Simons, Herbert W. 1990. *Preface to The Rhetorical Turn*. Ed. Herbert W. Simons, vii–xii. Chicago, IL: University of Chicago Press. http://dx.doi.org/10.7208/chicago/9780226759036.001.0001.

Skinner, Quentin. 1988. "A Reply to My Critics." In *Meaning and Context*, ed. James Tully, 231–88. London: Polity Press.

Smith, Laurajane. 2006. *The Uses of Heritage*. New York, NY: Routledge.

Smith, Laurajane, and Emma Waterton, eds. 2009. *Heritage, Communities and Archaeology*. London: Duckworth.

Starzmann, Maria T. 2008. "Cultural Imperialism and Heritage Politics in the Event of Armed Conflict: Prospects for an 'Activist Archaeology.'" *Archaeologies* 4 (3): 368–89. http://dx.doi.org/10.1007/s11759-008-9083-7.

Strecker, Ivo, and Stephen Tyler, eds. 2009. *Culture and Rhetoric*. New York, NY: Berghahn Books.

Trouillot, Michel-Rolph. 1995. *Silencing the Past: Power and the Production of History*. Boston, MA: Beacon Press.

Urban, Greg. 1996. *Metaphysical Community*. Austin: University of Texas Press.

Waterton, Emma, Laurajane Smith, and Gary Campbell. 2006. "The Utility of Discourse Analysis to Heritage Studies: The Burra Charter and Social Inclusion." *International Journal of Heritage Studies* 12 (4): 339–55. http://dx.doi.org/10.1080/13527250600727000.

Watson, Steve, and Emma Waterton. 2010. "Heritage and Community Engagement: Collaboration or Contestation?" *International Journal of Heritage Studies* 16 (1-2): 1–3. http://dx.doi.org/10.1080/13527250903441655.

Welsh, Scott. 2002. "Deliberative Democracy and the Rhetorical Production of Political Culture." *Rhetoric & Public Affairs* 5 (4): 679–707. http://dx.doi.org/10.1353/rap.2003.0020.

Williams, Raymond. 1976. *Keywords: A Vocabulary of Culture and Society*. New York, NY: Oxford University Press.

Wittgenstein, Ludwig. 1984. *Culture and Value*. Chicago, IL: University of Chicago Press.

Wojcieszak, Magdalena E., Young Min Baek, and Michael X. Delli Carpini. 2010. "Deliberative and Participatory Democracy? Ideological Strengths and the Processes Leading from Deliberation to Political Engagement." *International Journal of Public Opinion Research* 22 (2): 154–80. http://dx.doi.org/10.1093/ijpor/edp050.

Yack, Bernard. 2006. "Rhetoric and Public Reasoning: An Aristotelian Understanding of Political Deliberation." *Political Theory* 34 (4): 417–38. http://dx.doi.org/10.1177/0090591706288232.

Authenticity **2**

*Rhetorics of Preservation and the
Experience of the Original*

ANNA KARLSTRÖM

Authenticity is commonly defined as the quality of being true and genuine and is ascribed to objects that are in their original state. It is often set against fake and false, and it privileges the idea that appreciation and value grow the closer we come to the original state. Most scholars agree that authenticity is an important quality attached to cultural heritage. The concept of authenticity is widely used within contemporary heritage discourse, yet remains perplexing and slippery. Moreover, its usage evokes several paradoxes because the definition of authenticity is often taken for granted at the same time as contradictory and contested notions of authenticity occur.

On the one hand, we now witness a trend toward an explosion of meaning for the concept of authenticity. Current attempts to broaden the understanding of the concept have resulted in a recognition that authenticity is rooted in specific sociocultural contexts and corresponds to specific values, and that it can only be understood and judged within those specific contexts and according to those values (Labadi 2010: 78). In other words, there is no definite description of authenticity: it depends entirely on the situation and the context. This approach was formally accepted and institutionalized when the *Nara Document* (ICOMOS 1994) and its principles of diversity were included in

DOI: 10.5876/9781607323846.c002

UNESCO's (2005) *Operational Guidelines for the Implementation of the World Heritage Convention,* even though it existed informally long before that.

On the other hand, authenticity remains tied to conceptions of material, form, and fabric, as long as it is directed by and dependent on these institutionalized heritage structures. Embedded in these structures are the ideas that heritage values are universal, that heritage belongs to all humankind, and that heritage should be preserved for the future and preferably forever. The reason for this, I would argue, is that these structures, as well as the entire fields of archaeology and heritage, were not only developed in nineteenth century Europe (Smith 2006; Thomas 2004), but are still firmly entrenched in western worldviews. This paradoxical character of authenticity is the main challenge here and is also the primary reason to pursue a redescription.

Over the years, ongoing academic discussions on what exactly authenticity means to heritage and culture have resulted in a wide variety of approaches (Lindholm 2008). The materialist approach to authenticity, favoring the real and the original and focusing on form and fabric, lies at the heart of contemporary heritage management and conservation. This approach is institutionalized through the authorizing organizations of heritage, such as UNESCO and ICOMOS, and the charters and conventions enacted by them from the 1960s and on to today (Smith 2006: 53).

Within the broader field of heritage studies, a constructivist approach to authenticity has been agreed upon, where the idea of heritage as material has given way to the idea of heritage as social action (Byrne 2008, cf. the 'social turn' in heritage). Authenticity in this perspective is subjective and culturally constructed, not inherent in the object. It is context-dependent, negotiated, and even manipulated (Lowenthal 1985: 194), and originality and age are not always necessary attributes in order to value objects and sites as authentic (Holtorf and Schadla-Hall 1999: 243).

Even though the constructivist approach has been challenging and enlightening for the heritage debate, both approaches are organized around a dichotomy rooted in the western philosophical tradition. This dichotomy presents a problematic gap in our understanding of authenticity (Jones 2009: 133–34), as it does not take into account how people relate to heritage and the past, and it overlooks alternative non-western perspectives of heritage. In connection to her work in Scotland, Siân Jones (2010) recently extended the scope further by exploring an experienced and negotiable authenticity, arguing that authenticity is a product of the relationships between past and present, people, objects, and places. The experience and negotiation of authenticity has also been dealt with within the heritage tourism field, but in a slightly different manner, more focused on the construction of identity and culture (Scarangella 2010) and the self through a more philosophical existentialist authenticity (Wang 1999).

My redescription of the concept of authenticity in this chapter is inspired by the notion of performative authenticity, emphasizing the dynamic process of 'becoming' authentic through embodied practice (Knudsen and Waade 2010). It also derives its inspiration from Denis Byrne (1993) and his exploration of popular religious practices and beliefs in Thailand. Whereas some researchers in this field focus on the viewpoint of the performer (Zhu 2012; Alivizatou 2012), or from the perspectives of visitors to heritage sites (Kidd 2011; Guttormsen and Fageraas 2011), here I focus on the relationship that religious practitioners have with the material past, in which all, or some of, the above mentioned approaches to authenticity may be included. My approach to redescribing authenticity is to foreground the relationship between authenticity and alternative perceptions of materiality and preservation, and the experience of the original. It is also about acknowledging other worldviews, in which people relate to the material past through popular religious practices. Such alternative worldviews may appear in opposition to those on which contemporary heritage discourse was founded, but I argue here that they already operate simultaneously. In fact, alternative worldviews allow for this simultaneous possibility to a greater extent than do the materialist worldviews driving contemporary heritage discourse.

Sophia Labadi (2010: 66, 78) suggests that we may have come to an end with the concept of authenticity, so it would be more accurate to use the term 'post-authenticity' (cf. Lovata 2007 on 'inauthenticity'). I argue instead for a redescription of the concept, because a rejection of a word does not involve a rejection of an idea or a solution to the problem. The concept authenticity is pervasive in the heritage field and will continue to be so, and it should be acknowledged as complex and fluid. Dominant groups set heritage agendas over time, and recently developed critical approaches to heritage attempt to deconstruct these dominant heritage discourses by paying attention to difference, multivocality, and struggle, as well as by looking at the development of the entire discourse itself and analyzing its rootedness in the West (see Lafrenz Samuels, introduction to this volume).

In line with such aims, this chapter draws on local religious practices in Southeast Asia to demonstrate an authenticity built around performance, as an example for broadening the conceptual repertoire of authenticity. I consider local, or popular, religious practices as a means by which the material past (ancient objects and places) is contextualized and given meaning in everyday life. The main argument is that if we, as heritage practitioners, are prepared to include this alternative meaning, we can also start to accept alternative approaches to materiality and the understanding that change and sometimes even destruction are necessary for the appreciation of certain heritage expressions (Karlström 2009: 205–10). This in turn challenges western heritage discourse and questions its fundamental ideology of preservationism. We must understand local religious practices not only intellectually, but on a theoretical level, while also being prepared to grant popular religion equal value for modern rationalism (Byrne 2011: 6). Popular religion is a belief system and a practice to which the greater part of the world's population ascribes. A tolerance and inclusion of this system into the heritage discourse would thus correspond to the 'social turn' in heritage management, which is here to stay (Byrne 2009: 69, 87–88). By approaching authenticity through performance, as shown in the following examples, we might be able to re-think our position and allow the discourses of popular religion and heritage, and the two worldviews that they represent, to run parallel and coexist.

POPULAR RELIGION AND EMPOWERED OBJECTS

I was in Vientiane in 2012 and passed Ou Mong, one of the villages that make up the city. Curiosity led me to its temple. A brand-new *sim* (ordination hall) rose at the center of the temple compound. Its shiny and glittering appearance was striking. As I rested a while in the shade, I recalled the moment when I was here more than ten years ago, in December 2000, before I started my doctoral research. At that time, I witnessed how the ancient Ou Mong *sim* was completely demolished and leveled to the ground by the villagers while its original, authentic, murals crushed into small fragments and lost. The *sim* was almost a hundred years old. Its exterior was faded, but its interior, completely covered with murals illustrating the *Phralak-Phralam* (the Lao equivalent to the Indian *Ramayana*), was still perfectly intact. The *sim* was one of very few structures comprising depictions of this epic and one of the oldest in Vientiane. During the process of demolition, the villagers who were gathered at the temple site seemed happy indeed about the destruction, shouting and clapping their hands. One of the residents I spoke with, as the walls fell down before us, explained that the ancient *sim* had to be destroyed so that the new temple, which was under construction, could be empowered and made ready to use (Figure 2.1). The demolition of the *sim* was part of a merit-making act, which aimed at enhancing the prestige and beauty of the temple compound. The villagers in Ou Mong had saved money for years and finally the plan could be realized. Creating something new produces more merit than

FIGURE 2.1. *Destruction of the old Ou Mong* sim *in December 2000 (left) (photos courtesy of Alan Potkin), and the new building in March 2012 (right) (photo by the author).*

repairing an old object or structure. Therefore, the old structure was going to be replaced by a new one.

Later, I realized there was yet another explanation for the destruction. It was not the actual building with its original murals that was considered authentic, making it worthy of preservation. Instead, the spiritual values—connected to and residing in the building—were, and still are, the heritage the villagers wished to maintain. The old *sim* was the shell, the storage place for spiritual values. It had to be destroyed so that the spiritual values first could be liberated and then free to enter or 'pour through' into the new shell, the new *sim*, which was built as a result of the villagers' wish to gain merit. Destruction was in this case necessary for religious practices and beliefs to be maintained so that the new temple could be empowered with spirits and establish the connection between the villagers and their material past. The local heritage gained authenticity through the performed and embodied practice, which destruction and construction represented.

The temple destruction elicited reactions. Staff from the Ministry of Information and Culture's Heritage Department had tried, without success, to stop the destruction of what they regarded as one of the city's most valuable ancient structures. Some of the international scholars, working in the fields of archaeology and heritage management in Vientiane, also demonstrated their disapproval and counteracted the destruction of important Lao heritage by documenting the building and collecting fragments of its murals (Potkin 2001). The institutionalized materialist approach to authenticity dominates within Lao heritage management and practice and makes it against the law to destroy, damage, or change the national cultural heritage of Laos (see 2005 *National Heritage Law*), a view represented by the authorities and by professionals working in the heritage field. Officially, Lao professionals strongly support scientific conservation strategies, which portray local religious practices as destructive (Sayavongkhamdy 1996). To a certain extent and in a more unofficial way, these same professionals also acknowledge Buddhist notions of impermanence and nonlinear perceptions of time (Sayavongkhamdy 2009), but rarely do so in academic contexts. While this might be interpreted as yet another paradox, the majority of the Lao population (local professionals and non-professionals) in the course of everyday life participate in the institutionalized heritage discourse at the same time as they practice popular Buddhism. Science and popular religion appear compatible (cf. Byrne 2009: 76–78).

In Laos, like in many other Southeast Asian countries, popular Buddhism is the dominant religious practice. It includes the often overlapping practices of animism, Theravada Buddhism, and Hinduism. In canonical Buddhism, materiality is a matter of no concern: the notion of impermanence offers a continual circular motion, where everything cycles through birth, life, and death. Materiality in popular Buddhism, on the other hand, becomes extremely significant as people gain merit and tangible benefits through constantly performing material acts that are part of public worship and ritual (Holt 2009). Within this popular Buddhism, different sorts of objects, such as images, amulets, and *stupas* (mound-like structures containing Buddhist relics) serve as mediums. These representations are often referred to as 'reminders.' Of importance is neither the physical form and fabric of these reminders, but rather that the Buddha's attainment is symbolized by them, and as such, they act as a 'field of merit' (Tambiah 1970: 45). All such reminders are attributed with power, or rather *are power* (cf. Holbraad 2007: 189–225). By empowering objects, they become storage places for spiritual values, and it is the spiritual value that must be maintained. Empowering objects is therefore an important part of the everyday religious practices in Laos, and authenticity in popular Buddhism is measured according to the extent an object is empowered.

One particular episode during my fieldwork is instructive for illustrating the complexity of the relationship people have with their material past, and how authenticity is created and maintained through performance and the empowerment of objects. In February 2004, officials from the Ministry of

Information and Culture's office for Vientiane province were called to the main temple site in a village seventy kilometers north of Vientiane. Our excavation team, working in a neighboring village at the time, was also summoned. While digging for a new well in the temple area, a huge hollow tree trunk was found. The villagers were excited, because they were reminded of the traditional Lao epic about the giants from the north, who sent off a rocket from one of the northernmost provinces of Laos that landed here, and which they had now found (Viravong 1964). It was for this reason the authorities were asked to have a look and decide how to proceed. As the trunk was surrounded by clayish soil without any adjacent cultural layers, it was decided there was no need for an archaeological excavation. The trunk was pulled up by an excavator lent from the neighboring village. Of course, this event attracted many people. A sense of reverence seized the air, mixed with feelings of happiness, fear, thrill, alarm, joy, and sorrow. During the weeks that followed, people came traveling from all over the province to see the marvelous rocket. At this time of the year, village festivals, *Boun Ban*, are usually arranged. The timing was excellent, and the village decided to arrange the *Boun Ban* in honor of the installation of the rocket. For a couple of days, and during the *Boun Ban*, the huge tree trunk was standing in an upright position shielded by a party tent on the temple ground (Figure 2.2). Shrouded in pieces of cloth, and surrounded by candles, flowers, incense sticks, and small Buddha statues the tree trunk was the target to which people pushed their way through the crowd, to make offerings and pay their respect. They all wanted to be part of the process of empowering the object and, by doing so, add to and maintain its authenticity.

This event was of greatest concern for the staff of the Vientiane province office. They wanted to report it properly to the Ministry of Information and Culture in Vientiane and therefore searched for scientific data through which to connect and secure the importance of this event. For this purpose, I was allowed to scratch the trunk and carefully cut a piece. The wood sample was later analyzed and dated to be around three hundred years old. When the origin of a thing is confirmed, authenticity is involved. In this example, an authentication method of carbon-dating was used to verify the age of the tree trunk found at the temple site. This method presupposes a material authenticity, in opposition to a fake or copy, because an age determination for the tree trunk is possible only by analyzing the original, true piece of wood. Yet this kind of authenticity is not attached to the essence of, in this case, the piece of wood. Rather, the authenticity is a human construct, assuming that the viewer *believes* the wood is 'true.' The object itself does not determine its authenticity; the viewer does. Eight years after this occasion I visited the site again

FIGURE 2.2. *The tree trunk under excavation (above left). After it was excavated the tree trunk became an object of worship (right). The sign reading "Welcome to see the great rocket" invites bypassers to the temple site (below left) (photos by the author).*

and noted that the tree trunk was still there, at the temple, but somewhat deteriorated. It appeared that people were now allowed to share the spiritual power enveloped by the tree trunk by cutting pieces from it and keeping them as amulets, containers for its spiritual power. Highlighted here is a different conceptualization of authenticity within religious practice: authenticity through performance, instead of the material authenticity we achieve through, for example, the carbon-dating. As discussed above, this kind of authenticity concerns the extent to which things are empowered through social practice and includes the articulation of religious and spiritual values.

RESTORATION AND CHANGE

This different conceptualization of authenticity bears implications for the meaning of preservation as well. Preservation in a western heritage discourse often involves returning a structure to its previous state and focusing on form and fabric and material authenticity. In contrast, preservation in Lao society generally means returning the spiritual values to a structure by turning it into something new—for example as a result of adding or changing its physical form and fabric—whereby authenticity is maintained through a performative act. Accordingly, a redescription of authenticity might result in redescriptions of other concepts too, such as restoration and conservation, destruction and consumption, all of which relate to and depend on 'preservationism'— that is, restoration used as a tool to save heritage from destructive influences. By illustrating the complexity between the two extremes of conservation and impermanence, and between the different worldviews in which they exist, I argue we cannot continue to insist on a universal frame of reference that recommends preservationism.

This fundamentalist ideology of heritage preservation might even be dangerous, for example in the case of terrorism (cf. Holtorf 2006). The different worldviews I am referring to do not represent the dichotomies 'Western vs. Eastern', or 'Christian vs. Buddhist', or 'We vs. the Other' straight off. Different worldviews exist also in what seems a shared world, which are represented by popular religious beliefs and practices on one hand and by modern rationalism on the other, as discussed above. Thus, the purpose of illustrating this complexity with my examples from Laos is not to show how a proper 'Buddhist heritage management' should be carried out. My purpose is rather to open up heritage discourses to frames of reference other than those imposing preservation thanks to a materialist approach to authenticity and, moreover, to call for the creation of new heritage discourses, including the perceptions and values of local groups, might they be Buddhists or not.

The ongoing debate about whether to restore/reconstruct or conserve heritage remains often takes as its starting point the different perspectives of Eugène Viollet-le-Duc and John Ruskin in mid-nineteenth century Europe. Today, the term 'restoration' refers to the act of returning something to its authentic or former state, while not necessarily aiming at unity in style and without adding new material. If additions are allowed they must be distinguishable from the original. That is also how restoration is defined in the *Venice Charter for the Conservation and Restoration of Monuments and Sites* ('Venice Charter'), which was adopted by the international community in 1964. Whereas restoration aims at preserving and revealing historic and aesthetic values, based on respect for original materials, 'conservation' is today dominated by scientific methodology, knowledge, and values. Central to the contemporary field of conservation is a belief in scientific inquiry and the necessity to preserve the integrity of the physical object. Regardless of whether one argues for reconstruction, restoration, or conservation, the different approaches all pursue the same end: to maintain authenticity and the feeling of originality. Destruction and decay are regarded as threats to, and in opposition to, preservation. Moreover, the final stage in the restoration and conservation processes is a *complete* object or building, effacing its life history from construction to decay. The practices that occur in between are explained as religious in nature or too subjective to be taken into account in modern scientific heritage practices.

A typical Lao perspective sees what happens in between, concerning maintenance and restoration, as most meaningful. However, in this context the significance and meaning of the term restoration is different from the modern scientific heritage conservation practices detailed above. Restoration in the popular Lao perspective is similar or equivalent to creating something anew, such as building a new monument, interpreted as an act of merit-making, and it concerns the prestige of the original, rather than of the physical form and fabric of the original. For an alternative understanding of completion, of what happens in between, I return to the example of the Ou Mong temple site in Vientiane. Construction workers had already started to build a new *sim* at the temple compound when the demolition of the old *sim* was completed. As the walls grew higher, inscriptions with donors' names and the amounts of contribution were added, and signs were placed up on the temple yard communicating the same. The exact start date of the construction work is unknown, but it lasted over several years, until it arrived to its present state (Figure 2.1). Even after the installation ceremony, when the temple received its formal authority, building activities continued. Following the inherent meaning of the merit-making act, *the completion of a temple is less important than the process of its construction*. A temple under construction offers a chance to donate money or provide volunteer labor, which are ways of making merit. Adding, removing, and elaborating the material form of the temple over time are necessary parts of the merit-making act. With this more or less institutionalized maintenance practice, one can argue that the notion of completion does not exist in this context. The constant act of restoration is more important than the result of the restoration.

A parallel example of the significance of the process over anything else is the creation of a sand *mandala*, which appears in different contexts and also connects to the notion of impermanence. *Mandala* is a general term for any illustrations that model an idea of the cosmos, metaphysically or symbolically. It represents a microcosm of the universe, including the human body, the mind, and the surrounding world in which one lives. The term is of Hindu origin, but this metaphor is used in many other religions besides Hinduism and Buddhism, and the *mandala* representations look different within different religious practices. In Tibetan Buddhism, for example, a sand *mandala* is

FIGURE 2.3. *The process of creating a sand mandala (above left) and then immediately after destroying it and spreading the sand in the river (below left, middle, and right), demonstrating the notion of impermanence (photos by the author).*

occasionally created on the temple floor. It takes days to finish and several monks do the work. They 'paint' an intricate geometric pattern with colored sand, in a traditionally fixed design, which represents the objects of worship and contemplation of the Buddhist cosmology. After completion, the sand is brushed together and 'blown' away (Figure 2.3), to spread the blessings of the *mandala* and to emphasize its impermanence (Karlström 2005; Robinson and Johnson 1997: 34–42). The performance is the significant element here, and the degree of authenticity depends on the performer and the audience as well as the dynamic interaction between object, site, and experience, between individual agency and the external world (cf. Zhu 2012: 1498).

Returning to the concept of restoration further illustrates the complexity of the performative processes in which authenticity is created and/or maintained. Vientiane offers three examples of different restoration processes. The temple in the village Phonesay was originally built 500 years ago, but the only structure left from this period is a brick foundation in the corner of the temple compound, as well as a few Buddha statues located in different places in and around the temple. Close to the temple is also a *stupa*, which seemed to me in a very poor condition when I first visited the site. I later realized that the heap of bricks and the Buddha statues, some complete and others at different stages of decay (Figure 2.4), are not at all neglected, but rather looked after

FIGURE 2.4. *On top of and around the ancient* stupa *at the temple site in Phonesay, Buddha statues are restored, with elements constantly added and removed (photo by the author).*

with greatest care. Small pieces of leaf gold are added to the deteriorated corpses of the Buddha statues in an act of merit-making. Minor repairs as well as more extensive construction works are continuously carried out by villagers and monks to maintain the *stupa* and statues. These activities are important for the everyday use of and religious practice at the temple. It is through the repeated performances that the spiritual value of the objects is preserved. The statues and the *stupa* are empowered and authenticity created and/or maintained, and the value of the objects has nothing to do with their form and fabric, nor their age. Instead value accrues from what the objects represent, and the extent to which the objects are loaded with significance and power. The *stupa* and the Buddha statues at the Phonesay temple are not defined as historical documents, worthy of preservation because of their ancient origin and material authenticity, but instead present a strong example of designating authenticity through the performance of religious values because of their role in contemporary religious belief and practice.

Further, as was the case of Ou Mong, the demolished ancient *sim* was not valued for its material qualities. The demolition of the old *sim* and the

FIGURE 2.5. *Newly built Buddha statues on top of the ancient temple foundations (left), and the likewise newly constructed temple structure sheltering the powerful, ancient, and surviving Buddha statue (right) (photos by the author).*

construction of a new one illustrate another form of restoration compared to the maintenance of the *stupa* and Buddha statues in Phonesay, highlighting a slightly different practice, albeit related to the same philosophy. Whereas the Phonesay *stupa* and Buddha images act as representations of spirituality and require constant restoration through further additions and elaboration (such as the gold leaf), the Ou Mong *sim* was a shell or container, essentially a storage place for spiritual values, which had to be destroyed so that the spiritual values of the site and of the community could 'pour through' to the new temple and in that way be maintained. Despite these differences, the restoration practices share the same essential meaning: restoration is present-oriented and constantly in flux.

The excavations in Say Fong, another village in Vientiane, illustrate a third example of the complexity of establishing authenticity via performance. Say Fong is known popularly by the name "the village of 300 temples," because it acted as the religious center when Vientiane became the capital of the Lao kingdom 450 years ago. Two of the temple sites in the village were excavated: Vat Palei Lai and Vat Pa Mi (Figure 2.5). The largest is Vat Palei Lai, with numerous shrines and Buddha statues placed on top of a mound, which is the remains of a 1300-year-old *sim* and the main focus of excavation. There is a constant rebuilding and expansion of the site, and the new shrines and statues are empowered on a daily basis through different religious ceremonies, which create authenticity. At Vat Pa Mi, close to the river in the western outskirts of the village, there is only one small temple structure: a tiled concrete platform and a tin roof under which one single, sitting Buddha statue resides. Owing to its closeness to the river, the temple area is frequently flooded. When the 500-year-old temple was wiped out in the immense flooding of 1966, the Buddha statue was rescued. Our excavations started at Vat Paley Lai and attracted much interest and enthusiasm among residents in the village.

However, when it came to excavating Vat Pa Mi the enthusiasm changed to hesitation and anxiety, and a ceremony had to be performed before the excavation could start. Although they could be perceived as part of the same complex, further discussion with some of the residents in the village brought light to an issue of interpretation concerning the question of authenticity. *Stupas*, religious objects and images at Vat Paley Lai have to establish their own authenticity to become sacred and potent, something done through the daily religious practices carried out there. Created on top of ancient temple structures, these objects that are not at all ancient represent *religious* authenticity, which is secured through performance, as discussed earlier. However, at Vat Pa Mi the religious authenticity was already well established for the almost 500-year-old Buddha statue. One could then argue that this is more similar to the materialist authenticity of western heritage discourses, but I argue that it is not an authenticity built on form, fabric, and in this case, age. The Buddha statue is authentic on account of the power it possesses, having survived the flooding, which the temple did not. Such power may increase and decrease, and for this reason some Buddha statues need to be *revitalized* when their power has declined and sometimes even becomes exhausted. The Vat Pa Mi Buddha also acts as a reminder that authenticity gained through performance is associated with the performer rather than with the actual object. Authenticity appears to be more connected to self-realization and being truthful to oneself. Here we arrive full circle back to the introductory story about the Ou Mong *sim*, whose material authenticity in the end was subordinate to the villagers' being in the world.

RETHINKING PRESERVATION THROUGH AUTHENTICITY

If we now recall the introductory story about the demolition of the Ou Mong *sim*, we might ask ourselves which approach to heritage management would be the most appropriate. Is it possible to bridge the obvious gap between a sophisticated preservationist sensibility where the Lao cultural patrimony should be preserved, and the perceptions and priorities of the local community where the old *sim* is laid in ruins, the villagers make merit and by doing so maintain the authenticity of the place, partake in, and hand over the ever changing heritage of a Buddhist community? If it is possible, *how* can we then bridge this divide, to best meet as many demands as possible? Or is it desirable to even try? Can the *sim* be included in the heritage management process at all? These are all difficult questions with no simple or straightforward answers. General alternative strategies are not easily found when dealing with a constantly changing heritage. We might be better off debating preservation ethics in a way that respects situated, particular, and non-essentialist approaches. Imagination and sensitivity are needed to put heritage management into practice in a constructive and intelligent way, so that the people involved recognize their rights in justifying the same values that they consider important and sacred. A baseline for this approach must be to acknowledge the different worldviews one encounters and accept that western frames of reference cannot and should not be used unswervingly for other realities, other worldviews. There are different realities, rather than different appearances of reality. Henare, Holbraad, and Wastell (2007: 11), following Latour (2002), conclude this by stating that:

> For if cultures render different appearances of reality, it follows that one of them is special and better than all the others, namely the one that best *reflects* reality. And since science—the search for representations that reflect reality as transparently and faithfully as possible—happens to be a modern Western project, that special culture is, well, ours.

What some consider heritage might not at all be conceived or constructed in the same way by others. Similarly, what others consider sacred we cannot always conceive in the same way. Therefore, it is not only plurality and multivocality that is important; it is rather to acknowledge different worlds. Because if we just add alternative stories, we still use the same frames of reference, value systems, and discourses. Performative authenticity as illustrated here should not be understood only within the same frame of reference as that of material authenticity. It needs its own frame of reference. Further, heritage managers might practice a radical inclusivity, for example by granting equal value to popular religious discourses as to scientific heritage discourses, as well as acknowledging the double nature of heritage as both material and immaterial (see Preucel and Pecos in this volume). This does not mean that, having acknowledged the existence of different discourses and worldviews, heritage managers should have declared "Let them destroy their cultural heritage" in a case like Ou Mong. If scholarship, political commitment, and sensitivity are one and the same, then different worlds and realities must be engaged, and the differences and similarities examined in order to better understand and tolerate multiple frames of reference.

REFERENCES

Alivizatou, Marilena. 2012. "Debating Heritage Authenticity: Kastom and Development at the Vanuatu Cultural Centre." *International Journal of Heritage Studies* 18 (2): 124–43. http://dx.doi.org/10.1080/13527258.2011.602981.

Byrne, Denis. 1993. "The Past of Others: Archaeological Heritage Management in Thailand and Australia." PhD dissertation, Australian National University, Canberra.

Byrne, Denis. 2008. "Heritage as Social Action." In *The Heritage Reader*, ed. Graham Fairclough, Rodney Harrison, John H. Jameson, Jr., and John Schofield, 149–73. London: Routledge.

Byrne, Denis. 2009. "Archaeology and the Fortress of Rationality." In *Cosmopolitan Archaeologies*, ed. Lynn Meskell, 68–88. Durham, NC: Duke University Press. http://dx.doi.org/10.1215/9780822392422-004.

Byrne, Denis. 2011. "Thinking about Popular Religion and Heritage." In *Rethinking Cultural Resource Management in Southeast Asia: Preservation, Development, and Neglect*, ed. John N. Miksic, Geok Yian Goh, and Sue O'Connor, 3–14. London: Anthem Press.

Guttormsen, Torgrim Sneve, and Knut Fageraas. 2011. "The Social Production of 'Attractive Authenticity' at the World Heritage Site of Røros, Norway." *International Journal of Heritage Studies* 17 (5): 442–62. http://dx.doi.org/10.1080/13527258.2011.571270.

Henare, Amiria, Martin Holbraad, and Siri Wastell, eds. 2007. *Thinking Through Things: Theorising Artifacts Ethnographically*. London: Routledge.

Holbraad, Martin. 2007. "The Power of Powder: Multiplicity and Motion in the Divinatory Cosmology of Cuban Ifá (or *Mana*, Again)." In *Thinking Through Things: Theorising Artifacts Ethnographically*, ed. Amiria Henare, Martin Holbraad, and Sari Wastell, 189–225. London: Routledge.

Holt, John Clifford. 2009. *Spirits of the Place: Buddhism and Lao Religious Culture*. Honolulu: University of Hawaii Press.

Holtorf, Cornelius. 2006. "Can Less Be More? Heritage in the Age of Terrorism." *Public Archaeology* 5 (2): 101–9. http://dx.doi.org/10.1179/pua.2006.5.2.101.

Holtorf, Cornelius, and Tim Schadla-Hall. 1999. "Age as Artefact: On Archaeological Authenticity." *European Journal of Archaeology* 2 (2): 229–47. http://dx.doi.org/10.1179/eja.1999.2.2.229.

ICOMOS. 1994. *The Nara Document on Authenticity*. Paris: ICOMOS.

Jones, Siân. 2009. "Experiencing Authenticity at Heritage Sites: Some Implications for Heritage Management and Conservation." *Conservation and Management of Archaeological Sites* 11 (2): 133–47. http://dx.doi.org/10.1179/175355210X12670102063661.

Jones, Siân. 2010. "Negotiating Authentic Objects and Authentic Selves: Beyond the Deconstruction of Authenticity." *Journal of Material Culture* 15 (2): 181–203. http://dx.doi.org/10.1177/1359183510364074.

Karlström, Anna. 2005. "Spiritual Materiality: Heritage Preservation in a Buddhist World?" *Journal of Social Archaeology* 5 (3): 338–55. http://dx.doi.org/10.1177/1469605305057571.

Karlström, Anna. 2009. "Preserving Impermanence: The Creation of Heritage in Vientiane, Laos." PhD dissertation, Uppsala University, Uppsala.

Kidd, Jenny. 2011. "Performing the Knowing Archive: Heritage Performance and Authenticity." *International Journal of Heritage Studies* 17 (1): 22–35. http://dx.doi.org/10.1080/13527258.2011.524003.

Knudsen, Britta Timm, and Anne Marit Waade, eds. 2010. *Re-Investing Authenticity: Tourism, Place and Emotions*. Bristol, UK: Channel View Publications.

Labadi, Sophia. 2010. "World Heritage, Authenticity and Post-authenticity: International and National Perspectives." In *Heritage and Globalisation*, ed. Sophia Labadi and Colin Long, 66–84. London: Routledge.

Latour, Bruno. 2002. *War of the Worlds: What about Peace?* Chicago, IL: Prickly Paradigm Press.

Lindholm, Charles. 2008. *Culture and Authenticity*. Oxford: Blackwell Publishing.

Lovata, T. 2007. *Inauthentic Archaeologies: Public Uses and Abuses of the Past*. Walnut Creek, CA: Left Coast Press.

Lowenthal, David. 1985. *The Past is a Foreign Country*. Cambridge: Cambridge University Press.

Potkin, Alan. 2001. *Multimedia and Digital Imaging in Environmental and Cultural Conservation, Vat Ou Mong Peri-demolition Archive*. Vientiane, Laos: Cultivate Understanding Multimedia.

Robinson, Richard H., and Willard L. Johnson. 1997. *The Buddhist Religion: A Historical Introduction*. London: Wadsworth.

Sayavongkhamdy, Thongsa. 1996. *Prehistory in Laos*. Unpublished manuscript, Ministry of Information and Culture, Department of Museums and Archaeology, Vientiane, Laos.

Sayavongkhamdy, Thongsa. 2009. "Development of Museums in Laos." Paper presented at ASEAN Museum Directors' Symposium, Singapore. http://www.nhb.gov.sg/amds/downloads/51-56.pdf. Accessed April 10, 2012.

Scarangella, Linda. 2010. "Indigeneity in Tourism: Transnational Spaces, Pan-Indian Identity, and Cosmopolitanism." In *Indigenous Cosmopolitans: Transnational and Transcultural Indigeneity in the Twenty-first Century*, ed. Maximilian C. Forte, 163–88. New York, NY: Peter Lang Publishing.

Smith, Laurajane. 2006. *Uses of Heritage*. London: Routledge.

Tambiah, Stanley J. 1970. *Buddhism and the Spirit Cults in North-east Thailand*. Cambridge: Cambridge University Press.

Thomas, Julian. 2004. *Archaeology and Modernity*. London: Routledge.

UNESCO. 2005. *Operational Guidelines for the Implementation of the World Heritage Convention*. Intergovernmental Committee for the Protection of the World Cultural and Natural Heritage WHC–05/2. Paris: UNESCO.

Viravong, Maha Sila. 1964. *History of Laos*. [*Phongsavadan Lao*]. Trans. US Joint Publications Research Service. New York, NY: Paragon Books Reprint Corp.

Wang, Ning. 1999. "Rethinking Authenticity in Tourism Experience." *Annals of Tourism Research* 26 (2): 349–70. http://dx.doi.org/10.1016/S0160-7383(98)00103-0.

Zhu, Yujie. 2012. "Performing Heritage: Rethinking Authenticity in Tourism." *Annals of Tourism Research* 39 (3): 1495–513. http://dx.doi.org/10.1016/j.annals.2012.04.003.

Civil Society 3

Civil Society in the Field of Cultural Property
Protection during Armed Conflict

SIGRID VAN DER AUWERA

Recently the use of the concept of 'civil society' in the field of cultural heritage has increased significantly. In addition to governments and heritage workers, the communities that are heirs to cultural heritage (and thus members of civil society) are ever more being considered responsible for its maintenance and preservation. Moreover, the value of heritage for society is increasingly underlined by international heritage policies. The Council of Europe has clearly promulgated these ideas. The 2005 *Framework Convention on the Value of Cultural Heritage for Society* was epoch-making in this regard, due to the establishment of the concept of 'heritage communities' and of a legal basis for civil society engagement.

In the introduction to this volume, Kathryn Lafrenz Samuels points to a 'rhetoric revival,' which may have encouraged civil society activities in the field of cultural heritage. This evolution is clearly observed in the field of cultural heritage during armed conflict, in which a proliferation of civil society activities has been observed in recent decades, which the following illustrates by way of examples from this particular field of heritage management. Moreover, heritage is considered a form of rhetoric. This is also clearly observed during armed conflicts, in which promoting and destroying heritage sometimes presents a unique rhetorical strategy. For

DOI: 10.5876/9781607323846.c003

47

these reasons, I argue that a critical evaluation of civil society in the field of cultural heritage is necessary for understanding how and to what extent heritage practice is built upon a rhetoric of community, local responsibility, and an engaged citizenry.

Therefore in the following I begin by describing how the discourse of civil society has evolved in cultural heritage policy texts. I then turn to values attributed by different authors to a civil society in this field. By analyzing the *practice* of a civil society in cultural heritage protection during armed conflict as a case study, I argue for a more critical approach to civil society engagement in this field. A civil society seems to be well established when different non-governmental organizations (NGOs) are involved, but a true bottom-up approach including local communities is lacking. Moreover, the concepts 'civil society' and 'heritage communities' are rather problematic, since these actors could become the perpetrators of cultural property destruction. This observation makes advocating an actual bottom-up approach even more legitimate. Awareness-raising and education are considered a prerequisite for safeguarding heritage in societies where conflicts emerge.

CIVIL SOCIETY AND CULTURAL HERITAGE

The term 'civil society' only recently entered into the field of cultural heritage. Its growing significance is *inter alia* associated with current interest in bottom-up approaches for heritage conservation and volunteer projects for increasing engagement in local heritage. However, in discursive practice the meaning of the concept and its usefulness for the context of cultural heritage are often taken for granted. Civil society is a dynamic concept with a variety of meanings and interpretations, but it is held together by a central idea: civil society concerns communities that are based on a social contract among individuals. Hence, civil society can be expressed in terms of common bonds, or community (Delanty 2010: 2). Although the concepts of 'civil society' and 'community' are often used confusedly (especially in the field of cultural heritage), communities are considered a part of civil society. Communities are groups within civil society with a particular awareness of themselves in relation to other groups.

For our purposes here, I use the terms in the following manner. When I refer to 'communities,' I am either referring to a text in which this particular concept was used or I am referring to a specific section of civil society. In contrast to communities, 'civil society' refers instead to a certain aim of these communities (and other groups in society) to act publicly and change the current state order. Civil society is, for instance, described by Kaldor (2003: 585) as "the process through which individuals negotiate, argue, struggle against or agree with each other and with the centers of political and economic authority. Through voluntary associations, movements, parties, unions, the individual is able to act publicly." According to Encarnación (2003: 24), civil society is the domain of social life that is open, voluntary, self-generating, at least partly self-sustainable, autonomous from the state, and bound by a legal system of shared values. As a level of social organization, it is distinct from political society (i.e., political parties, governmental agencies, and the government itself) and from economic society (i.e., commercial firms and businesses). With these definitions another term associated with civil society is also cited: 'voluntary.' Civil society activities are voluntary, and voluntary associations are also part of civil society.

Although political theorists share some consensus on the meaning of the concept 'civil society,' debate continues regarding the groups that compose civil society. Civil society traditionally concerns groups functioning independently of the government and the market (non-governmental and non-profit). However, actors are often financed by states, and civil society organizations are increasingly involved in traditional state activities such as healthcare and social work. Nonetheless, civil society remains the domain situated between the state, the market, and the family, but the extent of this domain can depend on the responsibilities the government takes up. Moreover, increasingly political activities are transferred to international arenas, such as the European Union, the Council of Europe, and the United Nations. This internationalization has created a new playing field for civil society and an expansion of influence for non-governmental actors. Civil society contributes to processes of citizenship and democratization, which can no longer be situated between state borders alone. An international or global civil society is thus increasingly important for enhancing democracy on a supranational level. We see this mirrored in the field of cultural heritage, where heritage policies are increasingly developed and elaborated in the framework of international organizations, such as the UNESCO and the Council of Europe.

In the following, I outline the international context in which the concept of civil society entered into the field of cultural heritage. However, the European context is emphasized due to the significance of Council of Europe policies for the development of the concept in a cultural heritage context.

The emergence of the 'civil society' concept in the field of cultural heritage goes hand in hand with three other important developments in heritage discourse and policies, namely:

(1) the widening of the concept of cultural heritage from the intangible inheritance of cultural production to the recognition of both tangible and intangible heritage (cf. the UNESCO 2003 *Convention for the Safeguarding of the Intangible Cultural Heritage* and the Council of Europe's 2005 *Framework Convention on the Value of Cultural Heritage for Society,* also known as 'the Faro Convention');

(2) the shift in emphasis from unity to diversity, or from a heritage of humanity to heritage of local communities (cf. the 2003 UNESCO *Convention,* and the UNESCO 2005 *Convention on the Protection and Promotion of the Diversity of Cultural Expressions*); and

(3) the transition from conservation-oriented to value-oriented approaches for assessing the place of cultural heritage in society (cf. the 2005 Council of Europe *Framework Convention*).

These developments have encouraged civil society engagement in the field of cultural heritage. The widening of the concept of heritage and emphasis on cultural diversity stressed the importance of the heritage of local communities. A renewed attention to local identity, as the reverse side of globalization, requires a bottom-up approach to heritage management. Such an approach emphasizes that the government is not the sole stakeholder, as local communities—seen as the heirs to locally and culturally diverse heritage—are also responsible for its maintenance. Moreover, this framework acknowledges that if heritage is valuable for society, then society has to play a role in its preservation.

This philosophy is reflected in international policies. As early as 1996, the UNESCO World Commission on Culture and Development issued the report *Our Creative Diversity,* which pointed at the importance of engaging civil society in the field of cultural heritage:

> The commission, observing the discrepancy between the ends and means of heritage conservation, throughout the world, recommends that international efforts be made to mobilize the goodwill of volunteers of all ages to work as "Cultural Heritage Volunteers" under professional guidance and alongside professional staff. Their permanent mission would be to contribute to the preservation and enhancement of the human heritage, whether tangible or intangible, using modern techniques, in order to disseminate useful knowledge, enrich humanity's awareness of its heritage and promote deeper mutual understanding and respect between cultures. (UNESCO 1996: 14)

The focus of responsibilities concerning the protection of cultural heritage was shifting from a forum of conservation experts and governments to a more participatory approach involving local stakeholders. The *Operational Guidelines for the Implementation of the World Heritage Convention* (UNESCO 2005) defined these local stakeholders as private sector businesses, developers, owners, NGOs, and community groups. The UNESCO 2003 *Convention for the Safeguarding of the Intangible Cultural Heritage* also emphasizes the role of communities, as part of civil society, in the production, safeguarding, maintenance, and re-creation of intangible cultural heritage. This concern was restated and highlighted by the 2006 "Expert Meeting on Community Involvement in Safeguarding Intangible Cultural Heritage: Towards the Implementation of the 2003 Convention" (UNESCO 2006). Here the concept of community was used in order to point to the particular communities engaged in the production and recreation of elements of intangible heritage. However, I must point to some shortcomings. As UNESCO is a state-driven organization that respects the sovereign right of its members, the *nomination* of intangible cultural heritage still remains an exclusive right of the state concerned (I return to this point below). In a similar vein, the 2005 *Convention on the Protection and Promotion of the Diversity of Cultural Expressions* refers to the importance of civil society in promoting and protecting cultural diversity, of which cultural heritage is seen as a component.

Other global heritage organizations also incorporate this emphasis. According to the International Council of Museums (ICOM) *Code of Ethics*, adopted in Seoul in 2004, "the governing body should have a written policy in volunteer work which promotes a positive relationship between volunteers and members of the museum profession" (ICOM 2004: 1.17). Moreover, the concept of community participation in museums is becoming more firmly established and strongly promoted through ICOM initiatives such as eco-museums (Van der Auwera and Schramme 2011: 66–68), which do not simply describe the relationship between organisms, but rather the interaction with their whole physical environment—natural, fabricated and social (Davis 2011: 4)—and thus also the communities involved.

Heritage policies of the Council of Europe also demonstrate the intertwining of these processes. In 2001, an ambitious *Declaration on the Role of Voluntary Organisations in the Field of Cultural Heritage* was adopted by the Fifth European Conference of Ministers responsible for culture. This declaration was pivotal to the subsequent adoption of the Faro Convention, which already in Article 1 points to a "collective responsibility towards cultural heritage," "the role of cultural heritage in the construction of a peaceful and democratic society," and "greater synergy of competencies among all the public, institutional, and private actors concerned." The establishment of the concept of 'a heritage community' is a case in point here. Such a heritage community "consists of people who value specific aspects of cultural heritage which they wish, within the framework of public action, to sustain and transmit to future generations" (Article 2). This definition reveals a paradigm shift in how heritage is conceived in Europe: it involves people rather than objects, and the value for society is privileged. The implication is that society bears ever more responsibility for safeguarding this heritage. Section III consequently calls for "shared responsibility for cultural heritage and public participation" and created a legal basis for the promotion of civil society engagement in the field of cultural heritage with Article 11, titled "The Organization of Public Responsibilities for Cultural Heritage," and Article 12, titled "Access to Cultural Heritage and Democratic Participation."

Apart from discursive practices in policy texts, a growing number of volunteer initiatives and organizations actually engage in cultural heritage conservation and management, as illustrated in the *Inventory of Heritage Organisations in Europe* (2010), an overview of European NGOs active in the field of cultural heritage. Moreover, the growing number of conferences organized on this particular theme acknowledges its increasing importance. In 2009, for example, several Belgian heritage organizations took the initiative to organize the Conference "Heritage Care through Active Citizenship" in Mechelen, Belgium. This was followed in early 2010 by the Conference "Civil Society and Heritage." In 2010 too, the conference "Civil Society and Cultural Heritage in the Mediterranean" was organized as part of the EUROMED program (EUROMED 2011). Taking all of the above developments into account, we can consequently observe an increased attention directed to engaging civil society in the field of cultural heritage.

THE VALUE ASCRIBED TO CIVIL SOCIETY
FOR CULTURAL HERITAGE

The concept of civil society thus tends to be well established in heritage policy documents. Civil society organizations and initiatives are being founded at the same time that the concept is being incorporated into academic and professional parlance. Moreover, different authors ascribe specific values to civil society for cultural heritage. Rosenstein (2006: 1), for example, argues that processes of globalization and individualization have eroded a sense of community feeling, a sense of belonging to a certain group. Cultural heritage organizations can help to cultivate this sense of community belonging by creating a figurative meeting place. Thus, the aim of cultural heritage organizations is to bind communities together by promoting and safeguarding identities, traditions, and values. Through public programs that allow the sharing of cultural heritage, Rosenstein argues, civil society is also able to build bridges among different groups and communities.

Barber (2003: 81–84) also emphasizes the value of cultural heritage for community bonding. Cultural heritage allows us to see each other as parts of invisible entities bound by common characteristics that transcend our differences. However, these arguments start from the assumption that a sense of community feeling is necessary and valuable (I return to this assumption below). Moreover, Barber suggests that economic globalization leads to uniformity, and therefore the safeguarding of cultural heritage has become a political and ideological task for everyone, in order to preserve cultural diversity. This is associated with the idea that neither democracy nor civil society can exist without diversity and pluralism. Autonomous and diverse cultures should therefore be preserved and safeguarded from the monopolizing and homogenizing powers of globalization or, as Barber puts it, against a "McWorld" (2003: 81–84). Along the lines of such arguments, Beschaouch (2003: 90–91) argues that civil society should be engaged in preservation activities in order to promote cultural diversity.

Barber (2003: 80–81) goes even further in this rationale: in his view the maintenance and preservation of cultural heritage is essential for the establishment and maintenance of democracy itself. According to him, democracy should not only consider the opinions of the living but those of past generations as well, and these opinions are mirrored in heritage. He further argues that cultural heritage allows us to communicate with our ancestors and, thus, it should therefore be safeguarded in order to establish and maintain democracy. In this argument, Barber considers democracy as involving the whole of humanity. Democracy must thus not only give a voice to the living; it should also give a voice to those who have gone before, as they created welfare, habits, traditions, and heritage: the social capital on which our lives are built. The preservation and maintenance of cultural heritage is thus a democratic task (Barber 2003: 80–81). In this view, the destruction (and thus the non-maintenance) of cultural heritage opposes democracy, as observed more than once during armed conflicts. For example, the destruction of cultural property in Kosovo was used as a weapon of psychological warfare and was even an element in the ethnic cleansing process. Orthodox Serbs devastated Albanian Islamic religious heritage and vice versa. With these acts, both parties sought to exclude a part of the Kosovar past and thus any communication with a part of the country's ancestry.

CIVIL SOCIETY IN THE FIELD OF CULTURAL PROPERTY
PROTECTION DURING ARMED CONFLICT

Civil society thus plays a key role in fostering democracy in peaceful societies. Conflict situations may even generate a more intense mobilization of civil society, since a high degree of politicization and a less structured institutional setting feature in conflicts (Marchetti and Tocci 2009: 201). Furthermore, civil society seems to be well established in the protection of cultural heritage during and after armed conflicts, since by the beginning of the twentieth century a proliferation of NGOs in this field has been observed. Best known is the International Committee of the Blue Shield (ICBS), which was established in 1996 by the International Council of Museums (ICOM), the International Council on Monuments and Sites (ICOMOS), the International Federation of Library Associations (IFLA) and the International Council of Archives (ICA), later attended by the Co-ordinating Council of Audiovisual Archives Associations (CCAAA), and is formally recognized by UNESCO in the 1999 *Second Protocol to the Hague Convention on the Protection of Cultural Property during Armed Conflict.* After the looting of the National Museum in Baghdad in 2003, the proliferation of NGOs active in protecting cultural property during armed conflict became even more pronounced; my previous research accounted for more than 40 NGOs involved in this particular field (Van der Auwera 2012c: 177–213). Although the rapid growth of concern was mainly represented by NGOs, other civil society actions, such as non-institutionalized activities, occurred as well. In 2003, objects of the National Library of Baghdad were carried to the nearby mosque by neighbors under the surveillance of the Imam in order to save them (interview with Rene Teijgeler, September 21, 2011) and Great Ayatollah al-Said al-Sistani issued a *fatwa* in order to stop the looting of archaeological sites (Hamdani 2008: 226).

For the reasons described above, civil society activities involving cultural heritage protection during and after armed conflicts provide an excellent case-study for analyzing civil society practices in the field of cultural heritage more generally. However, another contextual condition shaping civil society during armed conflict is problematic for cultural heritage: the actual nature of the state in question. In normal circumstances, civil society needs to be permitted and protected by the state. Hence, its existence is determined by the degree of democracy or by the existence of basic rights and freedoms. When these rights and freedoms are curtailed, civil society is likely to develop beyond legal boundaries, often aiming to subvert the state (Marchetti and Tocci 2009: 203). During armed conflict, cultural property is not only protected by civil society; it seems also that civil society actors can be the main perpetrators of destruction.

Although the use of the term is controversial in this context, I argue that rebel groups and insurgents can also be characterized as civil society actors, in the sense of being non-state actors interacting with other actors in order to change the current state order (or, at least, as being established under the guise of this reason). In current armed conflicts, a politics of identity emerges (Van der Auwera 2012a), where identity (or sub-nationalism) is used in the process of political mobilization and heritage is used as a mirror for this identity. Elites are willing to fill the power vacuum. Therefore, they have to mobilize at a grassroots level and form 'imagined communities' (Anderson 2006), or rather 'difficult heritage communities' (translated, for this context, in line with 'difficult heritage'). The claims on the territory of 'others' have to be erased. Hence, cultural heritage symbolizing 'other' identities or communities is destroyed by these actors. This process of 'territorialization' (Smith 2009: 47–48) is part of the operation of ethnic cleansing. Heritage is thus used in nationalistic rhetoric by non-state actors in their struggle to fill the power vacuum (Van der Auwera 2012a).

This process was, for example, observed in Kosovo. During the Yugoslav period everything separating the people was banned from collective memory. When society became increasingly polarized after Josip Broz Tito's death in 1980, dissonant histories and nationalistic discourses re-emerged. These histories continually intensified and were (mis)used for nationalistic purposes. The destruction of memories that did not fit within these narratives went increasingly hand in hand with this process. Herscher and Riedlmayer (2000: 109–10) argue that competing narratives on cultural identity in Kosovo were pushed forward as a basis for competing claims on sovereignty over the territory. Cultural heritage was considered as proof for these claims and, as a consequence, suffered destruction.

Moreover, civil society actors (such as rebel groups) can become criminal organizations by engaging in illicit activities such as the looting of archaeological sites and museums and the subsequent illicit trade in looted antiquities. This looting and illicit trade can feed informal economies and fund insurgents, as was observed in Iraq (see Bogdanos 2008: 109–34). One could argue that these actors no longer belong to civil society, because they have become profit-making organizations. However, when they only engage in criminal activities in order to finance the struggle, so as to guarantee their continued engagement, they remain non-profit. When they cross the border of self-enrichment, they become profit-makers and leave the space of civil society.

Communities and civil society can, thus, be exclusive and inclusive, and in this way communities can take a civic or a radical form, very often being a resource for civic associations, but also for more radical kinds of collective mobilization (Delanty 2010: 35). The analysis of civil society during armed conflict by Marchetti and Tocci (2009) is very interesting in this regard and can be applied to a civil society in the field of cultural heritage during armed conflict. Their model points to the fact that civil society in the context of armed conflict can include 'civil' as well as 'less civil' organizations. Therefore, these authors prefer to use the term 'conflict society' (CoS), instead of civil society, which implies only 'civil' actors.

TOWARDS A BOTTOM-UP APPROACH

My previous inventory of civil society in the field of cultural heritage protection during armed conflict led to the conclusion that the main activities of the organizations involved were fact-finding missions, restoration projects, the adoption of statements (i.e., UNESCO and the Council of Europe), advocacy, and awareness-raising within the military and within antiquity-buying countries (Van der Auwera 2012c: 177–213). On the other hand, only a limited amount of involvement in awareness-raising exists within the conflict societies themselves, although organizations such as Society for the Preservation of Afghan's Cultural Heritage (SPACH) and Cultural Heritage without Borders (CHwB) are exceptions. However, such awareness-raising within local communities is essential because cultural property, in contemporary conflicts, is mostly destroyed by civilians and thus by civil society and community actors. The fact that civil society actors can also become perpetrators implies that the problem of cultural property destruction during armed conflict is strongly embedded within conflict societies. Multiple heritage perspectives must be highlighted, and bottom-up approaches must be encouraged. The communities that are heirs to cultural heritage, and thus also civil society, must play a role in the development of mutual respect for cultural heritage. Top-down approaches often fail to meet the needs of local communities. Bottom-up approaches (which are expected to feature civil society actors) are thus considered an asset. An awareness of the social context is needed, and a stakeholders' participatory approach is the most natural option in heritage management.

However, in practice, civil society activities related to the protection of cultural property during armed conflict are not true bottom-up activities (or, not true civil society activities). The field is, in particular, occupied by NGOs, which are often pejoratively referred to as Non-Grassroots Organizations (Marchetti and Tocci 2009: 204). Moreover, many NGOs active in this field are one-man initiatives or organizations without—or with few—grassroots

(Van der Auwera 2012b: 191–95). Mostly, these NGOs are international NGOs which have only limited bonds with the local population or none at all. However, some NGOs such as CHwB-Kosovo are willing to engage local communities. In this manner the organization endeavors to increase awareness and respect for the cultural heritage of diverse communities. Therefore, less institutionalized initiatives must also be encouraged.

Some striking examples were observed in Iraq. Abdelamir al Hamdani (2008: 226) heard of rumors spread by looters on the existence of a *fatwa* that allowed plundering when the profit financed the insurgency. These *fatwas* probably did not exist. However, Hamdani thought that such a *fatwa* could be a powerful instrument in the fight against looting. Therefore, he asked Great Ayatollah al-Said al-Sistani to assist in stopping the looting. Al-Sistani issued a *fatwa* prohibiting the looting of archaeological sites, and he requested that plundered artifacts be returned to the State Board of Antiquities and Heritage. Moreover, the archaeological site of Uruk was effectively protected against looters by the At-Tobe clan that lives nearby (Kila 2008: 180). The theoretical insight that the bonds engendered by non-voluntary groups (such as tribes, families, and communities) are often stronger and more tenacious than those of voluntary groups (Marchetti and Tocci 2009: 203) can thus be considered as an additional rationale to involve such groups.

Moreover, it is argued that projects mobilizing people around the care of cultural property can stimulate social cohesion. Bandarin, Hosagrahar, and Sailer Albernaz (2011) argue that cultural festivals have proven to be effective opportunities to strike up dialogue and to overcome barriers between different cultures. They name the UNESCO project in the Bamiyan province in Afghanistan as a case in point. A team of fifteen Afghans spent two years de-mining and removing unexploded ammunition from three sites at the heart of the Dragon Valley. Other projects such as the restitution of the Axum Obelisk to Ethiopia, the rebuilding of the Mostar Bridge in Bosnia and Herzegovina, and the safeguarding of the Angkor temple indicate that shared responsibility for preserving heritage for future generations is a factor in social cohesion (Bandarin, Hosagrahar, and Sailer Albernaz 2011: 20–21). However, these projects have to be carefully developed and thought over, since it is not a *sine qua non* that, for example, festivals overcome barriers between cultures. Such events can also be rather exclusive. In Northern Ireland, for example, past victories such as the Battle of the Boyne are celebrated. Parades are interpreted as celebrations of in-group solidarity and therefore as manifestations of Protestant dominance over the Catholic minority. Clearly, they intensify political and cultural differences and often result in violence (Conteh-Morgan 2004: 81–82).

In Kosovo, NGOs and international organizations working on the restoration of destroyed heritage often claim that their work stimulates dialogue and reconciliation between different communities. Moreover, according to Sali Shoshi, the Director of CHwB-Kosovo, EU funding is easier to obtain when reconstruction projects are framed in reconciliation efforts that involve different communities (interview with Sali Shoshi, October 26, 2011). Although I acknowledge that such a project can be successful, such success must not be assumed. More research into the factors of success versus failure associated with these projects is urgently needed. Moreover, it is questionable as to whether such projects do not cater to 'imagined' or 're-invented communities' and thus to communities of which the existence was exaggerated in the process of political mobilization at the start of the conflict. In the end, awareness-raising activities must also lead to an awareness that homogeneous groups are social constructions too, and that the formation of identity is a multilayered process.

Finally, let us return to the international heritage policies, increasingly focused as they are on civil society and communities. Although the *Framework Convention* of the Council of Europe is pointing to the value of heritage in post-conflict resolution and prevention (Article 7c) and to the responsibility for respecting the cultural heritage of others as much as their own heritage (Article 4b), the risks of community and civil society involvement must be further highlighted. According to the Faro Convention, a heritage community "consists of people who value specific aspects of cultural heritage which they wish, within the framework of public action, to sustain and transmit to future generations" (Article 2b). Heritage communities destroying the cultural heritage of other communities are thus heritage communities too. Hence, I argue the concept of heritage communities should refer to the need for inclusiveness of these communities, and the effects of 'difficult heritage communities' may thus not be ignored. Moreover, as highlighted above, the UNESCO 2003 *Convention for the Safeguarding of the Intangible Cultural Heritage* emphasizes the role of communities in the production, safeguarding, maintenance, and recreation of intangible cultural heritage. Nevertheless, as UNESCO is a state-driven organization that respects the sovereign rights of its members, the nomination of intangible cultural heritage still remains an exclusive right of the state concerned. This is particularly problematic in countries which are vulnerable to identity-bound conflict, where the heritage of cultural minority communities may be excluded. Effective bottom-up strategies challenging the 'Authorized Heritage Discourse' (Smith 2006) still appear to be insignificant in this context. A multilayered approach to heritage and its communities is thus desirable. Belonging should not be represented as a final once and for all solution or, as Fraser (2008: 131) puts it, lead to a situation in which group members are bound by and have to conform to a collective identity.

CONCLUSION

The idea of civil society has increasingly entered heritage discourse, in policy as well as academic parlance. Moreover, a proliferation of NGOs, which are identified as civil society actors, has sprung up in the field of cultural heritage and in particular in the context of heritage protection during armed conflict. In heritage parlance the concept of civil society is associated with community participation, an engaged citizenry, and voluntary associations. Bottom-up approaches tend to be taken for granted as being part of civil society activities in the field of cultural heritage. Nevertheless, an evaluation of so-called civil society activities in the field of cultural heritage protection during armed conflict is not encouraging. The practice of NGOs in the field is instead top-down, and local communities are not consulted and are often themselves the perpetrators of cultural heritage destruction during armed conflicts. In some instances, however, communities are involved in NGO work. Yet in such instances the assumption is often to involve communities as opposing stakeholders, ignoring further that the concept of communities as homogeneous groups is a social construct. Therefore, different forms of belonging can be identified, and must be highlighted. Civil society activities in the field of cultural heritage must consequently point to the importance of developing inclusive, pluralistic, multilayered, and democratic heritage communities.

REFERENCES

Anderson, Benedict. 2006. *Imagined Communities*. 2nd ed. London: Verso.

Bandarin, Fransesco, Jyoti Hosagrahar, and Frances Sailer Albernaz. 2011. "Why Development Needs Culture." *Journal of Cultural Heritage Management and Sustainable Development* 1 (1): 15–25. http://dx.doi.org/10.1108/20441261111129906.

Barber, Benjamin R. 2003. "Managing Europe's Cultural Heritage: A Democratic Perspective." In *Visies op erfgoed in Vlaanderen en Europ/ Optique de gestions du partimoine en Flandres et en Europe*, ed. Joris Capenberghs, Jann Cools, and Patrick De Rynck, 80–84. Antwerp, Belgium: Culturele Biografie Vlaanderen vzw.

Beschaouch, Azedine. 2003. "Towards an Ethics of Social Integration and Participation Practices in Cultural Heritage Management." In *Visies op erfgoed in Vlaanderen en Europa: Optique de gestions du partimoine en Flandres et en Europe*, ed.

Joris Capenberghs, Jann Cools, and Patrick De Rynck, 130–33. Antwerp, Belgium: Culturele Biografie Vlaanderen vzw.

Bogdanos, Matthew. 2008. "Thieves of Baghdad." In *The Destruction of Cultural Heritage in Iraq*, ed. Peter G. Stone and Joanne Farchakh, 109–34. Woodbridge, UK: The Boydell Press.

Conteh-Morgan, Earl. 2004. *Collective Political Violence: An Introduction to the Theories and Cases of Violent Conflicts*. London: Routledge.

Davis, Peter. 2011. *Eco Museums: A Sense of Place*. 2nd ed. London: Continuum.

Delanty, Gerard. 2010. *Community*. 2nd ed. London: Routledge.

Encarnación, Omar G. 2003. *The Myth of Civil Society: Social Capital and Democratic Consolidation in Spain and Brazil*. New York, NY: Palgrave. http://dx.doi.org/10 .1057/9781403981646.

EUROMED (Euro-Mediterranean Networks). 2011. EUROMED homepage. http://www.euromedheritage.net. Accessed December 7, 2011.

Fraser, Nancy. 2008. "Rethinking Recognition: Overcoming Displacement and Reification in Cultural Politics." In *Adding Insult to Injury: Nancy Fraser Debates Her Critics*, ed. Kevin Olsen, 129–41. London: Verso.

Hamdani, Abdelamir al. 2008. "Protecting and Recording Our Archaeological Heritage in Southern Iraq." *Near Eastern Archaeology* 71 (4): 221–29.

Herscher, Andrew, and Andras Riedlmayer. 2000. "Monument and Crime: The Destruction of Historic Architecture in Kosovo." *Grey Room* 1: 108–22. http://dx.doi.org/10.1162/152638100750173083.

ICOM. 2004. *ICOM Code of Ethics*. Paris: ICOM.

Inventory of Heritage Organisations in Europe. 2010. "Inventory of Heritage Organisations in Europe." http://www.heritage-organisations.eu/page?page=home2&lng=1. Accessed October 26, 2010.

Kaldor, Mary. 2003. "The Idea of Global Civil Society." *International Affairs* 79 (3): 583–93. http://dx.doi.org/10.1111/1468-2346.00324.

Kila, Joris D. 2008. "The Role of NATO and Civil Military Affairs." In *Antiquities under Siege: Cultural Heritage Protection after the Iraq War*, ed. Laurence Rothfield, 175–92. Lanham, MD: AltaMira Press.

Marchetti, Raffaele, and Nathalie Tocci. 2009. "Conflict Society: Understanding the Role of Civil Society in Conflict." *Global Change, Peace & Security* 21 (2): 201–17. http://dx.doi.org/10.1080/14781150902872091.

Rosenstein, Carol. 2006. *How Cultural Heritage Organizations Serve Communities: Priorities, Strengths, and Challenges*. Washington, DC: The Urban Institute.

Smith, Anthony D. 2009. *Ethno-symbolism and Nationalism: A Cultural Approach*. London: Routledge.

Smith, Laurajane. 2006. *The Uses of Heritage*. London: Routledge.

UNESCO. 1996. *Our Creative Diversity. Report of the UNESCO World Commission on Culture and Development, CLT-96/WS6*. Paris: UNESCO.

UNESCO. 2005. *Operational Guidelines for the Implementation of the World Heritage Convention*. Intergovernmental Committee for the Protection of the World's Cultural and Natural Heritage, World Heritage Centre, (Revised) February 2, WHC. 05/2. Paris: UNESCO.

UNESCO. 2006. *Expert Meeting on Community Involvement in Safeguarding Intangible Cultural Heritage: Towards the Implementation of the 2003 Convention. CLT/CH/ITH/DOCEM0306 REV.1*. Paris: UNESCO.

Van der Auwera, Sigrid. 2012a. "Contemporary Conflict, Nationalism, and the Destruction of Cultural Property during Armed Conflict." *Journal of Conflict Archaeology* 7 (1): 49–65. http://dx.doi.org/10.1179/157407812X13245464933821.

Van der Auwera, Sigrid. 2012b. *De bescherming van culturele goederen tijdens gewapende conflicten: naar een integrale preventiestrategie*. Antwerp, Belgium: Universiteit Antwerpen.

Van der Auwera, Sigrid. 2012c. *De bescherming van culturele goederen tijdens gewapende conflicten: naar een integrale preventiestrategie. Bijlage II: Inventaris*. Antwerp, Belgium: Universiteit Antwerpen.

Van der Auwera, Sigrid, and Annick Schramme. 2011. "Civil Society Action in the Field of Cultural Heritage: A European Perspective." *Heritage & Society* 4 (1): 59–81. http://dx.doi.org/10.1179/hso.2011.4.1.59.

Cultural Diversity 4

*Cultivating Proud and Productive
Citizens in Belizean Education*

ALICIA EBBITT MCGILL

Recognition of the complicated and multifaceted relationships between heritage and society is nothing new
(Kohl and Fawcett 1995; Smith 2006; Pyburn 2007;
Labadi and Long 2010). Smith (2006) notes the role
of heritage as a social process involving many actors.
On national levels, heritage is frequently a tool implemented by nation-states in developing "solidarity and
common cultural life" (De Cesari 2010: 309). Through
heritage policies and practices related to conservation,
tourism, research, and education nation-states utilize
culture and heritage rhetoric to construct and promote
national identity, manage cultural diversity, and cultivate a productive citizenry. These processes define and
reinforce ideologies about what both 'culture' and 'heritage' are and how they should be used and managed.

While global and national discourses of culture and
heritage limit interactions with and interpretations of
cultural heritage (see chapters by Adams, Baird, and
Rodéhn in this volume), such processes have been
found to influence but not dictate the lives of local
actors, who reinterpret heritage ideologies for their
own agendas (e.g., Askew 2010; McGill 2011, 2012;
Meskell 2012; Salazar 2010). For example, state cultural
heritage rhetoric is commonly transmitted via national
education initiatives and reproduced by teachers and
students. But, teachers and students also produce and

DOI: 10.5876/9781607323846.c004

transform cultural knowledge in educational contexts. Thus, an examination of schooling and curriculum related to culture and heritage can enrich understandings of the relationship between a state and its citizens by revealing power structures and individuals' responses to such discourses. Rodéhn's chapter on democracy and democratization in this volume demonstrates how museums are another institutional context for examining specific rhetoric and ideology about civic identity and citizenship.

In this chapter, I examine negotiations of heritage ideologies between the Belizean state and its citizens via the context of heritage education. In Belize, heritage plays a fundamental role in national identity narratives. State messages about the country's rich cultural diversity are promoted through archaeological research, tourism, and education. Here I draw from sixteen months of ethnographic research in Belize with a focus on interviews with national scholars involved in heritage research and education, and analysis of national social studies curricula. I demonstrate how global structures and ideologies related to heritage and cultural difference are used and transformed in Belizean education for national agendas related to cultural identity, nationalism, and development. I show how social and political inequalities are obscured under the guise of promoting national unity and celebrating cultural diversity in cultural education and reveal limitations of state ideologies by discussing how teachers negotiate these messages. Such findings are applicable to modern heritage projects entangled in these issues, such as heritage management, tourism, archaeological research, and education policy.

RESEARCH CONTEXT

Data presented here came from ethnographic interviews conducted in 2006 with Belizean social science scholars (cultural anthropologists, archaeologists, sociologists, and historians) who work in national heritage institutions and/or were involved in the construction of heritage education curriculum for primary schools. These individuals had strong opinions about the economic, political, and cultural values of archaeological practice and heritage management, as well as the integration of Belizean cultural heritage into the national education system. Teachers' comments were collected in interviews at government primary schools in 2005, 2008, and 2009 in Crooked Tree and Biscayne Villages: two rural African-descendant Kriol communities in north-central Belize located close to Maya archaeological sites.[1]

As Belize is an ethnically, racially, and linguistically diverse country, the relationship between cultural diversity, heritage, nationalism, and education is quite complex. The colonial history of Belize has created a race/class/ethnicity matrix (*sensu* Johnson 1998) that affects interactions between cultural groups, self-determination efforts of individual communities, and constructions of national identity. The current ethnic population of Belize consists primarily of Kriols (descendants of British settlers and West African peoples), Mestizos (Spanish-speaking immigrants from Central American countries), Garifuna (descendants of Indigenous Carib peoples and West African populations), Yucatec, Mopan, and Kekchi Maya peoples, Mennonites, Lebanese, East Indians, Chinese, and people of European and North American descent. A colonial history of racially divided labor forces (e.g., enslaved African people forced into timber extraction) and cultural discrimination (e.g., Maya groups' ancestral rights to land being challenged by some Belizeans) have contributed to modern racial and ethnic stereotypes and divisions in the country. Although many Belizeans have multi-ethnic backgrounds, social, racial, political, and economic tensions continue and are exacerbated by recent demographic shifts such as the majority population in Belize changing from Belizean Kriol to Mestizo due to emigration and immigration, respectively.

Belize gained independence from Great Britain in 1981, and philosophies about the best practices and policies for national and economic development have been debated since the 1950s. Today, the cultivation of Belizean citizens who are proud of their heritage is a state agenda, considered integral to national development. To this end, curricula and other school practices function as cultural policies implemented to manage cultural difference, emphasize certain forms of cultural heritage, and promote national unity. The current Belizean primary school social studies curriculum includes sections on diverse contemporary groups and practices. In addition, there are educational projects that focus on specific aspects of Belizean heritage. The African and Maya History Project (AMH) was first used in Belizean schools in 2004. AMH consists of six textbooks, accompanying teacher guides, and supplemental materials that highlight ancient African and Maya civilizations and modern African and Maya cultural practices. The textbooks were written by social science scholars, evaluated by teachers, and tested in several classrooms before the final texts were published. AMH is one of many forms of state rhetoric in Belize that aims to promote and manage cultural diversity and heritage.

EDUCATION, NATIONAL IDENTITY, AND CULTURAL DIVERSITY

Educational systems and practices play prominent social and political roles in society (Friedman Hansen 1979; Levinson, Foley, and Holland 1996). In schools, specifically, cultural values, expectations, and behaviors (including those about cultural identity and heritage) are defined, promoted, and transmitted to educators and students (Bourdieu and Passeron 1977). Althusser (1971) even suggests education functions as an ideological state apparatus. Seen in this way, schools reinforce cultural hegemony and affect the formation of citizens by conveying and replicating 'common sense' understandings about social order (following Gramsci 1971), including concepts and categories about cultural diversity. According to Spring (2004: 3), "schooling supports the political needs of the nation-state through education and disciplining a loyal, patriotic citizenry imbued with nationalism and acceptant of the legitimacy of the state." Schools are not, however, merely centers of cultural reproduction. In schools, as constructs of national identity are defined and reinforced in curricular and social practices, citizens and identities are culturally produced and knowledge is consumed and transformed in creative ways (Levinson, Foley, and Holland 1996 and see for example Coe 2005; Gustafson 2009; Hall 2002; Levinson 2001). I briefly discuss these processes of negotiation in the conclusion of this chapter.

Cultural education is an increasingly common and perhaps even global phenomenon (Sutton 2005), wherein 'culture' and 'diversity' are mobilized and managed to address national ethnic and racial politics, offering "human beings particular views of themselves and the world" (Giroux 1991: 56). The field of anthropology has struggled with the culture concept since its inception. One of the greatest challenges in debates about culture is describing the ever-changing and historically situated practices of social actors in a way that acknowledges fluidity and does not reify diverse processes (this debate is broad, but see Abu-Lughod 1991; Kroeber and Kluckhohn 1952; and Turner 1993). Certainly the history of the usage of the culture concept influences cultural education and heritage practices today. Indeed, the ongoing paradox of not essentializing culture is an ever-present challenge in education focused on ethnicity. In this chapter, I describe the political agendas for using certain forms of culture in education and the rhetoric of the value of diversity in Belize.

Curricula related to cultural diversity in the past and present can be especially politicized in comparison with other school subjects because certain forms of heritage can be privileged and promoted over others, and hidden or overt messages related to how citizens should contribute to social, political, and economic development are often conveyed. Coe's (2005) work on Ghanaian education, for example, explores state appropriation of local cultural traditions into curriculum (such as drumming and dancing), transforming practices from local culture to an official, nationalized cultural package. Levinson (2001) also demonstrates the ways the Mexican state attempted to mute cultural difference in the classroom by emphasizing national values of equality, solidarity, and group unity through curriculum and other school practices.

Culture and diversity can also be used to fit global cultural heritage models. For example, representations and celebrations of cultural diversity are tied to efforts to overcome past social injustices and highlight the value of cultural difference for all of humanity. In a critique of the World Heritage movement, Kirshenblatt-Gimblett (2006) suggests these practices create a kind of paradox between identifying cultural diversity as a human right and claiming it as universal heritage. While integrating multiple voices and forms of heritage into education may enable a celebration of the cultural heritage of particular groups that have been historically excluded, a common critique of this form of multiculturalism is that it also risks "concealing social politics" and questions of inequalities (De Cesari 2010: 310, citing Fraser 2000) and internationalizing local culturally relative practices under the guise of universal cultural diversity (Kirshenblatt-Gimblett 2006; Harrison 2013). These complexities of local, national, and international uses of 'culture' and 'diversity' are what I sought to explore within educational contexts in Belize.

STATE RHETORIC ABOUT CULTURE AND HERITAGE IN EDUCATION

Most cultural education sections in the primary school Belizean social studies curriculum (i.e., the 2001 Primary School Social Studies Curriculum for Standards IV and V) focus on providing students with a general introduction to the cultural practices of ethnic groups that make up the cultural fabric of the nation. AMH, as mentioned above, is more specific in focus, highlighting African and Maya civilizations. There are several national goals for cultural education like AMH in Belize, but the majority are structured around the creation and governance of a "culturally educated citizenry" (Stone 2007: 290). The national goals of cultural education in Belize, as well as the values of incorporating culture and heritage into educational programming, were expressed in interviews I conducted. What I determined is that in Belizean education reified versions of culture and heritage are often considered a kind of 'cure-all' for addressing social problems. National education programs utilize culture and heritage to promote a vision of a unified national identity and to minimize colonial legacies. The programs also seek to manage difference in the hopes of assuaging ethnic conflicts, minimizing crime, motivating young people to become more engaged in national development, and sustaining cultural traditions in the face of the perceived homogenizing effects of globalization.

The enculturation of young people into national identity ideology is an important and frequent component of nation-building. Many Belizean scholars agreed that learning about the country's heritage and modern cultural groups would increase student understanding of their national identity. The relationship between heritage and national identity can be quite important in postcolonial nations such as Belize in which, historically, colonial powers highlighted certain forms of cultural heritage and excluded and/or misrepresented others.

Ethnic diversity and heritage education initiatives, like AMH, were developed partly in response to colonial structures, with the hopes of defining and promoting a uniquely Belizean identity. The inspiration and vision statement for the construction of AMH textbooks demonstrates this desire to move beyond colonial history: "The overall purpose of the [AMH] project is to strengthen pride in Belize's African and Maya heritage to complement the pride we have in western civilization that dominates our worldview today . . . The project aims to positively contribute to the building or strengthening of knowledge, skills, and values consistent with the long-term development of an invigorated, assertive, self-enriching, national Belizean identity" (Cal 2004: back cover).

Both legacies of colonial institutions and a colonial mentality that devalued Belizean heritage are blamed for problems with political, cultural, and economic development. One teacher I spoke with told me that the deterioration of Kriol culture was a result of 'colonialized' minds taught to embrace everything British and reject Kriol language and cultural traditions. Noncolonial culture and heritage are considered important tools in overcoming these legacies. I talked at length with Xaxier Choc, Director of the National Archaeology Organization, about public archaeology projects and heritage education in Belize. In this personal interview, I asked him to discuss the value of projects like AMH (which he helped to write) and asked what he thought archaeology could contribute to Belizean society. Choc suggested that cultural heritage can be powerful in helping a nation move on from its history and also suggested that national pride and self-identity are crucial to development:

Well I think for a developing country, all nations . . . all cultures need icons. We need things that make us feel proud of who we are, and I think that archaeology lends itself to that . . .

We have the sort of developing country mentality, you know, [that] we can't compete with anybody else, but if you take archaeology and show them 'look, the first Belizeans were among the most advanced societies in the world,' it gives them a sense that we can achieve . . . I think one of the most important things . . . for archaeology within the school curriculum is to do just that, is to give people a sense of who we are. That we are this mixed group of people with a rich heritage and that one of those branches of our heritage can still be compared with all the world's greatest civilizations. And then it will give them a sense of pride and to believe in themselves.

Much of the emphasis on heritage in Belize focuses on a Maya past; however, some national actors also identify the need for teaching about contemporary cultural diversity in relation to Belizean national identity. Christina Pop, a curriculum designer, cultural activist, and previous Director of the National Social Research Organization, talked about the importance of cultivating pride and cultural awareness through education. Pop helped facilitate the development of AMH textbooks, activities, and training workshops for teachers. I asked her about the agendas for the AMH project and her thoughts on students learning about archaeology and national heritage. Christina discussed her concerns that teachers did not know how to teach about the complexities of cultural identity and suggested that many students are confused about their diverse cultural backgrounds. She said that one of the most important aspects of teachers learning about Belizean cultural history was that they would develop a better understanding of current cultural dynamics and teach this to young citizens.

Identifying and promoting heritage are often considered integral steps in the construction of an 'imagined community' (Anderson 1991) and a cohesive nation-state. Connections between nationalism and heritage have been explored by a variety of scholars (Anderson 1991; Hamilakis 2007; Handler 1985; Kohl and Fawcett 1995; Meskell 1998; Pyburn 2007). Drawing from Handler's (1985) work on Canadian heritage and nationalism, De Cesari (2010: 307) argues that through nationalist efforts, heritage and culture are framed and reified as components central to national identity, suggesting that heritage and culture are something "which a nation must *possess* in order to exist as such" (emphasis in original). State interests in defining national identity by promoting specific cultural characteristics and aspects of heritage (such as Choc's suggestion that "all nations . . . all cultures need icons") reinforces the reification of cultural identities and heritage as "essentialized, fixed, and monologic" (De Cesari 2010: 310, citing Fraser 2000). This process, which focuses on culture, ethnicity, and heritage as physical entities and possessions, de-emphasizes the social and lived aspects of these concepts.

Managing Cultural Difference and Addressing Social Problems

Because of Belize's complex cultural, ethnic, and racial history, contemporary diversity, and shifting demographics over the last decades, there is concern about how to define national identity in a way that addresses and incorporates many cultures. During the colonial era, ethnic divisions were reinforced through divisions of labor and racialized stereotypes as an effort to 'divide and conquer.' Another national agenda of Belizean cultural education is to minimize ethnic tensions and colonial legacies of dividedness. Cultural education plays a role in constructing "'unity' out of difference" (Hall 1991: 166) by emphasizing specific forms of cultural identities, practices, and heritage as part of the tapestry of Belizean identity. A major theme in Belizean cultural education is diverse ethnic groups living together as one, following a common national slogan, *Aal a wi da wan* (We are all one).

This goal of unity is shared by many national actors. Christina Pop and I discussed the fact that some teachers are frustrated with the AMH project and choose not to teach the AMH materials. In a personal interview, she suggested that this was because teachers were unsure why the AMH content was being integrated into the curriculum and were unfamiliar with the project's philosophy, which according to Pop was to create a unified sense of Belizeanness. Pop felt that this was crucial to moving beyond ethnic dividedness and that for her, critical issues in society could be addressed by having students learn about contemporary cultural groups and shared identities:

And one of the main things I always tell people is even though you might look a certain kind of way if you start going into your family tree, you will find a lot of characters in there . . . Eighty percent of Belizeans, have African, European, and Maya . . . That means the majority of us have so much in common. So why is it that we are unable to get ahead? Why do we have dividedness? Why do we have the crime that we do? Why is it that we are so quick to say, 'oh that person's a Maya, so therefore I have nothing in common with them.' . . . I'm like, here we are twenty-five years later. What do we call a Belizean identity? How do you know you're a Belizean?

The unique character of Belize's diverse heritage and concerns about colonialism's influences on cultural dynamics are also referenced in an early edition of a common social studies textbook (Leslie 1983: 73):

Belize has its own rich culture which includes the heritage of the different ethnic groups of Belize . . . For much of our history, the natural interaction of cultures which co-exist within one community was inhibited by the colonial policy of divide and rule, which ensured that our various cultures remained largely isolated from, and suspicious of each other, and that the colonizer's culture remained dominant. An essential part of the decolonization process must therefore be the elimination of all colonially inherited prejudices about each other's cultures.

The historical origins of our people and the more recent influences upon our culture have produced diversity. Out of this diversity we must seek unity, while recognizing the value of our different customs and traditions.

In addition to culture being essential to definitions of national identity, as discussed previously, determining how to manage cultural difference is also an international process. Wilk's (1995, 1996) analyses of beauty pageants demonstrates the ways a global format can be used to domesticate diversity through 'structures of common difference.' In the Belizean context, cultural education is a particularly persuasive structure of common difference. Cultural education in Belize focuses on teaching students about 'safe culture' including cultural traits and practices associated with various ethnic groups (music, dance, food, and traditions). This promotes diversity in forms that are easy to manage and contain, and difference is 'domesticated' by "channeling potentially dangerous social divisions" into the realm of cultural traditions (Wilk 1996: 218).

Through cultural education, it is possible to accommodate cultural pluralism and celebrate difference without addressing the social politics of diversity and issues like ethnic tension, racism, colonial history, and social inequalities, all of which exist in Belize. These ostensibly 'safe' and neutral versions of culture in the curriculum also avoid broader political debates about cultural representation and rights, and misconceptions about certain ethnic groups having cultural privileges. And as Wilk suggests, such processes can (often unintentionally) "end up emphasizing and exacerbating the divisions they are meant to minimize or control" (1996: 218). One example of such debates involves ongoing land tenure disputes between Maya communities, the federal government, and large corporations in southern Belize. Court cases over communal land ownership and property rights in Maya communities are commonly addressed in popular media, political discourse, and came up in my interviews with teachers and other social actors. In commentaries to online media coverage of these land tenure cases as well as on public radio shows, some Belizeans accused Maya communities of seeking 'special treatment.' Cultural groups who were long discriminated against are incorporated into Belizean cultural education in an effort to redefine national identity and move beyond colonial forms of cultural exclusion, but cultural education does not focus on social and political controversies like land tenure disputes.

This is similar to many cultural education programs in the United States, which according to Zimmerman (2002: 4) enable racial and cultural groups to "enter the story, provided that none of them questions the story's larger themes of freedom, equality, and opportunity." Although Belize's diverse and vibrant local cultures are promoted in cultural education, citizens also learn through school curricula, visits to archaeological sites and museums, and national symbols that certain historical details and forms of material culture heritage are especially significant aspects of Belizean heritage. For example, Kriol history is not a focus of the AMH project. Instead, the texts highlight Ancient, Historic, and Modern Maya populations (with information on Ancient Maya civilizations and the Caste Wars) and the prehistory of major kingdoms and cultural groups in continental Africa. An emphasis on Ancient Maya civilization also dominates archaeological tourism, research, and heritage preservation efforts in the country (McGill 2012). The discrepancy between the types of culture and heritage promoted in national rhetoric and the diversity of Belize is noted by many citizens. The Maya-centric focus in archaeology and tourism causes concerns among non-Maya peoples about resource competition and recognition on a national and global stage, and many individuals have strong feelings about cultural preservation. Kriol people I interviewed remarked that the Maya and Garifuna groups do a better job maintaining their cultures, adding to extant racial and ethnic dynamics involved in the construction of identities. However, there are few winners in this scenario because Ancient Maya heritage is often co-opted as national heritage, which distances contemporary Maya groups from engaging with archaeological sites as well (Parks 2011).

These sorts of ethnic tensions and concerns were what national scholars were hoping to avoid when designing curriculum focused on cultural diversity in the present and the rich Maya heritage of the past, but these efforts are complicated by the economic and political resources (such as tourist revenue and land rights) at stake. Current national initiatives, such as the establishment of the first ever Belize History Association and efforts to craft a Belizean

National Cultural Policy, will continue to struggle with the challenge of defining unified national identity while at the same time acknowledging complex social histories and celebrating cultural diversity.

CULTIVATING A PRODUCTIVE CITIZENRY

Another state agenda for the construction of cultural education in Belize is the development of productive citizens. This goal is explicitly identified in the vision statement of the AMH project as they emphasize the development of skills and knowledge of an active national citizenry by using terms like "invigorated, assertive, self-enriching" (Cal 2004: back cover).

For many Belizeans I interviewed, an important aspect of an engaged citizenry is an appreciation for cultural heritage. This ideology is tied to concerns about economic growth and national development. Actors I spoke with argued that by learning about culture in the past and present, Belizean children will become more active and productive and contribute more to the national economy. Manuel Jimenez, a Belizean historian involved in the AMH project, told me a goal of AMH was enhancing student pride in their heritage in order to increase their involvement and productivity in the Belizean state. Teacher Albert, a Crooked Tree school teacher, often expressed frustration with his students to me, other teachers, and even in the classroom. He lamented that his students were lazy, disinterested in academics, and did not perform well in school. In a conversation about cultural education, Teacher Albert suggested that texts about Maya Civilization (like AMH) might influence his students to think more about and preserve their own culture, and that this might also make them more motivated and engaged in school.

Archaeological and cultural tourism are additional ways culture and heritage are tied to national development. Adams' chapter in this volume identifies similar connections between tourism and development in 'less developed' countries and demonstrates how this ideology is also often connected to rhetoric about equity and poverty alleviation, goals frequently not achieved due to broader global politics and inequalities. Tourism is a major contributor to the Belizean economy with many programs highlighting cultural heritage. Tourism is also incorporated into education. For one primary school grade level, there is an entire unit on tourism, with a focus on career opportunities. The Belize Tourism Board (BTB), a statutory board in the Ministry of Tourism, has even published its own school curriculum, *Training Modules in Tourism*. The national and BTB tourism-based curricula are designed to teach young people how to become good tour guides and ambassadors for their country. Teachers I interviewed told me it is important for children to learn about cultural heritage and local history so they can share this information with tourists. The BTB (Belize Tourism Board 2004: 98) echoes these sentiments: "Belizean people ought to be proud of their culture and be happy to share it with tourists."

Rhetoric suggesting citizens need to learn about specific versions of culture and heritage to 'know who they are' and 'share with others' emphasizes a 'deficit model' of cultural education, where it is assumed that local people need to be taught about their heritage in order to appreciate it (see Schadla-Hall 2006 for a discussion of a deficit model of public archaeology). This is an inaccurate representation of Belizean citizens' knowledge about cultural heritage. As I demonstrate below, many individuals are in fact quite savvy to heritage politics and recognize the power of claiming and promoting different forms of cultural identity on a local, national, and global scale.

NEGOTIATIONS OF STATE RHETORIC

State ideologies concerning cultural diversity, citizenship, and cultural heritage are powerful influences for Belizean constructions of identity. However, teachers and students are also cultural agents in educational processes—they replicate national rhetoric about culture and heritage but also challenge and transform these messages.

One way that ideas about reified versions of culture and heritage influence teachers is by intensifying anxiety about cultural 'loss.' The idea that culture and heritage are possessed by people suggests that some people have culture and heritage while others do not and also implies that culture and heritage can be lost. Many teachers I spoke with expressed concerns about cultural preservation and the future of Kriol identity. Teacher Albert and Teacher Ranicia both refer to the process of cultural 'loss' in their comments below regarding threats to Kriol culture. While emphasizing the importance of cultural education, Teacher Ranicia expressed frustration about the influences of globalization, saying: "I think the Kriols lost their sense of identity because they mix with all the other ethnic groups and they don't practice their own culture . . . I think the younger generation lost touch completely . . . They don't know what the Kriol culture is all about." Teacher Albert also discussed the power of outside cultural influences:

Back in our days, the only thing we used to listen to were our parents.
Nowadays children have television to listen to, they have all this entertain-

ment, that they're fastly forgetting their culture . . . Every day they're losing [their culture], and they're more into this . . . American thing . . . everything is Americanized.

Although there are concerns about the sustainability of Kriol identity and practices, Kriol culture and heritage are alive and well known to Kriol people and other ethnic groups. Kriols participate in their own forms of cultural education (e.g., story-telling and sharing knowledge about environmental resources and hunting practices) that do not conform to the 'official' versions of culture and heritage.

Many Crooked Tree and Biscayne community members I spoke to recognized the national focus on Maya heritage through archaeology and tourism, acknowledged the increasing economic value of heritage, and identified a need for preserving and emphasizing aspects of local identity. One effort that addresses both community concerns about 'cultural loss' and the emphasis of certain forms of cultural heritage over others in Belize is the construction of new kinds of cultural practices and traditions. Several traditions and festivals that draw upon already existing cultural practices have been developed in Crooked Tree in the last fifteen years. These include the Tilapia Fest, Cashew Fest, and adoption of 'traditional' cultural costumes for local young girls to wear in school and community performances.

In Belize, teachers also participate in 'everyday acts of resistance' (Scott 1987) to state institutions by gossiping about the government and education programs, choosing not to utilize some textbooks in their classrooms, and deciding not to participate in national education events such as the Festival of the Arts and the Social Studies Bowl. Further, in classes about culture and heritage, teachers construct alternative narratives as they struggle to express complex cultural realities for themselves and their students.

The processes of negotiating and responding to state messages about cultural and national identity by citizens is interesting in anthropological work, as it reflects the relationship between structure and agency and demonstrates youth involvement in the production of cultural knowledge. In other work, I address specific aspects of the curriculum and how these are interpreted by teachers (McGill 2011) and children (McGill 2012). My goal in this chapter was to provide a detailed case study that highlighted the role of concepts of culture and diversity within heritage rhetoric through cultural education initiatives in Belize.

Both state usage of concepts of culture and heritage and local reactions to these practices demonstrate the ways a range of actors navigate heritage ideologies. The processes I describe in this chapter reveal power imbalances that exist between a state and its citizens even in efforts to define national identity and celebrate cultural diversity. This demonstrates the need for heritage scholars to be mindful of the uses of rhetoric about cultural diversity and heritage in formal educational contexts and the need for careful examination of the definitions of these terms.

NOTE

1. Pseudonyms for individuals and organizations are used to protect the interests of research participants.

REFERENCES

Abu-Lughod, Lila. 1991. "Writing Against Culture." In *Recapturing Anthropology*, ed. Richard G. Fox, 137–62. Santa Fe, NM: School of American Research.

Althusser, Louis. 1971. "Ideology and the Ideological State Apparatuses." In *Lenin and Philosophy and Other Essays*, ed. Louis Althusser, 127–88. New York, NY: Monthly Review Press.

Anderson, Benedict. 1991. *Imagined Communities: Reflections on the Origin and Spread of Nationalism*. New York, NY: Verso.

Askew, Marc. 2010. "The Magic List of Global Status: UNESCO, World Heritage, and the Agendas of States." In *Heritage and Globalization*, ed. Sophia Labadi and Colin Long, 19–44. New York, NY: Routledge.

Belize Tourism Board. 2004. *Training Modules in Tourism: Section 2—Standard Four to Standard Six*. Belize City: Belize Tourism Board.

Bourdieu, Pierre, and Jean-Claude Passeron. 1977. *Reproduction in Education, Society, and Culture*. Beverly Hills, CA: Sage Publications.

Cal, Angel. 2004. *Belize: Maya Civilizations, Student's Handbook (Primary School—Upper Division)*. Belmopan: Center for Multi-cultural Studies and University of Belize Press.

Coe, Cati. 2005. *Dilemmas of Culture in African Schools: Youth, Nationalism, and the Transformation of Knowledge*. Chicago, IL: University of Chicago Press.

De Cesari, Chiara. 2010. "World Heritage and Mosaic Universalism: A View from Palestine." *Journal of Social Archaeology* 10 (3): 299–324. http://dx.doi.org/10.1177/1469605310378336.

Fraser, Nancy. 2000. "Rethinking Recognition." *New Left Review* 3: 107–20.

Friedman Hansen, Judith. 1979. *Sociocultural Perspectives on Human Learning:*

Foundations of Educational Anthropology. Long Grove, IL: Waveland Press.

Giroux, Henry. 1991. "Modernism, Postmodernism, and Feminism: Rethinking the Boundaries of Educational Discourse." In *Postmodernism, Feminism, and Cultural Politics: Redrawing Educational Boundaries*, ed. Henry Giroux, 1–59. New York: State University of New York Press.

Gramsci, Antonio. 1971. *Selections from the Prison Notebooks*. London: Lawrence and Wishart.

Gustafson, Bret. 2009. *New Languages of the State: Indigenous Resurgence and the Politics of Knowledge in Bolivia*. Durham, NC: Duke University Press. http://dx.doi.org/10.1215/9780822391173.

Hall, Kathleen. 2002. *Lives in Translation: Sikh Youth as British Citizens*. Philadelphia: University of Pennsylvania Press.

Hall, Stuart. 1991. "Old and New Identities, Old and New Ethnicities." In *Culture, Globalization, and the World-system: Contemporary Conditions for the Representation of Identity*, ed. Anthony D. King, 41–68. Binghamton: State University of New York Press.

Hamilakis, Yannis. 2007. *The Nation and Its Ruins: Antiquity, Archaeology, and National Imagination in Greece*. Oxford: Oxford University Press.

Handler, Richard. 1985. "On Having a Culture: Nationalism and the Preservation of Quebec's Patrimony." In *Objects and Others: Essays on Museums and Material Culture*, ed. George Stocking, 192–217. Madison: University of Wisconsin Press.

Harrison, Rodney. 2013. *Heritage: Critical Approaches*. Abingdon / New York, NY: Routledge. http://dx.doi.org/10.1093/oxfordhb/9780199602001.013.021.

Johnson, Melissa A. 1998. "Nature and Progress in Rural Creole Belize: Rethinking Sustainable Development." PhD Dissertation, Department of Anthropology, University of Michigan, Ann Arbor.

Kirshenblatt-Gimblett, Barbara. 2006. "World Heritage and Cultural Economics." In *Museum Frictions: Public Cultures/Global Transformations*, ed. Ivan Karp, Corinne A. Krantz, Lynn Szwaja, and Tomás Ybarra-Frausto, 161–202. Durham, NC: Duke University Press. http://dx.doi.org/10.1215/9780822388296-008.

Kohl, Phillip, and Clare Fawcett, eds. 1995. *Nationalism, Politics, and the Practice of Archaeology*. Cambridge: Cambridge University Press.

Kroeber, Alfred, and Clyde Kluckhohn. 1952. *Culture: A Critical Review of Concepts and Definitions*. Cambridge, MA: Peabody Museums, Harvard University.

Labadi, Sophia, and Colin Long, eds. 2010. *Heritage and Globalisation*. London: Routledge.

Leslie, Robert. 1983. *A History of Belize: Nation in the Making*. Benque Viejo, Belize: Cubola Productions.

Levinson, Bradley. 2001. *We Are All Equal: Student Culture and Identity at a Mexican Secondary School, 1988–1998*. Durham, NC: Duke University Press. http://dx.doi.org/10.1215/9780822381075.

Levinson, Bradley, Douglas Foley, and Dorothy Holland, eds. 1996. *The Cultural Production of the Educated Person: Critical Ethnographies of Schooling and Local Practices*. Albany: State University of New York.

McGill, Alicia Ebbitt. 2011. "Dis da fi wi Hischri?: Archaeology Education as Collaboration with Whom? For Whom? By Whom?" *Archaeological Review from Cambridge* 26 (2): 153–70.

McGill, Alicia Ebbitt. 2012. "'Old Tings, Skelintans, and Rooinz': Belizean Student Perspectives about Archaeology." *Chungara, Revista de Antropologia Chilena* 44 (3): 475–85.

Meskell, Lynn, ed. 1998. *Archaeology under Fire: Nationalism, Politics, and Heritage in the Eastern Mediterranean and Middle East*. London: Routledge. http://dx.doi.org/10.4324/9780203259320.

Meskell, Lynn. 2012. *The Nature of Heritage: The New South Africa*. London: Wiley-Blackwell.

Parks, Shoshaunna. 2011. "Winning Title to Land but Not to Its Past: The Toledo Maya and Sites of pre-Hispanic Heritage." *International Journal of Cultural Property* 18 (1): 111–29. http://dx.doi.org/10.1017/S0940739111000063.

Pyburn, K. Anne. 2007. "Archaeology as Activism." In *Cultural Heritage and Human Rights*, ed. Helaine Silverman and D. Fairchild Ruggles, 172–83. New York, NY: Springer Press. http://dx.doi.org/10.1007/978-0-387-71313-7_10.

Salazar, Noel. 2010. "The Glocalisation of Heritage through Tourism: Balancing Standardisation and Differentiation." In *Heritage and Globalization*, ed. Sophia Labadi and Colin Long, 130–46. New York, NY: Routledge.

Schadla-Hall, Tim. 2006. "Public Archaeology in the Twenty-First Century." In *A Future for Archaeology: The Past in the Present*, ed. Robert Layton, Stephen Shennan, and Peter G. Stone, 75–82. Walnut Creek, CA: Left Coast Press.

Scott, James C. 1987. *Weapons of the Weak: Everyday Forms of Peasant Resistance*. New Haven, CT: Yale University Press.

Smith, Laurajane. 2006. *Uses of Heritage*. London: Routledge.

Spring, Joel. 2004. *How Educational Ideologies are Shaping Global Society: Intergovernmental Organizations, NGOs, and the Decline of the Nation-State*. Mahwah, NJ: Lawrence Erlbaum.

Stone, Michael. 2007. "Cultural Policy, Local Creativity and the Globalization of Belize." In *Taking Stock: Belize at 25 Years of Independence*, ed. Barbara Balboni and Joseph Palacio, 289–309. Benque Viejo, Belize: Cubola Productions.

Sutton, Margaret. 2005. "The Globalization of Multicultural Education." *Indiana Journal of Global Legal Studies* 12 (1): 97–108. http://dx.doi.org/10.2979/GLS .2005.12.1.97.

Turner, Terence. 1993. "Anthropology and Multiculturalism: What is Anthropology that Multiculturalists Should be Mindful of It?" *Current Anthropology* 8 (4): 411–29.

Wilk, Richard. 1995. "Learning to be Local in Belize: Global Systems of Common Difference." In *Worlds Apart: Modernity through the Prism of the Local*, ed. Daniel Miller, 110–33. London: Routledge.

Wilk, Richard. 1996. "Connections and Contradictions: From the Crooked Tree Cashew Queen to Miss World Belize." In *Beauty Queens on the Global Stage: Gender, Contests, and Power*, ed. Colleen B. Cohen, Richard R. Wilk, and Beverly Stoeltje, 217–32. New York, NY: Routledge.

Zimmerman, Jonathan. 2002. *Whose America? Culture Wars in the Public Schools.* Cambridge, MA: Harvard University Press.

Cultural Property 5

*Building Communities of Stewardship beyond
Nationalism and Internationalism*

Alexander A. Bauer

In February 2006, the Metropolitan Museum of Art
and the Republic of Italy reached a landmark agreement. The museum would turn over to Italy twenty
artifacts obtained by the museum, including the famed
Euphronios Krater and a set of silver looted from the
site of Morgantina, in exchange for rotating four-year
loans of similarly important works over the next forty
years (Metropolitan Museum of Art and Republic of
Italy 2006). In the months and years leading up to this
agreement, whose implications I discuss further below,
and similar agreements with other major collecting
museums in the United States, such as the Museum
of Fine Arts, Boston, The Cleveland Museum, and the
Getty Museum, debates intensified about what 'cultural
property' is, why it is important, and who has the right
to own it. Panicked from the 2002 conviction of the
highly regarded antiquities dealer Frederick Schultz
and from the investigations leading to the 2005 indict-
ments in Italy of dealer Robert Hecht and Getty curator of antiquities Marion True, an international group
of major collecting museums issued an existential plea
in the form of a *Declaration on the Importance and
Value of Universal Museums* (Art Institute of Chicago
et al. 2004), in which they argued against the return
of objects "acquired in earlier times" under "different
sensitivities and values" and which since "have become

DOI: 10.5876/9781607323846.c005

81

part of the museums that have cared for them, and by extension part of the heritage of the nations which house them" (4). The museums—and their sympathizers—openly expressed fears that if such actions against dealers were allowed to stand and museums were forced to return objects to their countries of origin, the museums would soon be emptied of their collections.

Against the backdrop of the 2001 detonation of the Bamiyan Buddhas by the Taliban and the looting of the Iraq Museum following the US invasion in 2003, these fears were compounded by concerns over the safety of objects in other countries and at the mercy of what were seen by many as narrow-minded parochial and nationalist interests. The reinvigorated debate over who has the right to own and control cultural property played out in public symposia held in New York City and elsewhere, with the most impassioned defenses of museums and collecting practices coming from James Cuno (2008, 2009), then Director of the Art Institute of Chicago (and now Director of the Getty Trust), and Kwame Anthony Appiah (2006), a professor of moral philosophy at Princeton. Nation-states' assertions of cultural property ownership and efforts to repatriate such material, both Cuno and Appiah argued, advocates divisive and dangerous interests of nationalism over the cooperative and cosmopolitan view that cultural property belongs not to a specific nation but the world as a whole.

These arguments were not new, but rather represented the latest iteration of a debate defined over thirty years ago by legal scholar John Henry Merryman (1986) as a struggle between 'cultural internationalism' on one hand and 'national retention' on the other. This oppositional construct was the dominant framework for understanding and interpreting cultural property debates for at least the past thirty years and through Italy's agreements with the Met and other museums. In the aftermath of these agreements, however, there is a new sense that the standard terminology may have finally run its course, and we may be witnessing new ways of engaging with 'cultural property' beyond the tired binaries of 'nationalism' and 'internationalism' (Bauer 2008).

This chapter aims to describe and analyze the significance of two interrelated trends: (1) that the past thirty years has witnessed a shift away from 'cultural property,' with its Western legal connotations of alienability and labor-based exchange value, and toward 'cultural heritage' as the preferred term representing the objects and traditions claimed by different communities or groups as rightfully theirs to control and dispose of as they wish; (2) that part of this shift has entailed a move away from the dualist framework of 'cultural internationalism' and 'cultural nationalism,' which has essentially defined the conflicts over such cultural expressions until recently. What is less clear is what kinds of new relationships and perspectives are developing in its stead. Part of this chapter thus aims to explore how changing terminologies and frameworks of practice over 'cultural property' act recursively to generate new entailments between people and the cultural expressions we value collectively and alone. My discussion is primarily focused on developments in the policy arena involving the Euro-American antiquities market and collecting museums for two reasons: first, this arena is where the term 'cultural property' first emerged and continues to be employed—in most other contexts (indigenous rights, historic preservation, intangible heritage), the term 'cultural heritage' is now used; second, recent legal developments in this arena are forcing significant transformations in museum practice, and these changes merit attention. In the following sections, I introduce the concept of 'cultural property' and its critiques, the recent developments that have changed the parameters of the debate, and prospects for the future of both the term itself and how we engage with the cultural material it purports to represent. Since these debates have taken place over the past three decades or so, it is hoped that the case of 'cultural property' can provide an important opportunity to consider the relationship of terminological shifts to changing social practices and engagements with heritage over time.

'CULTURAL PROPERTY' AND ITS CRITICS

With its origins in rules of conduct during war and how to prevent wartime destruction of cultural monuments and artwork, the concept of 'cultural property' grew over the course of the twentieth century to refer to (mainly movable) art objects and antiquities that have cultural value for individuals and groups and have often ended up on museum shelves (Blake 2000; Merryman 2005; Prott and O'Keefe 1992). The first use of the term 'cultural property' in a legal or policy context appears in the 1954 *Hague Convention for the Protection of Cultural Property in the Event of Armed Conflict,* which established an international standard for protecting art and cultural monuments from destruction in times of war. But while that may have been the first use of the English term (the relation of language to power itself being an important issue, though a bit beyond the scope of this chapter), it followed upon a longer tradition in France and other civil law systems dealing with similar *'biens culturels'* (literally 'cultural goods'). Whether talking about 'property' or 'goods,' however, these initial usages clearly denoted a narrow set of things (indeed, physical 'things') deemed worthy of protection, and certainly regarded them as a kind of property, if perhaps a special class (Crewdson 1984). This view of 'cultural property' was reinforced in the landmark UNESCO 1970 *Convention on the Means of Prohibiting and Preventing the Illicit Import, Export and Transfer of Ownership of Cultural Property*, whose aim was to crack down on the growing problem of looting at archaeological sites and the illegal trade in antiquities. As of the time of writing this chapter, the 1970 UNESCO *Convention* has been signed and/or ratified by 125 nations, some of which required separate domestic implementing legislation, such as the United States' 1983 *Convention on Cultural Property Implementation Act*, which, among other things, established the Cultural Property Advisory Committee to guide US policy in this area (I mention all of this to illustrate how pervasive the term 'cultural property' has become as a result of the 1970 UNESCO *Convention*).

By the 1980s, then, 'cultural property' had become the dominant legal and scholarly term for objects, monuments, and other tangible products of historical and artistic value. And as with the development of all such terms, soon different schools of thought developed around what the term meant and how it should be dealt with. Of central concern was the problem of how one should go about interacting with cultural property—could it be owned or disposed of by a private individual, or does it belong to a particular group, or perhaps the world as a whole?—and who has the right to decide. In spite of some notable attempts to avoid polarization of the issue (e.g., Bator 1982), the discussion soon became framed as one pitting 'cultural internationalists' against 'cultural nationalists.' These contrasting perspectives were exemplified, in Merryman's (1986, 2005) view at least, by the differing approaches to 'cultural property' articulated in the 1954 *Hague Convention* and in the 1970 UNESCO *Convention*, respectively. While the former's preamble declares that "damage to cultural property belonging to any people whatsoever means damage to the cultural heritage of all mankind," which Merryman argues recognizes a global interest in (and thus right to circulate) any and all cultural property, the latter convention advocates a more narrow, national interest in that it allows each nation to define what should be considered 'cultural property' in its borders, and to decide how, or even if, that material will be shared with the world.

In a series of influential essays, Merryman (1986, 1988, 1989, 2005) has argued that the 'nationalist' perspective embodied by the 1970 UNESCO *Convention* and subsequent policy represented a dangerous move away from the shared concern with and responsibility for cultural material exemplified by the 1954 *Hague Convention*. He felt that it advocated a narrow parochialism pitting cultures against each other (a point echoed in Appiah 2006; Lowenthal 1998) and, even worse, would serve to undermine the world's great museums and collections that celebrated human achievement. Merryman's argument has been criticized on several grounds, however, most notably for being more about advancing the liberalization of trade in antiquities than combating ethnocentrism. As sharply noted by Prott (2005: 228), for example, the 'internationalist' view hardly meant shared custody, but rather the right of anyone to own such objects, made possible through their free circulation in the global marketplace, a situation which in practice "looks far more like cultural imperialism, based as it seems to be on the activities of those from wealthy countries with each other and with poorer states whose cultural resources are flowing in one direction, without an equal exchange."

So the terms of the debate over 'cultural property' were set, with 'cultural internationalists'—mainly dealers, collectors, and the museum community in so-called 'market nations'—advocating for a robust, if not entirely 'free' trade in art and antiquities, on one side, and on the other 'cultural nationalists'— mainly archaeologists and political actors and activists of so-called 'source nations'—pushing for greater restrictions on the antiquities market and the repatriation of objects thought to be looted from archaeological sites. But to many in the latter group, a large part of the problem was the term 'cultural property' itself, which both failed to encompass all that it was meant to describe and reinforced a view of cultural materials as being alienable property, due to its history as a term within Western legal systems.

Specifically, objections to 'cultural property' developed around four main issues. First and perhaps most important, 'property' connotes alienability and personal sovereignty over an object, so that an owner of that property may dispose of it as he or she sees fit. The problem with this view is most famously illustrated by Sax (1999), who observed that an owner would be well within his or her rights to "play darts with a Rembrandt" he or she owned, a point underscored even more vividly by the Taliban's 2001 destruction of the Bamiyan Buddhas, which were legally theirs to destroy in spite of international outcry (for two very different perspectives on the destruction of the Bamiyan Buddhas, see Cuno 2006; Meskell 2002). Related to the previous one, a second problem with the term 'property' is that a central goal of property law is to protect the rights of its owner, and as Blake (2000: 65–66) writes, "[i]t is problematic to apply a legal concept involving the rights of the possessor to the protection of cultural resources which may involve a severe curtailment of such rights and the separation of access and control from ownership." If even the expansion of moral rights legislation (such as the 1990 *Visual Artists Rights Act* in the US, which protects some artists' rights in their work even after it is sold) has faced resistance, the idea that another community or nation can dictate how an object is displayed or demand its return because of its symbolic importance would seem completely antithetical to the core goals of property law (though it is this very right which is recognized by the 1990 *Native American Graves Protection and Repatriation Act* [NAGPRA], a point I will return to later).

The third and fourth problems with the term 'cultural property' regard the inadequacy of 'property' to account for all it is meant to encompass in this particular context. Using the word 'property' does not seem to leave room for the dimensions of preservation and protection that are core concerns of cultural property policy. Much cultural property is considered as one would an 'inheritance,' something to be safeguarded and passed down to future generations as a kind of trust (and in fact, some art and cultural property cases have been treated as a part of trust law). From this perspective, if one happens to own a Rembrandt, that owner is more like a caretaker and has the obligation not to play darts with it, but rather preserve it for future generations to enjoy. Such an obligation forms no part of Western property law. Finally, using 'property' in 'cultural property' makes it difficult to include those many things considered 'cultural property' that are not tangible or moveable, such as ideas, traditions, symbolic landscapes, etc. As Prott and O'Keefe (1992) argue, the kinds of things meant to be protected by 'cultural property' law falls into five categories: (1) movable objects, (2) immovable monuments and sites, (3) traditional knowledge and practices, (4) ceremonies and performances, and (5) information about the other four—of which only the first two fit easily within Western legal categories of 'property,' with the third being partly, if inadequately, dealt with in intellectual property (IP) law.

Since the 1970 UNESCO *Convention*, efforts were thus made to find a replacement for the term 'property' and its connotations of alienability within the Western capitalist framework. It must be remembered that the term 'property' was not universally used, as other nations and languages used words with varying connotations. As mentioned previously, several nations used *'biens culturels'* or some correlate to refer to the material being protected, while in other contexts *'patrimoine'* and its variants were employed. Many policymakers have considered these terms preferable to the more narrow, capitalism-based 'property,' and debates over terminology (unsurprisingly) featured prominently in the drafting of the UNIDROIT 1995 *Convention on Stolen or Illegally Exported Cultural Objects*, which ultimately settled on 'cultural objects' when the text was finalized. In a key article, legal scholars Lyndel Prott, who served as an advisor to UNESCO for many years, and Patrick O'Keefe suggested that 'cultural heritage' was a better term for recognizing the cultural embeddedness of objects within communities, and the deeply emotional connection that people have with such objects (Prott and O'Keefe 1992). With increasing concerns over protecting the so-called 'intangible heritage' since the late 1990s, 'cultural heritage' is becoming more widely adopted as the preferred term for all such cultural products.

Another important shift has taken place in the rhetoric about peoples' relationships to cultural objects, with a move away from thinking about objects in terms of 'ownership' toward terms that emphasize shared responsibility and collaborative practice. In the early 1990s, two landmark laws recognizing indigenous communities' heritage claims, NAGPRA in the US and the 1993 *Native Title Act* in Australia, were passed. Both these laws, either directly or indirectly, led to the development of new kinds of attitudes around sites and objects of heritage, emphasizing dialogue and what Paterson (2005: 62) calls a "caring and sharing" approach that moved away from zero-sum solutions. While neither law really introduced a new terminology for cultural property, both represent a significant move away from thinking about heritage as property within the context of law (see also Brown 2003, 2004).

In 1997, Peter Welsh (1997) suggested adopting Annette Weiner's (1992) term 'inalienable possessions' for describing cultural objects, as a way of recognizing groups' ongoing connection to—and sense of rights over—objects that may not be in their possession and may be widely distributed in collections around the globe. A more widely used alternative is that of 'stewardship,' a central concept in the revised Society for American Archaeology's *Code of Ethics* in 1996 (Lynott and Wylie 2000; Wylie 2005). While the "Stewardship Principle" (Principle #1) within the SAA *Code* is more broadly construed as a way of guiding how archaeologists stand in relationship to the archaeological record as a whole, the idea of stewardship (along with Principle #3, "Commercialization") presents an important alternative to ownership. In spite of its wide use, however, even 'stewardship' fails to get around the problem of who gets to play the role of 'steward' and on what basis. 'Universal museums,' after all, declared themselves stewards of the world's heritage for the sake of all peoples, using this as a rationale for their continued possession of cultural property that some groups would rather see returned to their countries of origin. As long as cultural objects were bought and sold among participants, efforts to shift the discourse—such as the attempt to substitute the term 'heritage' for 'property,' or 'stewardship' for 'ownership'—had limited effect.

DEVELOPMENTS IN THE NEW MILLENNIUM

Several legal and policy developments over the past decade have had a significant impact on cultural property disputes and, in turn, on a general departure from 'property' within this discourse. In spite of the plea of the 'Universal Museums,' the general trend has been a move away from a largely unfettered market in antiquities in favor of the rights of individual nations to dictate the terms under which objects are exchanged. As referenced earlier, in 2002 and 2003 a key criminal decision in the US against antiquities dealer Fredrick Schultz on top of the prior conviction in the United Kingdom of his conspirator, Jonathan Tokeley-Parry, definitively established that US courts would enforce other nations' patrimony laws (Gerstenblith 2006; Yasaitis 2005). At the same time, source nations have also increased their prosecution of antiquities traffickers at home and abroad, with the trials in Italy of the well-known art dealer Robert Hecht and past curator at the Getty Museum, Marion True, serving as the most high-profile examples (for more on these cases, see Watson and Todeschini 2006). Together, these cases have changed the calculus for recovering cultural property internationally and have already had a significant impact on the international trade in antiquities.

A second development came from several important 'market' nations, who somewhat unexpectedly ratified the 1970 UNESCO *Convention* after thirty years and then passed new cultural property laws aimed at cracking down on the international trade in antiquities. One of the longstanding weaknesses of the 1970 UNESCO *Convention* was that some of the most prominent market nations were not signatories (the US was a significant exception, having become a signatory in 1972 and then having implemented it into US law in 1983). Without the participation of many 'market' countries, where most of these objects were bought and sold, the convention's effect on antiquities trafficking remained more moral than legal. However, the situation has changed since the late 1990s, with France signing the convention in 1997, the United Kingdom and Japan in 2002, Switzerland in 2003, Germany in 2007, and Belgium and the Netherlands in 2009.[1]

It is against this backdrop of increasing acceptance on the part of market nations to join international efforts against antiquities trafficking and the increasingly successful prosecutions of smugglers that major collecting museums have begun entering into agreements to return objects to their countries of origin, such as that between the Metropolitan Museum of Art and the Republic of Italy that I discussed at the beginning of this chapter. To see these developments as the culmination of the struggle between 'cultural internationalism' and 'cultural nationalism,' in which the latter has finally prevailed, is to miss the significance of this moment. Rather than simply being the inevitable result and outgrowth of changing trends in the legal sphere, these agreements should be seen as the key turning point in the past forty years regarding how 'cultural property' is defined and how people and groups stand in relation to it. It seems that 'property' may finally be an outmoded term for the objects and other parts of culture claimed by communities as part of their heritage. The ongoing nature of heritage claims, such as that of the so-called 'Elgin Marbles' held by the British Museum for almost two centuries, have long illustrated that legal statutes of limitations regarding the ownership of 'property' do not settle such disputes. What NAGPRA and the more recent agreements between individual museums and various communities and governments have done is recognize that ongoing claims require moving beyond traditional property law approaches toward more creative and often non-legal remedies. In terms of the rhetoric of heritage, these new laws and agreements show that changes in rhetoric and terminology can both reflect changing attitudes and also help to promote alternative subjectivities of heritage.

CULTURAL PROPERTY BEYOND 'NATIONALISM' AND 'INTERNATIONALISM'

This new state of affairs seems to have finally offered ways for adversaries in the cultural property debates to work together, and in turn has thus provided new conditions for relating to cultural objects beyond the rhetoric of 'property.' In a manner not dissimilar to NAGPRA and its aftermath, agreements such as those between the Met and Italy have helped to establish new social relations among previously adversarial parties and act to bind the participants together in a cooperative framework of reciprocity. The Met-Italy agreement, for one, stipulates that following the return of the objects from the Met to Italy, objects "of equal beauty and historical and cultural significance" are to be offered by Italy in return in rotating four-year loans, with the pieces originally returned by the Met among the possible pieces to be circulated. Aside from the marketing benefits of such an arrangement for the museum, by putting time constraints on the opportunity for viewing the special objects, it has the more substantial effect of creating a community of exchange partners around particularly compelling or valuable materials, whose circulation acts both to reinforce these social obligations of reciprocity and to change the status of the objects circulated away from that of alienable property and toward one of shared heritage (Bauer 2015). Rather than the zero-sum situation of 'cultural property,' where the ownership of the objects is most important, these new arrangements acknowledge the ways in which objects are linked to people and yet may circulate among many groups who feel connected to and responsible for them. Interestingly from a rhetorical standpoint, when the Metropolitan Museum initially agreed to return several objects to Italy, they remained on display at the Met with only the tags changed to read that they were there on loan from the Republic of Italy. They were thus figuratively 'returned,' or recognized as 'inalienable possessions' along the lines of Welsh's (1997) argument, before they were physically circulated back to Italy in exchange for other objects.

Perhaps more significant than the return of objects is their new position in a system of circulation and exchange of objects of heritage, which essentially allows several groups to be connected to the objects and, through their circulation, to each other. We might thus understand what has been created by these reciprocal loan arrangements to be a kind of *kula* ring of important antiquities moving among previously competing parties. Like *kula*, this circulation of antiquities has the effect of creating new kinds of 'metaphysical communities'—communities that conceive of themselves as communities (Urban 1996)—around the ideas and discourses of stewardship and shared heritage (Bauer 2015). It is a move away from the community offered in the 'Universal Museum' declaration (Art Institute of Chicago et al. 2004) and toward one that is pragmatically brought into being by new social relationships of sharing and reciprocity.

While it is still early to fully assess these new developments and determine the robustness of the new communities that are arising from them, there is reason to believe that the vision I am offering here is in fact coming into focus. Since the Getty Museum's own 2007 agreement with the Italian Ministry of Culture, long-term partnerships have been established between the Getty and the National Museums of Florence and Naples and between the Sicilian Ministry of Culture and Sicilian Identity, which has facilitated an exchange of both significant artworks and expertise, particularly regarding the protection and conservation of collections.

A different kind of museum collaboration, perhaps one that is closer to the development of a distinct 'community' is that of the French Regional and American Museum Exchange (FRAME) organization, which was founded in 1999 to share cultural materials and collections and to promote the exchange of information, personnel, technology, and other resources among its member museums.[2] Now comprised of fourteen museums in North America, including such major museums as the Cleveland Museum of Art, the Minneapolis Institute of Arts, and the Los Angeles County Museum of Art, together with the regional museums of twelve cities in France, FRAME boasts a collaboratively shared collection of over two million artworks, and has mounted fourteen major exhibitions that traveled to eighteen cities in Europe and North

America. While objects within the FRAME organization are still part of the individual museums' collections, the partnership does shift the focus away from regarding the collections as individually owned and toward a consideration of them as a shared resource (Salmore 2008). Such a consortium-type sharing arrangement thus acts as another feasible alternative to the increasingly outdated mentality of simple cultural property ownership.

But rather than seeing these developments as something radically new, the redescription of 'cultural property' as a *kula* of heritage may be the culmination of a half century of changing attitudes and policies regarding objects of heritage. In fact, these types of engagements with heritage objects were envisioned in the preamble to the 1970 UNESCO *Convention*, which reads in part, "the interchange of cultural property among nations for scientific, cultural and educational purposes increases the knowledge of the civilization of Man, enriches the cultural life of all peoples and inspires mutual respect and appreciation among nations." As this quote illustrates, the goal of the 1970 *Convention* was not simply the repatriation and retention of objects by individual nations, but the recognition of heritage rights that would allow for globally collaborative arrangements of heritage circulation outside of the market system. What we may finally be witnessing is the development of just such arrangements.

CONCLUSION

The terminological shifts from 'cultural property' to 'heritage' and 'cultural objects,' and from 'ownership' to 'stewardship' and its alternatives that have taken place over the past few decades show us that such redescription occurs on several fronts and not necessarily in a linear way. Conventions and other documents provide a particularly visible and top-down way to establish new terminologies and approaches, but the voices of individual scholars and experiments with new forms of practice also significantly impact the debate. Both participatory and deliberative models of democratic practice play a vital role in changing the rhetorics and developing new policies around objects of heritage. The collaborative approaches encouraged by NAGPRA, the new loan arrangements, and cooperative networks such as FRAME all illustrate the impact that participatory action has in creating new modes of engagement. But the drafting of NAGPRA itself, as with UNESCO 1970 and UNIDROIT 1995, each of which have had a tremendous impact on how 'cultural property' is defined and dealt with, all resulted from the slow, often messy, and seemingly inconsistent deliberative approach to policymaking.

In the end, the term 'cultural property' may not need to disappear, as new ways of thinking about and dealing with cultural property are creating new relationships among participants and with the objects themselves. As I have attempted to illustrate, long-term loan and other kinds of agreements among previously adversarial parties may reflect for cultural materials a new spirit of collaborative practice centered around notions of shared stewardship. But more than simply reflecting new attitudes, I contend that such practices act recursively to establish and reinforce new forms of social relations among them. In this way, new 'metaphysical communities,' such as more formally in the FRAME consortium, and more informally through patterns of practice, may already be seen as emerging around notions of stewardship and shared heritage beyond 'nationalism' and 'internationalism.'

NOTES

1. For a complete list of signatories, see http://www.unesco.org/eri/la/convention .asp?KO=13039&language=E, accessed December 26, 2012.

2. See http://www.framemuseums.org/.

REFERENCES

Appiah, Kwame Anthony. 2006. *Cosmopolitanism: Ethics in a World of Strangers*. New York, NY: W. W. Norton.

Art Institute of Chicago, Bavarian State Museum, State Museums of Berlin, Cleveland Museum of Art, J. Paul Getty Museum, Solomon R. Guggenheim Museum, Los Angeles County Museum of Art, Louvre Museum, The Metropolitan Museum of Art, New York The Museum of Fine Arts, et al. 2004. "Declaration on the Importance and Value of Universal Museums." In *Icom News*, vol. 2004–1. http://icom.museum/fileadmin/user_upload/pdf/ICOM_ News/2004-1/ENG/p4_2004-1.pdf. Accessed December 26, 2012.

Bator, Paul M. 1982. *The International Trade in Art*. Chicago, IL: University of Chicago Press.

Bauer, Alexander A. 2008. "New Ways of Thinking About Cultural Property." *Fordham International Law Journal* 31: 690–724.

Bauer, Alexander A. 2015. "The Kula of Long-term Loans: Cultural Object Itineraries and the Promise of the Postcolonial 'Universal' Museum." In *Things in Motion: Object Itineraries in Anthropological Practice*, ed. Rosemary A. Joyce and Susan D. Gillespie. Santa Fe, NM: School of Advanced Research Press.

Blake, Janet. 2000. "On Defining the Cultural Heritage." *International and Comparative Law Quarterly* 49 (1): 61–85. http://dx.doi.org/10.1017/S002058930 006396X.

Brown, Michael F. 2003. *Who Owns Native Culture?* Cambridge, MA: Harvard University Press.

Brown, Michael F. 2004. "Heritage as Property." In *Property in Question: Value Transformation in the Global Economy*, ed. Katherine Verdery and Caroline Humphrey, 49–68. Oxford, UK: Berg.

Crewdson, Richard. 1984. "Cultural Property: A Fourth Estate?" *Law Society's Gazette* 18: 126–29.

Cuno, James. 2006. "Beyond Bamiyan: Will the World be Ready Next Time?" In *Art and Cultural Heritage: Law, Policy, and Practice*, ed. Barbara T. Hoffman, 41–46. New York, NY: Cambridge University Press.

Cuno, James. 2008. *Who Owns Antiquity? Museums and the Battle over Our Ancient Heritage*. Princeton, NJ: Princeton University Press.

Cuno, James. 2009. *Whose Culture? The Promise of Museums and the Debate over Antiquities*. Princeton, NJ: Princeton University Press.

Gerstenblith, Patty. 2006. "Recent Developments in the Legal Protection of Cultural Heritage." In *Archaeology, Cultural Heritage, and the Antiquities Trade*, ed. Neil Brodie, Morag M. Kersel, Christina Luke, and Kathryn W. Tubb, 68–92. Gainesville: University Press of Florida.

Lowenthal, David. 1998. *The Heritage Crusade and the Spoils of History*. Cambridge: Cambridge University Press. http://dx.doi.org/10.1017/CBO9780511523809.

Lynott, Mark J., and Alison Wylie. (Original work published 1995) 2000. "Stewardship: The Central Principle of Archaeological Ethics." In *Ethics in American Archaeology*, 2nd revised ed., ed. Mark J. Lynott and Alison Wylie, 35–39. Washington, DC: Society for American Archaeology.

Merryman, John Henry. 1986. "Two Ways of Thinking About Cultural Property." *American Journal of International Law* 80 (4): 831–53. http://dx.doi.org/10.2307 /2202065.

Merryman, John Henry. 1988. "The Retention of Cultural Property." *U.C. Davis Law Review* 21: 477–513.

Merryman, John Henry. 1989. "The Public Interest in Cultural Property." *California Law Review* 77 (2): 339–64. http://dx.doi.org/10.2307/3480607.

Merryman, John Henry. 2005. "Cultural Property Internationalism." *International Journal of Cultural Property* 12 (1): 1–29. http://dx.doi.org/10.1017/S094073910 5050046.

Meskell, Lynn M. 2002. "Negative Heritage and Past Mastering in Archaeology."

Anthropological Quarterly 75 (3): 557–74. http://dx.doi.org/10.1353/anq.2002.0050.

Metropolitan Museum of Art and Republic of Italy. 2006. "Agreement." *International Journal of Cultural Property* 13: 427–34.

Paterson, Robert K. 2005. "The 'Caring and Sharing' Alternative: Recent Progress in the International Law Association to Develop Draft Cultural Material Principles." *International Journal of Cultural Property* 12 (1): 62–77. http://dx.doi.org/10.1017/S0940739105050058.

Prott, Lyndel V. 2005. "The International Movement of Cultural Objects." *International Journal of Cultural Property* 12 (2): 225–48. http://dx.doi.org/10.1017/S0940739105050125.

Prott, Lyndel V., and Patrick J. O'Keefe. 1992. "'Cultural Heritage' or 'Cultural Property?'" *International Journal of Cultural Property* 1: 307–20.

Salmore, Amy M. 2008. *Une relation privilégiée: The French Regional & American Museums Exchange, Arts, and Administration Program*. Eugene: University of Oregon.

Sax, Joseph L. 1999. *Playing Darts with a Rembrandt*. Ann Arbor: University of Michigan Press.

Urban, Greg. 1996. *Metaphysical Community*. Austin: University of Texas Press.

Watson, Peter, and Cecilia Todeschini. 2006. *The Medici Conspiracy: The Illicit Journey of Looted Antiquities from Italy's Tomb Raiders to the World's Greatest Museums*. New York, NY: Public Affairs.

Weiner, Annette B. 1992. *Inalienable Possessions: The Paradox of Keeping-While-Giving*. Berkeley: University of California Press. http://dx.doi.org/10.1525/california/9780520076037.001.0001.

Welsh, Peter H. 1997. "The Power of Possessions: The Case against Property." *Museum Anthropology* 21 (3): 12–18. http://dx.doi.org/10.1525/mua.1997.21.3.12.

Wylie, Alison. 2005. "The Promise and Perils of an Ethic of Stewardship." In *Embedding Ethics*, ed. Lynn M. Meskell and Peter Pels, 47–68. London: Berg.

Yasaitis, Kelly E. 2005. "National Ownership Laws as Cultural Property Protection Policy: The Emerging Trend in *United States v. Schultz*." *International Journal of Cultural Property* 12 (1): 95–113. http://dx.doi.org/10.1017/S094073910505006X.

Democratization 6

*The Performance of Academic Discourse
on Democratizing Museums*

Cecilia Rodéhn

The study of democratization has become a growth
industry in museum and heritage studies with one target in mind: arguing for a correction of past heritage
performances. This has resulted in a flourishing theoretical debate as well as practical and methodological
advancements in the global heritage sector. Although
museums have been scrutinized in terms of their democratic performance, the role of researchers has thus far
been overlooked.

The issue of democratization typically is explored
from a one-sided western perspective, the constant
rehashing of which serves to reinforce and recreate the
power-structures entrenched in western definitions
of democratic heritage. 'Democracy' therefore would
profit from reexamination in a global context. At the
same time, we need to acknowledge democratization
discourses as performances with real effects if we wish
to begin transforming the power of its rhetoric to redescribe democratization and find more useful ends. Thus,
this chapter aims to discuss the discourse on democratizing museums and seeks to answer the following
questions: how do we, the scholarly community, write
about democracy and democratization processes? And
in doing so, how do we become part of the processes
we are writing about?

DOI: 10.5876/9781607323846.c006

In order to identify how issues of democratization are presented in museum and heritage discourses, I have analyzed 140 articles and books published between 1982 and 2012. The material varies and ranges across journals and books located within the field of museum and heritage studies with the effort to find articles by scholars originating from, and focusing on, museums all over the world. In order to distinguish the discussion on democratization from the general museological and heritage discourse, which also has a democratic character, I have focused on those texts that use the words 'democracy,' 'democratic,' and 'democratization.' I regard their use as a statement that the writers particularly seek to engage in a discussion of these topics. Because citing the entire corpus of such works would produce an unwieldy text in what follows, I have instead focused on representative texts so as to highlight some issues for discussion.

DEMOCRACY AND DEMOCRATIZATION AS PERFORMANCES

In order to answer the posed questions I approach the issue from the angle of performance theory. Following Taylor (2004: 381–82) I hold that performance theory is both a methodological lens for examining texts, but also an epistemological analysis for revealing discourses. Therefore, I draw on Austin (2007: 177), who claims that "by saying or in saying something we are doing something." I also follow Schechner (2002: 220–24), who states that all 'doings' can be studied as performances that include executions of power. Performance theory is here used as a method to examine text in order to discuss the dominant message, subject matter, and characteristics of the text. It is also a means to discuss scholarly publications as performances imbued with, and as acting out, power and cultural meaning. Scholarly publications are here more specifically understood as performances of democracy and democratization processes. Using this approach, I hold that democracy and democratization processes are not only the processes that can be observed in museums or at heritage sites, but that researching and writing about democratization must also be regarded as part of that process.

Researchers, when discussing democracy and democratization, are party to creating the standards, norms, and methods for how to proceed when making heritage democratic. Inspired by Alexander, Anderson, and Gallegos (2004) and Lamm Pineau (1994), I hold that scholarly publications can be regarded as descriptive, repetitive actions that must be analyzed in relation to a web of power relations and social norms. The body of scholarly publications can therefore be seen as an ongoing collection of performances of democratization processes that influence not only each other, but also the practical work in museums and at heritage sites. Analyzing democratization as textual performances shows that the lived experience of museum workers is different from the one described in texts. Although scholarly publications and practical museum work intersect and feed knowledge between one another, the scholarly performance has a dominant role and museum workers often adjust their work accordingly. South African museum practice is one example of how scholarly publications associated to the theoretical framework of 'new museology' has become the blueprint for democratization to which museum workers often refer when explaining their practice (Rodéhn 2008: 53). Similarly, the work of Hildegard Vieregg exemplifies how museological research is used in Latin America to promote post-colonial museums. She also suggests that museums in Eastern Europe should appropriate museological research to "encourage the democratic process" (Vieregg 1999: 25). Therefore we need to acknowledge the dominant role that scholars play in democratization processes. For this reason I have focused on the discourse to align the responsibility of researchers and the active role they have in shaping democracy and democratization processes.

THE TEMPORAL ASPECTS OF DEMOCRACY AND DEMOCRATIZATION

In order to understand how democracy and democratization processes are performed, we need to consider their temporal aspects. I have, to begin with, constructed a timeline through which different arguments concerning democratization typically unfold, wherein the changing and recurrent patterns and discourses can be located in order to enable a deconstruction of what democratization entails. There are many ways of considering time, but it is commonly referred to as the means for structuring lived experience, or relating to the 'present', the 'past,' and the 'future.' Time is both a way to describe and analyze social occurrences, but it is also a lived experience. Moreover, these analytical and experiential functions are interlinked. Munn (1992: 93–94) suggests that time is a theoretical examination of a basic sociocultural process in which temporality is constructed. This means that time refers to how groups create, understand, and negotiate time while also acknowledging that groups construct time differently.

Munn (1986: 11–13; 1992: 93–94, 104) and Giddens (1984: 133) suggest that actors are not merely 'in' time and space but also create that time and space that they are 'in.' This means that actors (e.g., scholars) live and act in a time that they also socially construct. Furthermore, actors (e.g., scholars) are active participants who negotiate, renegotiate, and create time in the form of relations between themselves and temporal reference points that are also spatial. Therefore, scholars are not only affected by the time that they are 'in,' but they also create the sociocultural time that democratization plays out 'in.' By writing about democratization they are creating and recreating an academic time of democratization, which is not necessarily the same time that their subject of study is 'in.'

Hence, there are potentially many different kinds of democracies and democratization processes, but they are nevertheless performed in very similar ways no matter the time that scholars are 'in.' This can clearly be seen in how democratization is related to temporal aspects such as concepts of the 'past,' 'present,' and 'future.' I argue below that this temporal structuring of democratization is central not only to how democratization is understood but also to how it is constructed in texts. The 'past' is often perceived as something negative, the 'present' is seen as transformative, and the 'future' is constructed as democratic. Therefore, democratization is argued in specific ways in scholarly publications, and these arguments are, as I will show below, repeated over time as they are re-performed and interlinked. Thus the concept of time assists in revealing the power of rhetoric hidden within the discourses of democratization of heritage and discloses the need to revisit definitions in order to contribute to a redescription.

Discussions on democratization go back as far as the 1800s, and perhaps even further. It was, however, not recognized until the 1950s and 1960s that museums should in earnest commit to the democratization of heritage (Bennett 1998: 25–35; Cameron 1982: 180). During the 1970s and 1980s a critical museum discourse emerged. It focused on (mis)representations of heritage so as to offer suggestions toward fair and equal representation in order to make museums more appealing to all groups in society (Cameron 1982: 178–80; Ames 1988: 157). Emerging out of this discussion was the issue of access that surfaced during the 1990s. Access was discussed, for example, in relation to museums' authoritarian role (Kaplan 1994), how museums could be more welcoming to visitors (Hooper-Greenhill 1995: 5), how different pedagogical techniques could provide access to visitors (Macdonald 1998: 16), and furthermore, how collections and the knowledge that museums' provided might be accessed (Ames 1992: 16)

During the late 1990s and 2000s, the discussions centered on three different but entangled themes: (1) the social role of the museum, (2) participation, and (3) social inclusivity. The first was explored in relation to political issues pertaining to society. Museums, it was stressed, should assist in educating people about the wrongdoings of past regimes and encourage people to participate in democratic culture and rewrite history (e.g., Rassool 2006; Vieregg 1999: 32; Bădică 2010: 288; Leach 2009: 152). Museums were also variously seen as a place where differences in the society could be dealt with, or as a democratic agent of change (Sevcenko 2010: 21; de Wenden 2007: 27–28; Salazar 2011: 130). The second theme, issues of participation, drew on discussions during the 1970s of the museum as a temple or a forum (e.g., Choi 2010; Nissley and Casey 2002; Message 2007). Scholars stressed the need for people to participate in the production of heritage in order to deconstruct the museums' authoritarian role and bridge the gap between professionals and visitors so that subaltern voices, memories, and representations could be made (Burch 2010: 227; Cameron 2005; Davis 2004; Black 2005: 64; Henning 2011; Message 2007: 236). The third theme, social inclusivity, emerged especially during the latter part of 2000s. It was argued that museums should partake in a dialogue with marginalized groups in society in order to challenge normative representations (e.g., western/Eurocentric) of heritage and balance the narrative (dos Santos 2012; Shatanawi 2012: 65). Museums, it was stressed, should also act in society in order to assist in furthering democratic values such as freedom of expression. Scholars also addressed the need to promote citizenship, work for social inclusion, and assure that museums actively contribute to the reconciliation of conflicting groups in order to democratize a diverse society (Sandell 2003: 55; Golding 2006; Sandhal 2006).

Overall, scholarly discussions centered on arguments in favor of realizing democratization in museums. Therefore the focus has been on evaluating approaches, representations, and performances in museums. The consequence is that when a method is articulated as being used in order to realize democratization, it is often given a positive character. Along these lines, the 'present' is contrasted to the 'past,' so that a temporal difference is created between what is considered undemocratic (the 'past') and the practices that seek to implement democratization (the 'present'). There are scholars, however, that critique the 'present' methods used by museums to become democratic as being patronizing and misguiding (e.g., Appleton in Mason 2004: 49–51). Arguments about democratization also tend to be treated in the same way regardless of whether the text is produced in 1982 or in 2012. Democratization in museums is, therefore, performed as something that has not happened and that museums should strive to fulfill. It is as if, in the eyes of scholars, museums can never really become democratic no matter how hard they try to implement the approaches and suggestions that scholars recommend. Thus what I am arguing for in this chapter is a greater understanding of, and more research into, the reciprocity between scholarly publications and practical work in museums.

The corpus of scholarly articles I have analyzed explore democratization processes in different contexts, places, spaces, and times. The articles are moreover produced by scholars during different times, from various academic disciplines, and from various academic institutes all over the world. Despite these variations, the texts explore and express democracy and democratization processes in similar ways. Discussions center on themes such as public sovereignty, equality, participation, and rights, and reach similar conclusions. Thus definitions of democracy and democratization in museum settings rest on assumptions implicit to western frameworks, deriving mainly from Anglo-Saxon theory and methodology. Consequently, the scholarly debate feeds particular kinds of knowledge and perspectives into the heritage sector, to which I now turn.

DEFINING DEMOCRACY

Democracy is contested and debatable. Much confusion surrounds the term as it is both a descriptive label and a desirable value (Whitehead 2002: 7; Jakobsen and Kelstrup 1999: 11). It is commonly referred to as 'government of the people,' which is also why democracy is so attractive; it refuses to accept anything as justifiable if it does not originate from the people (Jakobsen and Kelstrup 1999: 19; Held 1987: 17–18, 363–64). Although there is much debate on how to define democracy, this debate does not appear in literature on museum and heritage studies. The term is in most cases taken for granted and therefore not defined, or it is understood as something that does not need further conceptualization. Scholars therefore construct democracy as having a fixed and universal value ready to be applied in all different circumstances. This, and here I draw on Held (1987: 17, 363–64), is because democracy seems to legitimate contemporary political life since decisions seem justified and reasonable if they are democratic. In this way democracy is understood as having the sole right to define what is politically correct.

Although most scholars do not define democracy, it is implicit in their texts what they suggest. In the few cases that democracy is actually defined, scholars draw on the etymological meaning of the Greek word. There are also alternative definitions like that given by Golding (2006: 316), who stresses the term 'thick democracy,' which "highlights a need to reconfigure notions of the rights and responsibilities of citizens in a new context, one of a global political economy that transcends the nation state." Both these definitions, however, are problematic since neither offer a precise explanation, but are vague descriptions of a broad subject. So defining democracy as 'government of the people' is far more difficult than researchers within museum and heritage studies admit, hence scholars need to identify and define who 'the people' are and how they should govern.

Therefore, it is highly problematic that literature within museum and heritage studies seldom defines who 'the people' are. 'The people' is a multifaceted term to work with since groups of people are composed of individuals with different ages, genders, ethnicities, religious and economical backgrounds, etc. It is apparent when analyzing discussions that 'the people' bear a certain connotation, specifically addressed to those groups understood as marginalized in society. Such groups are for example indigenous people, immigrant groups, and the less economically privileged (e.g., de Wenden 2007; Black 2005; Message 2007). This means that 'the people' are not everyone in society but those that are experienced as excluded. Although the effort is to produce theories and methodologies in order to include these groups, the democratic discourse continues to reproduce them as outsiders to the heritage project. These groups are constantly explored as 'the other,' and this means that democratization of heritage is not about 'the self' but instead about 'the other.' Consequently, 'the people' are reproduced as not being included, and in so doing, museums are portrayed as undemocratic.

I argue that the focus on marginalized groups has consequences for the practical work in museums because democratization is performed as a correction. Scholars often focus on misrepresentations of people's cultures during past regimes (e.g., Cameron 1982). This includes a discussion on how heritage in the 'past' was represented from a dominant and biased western/Eurocentric perspective. Scholars writing on South African museums especially evoke this perspective. For instance, Dubin (2006) explores how museums marginalized different African groups' heritage during apartheid. He explores how museums negotiate the previous misrepresentation of a people's heritage and how representations were corrected to become more inclusive and democratic. Rassool (2006: 288–311) discusses how museums were part of the reconstruction of society during the post-apartheid social environment and prompted participation and construction of new social memories in "democratic community museums." Rassool explains that community museums are places where the community can come together to share memories and participate, creating a heritage from which they were previously excluded.

In previous work on South African museums (Rodéhn 2008), I have argued that scholars writing on the democratization process argue their case from the binary opposition between dominator and subjugated, which also remains the basis for museological democracy debates elsewhere. So the term 'democratization' is understood and performed in scholarly publications as a critique of what is considered normative and a critique of how things were done in museum in the past. Although scholars try to break with past norms, post-colonial influenced museological writing continues to build on the epistemology of the dominator in its constant rejection of the 'past' (e.g., Kaplan 1994).

Drawing on Jakobsen and Kelstrup (1999: 19) and Held (1987: 17–18, 363–64), I argue that democratization is performed as a critique of the past because democracy is considered a means for restraining the state's execution of power and a mechanism that grants legitimacy for decisions. When scholars stress the need to incorporate marginalized peoples' heritage in museums, it is understood as deconstructing hegemonic interests (e.g., Shatanawi 2012; dos Santos 2012). Aspects such as participation, access, and community museums play a particular role in such arguments because they imply a sense of direct democracy of 'the people.' It should, however, be acknowledged that the kind of direct democracy that scholars stress are seldom fully realized, since 'the people' are not entirely free to make decisions as their participation in a democratic heritage is played out according to normative heritage structures. Furthermore, democracy is sometimes also hampered by the hierarchal social structures that exist among 'the people.' It is often the voices of the elite within the marginalized group that are heard, with the result that the truly marginalized people remain silenced.

Another issue of scholarly concern is the rights of 'the people,' articulated as the right to access, represent, and participate in heritage productions. The bottom-up approach is something that is stressed especially in decision-making processes, noted, for example, in discussions on eco-museums (e.g., Davis 2004; Rassool 2006; dos Santos 2012). Nevertheless, it is rights that are discussed, whereas the obligations and responsibilities of 'the people' are seldom addressed. Thus 'the people' are understood as passive participants, rather than being responsible for enforcing democratization or upholding a democratic heritage. Instead, that responsibility is directed to heritage professionals, which means that democratization is performed as the obligation and responsibility of museums.

Furthermore, the literature seems to suggest that everyone wants to, or should, participate in a democratic heritage. However, there are also groups in society that disagree with the normative definitions of democratic heritage and do not want to participate in it. Should these groups be excluded in discussions of heritage and in representations in museums because they do not comply with what is considered normative? Or should they be educated in the normative definition of a democratic heritage, and in doing so, are museums and scholarly publication not the very kind of authorities they endeavor to avoid being and that scholars write they should not be? This is an issue that needs further exploration because the values that the museum and heritage discourse have stipulated as democratic are not 'democratic enough' to incorporate ideals that are considered undemocratic.

DEFINING DEMOCRATIZATION PROCESSES

Democratization processes are, like democracy, seldom defined in texts about museums and heritage. However, from the content of discussions it is possible to conclude that scholars view democratization as a process of turning museums around from an unjust situation to one of democratic governance. Ames (1992: 24), for example, writes that "democratization of museums not only means extending access to a wider range of people, but also entails the obligation to *work to make the people come*" (emphasis in original). Whereas this sort of explanation represents most writings in favor of museum democratization, Schwenkel (2009) offers a different understanding. She writes that "democratization practices, however, are selective, ambiguous, and at times involuntary" (2009: 174). Although she does not define the term in her writings, she acknowledges that democratization is not a static, but plural, phenomenon.

'Democratization' is as equally complicated a term to explain as 'democracy.' Democratization processes often unfold as an ongoing unstructured array of social negotiations and should be understood as such. Nevertheless, a way to structure the democratization process is needed in order to understand how scholars perform democratization through the medium of their writing. Thus I return to the concept of time as a way to describe, structure, and analyze social occurrences. To organize how time is constructed in scholarly writings on democratization processes, I use Silander's (2005: 195) model that divides democratization processes into three different phases: (1) *pre-transition*, a phase of liberation in a non-democratic environment accompanied by a phase of unity; (2) the *transition* phase that refers to a political change, for example, from a dictatorship to a democratic society; and (3) the *consolidation* phase, a long period during which institutions and values become stable. Silander's model corresponds to how scholars understand democratization processes and allows me to create temporal reference points from which to account for democratization and reveal how scholars perform it. It also allows me to deconstruct democratization through its own rationalization and to highlight that scholars favor certain phases while others appear less important.

Using Silander's model, my research has shown that the pre-transition phase is not of particular interest to scholars (for an exception see Chapter 15 of this volume). Seldom investigated or analyzed, pre-transition is simply considered a prelude to actual democratization processes when it is mentioned at all. Work that happens in museums before, for example, a political transition is not acknowledged as important to the democratization process. Most publications focus on the transition phase, which becomes synonymous with the democratization process. This process is seldom analyzed when it actually occurs, but rather in its aftermath. Thus scholars often take on a moral role, highlighting atrocities in order to stress change (e.g., Sandhal 2006: 32). The transition phase is promoted, celebrated, and often expressed almost in a revolutionary and romantic tone. The consolidation phase, meanwhile, is sometimes studied but not to the same degree as the transition phase. When studied, it is explained as the outcome of the supposed paradigm shift or as a period being on the verge of a democracy. The consolidation phase is also given attention when the institution can prove that they have bettered themselves and contemplated the moral lessons of democratization (e.g., Sevcenko 2010). In sum, scholars actively favor processes that appear sensational or dramatic, while the more peaceful processes are overlooked or neglected. Consequently, scholars limit the understanding of which phase a museum is 'in' when experiencing a democratization process, and therefore I suggest that democratization processes, as they are performed in scholarly publications, are highly selective and biased.

The temporal understanding of democratization in scholarly publication is thus performed as an evolving process that is expressed as having a beginning and an end. This has consequences for the heritage sector because in order to be seen as a democratic museum, the museum must constantly produce a heritage that is different from the previous one. Although museums are persistent in striving to become more democratic and implementing changes, they are nevertheless seldom considered democratic by scholars and therefore remain situated in a state of permanent transition within the democratization process. Also, in order for museums to appear democratic they need to constantly be changing, but in changing they are also experienced as not yet democratic.

I suggest, therefore, that the democratization of heritage is best understood as eclectic negotiations of power, ideas, and interests: processes where the past and the present are intertwined, superimposed, and interrupted all at the same time. It is a process where personal and academic agendas constantly are rejected and affirmed by different actors. In keeping with Whitehead (2002: 26–32), I argue that democratization should be understood as a long process of open-ended social constructions. I propose, therefore, that the way scholars present democratization may not correspond to the lived experience of museum workers.

Fostering democratization 'in practice' is complex, involving negotiations of many different actors, material cultures, documents, and power relations so that democratization is performed as networks of actions with uncertain outcomes. When scholars on the other hand perform democratization, the process is controlled by the writer, who can regulate the outcome. S/he often performs democratization in a manner that corresponds to the preconditioned and supposedly universal values associated with democracy and democratization, to which I now will turn.

A WESTERN CONSTRUCT

Democratization processes are neither fully stable, nor entirely predetermined, and therefore if understood as contextually variable, democratization processes cannot be defined by some fixed and timeless criterion (Whitehead 2002: 7, 18, 20, 26–32). Yet my research has shown that scholars treat the concept as having a fixed and stable definition that is constructed around values of access, inclusivity, participation, and representation. Heritage is furthermore explored from a western perspective and an Anglo-Saxon theory and methodology. Building on the work of Silander (2005: 142–43), I argue that democracy in the context of museum practice has come to symbolize the powerful western project that includes appropriations of western political standards and values.

One example of western discourse in museum and heritage studies is how democracy is defined as 'government of the people' by drawing on the etymological meaning of the Greek word, as explained above. The definition is problematic as it constructs democracy on a classical Mediterranean framing. Democracy is positioned in relation to the 'cradle of western civilization,' which creates a sense of legitimacy and origin. Antiquity has served as a nationalistic marker and a symbol of political virtue, wisdom, and taste, not only within a European context but also in the context of colonized areas (Rodéhn 2008: 188). Therefore this definition becomes more problematic than it seems at first glance, as democracy is performed as originating, and being, European. It is connected to various Eurocentric nationalisms, and the legacy of classical antiquity has in many cases been appropriated to exclude other groups. Democracy is thus created, constantly recreated, and maintained as a western construct through its definition, which results in an exclusion of alternative explanations.

Another issue is that texts in museum and heritage studies portray democratization as an evolutionary process. The approach is similar to a Social Darwinist approach to analyzing social development. In order for democracy to assume its unique position it needs to be polarized against something, e.g., past regimes or past times. Past regimes are expressed as 'the other' in comparison to democracy, thus democratization is performed as making a difference (e.g., Dubin 2006; Rassool 2006). As a result, scholars specifically explore how museums and heritage change and are changed. It also affects heritage practitioners because in order for museums to appear democratic, they have to be seen as doing something different from before, as leaving the past behind and evolving to something better. Again, treating democratization processes as an evolutionary process is a western construct with a tainted legacy connected to the subjugation of other groups. This fact is, nevertheless, overlooked when arguing in favor of democracy, which is peculiar since scholars within museum and heritage studies have engaged in an animated post-modern and post-colonial critique deconstructing these same evolutionary narratives.

Consequently, in order to know how ideas of democracy and democratization processes are upheld and furthered in museum and heritage studies, it is necessary to examine the power base, and the existing and ongoing centrality of western and Anglo-Saxon discourse. Scholars need to be more careful in how we portray democracy and democratization, and we need to be aware of how our texts form part of western democracy promotion. In keeping with Silander (2005: 140), I argue that democracy promotion can be understood almost as a missionary movement, which is dangerous because instead of leading to democracy it can result in conflict and domination. The way scholars appropriate western and Anglo-Saxon values has taken on almost imperial and colonial proportions as their writings enforce Eurocentric values of democracy in other cultural contexts. The power invested in western discourses, from which so many post-colonial countries have tried to rid themselves, are now enforced again through this discourse. The quest for equality results in camouflaging unequal political power distributions.

CONCLUSION

In this chapter, I have emphasized the need to be more aware of the way we write about democracy and democratization processes. In this respect I return to Austin's (2007) claim: in saying something we are doing something. Consequently, in writing about democracy we are 'doing' what we are writing about and co-creating the conditions for democracy and democratization in museums. Furthermore, as I argued above, these writings must be regarded as ongoing performances that influence one another. Academic writing represents an active participant to creating heritage, on par with the everyday work of heritage practitioners. Although our constructions of democracy and democratization operate in a discursive space, they influence the practical side of heritage work to a great extent. Scholarly publications are evoked in policy documents, in political speeches, and are used as reference material for heritage professionals in their work with exhibitions, collections, and pedagogic activities.

Our textual production involves execution of power; this power, however, is largely concealed in our quest for more just and equal heritage expressions. There is, nevertheless, a great need to acknowledge the western power that we promote in our writing. The western Anglo-Saxon discourse has taken on missionary proportions similar to that of imperial and colonial projects in that it imposes cultural values upon other groups. Therefore, we need to ask ourselves: are we driving a political project, or rather, what kind of political project are we driving? Considering these questions can hopefully make us more aware of our active participation in democratization processes.

REFERENCES

Alexander, Bryant Keith, Gary Anderson, and Bernardo Gallegos. 2004. *Performance Theory in Education: Power, Pedagogy and the Politics of Identity*. Mahwah, NJ: Laurence Erlbaum Associates.

Ames, Michel M. 1988. "A Challenge to Modern Museum Management: Meshing Mission and Market." *International Journal of Museum Management and Curatorship* 7 (2): 151–57. http://dx.doi.org/10.1080/09647778809515116.

Ames, Michel M. 1992. *Cannibal Tours and Glass Boxes: The Anthropology of Museums*. Vancouver: University of British Columbia Press.

Austin, John Langshaw. 2007. "How to Do Things with Words, Lecture II." In *The Performance Studies Reader*, ed. Henry Bial, 177–86. London: Routledge.

Bădică, Simina. 2010. "Same Exhibitions, Different Labels? Romanian National Museums and the Fall of Communism." In *National Museums: New Studies from Around the World*, ed. Simon Knell, Peter Aronsson, Arne Bugge Amundsen, Amy Jane Barnes, Stuart Burch, Jenifer Carter, Viviane Gosselin, Sarah Hughes, and Aalan Kirwan, 272–90. London: Routledge.

Bennett, Tony. 1998. "Speaking to the Eyes: Museums, Legibility and the Social Order." In *The Politics of Display: Museums, Science, Culture*, ed. Sharon Macdonald, 25–35. London: Routledge.

Black, Graham. 2005. *The Engaging Museum: Developing Museums for Visitor Involvement*. London: Routledge.

Burch, Stuart. 2010. "Taking Part: Performance, Participation and National Art Museum." In *National Museums: New Studies from Around the World*, ed. Simon Knell, Peter Aronsson, Arne Bugge Amundsen, Amy Jane Barnes, Stuart Burch, Jenifer Carter, Viviane Gosselin, Sarah Hughes, and Aalan Kirwan, 225–47. London: Routledge.

Cameron, Duncan. 1982. "Museums and Public Access: The Glenbow Approach." *International Journal of Museum Management and Curatorship* 1 (3): 177–96. http://dx.doi.org/10.1080/09647778209514832.

Cameron, Fiona. 2005. "Contentiousness and Shifting Knowledge Paradigms: The Roles of History and Science Museums in Contemporary Societies." *Museum Management and Curatorship* 20 (3): 213–33. http://dx.doi.org/10.1080/09647770500502003.

Choi, Sunghee. 2010. "Rethinking Korean Cultural Identities at the National Museum of Korea." In *National Museums: New Studies from Around the World*, ed. Simon Knell, Peter Aronsson, Arne Bugge Amundsen, Amy Jane Barnes, Stuart Burch, Jenifer Carter, Viviane Gosselin, Sarah Hughes, and Aalan Kirwan, 290–301. London: Routledge.

Davis, Peter. 2004. "Ecomuseums and the Democratization of Japanese Museology." *International Journal of Heritage Studies* 10 (1): 93–110. http://dx.doi.org/10.1080/135 2725032000194268.

dos Santos, Paula Assuncão. 2012. "Museu da Maré: A Museum Full of Soul." *Curator* 55 (1): 21–34. http://dx.doi.org/10.1111/j.2151-6952.2011.00118.x.

Dubin, Steven C. 2006. *Transforming Museums: Mounting Queen Victoria in a Democratic South Africa*. New York, NY: Palgrave Macmillan.

Giddens, Anthony. 1984. *The Constitution of Society: Outline of the Theory of Structuration*. Cambridge, UK: Polity Press.

Golding, Viv. 2006. "Learning at the Museum Frontiers: Democracy, Identity, and Difference." In *Museum Revolutions: How Museums Are Change and Are Changed*, ed. Simon Knell, Sharon MacLeod, and Sheila Watson, 315–29. London: Routledge.

Held, David. 1987. *Demokratimodeller från klassisk demokrati till demokratisk autonomi*. [*Models of Democracy: From Classical Democracy to Democratic Autonomy*]. Trans. Stefan Jordsebrandt Annika Persson, and Tore Winqvist. Gothenburg, Sweden: Daidalos.

Henning, Michelle. 2011. "New Media." In *A Companion to Museum Studies*, ed. Sharon Macdonald, 302–18. London: Routledge.

Hooper-Greenhill, Eilean. 1995. "Museums and Communication: An Introductory Essay." In *Museum, Media, Message*, ed. Eilean Hooper-Greenhill, 1–14. London: Routledge. http://dx.doi.org/10.4324/9780203456514_chapter_1.

Jakobsen, Uffe, and Morten Kelstrup. 1999. "Studiet af demokrati og demokratisering." In *Demokrati og Demokratisering: Begreber og Teorier*, ed. Uffe Jakobsen and Morten Kelstrup, 7–39. Copenhagen, Denmark: Förlaget Politiska Studier.

Kaplan, Flora, ed. 1994. *Museums and the Making of "Ourselves": The Role of Objects in National Identity*. London: Routledge.

Lamm Pineau, Elyse. 1994. "Teaching is Performance: Reconceptualizing a Problematic Metaphor." *American Educational Research Journal* 31 (1): 3–25. http://dx.doi.org/10.3102/00028312031001003.

Leach, Michael. 2009. "Difficult Memories: The Independence Struggle as Cultural Heritage in East Timor." In *Places of Pain and Shame: Dealing with 'Difficult Heritage,'* ed. William Logan and Keir Reeves, 144–62. London: Routledge.

Macdonald, Sharon. 1998. "Exhibitions of Power and Powers of Exhibitions: An Introduction to the Politics of Display." In *The Politics of Display: Museums, Science, Culture*, ed. Sharon Macdonald, 1–24. London: Routledge.

Mason, Rhiannon. 2004. "Conflict and Complement: An Exploration of the Discourses Informing the Concept of the Socially Inclusive Museum in Contemporary Britain." *International Journal of Heritage Studies* 10 (1): 49–73. http://dx.doi.org/10.1080/1352725032000194240.

Message, Kylie. 2007. "Museums and the Utility of Culture: The Politics of Liberal Democracy and Cultural Well-Being." *Social Identities* 13 (2): 235–56. http://dx.doi.org/10.1080/13504630701235846.

Munn, Nancy D. 1986. *The Fame of Gawa: A Symbolic Study of Value Transformation in Massim (Papua New Guinea) Society*. Cambridge: Cambridge University Press.

Munn, Nancy D. 1992. "The Cultural Anthropology of Time: A Critical Essay." *Annual Review of Anthropology* 21 (1): 93–123. http://dx.doi.org/10.1146/annurev.an.21.100192.000521.

Nissley, Nick, and Andrea Casey. 2002. "The Politics of Exhibition: Viewing Corporate Museums through the Paradigmatic Lens of Organization Memory." *British Journal of Management* 13 (S2): 35–45. http://dx.doi.org/10.1111/1467-8551.13.s2.4.

Rassool, Ciraj. 2006. "Community Museums, Memory Politics, and Social Transformation in South Africa: Histories, Possibilities, and Limits." In *Museum Frictions: Public Cultures/Global Transformations*, ed. Ivan Karp, Corinne A. Kratz,

Lynn Szwaja, and Tomás Ybarra-Frausto, 286–321. Durham, NC: Duke University Press. http://dx.doi.org/10.1215/9780822388296-016.

Rodéhn, Cecilia. 2008. "Lost in Transformation: A Critical Study of Two South African Museums." PhD dissertation, Centre for Visual Arts, University of KwaZulu-Natal, Pietermaritzburg, South Africa.

Salazar, Juan Francisco. 2011. "The Mediations of Climate Change: Museums as Citizens' Media." *Museums and Society* 9 (2): 123–35.

Sandell, Richard. 2003. "Social Inclusion, the Museum, and the Dynamics of Sectoral Change." *Museum and Society* 1 (1): 46–62.

Sandhal, Jette. 2006. "The Interpretation of Cultural Policy, by and for Museums: A Museum as an Embodiment of Cultural Policies?" *Museum International* 58 (4): 29–36. http://dx.doi.org/10.1111/j.1468-0033.2006.00580.x.

Schechner, Richard. 2002. *Performance Studies: An Introduction*. London: Routledge.

Schwenkel, Christine. 2009. *The American War in Contemporary Vietnam: Transnational Remembrance and Representation*. Bloomington: Indiana University Press.

Sevcenko, Liz. 2010. "Sites of Conscience: New Approaches to Conflicted Memory." *Museum International* 62 (1/2): 20–25. http://dx.doi.org/10.1111/j.1468-0033.2010.01720.x.

Shatanawi, Mirjam. 2012. "Engaging Islam: Working with Muslim Communities in a Multicultural Society." *Curator* 55 (1): 65–79. http://dx.doi.org/10.1111/j.2151-6952.2011.00121.x.

Silander, David. 2005. *Democracy From The Outside-In? The Conceptualization and Significance of Democracy Promotion*. Gothenburg, Sweden: Växjö University Press.

Taylor, Diana. 2004. "Translating Performance." In *The Performance Studies Reader*, ed. Henry Bial, 381–86. London: Routledge.

Vieregg, H. K. 1999. "The Interrelationship between Museology and Globalization: Case Studies on Historical Prototypes and a Future Subject." *International Journal of Heritage Studies* 5 (1): 21–34. http://dx.doi.org/10.1080/13527259908722244.

de Wenden, Catherine Wihtol. 2007. "Immigration and Cultural Rights: Political Recognition and Cultural Acceptance." *Museum International* 59 (1/2): 24–29. http://dx.doi.org/10.1111/j.1468-0033.2007.00591.x.

Whitehead, Laurence. 2002. *Democratization: Theory and Experience*. Oxford: Oxford University Press. http://dx.doi.org/10.1093/0199253285.001.0001.

Difficult Heritage 7

Coming 'to Terms' with Sicily's Fascist Past

Joshua Samuels

In the last twenty years, concepts of dissonant, difficult, negative, and undesirable heritage have emerged to help describe the ways in which sites, time periods, or events associated with violence, trauma, or embarrassment are today being preserved or memorialized. This chapter discusses what these different terms achieve rhetorically: how the choice of word affects, intentionally or otherwise, our methodological approach to and interpretation of the bundled relationships between past and present. I suggest that the use of these terms says a great deal about what one expects to see, and has the potential to overshadow more nuanced appreciations of everyday heritage practices on the ground, including potential strategies for their future management as cultural resources. I contextualize this discussion within my own frustration in coming 'to terms' with the material heritage of Italian Fascism in the Sicilian countryside, a heritage which many would assume to manifest 'difficult' characteristics.

TERMINOLOGICAL TRAJECTORIES

Although the scholarship on difficult heritage is fairly recent, the idea has been a part of the official discourse on heritage management for quite some time. The slave-depot island of Gorée in Senegal and

DOI: 10.5876/9781607323846.c007

the Auschwitz-Birkenau concentration camp in Poland were among the very first sites inscribed on the World Heritage List in 1978 and 1979, respectively. Although UNESCO made a point of its intentions "to restrict the inscription of other sites of a similar nature" (UNESCO 1979), a few others have made it onto the list, including the Genbaku Dome Peace Memorial in Hiroshima in 1997 and Robben Island in 1999 (Labadi 2005: 95; Rico 2008).

Much of the academic discussion on managing the material legacies of these kinds of sites makes reference to Tunbridge and Ashworth's (1996) *Dissonant Heritage: The Management of the Past as a Resource in Conflict*. Here, the authors argue that heritage is a narrative that is constructed, consciously or unconsciously, to achieve certain ends. Because there are an infinite number of ways to interpret the past, conflict and contestation become an implicit part of the construction of historical narratives: particular attributes are emphasized while others are downplayed, ignored, or silenced (Trouillot 1995). Tunbridge and Ashworth (1996) propose 'dissonance' as the word that best captures the inherently conflictual nature of heritage narratives, a cacophonous disharmony analogous to simultaneously "holding mutually inconsistent attitudes or the existence of a lack of consonance between attitudes and behavior" (1996: 20). They understand dissonance as an inalienable attribute of heritage and its management; however, it is particularly pronounced in heritage sites associated with war, pogrom, persecution, injustice, violence, and atrocity. In these cases, dealing with dissonance can be extremely challenging.

Tunbridge and Ashworth (1996: 5) focus on the heritage of atrocity, developing a model for heritage management based on production and consumption primarily in the context of tourism. The flurry of complementary concepts that have emerged since then grapple with more subtle forms of dissonance, with less of an emphasis on heritage as a product to be marketed and consumed and more as a component of complex personal, socio-political, or national identity politics. For example, an important turning point in this literature is Meskell's (2002) discussion of the World Trade Center and the Bamiyan Buddhas as examples of 'negative heritage,' which she describes as a "conflictual site that becomes the repository of negative memory in the collective imaginary" (2002: 558). Meskell's interest is in the different ways that sites of negative heritage are mobilized to 'master' past traumas, for example through erasure or as rehabilitative didactic testimonies. Significantly, she draws out how 'negativity' is not intrinsic to the site itself, but actively constructed: the negativity is contingent and subjectively experienced.

Dissonance is also at the forefront of Macdonald's (2006) analysis of changing management strategies for the Nazi Rally Grounds in Nuremberg. She introduces the concept of 'undesirable heritage,' referring to the "physical remains of the past [that] offer up an identity that many of those in the present wish to distance themselves from, even while, at the same time, recognizing . . . as fully part of their history" (2006: 11). Describing the same material, Macdonald (2009: 1) shifts her terminology to 'difficult heritage,' defined as "a past that is recognized as meaningful in the present but that is also contested and awkward for public reconciliation with a positive, self-affirming contemporary identity." 'Difficult heritage' appears to be taking off as the term of choice in more recent scholarship. It is in the title of Logan and Reeves's (2009) edited volume on places of pain and shame, as well as Burström and Gelderblom's (2011) article on the remains of the Nazi Harvest Festival in Bückeberg. The International Committee for Museums and Collections of Archaeology and History organized their 2011 conference in Helsinki around the theme of "Museums and Difficult Heritage." A final, recent addition to the literature centers around the idea of 'abjection,' variously described in reference to sites that are wretched, ruined, nauseating, or pitiful (e.g., Buchli and Lucas 2001; González-Ruibal 2006, 2008; Pétursdóttir 2013). Deploying this term as 'abject heritage' is still taking shape; Herscher (2010) uses it to describe the old-fashioned and obsolete buildings in Kosovo that had to be destroyed in the name of Socialist modernity, while Smith (2012) uses it to discuss abandoned, unfinished, or disruptive spaces that can be engaged ironically as an intervention into traditional models of heritage (what he calls 'counter-tourism').

At the risk of over-generalizing, I suggest that dissonant, negative, undesirable, difficult, and abject heritage refer to more or less the same thing, namely the challenge of what to do with the material remains of an historical period, site, or event that is today generally perceived as problematic for one reason or another. But as terms like these begin to circulate more widely, especially given increasing global interest in dark and thanatourism (Lennon and Foley 2000; Sather-Wagstaff 2011; Sharpley and Stone 2009; Timm Knudsen 2011), it is worth taking stock of what they achieve rhetorically. In the discussion that follows, I will identify some of the potential problems that these terms collectively introduce, and highlight how a particular approach to one of them—difficult heritage—may help mitigate these pitfalls.

'Dissonant,' 'negative,' and 'abject' are powerful adjectives; as an attribute of 'heritage' they are jarring and unsettling. 'Difficult' is not quite as evocative, and 'undesirable' even less so. Nonetheless, all of these terms effectively upset traditional conceptions of heritage as a (beneficial) inheritance of wealth, land, tradition, or resources, highlighting instead the idea of inheritance as a burden. However, I believe there is a methodological danger in overemphasizing certain sites or events as difficult, negative, or dissonant in that it predisposes us to particular ways of researching, analyzing, and eventually managing them as heritage resources. For example, calling a site a 'place of pain and shame' (Logan and Reeves 2009) implies that people should be ashamed of it. While this assumption may be valid, it might not be the most beneficial way to structure research and management plans. For this reason, care must be exercised in how these terms are deployed.

'Ambivalent heritage,' as outlined by Breglia (2006) and Chadha (2006), may serve as a useful intervention. Ambivalence literally means "both strength": it was coined by a German psychologist in 1910 to suggest the experience of having simultaneous conflicting feelings (Graubert and Miller 1957). This places the word squarely within Tunbridge and Ashworth's (1996) discussion of 'dissonance.' However, while 'dissonance' suggests a state of violent psychic discord, the 'ambivalence' described by Breglia and Chadha—regarding the ruins of Maya temples and a colonial cemetery in Calcutta, respectively—is far less dramatic.

While 'difficult' heritage may lack the evocative bite of its alternatives, I believe this potential weakness may be an asset and the reason for its terminological ascendancy. The rhetorical strength of 'difficult heritage' lies in a recognition of the everyday ambivalence at its core, giving it an advantage over the dramatic fireworks of its 'dissonant' and 'negative' variants. Ideally, 'difficult heritage' should draw attention to the process of dealing with problematic pasts most appropriately; the difficulty refers to the practice of heritage-making, not the site or event itself. While this nuance is built into the heart of Meskell's (2002) conceptions of 'negative heritage,' it gets obscured by the hyperbole of negativity. 'Difficult heritage' should strive to be powerful and evocative yet still retain as much ambivalence as possible. The rhetoric of shame and violence, while forceful and appealing from a didactic perspective, may prove counter-productive as a research methodology and, ultimately, as a management strategy.

FASCIST AGRICULTURAL REFORM IN SICILY

As an example, my experience researching Italian Fascism in Sicily confounded my preconceived ideas about what constitutes a negative or dissonant heritage. Fascist Italy's violent political repression, colonial brutality, and alliance with Nazi Germany place it firmly within the purview of negative, undesirable, and difficult heritage (Ebner 2011). However, its memory and material remains are rarely understood in exclusively negative terms. The buildings and monuments are permitted to have artistic or architectonic merit in a way that is simply not possible in the case of works by Albert Speer, Hitler's chief architect; there is a palpable nostalgia for the past that is not poisoned by the politics of the period. This may in part be due to the lack of a proper 'taking account' of Italy's Fascist past, what Battini (2007) describes as Italy's "missing Nuremberg." Not putting Fascism on trial enabled a "selective and partial public memory" (Battini 2007: 26) of the Fascist period to take hold in Italy. As a result, unlike the example of post-war Germany chronicled by Macdonald (2006, 2009), there has been little public discourse about what Italians should do with Fascism's material remains, and there is no officially endorsed national narrative through which to think about the Fascist past.

This has translated into an awkward relationship with Fascism as an historical period, as well as the material objects it left across Italy and its colonies—buildings, monuments and landscapes. While Macdonald (2006, 2009) describes "coming to terms with the past" (*vergangenheitsbewältigung*) as something of a national obsession in Germany, this has simply not been the case in Italy. Neither Fascism nor its material remains have been 'put on trial'; the past, however dissonant, has been left as is.

My research into heritage dissonance and the Fascist past focused on a series of land reforms and building programs undertaken in western Sicily in the late 1930s and early 1940s. For centuries, southern Italian agriculture had been dominated by large semi-feudal estates called *latifondi*. By the late nineteenth century, these great estates were owned by typically absent landlords who leased their properties to middlemen who would, in turn, sublet small parcels out to individual farmers in year-long contracts, extorting money and produce in the process (Hilowitz 1976; Pluciennik, Mientjes, and Giannitrapani 2004; Schneider and Schneider 1976). The farmers themselves did not live on the fields they worked, but commuted to them from large towns and cities. Because farmers would often have small stakes in multiple properties, they would commute from the town where they lived to the fields that they worked, typically spending their nights in rented quarters at the *latifondo*'s central buildings, the *baglio* or *masseria*, and only returning home on the weekends. Not only were the *latifondi* economically unjust, but they were agriculturally underproductive, and their insularity opened up a space for nascent Mafia networks to emerge as a force for maintaining discipline and order in the countryside (Blok 1975; Lupo 2009: 11; Smith 1968: 466).

In an attempt to modernize Sicilian agriculture, as well as substitute the power of the State for that of the landowners and their Mafia enforcers, the Fascists developed a rural-urbanism in Sicily centered around custom-built

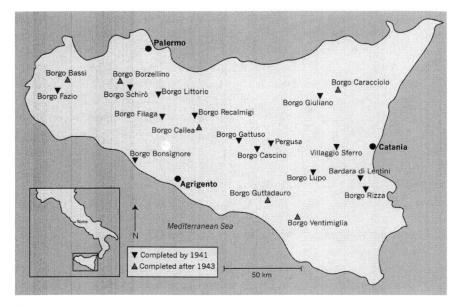

FIGURE 7.1. *Major* borghi *built under Fascism, not including agricultural experimentation centers, roadworker (*cantoniere*) villages, or extensions of earlier* latifondo *estates. For a complete discussion see Dufour (2005), La China (2008), Pennacchi (2008), and Samuels (2012).*

agricultural centers called *borghi* (sing. *borgo*), in dialogue with similar projects in the Pontine Marshes south of Rome and Italy's African colonies in Eritrea, Ethiopia, Somalia and Libya. Through the Agency for the Colonization of the Sicilian *Latifondo* (ECLS), the government built over twenty of these centers across the island (Figure 7.1), each consisting of a central piazza bounded by the church, school, Fascist Party headquarters (the *Casa del Fascio*), agriculture office, post office, shop, medical dispensary, police station, *trattoria*, and services. Landowners in the area around each *borgo* were required to set aside portions of their property for individual farmers, providing them each with an agricultural plot that included a farmhouse where their families would live full-time. Only the people staffing the *borgo*'s offices and services were intended to live within its confines; the bulk of the resettled population was to be housed in the new homesteads. The plans called for a *borgo* every 10 km, serving approximately 240 farmsteads in the immediate vicinity of each; in this way, the *borghi* and farmhouses would form a comprehensive rural-urban fabric. This vision was evocatively summarized by Edoardo Caracciolo (1942:

286), a prominent Sicilian architect responsible for designing Borgo Gatusso, who described Sicily's 'new urbanism' as "the pulverization of the city center onto the agricultural surface, or as an organization of urban character over vast extensions of rural space."

It is very appealing to seek out the dark side of Fascist planning of this kind, especially in the context of land reform. Arguments have been made that land reform was also social reform, an attempt to purge the Sicilian peasantry of their perceived pathologies and control their activities, essentially using land tenure as a form of internal colonialism to bring them into line with a Fascist conception of modernity (Ben-Ghiat 2001; Ghirardo and Forster 1985; Mariani 1976; Martinelli and Nuti 1978: 272). This provides a comforting counter-balance to what might otherwise be interpreted as massive public works projects aimed at transforming landscapes in order to improve the lives of thousands of farmers across the island. Without a subtext of social conditioning, undercurrent of menace, and the threat of reprisal, Fascist land reclamation risks seeming like a rather positive thing—at the very least a valiant effort—dangerously close to the very similar public works projects undertaken in the New Deal (Ghirardo 1989). Regardless of whether we interpret the New Deal as essentially Fascist, or Fascist land reform as essentially virtuous, their proximity is very disruptive; there appears to be a need to underscore Fascism's sinister motives in order to disambiguate the two projects and stay on the 'right' side of history. It seems essential that Fascism and its material remains be adequately problematized.

Today, roughly 40 percent of the *borghi* built during the Fascist period, and most of their associated farmhouses, are abandoned or in a very poor state of repair. The Fascists were aware that convincing farmers and their families to leave behind the civic and social comforts of the city would be difficult, but their attempts to make the countryside hospitable through the *borghi* were largely unsuccessful. Most people simply did not like being isolated year-round in their farmhouses, distant from the social fabric of their old towns. As Barbera (2002: 156) starkly observes, "it makes no sense to have a piazza without a city, dispersed in a desolate countryside." The construction of farmhouses and *borghi* also frequently preceded the necessary infrastructure, so that fundamental resources like water were either unavailable or insufficient for the surrounding population's needs. A cynical argument holds that, under Fascism, the government was primarily interested in the appearance of progress, for propagandistic purposes; whether the *borghi* and farmhouses were functional in practice was not as much of a concern. Furthermore, the Fascists' focus on grain was never a particularly good idea (Hazan 1933: 496–99), though it did

FIGURE 7.2. *Borgo Borzellino perched above a rest stop along the SS 624 (photo by the author).*

fit in nicely with the goals of the Battle for Wheat. Launched on June 20, 1925, the Battle for Wheat aimed to make Italy self-sufficient in grain production, part of a larger autarkic push to rid the country of its dependence upon foreign food imports. However, by the twentieth century there was simply not enough water in the Sicilian interior to produce wheat efficiently, and the problem compounded when competition from other grain-producing nations brought down global market prices. But the most significant reason for the failure of many *borghi* was the growing availability of automobiles in the late 1950s and 1960s. Cars made the need to settle farmers directly on their fields completely unnecessary: whereas before it could take two or more hours to reach the fields on foot or by donkey, the trip now took a matter of minutes. Notably, a reason that is rarely given to explain the *borghi*'s abandonment is their association with Fascism. One exception is Borgo Caracciolo, which was built on land expropriated from Duke Nelson and destroyed in the mid-1960s by his family after they had regained title. Here, erasure was very clearly a strategy to wipe the traces of the Fascist past away.

Today, most of the abandoned villages are crumbling silently, insular pockets of rubble tucked away within the vast expanses of countryside. Others have a slightly more public presence: Borgo Borzellino's remains were effectively pedestaled by the SS 624 highway, completed in the late 1990s, that runs from Palermo to Sciacca (Figure 7.2). A rest area alongside the road serves as a convenient viewing platform that turns the *borgo* into something akin to a museum exhibit, allowed to be seen but not touched. Following González-Ruibal (2005) and Macdonald (2006, 2009), abandonment can be read as an active choice in which decay is used as a past-mastering strategy (Meskell 2002): allowing the relics of Fascist building programs to rot in public serves as a subtle commentary on that phase of Italian history. Indeed, for years I was convinced that the SS 624 rest area was intentionally sited below Borgo Borzellino to encourage passerby to pause and reflect upon its ruination.

DIFFICULT HERITAGE?

I took a similar line, predicated on the assumption that the *borghi* were sites of negative or difficult heritage, in my interpretation of the many plans that have been put forward throughout the decades to re-use or transform Fascist *borghi*. My logic was that adapting these spaces to new purposes effectively absolves them of their association with Fascism. For example, a 2009 project proposed by Sicily's Agency for Agricultural Development (ESA) aims to 're-qualify' several *borghi* as waypoints along a bicycle and trekking route. ESA was created in 1965 out of the ashes of the Agency for Sicilian Agricultural Reform (ERAS), which itself developed out of the Fascist ECLS, which had in turn absorbed the Vittorio Emanuele III Institute for the Reclamation of Sicily that had been founded just a few years after Mussolini came to power. There is a very clear trajectory in the agency's mission and person-nel from 1925 until today; indeed, ERAS and ESA continued to build new borghi surrounded by farmhouses into the late 1960s, with about as much success as before. However, in recent years ESA has been struggling to jus-tify its existence: once they finally stopped building the ill-fated *borghi*, they began focusing on renting out tractors and heavy equipment to farmers who could not afford their own. In recent years they have been providing technical expertise and investigating greener approaches to agriculture, but there is a sense that they have lost their mandate. This new project is one of the ways that ESA hopes to reaffirm its relevance (ESA 2009).

The project is titled *Via dei Borghi*, and is designed to develop 'slow tourism' across Sicily's rural landscapes (ESA 2009). Under the plan, ten of the eighty-six rural *borghi* built between 1926 and 1967 will become tourist portals and activity centers with particular themes, focusing on either natural or cultural heritage (e.g., cheese or wine production, protected forests, archaeological sites). Half of the selected *borghi* belong to the agency's Fascist period, and the others from its post-war incarnations. They will not be converted into hotels or bed and breakfasts—ESA does not want to immerse itself too directly in the tourism business—but the hope is that, by providing a clear route and spe-cific itineraries, they will encourage the development of agricultural tourism in the surrounding areas. The project description relies on rhetorical tropes of sustainability, green tourism, and rural heritage. ESA argues that farmers need to emphasize the regional specificity of their produce, as a mark of its quality and desirability, and diversify their sources of income. Through the *Via dei Borghi*, ESA hopes to develop an international interest in Sicily's agricultural landscapes, traditions, and products.

ESA's plan is the latest in a broad trend toward adapting *borghi* for new purposes. For example, in 2005 the city of Carlentini approved a contract to begin restoration work at nearby Borgo Rizza. The plan was to 're-functionalize' the *borgo* as a study center and tourist portal serving the activities and archaeological sites in the surrounding area, including the nearby Bronze Age rock-cut tombs of Pantalica. Another example is Borgo Ventimiglia, which was still under construction when the Allies landed on July 10, 1943. According to Ciriacono (2003), approximately three hundred settlers were distributed in the area in farmhouses on thirty-eight plots; these farmhouses were the site of the July 13, 1943 Piano Stella massacre, in which American troops are said to have killed several unarmed settlers. Of all the *borghi*, Ventimiglia might therefore seem to be the one most in need of rehabilitation, from both its Fascist and potential war-crime past. It is therefore fitting that since 1988, it has been used as a residential alcohol-dependency recuperation center. The center's website describes its buildings as "of very recent construction, immersed in greenery and comprised of accommodation furnished with every comfort, rooms for reading and recreation, equipped laboratories, an auditorium, and private chapel."[1] Borgo Ventimiglia's rehabilitation is complete; it has been 'clean' for decades. Other *borghi* have also been transformed into rehabilitation centers. Bardara di Lentini, also known as Villaggio Biviere, once served as a center for the "recuperation and placement of handicapped people" called *Nuova Vita* ("New Life"), according to a rusting sign hanging from one of its gates. And in 2005, a charismatic priest in Troina had plans to turn Borgo Giuliano, which is barely standing, into a medical center to provide free check-ups for the local geriatric population (Catania 2006: 157–59). One commentator has suggested transforming Borgo Bassi into a retirement community, dedicated to the memory of the village's final resident, Padre Michele di Stefano, who was murdered in his sleep in February of 2013 by a parishioner (TP24.it 2013).

As mentioned above, it is tempting to interpret the trend in re-functionalizing or re-qualifying *borghi* in line with that of abandonment and decay: by using these spaces to rehabilitate people in the present, the buildings are absolved of their historic ties to Fascism, colonialism, totalitarian control, and manipulative social engineering. Unfortunately, these interpretations say far more about my own opinions and assumptions about Fascism and the way it is understood as a form of heritage. What I was compelled to recognize, indeed what I actively resisted understanding, is that Fascism is not something that the *borghi*

FIGURE 7.3. *Schoolhouse plaque at Borgo Bonsignore (photo by the author).*

necessarily need to overcome. The focus on rehabilitation, re-functionalization, and social service is not about past mastering (Meskell 2002): it has far more to do with pragmatism than politics.

This is particularly true of the Fascist *borghi* that are still occupied today. Some, like Borgo Lupo, Borgo Gattuso (now Petilia), and, until a few years ago, Borgo Bassi contain a handful of families who have transformed the old municipal buildings into residences. Borgo Callea is quite active, and Borgo Cascino even has a small restaurant. Tenancy in these *borghi* is technically illegal, but generally uncontested; the buildings were empty, so why not move in? Who built them does not seem to matter. This was made clear to me on my first visit to Borgo Bonsignore, in July of 2006. Standing in the middle of the piazza, I was immediately drawn to the old schoolhouse. A plaque on the wall depicts a book, a musket, a shovel, a head of wheat, and a Rationalist building (Figure 7.3). This is rich Fascist symbolism: the building evokes the *borgo* itself, the wheat and the shovel refer to the Fascist valorization of rurality and the Battle for Wheat, while the book and the gun refer to the slogan "*libro e moschetto, fascista perfetto*" ("a book and a musket make the perfect Fascist"). I met the school's occupants sitting beneath a portico in the back. Two are daughters of a *primo colono*, one of the *borgo*'s first occupants, and have been living there seasonally since the 1970s; their brother lives in the original farmhouse.

After trekking from *borgo* to *borgo* and talking to people I met in the fields, I was finding it difficult to get anyone to speak negatively, as I expected they would, about the effects of Fascist land reform. I wanted to hear stories about forced relocation, colonial control, and Fascist indoctrination; overcoming these past abuses through the conspicuous decay, public defacement, or rehabilitative transformation of Fascist buildings was the heritage narrative I was expecting to construct. In a final attempt to conform my data to this narrative, I asked the schoolhouse's occupants what it was like to be living in a building so heavily burdened with the symbolism of the former regime. "It's good," replied one of the sisters. "But surely it's strange to be living in the shadow of the tower of the *Casa del Fascio*?" "Pardon?" "Surely you feel oppressed when you look at the . . ." "It's a water tower. It provides water for the *borgo* and its surroundings," she said with a shrug. Her answer was matter-of-fact: what else was there to say?

This brief interaction underscored how my own understanding of Fascist land reform, based on a model of negative or dissonant heritage, assumed it should be shameful, troubling, or unsettling to the people currently occupying Sicily's agricultural landscapes. I realized that I had imposed this negativity onto Fascism's material remains. Although I have no intention of becoming a Fascist apologist and am confident that my particular view of Italian Fascism is entirely justified, I had to radically reframe my analysis in order to encompass my Sicilian informants' experience. For many of them, the Fascist land reforms and building programs are understood to have been rather a good thing for the island and its inhabitants, or at least a step in the right direction. They will criticize the Fascist regime for its alliance with Hitler and entrance into World War II, and occasionally for the racial laws enacted in 1938 and Italy's colonial endeavors, but for the most part the legacy of Fascism in the parts of Sicily where I conducted research is relatively benign and untroubling.

My informants display a remarkable ability to separate Fascism's material remains from the regime itself: Mussolini's various abuses, from political repression, colonialism, racial and religious discrimination, the Nazi alliance, and WWII, do not adhere to the building programs his government engendered. Fascism therefore enters minimally into residents' construction of Borgo Bonsignore as a place. An outsider like myself might feel its dark aura attaching itself to the old buildings, but this is not the case for the local populations interacting with them. There are three main reasons for this. The first is that the construction and distribution of *borghi* and farmhouses was embedded within local landscapes and networks of power, rather than simply being imposed from above (Samuels 2010). Second, because the idea of building farmhouses and *borghi* continued in more or less the same way well into the 1960s, and since the idea of land reclamation had a long history before Fascism, there is a strong case to be made that the *borghi* are not intrinsically Fascist, but part of a larger history of land reclamation across Italy (Novello 2003; Stampacchia 2000). Third, the potential utility of the buildings and other infrastructure constructed under Fascism supersedes any historical baggage they may carry. There is a pragmatism at work here: if the old structures can be made useful, they should be used; if not, they may be left to crumble. This is akin to the strategies of banalization that Macdonald describes at Nuremberg, except that the buildings' mundane usefulness is an end unto itself rather than part of an overarching *vergangenheitsbewältigung*. Over the years, the opportunism of individuals, priests, and development agencies has in many cases transformed the *borghi* into homes, rehabilitation centers, art projects, or storage areas, allowing them to shed their Fascist skin. However, I do not believe that these re-uses constitute an explicit attempt at rehabilitation because, as far as the *borghi* are concerned, the Fascist past does not seem to require mastering.

For local communities, the buildings manage to resist any ideological association with totalitarianism, despite having been built under Fascist land reclamation programs. And even when the buildings' Fascist origins are explicitly acknowledged, they are neutralized in one way or another. A very common refrain across Sicily and throughout Italy is that during the Fascist period you could leave your doors unlocked without fear of being burgled. This is usually followed by a chronicle of all the dangers of today, the constant stream of rape, robbery, and murder reported in the newspapers and on television. Whether or not the streets were indeed safer under Fascism (the threat of squadrist violence seems to undermine the argument somewhat), peoples' nostalgia for what they perceive to have been a safer and simpler time is entwined with their memory of the regime. Many of my informants also felt that the Fascists did a great deal of good for the settlers, or at the least made a genuine effort to improve their lives, by building the *borghi* and obligating landowners to settle them on individual plots with a farmhouse. Despite the ultimate failure of the Fascist 'new urbanism,' hundreds of kilometers of new roads and irrigation canals were built. Progress was made, even though it was not enough, and it is easy to blame the advent of WWII for stunting the government's goals.

CONCLUSION

What does it mean when what you consider to be a difficult heritage turns out not to be very difficult for those who live with it? As I see it, there are three possible ways forward. The first is to take what my informants tell me at face value, and appreciate how Italian Fascism, at least as it touched their own lives, was not really all that bad. On the opposite end of the spectrum, I could take strength in how my own position as an outsider has enabled me to see how thoroughly my informants have failed to adequately 'come to terms' with the past. This is the conclusion that Burström and Gelderblom (2011) arrive at regarding the site of the Nazi Harvest Festival site: they feel a responsibility as professional heritage practitioners to open up this kind of reckoning, even over the objections of many local stakeholders. Finally, I could simply fail to appreciate the nuance and elegance of Sicilians' ability to incorporate a difficult past into their everyday lives. They may be on to something, providing a blueprint for seamless post-conflict reconstruction based upon pragmatic re-use. Putting the buildings to work, rather than banalizing or rehabilitating them, turns the page on their past to focus on their productive potential in the present.

The difficulty in 'difficult heritage' is not the site or event itself, but dealing with these ambiguities. What is deeply problematic for some may not necessarily be so for others. Different actors or agencies may stress the importance of a public reckoning with the past's material remains, while other see erasure and forgetting as an appropriate means to move forward. I still believe strongly that Italy could use a national dialogue that appropriately contextualizes the memory and material remains of Mussolini's regime; in the context of Fascist *borghi*, this would involve explicitly linking these seemingly quaint and bucolic villages to the physical, political, social, and colonial violence within which they were embedded. However, interventions like this are difficult in practice and ethically complex: do I really have the right to tell someone they should be ashamed of their past? While heritage practitioners need not withhold judgment, it is important to appreciate the various perspectives if the goal is to generate productive dialogue that will result in viable management strategies. For this reason I advocate an approach to 'difficult heritage' that recognizes how mundane ambivalence may have more relevance than dramatic dissonance.

NOTE

1. http://www.associazioneoasi.org/ita/.

ACKNOWLEDGMENTS

The research described here was conducted with the generous support of the Wenner-Gren Foundation, the Barbieri Endowment at Trinity College, the Department of Anthropology at Stanford University, and the Stanford Archaeology Center.

REFERENCES

Barbera, Paola. 2002. *Architettura in Sicilia tra le due guerre*. Palermo, Italy: Sellerio.

Battini, Michele. 2007. *The Missing Italian Nuremberg: Cultural Amnesia and Postwar Politics*. New York, NY: Palgrave Macmillan. http://dx.doi.org/10.1057/9780230607453.

Ben-Ghiat, Ruth. 2001. *Fascist Modernities: Italy, 1922–1945*. Berkeley: University of California Press.

Blok, Anton. 1975. *The Mafia of a Sicilian Village, 1860–1960: A Study of Violent Peasant Entrepreneurs*. New York, NY: Harper & Row.

Breglia, Lisa. 2006. *Monumental Ambivalence: The Politics of Heritage*. Austin: University of Texas Press.

Buchli, Victor, and Gavin Lucas. 2001. "The Absent Present: Archaeologies of the Contemporary Past." In *Archaeologies of the Contemporary Past*, ed. Victor Buchli and Gavin Lucas, 3–18. London: Routledge.

Burström, Mats, and Bernhard Gelderblom. 2011. "Dealing with Difficult Heritage: The Case of Bückeberg, Site of the Third Reich Harvest Festival." *Journal of Social Archaeology* 11 (3): 266–82. http://dx.doi.org/10.1177/1469605311417054.

Caracciolo, Edoardo. 1942. "La Nuova Urbanistica nella Bonifica del Latifondo Siciliano." In *Il Latifondo Siciliano*, ed. Ente per la Colonizzazione del Latifondo Siciliano, 279–319. Palermo, Italy: Ministero dell'Agricoltura e delle Foreste.

Catania, Enzo. 2006. *San Teodoro perla nei Nebrodi: Una storia d'autore dalle origine a oggi*. Origgio, Italy: Agar.

Chadha, Ashish. 2006. "Ambivalent Heritage: Between Affect and Ideology in a Colonial Cemetery." *Journal of Material Culture* 11 (3): 339–63. http://dx.doi.org/10.1177/1359183506068809.

Ciriacono, Gianfranco. 2003. *Le stragi dimenticate: Gli eccidi americani di Biscari e Piano Stella*. Ragusa, Italy: Coop. C.D.B.

Dufour, Liliane. 2005. *Nel segno del Littorio: Città e campagne siciliane nel ventennio*. Caltanissetta, Italy: Lussografica.

Ebner, Michael R. 2011. *Ordinary Violence in Mussolini's Italy*. Cambridge: Cambridge University Press.

ESA (Ente Sviluppo Agricolo Regione Siciliana). 2009. *Progetto di Riqualificazione dei Borghi Rurali dell'Ente di Sviluppo Agricolo.* Palermo, Italy: Ente Sviluppo Agricolo Regione Siciliana.

Ghirardo, Diane, and Kurt Forster. 1985. "I Modelli delle Città di Fondazione in Epoca Fascista." In *Storia d'Italia, Annali 8: Insediamenti e terretorio,* ed. Cesare De Seta, 627–74. Milan, Italy: Einaudi.

Ghirardo, Diane Y. 1989. *Building New Communities: New Deal America and Fascist Italy.* Princeton, NJ: Princeton University Press.

González-Ruibal, Alfredo. 2005. "The Need for a Decaying Past: An Archaeology of Oblivion in Contemporary Galicia (NW Spain)." *Home Cultures* 2 (2): 129–52. http://dx.doi.org/10.2752/174063105778053355.

González-Ruibal, Alfredo. 2006. "The Dream of Reason: An Archaeology of the Failures of Modernity in Ethiopia." *Journal of Social Archaeology* 6 (2): 175–201. http://dx.doi.org/10.1177/1469605306064239.

González-Ruibal, Alfredo. 2008. "Time to Destroy: The Archaeology of Super-modernity." *Current Anthropology* 49 (2): 247–79. http://dx.doi.org/10.1086/526099.

Graubert, David N., and Joseph S. A. Miller. 1957. "On Ambivalence." *Psychiatric Quarterly* 31 (1–4): 458–64.

Hazan, Nissim William. 1933. "The Agricultural Program of Fascist Italy." *Journal of Farm Economics* 15 (3): 489–502. http://dx.doi.org/10.2307/1231067.

Herscher, Andrew. 2010. *Violence Taking Place: The Architecture of the Kosovo Conflict.* Stanford, CA: Stanford University Press.

Hilowitz, Jane. 1976. *Economic Development and Social Change in Sicily.* Cambridge: Schenkman Publishing Company.

La China, Maria Lina. 2008. "Borghi di Sicilia: Sviluppi possibili: Inventario dei borghi rurali 'fondati' dal 1920 al '70." Unpublished postdoctoral thesis, Facoltà di Architettura, Università degli Studi di Palermo.

Labadi, Sophia. 2005. "A Review of the Global Strategy for a Balanced, Representative, and Credible World Heritage List, 1994–2004." *Conservation and Management of Archaeological Sites* 7 (2): 89–102. http://dx.doi.org/10.1179/135050305793137477.

Lennon, John J., and Malcolm Foley. 2000. *Dark Tourism: The Attraction of Death and Disaster.* London: Continuum.

Logan, William, and Keir Reeves, eds. 2009. *Places of Pain and Shame: Dealing with 'Difficult Heritage.'* New York, NY: Routledge.

Lupo, Salvatore. 2009. *History of the Mafia.* New York, NY: Columbia University Press.

Macdonald, Sharon. 2006. "Undesirable Heritage: Fascist Material Culture and Historical Consciousness in Nuremberg." *International Journal of Heritage Studies* 12 (1): 9–28. http://dx.doi.org/10.1080/13527250500384464.

Macdonald, Sharon. 2009. *Difficult Heritage: Negotiating the Nazi Past in Nuremberg and Beyond*. New York, NY: Routledge.

Mariani, Riccardo. 1976. *Fascismo e 'Città Nuove*. Milan, Italy: Feltrinelli.

TP24.it. 2013. "Ad un mese dall'omicidio di Don Michele Di Stefano tante ipotesi, nessuna pista concreta." March 30. http://www.tp24.it/2013/03/30/cronaca/ad-un -mese-dallomicidio-di-don-michele-di-stefano-tante-ipotesi-nessuna-pista -concreta/72017. Accessed April 12, 2013.

Martinelli, Roberta, and Lucia Nuti. 1978. "Le Città Nuove del Ventennio da Mussolinia a Carbonia." In *Le Città di Fondazione*, ed. Roberta Martinelli and Lucia Nuti, 271–93. Venice, Italy: CISCU-Marsilio.

Meskell, Lynn. 2002. "Negative Heritage and Past Mastering in Archaeology." *Anthropological Quarterly* 75 (3): 557–74. http://dx.doi.org/10.1353/anq.2002.0050.

Novello, Elisabetta. 2003. *La bonifica in Italia: Legislazione, credito e lotta alla malaria dall'Unità al fascismo*. Milan, Italy: FrancoAngeli.

Pennacchi, Antonio. 2008. *Fascio e martello: Viaggio per le città del duce*. Rome, Italy: Laterza.

Pétursdóttir, Þora. 2013. "Concrete Matters: Ruins of Modernity and the Things Called Heritage." *Journal of Social Archaeology* 13 (1): 31–53. http://dx.doi.org/10 .1177/1469605312456342.

Pluciennik, Mark, Antoon Mientjes, and Enrico Giannitrapani. 2004. "Archaeologies of Aspiration: Historical Archaeology in Rural Central Sicily." *International Journal of Historical Archaeology* 8 (1): 27–65. http://dx.doi.org/10.1023/B:IJHA .0000025716.86719.af.

Rico, Trinidad. 2008. "Negative Heritage: The Place of Conflict in World Heritage." *Conservation and Management of Archaeological Sites* 10 (4): 344–52. http://dx.doi .org/10.1179/135050308X12513845914507.

Samuels, Joshua. 2010. "Of Other Scapes: Archaeology, Landscape, and Heterotopia." *Archaeologies* 6 (1): 62–81. http://dx.doi.org/10.1007/s11759-010 -9129-5.

Samuels, Joshua. 2012. *Reclamation: An Archaeology of Agricultural Reform in Fascist Sicily*. PhD dissertation, Department of Anthropology, Stanford University, Stanford, CA.

Sather-Wagstaff, Joy. 2011. *Heritage that Hurts: Tourists in the Memoryscapes of September 11*. Walnut Creek, CA: Left Coast Press.

Schneider, Jane, and Peter T. Schneider. 1976. *Culture and Political Economy in Western Sicily*. New York, NY: Academic Press.

Sharpley, Richard, and Philip R. Stone, eds. 2009. *The Darker Side of Travel: The Theory and Practice of Dark Tourism*. Bristol, UK: Channel View Publications.

Smith, Denis M. 1968. *A History of Sicily: Modern Sicily after 1713*. New York, NY: Viking Press.

Smith, Phil. 2012. *Mythogeographic Performance and Performative Interventions in Spaces of Heritage-Tourism*. PhD dissertation, School of Humanities and Performing Arts, University of Plymouth, Plymouth, UK.

Stampacchia, Mauro. 2000. *"Ruralizzare l'Italia!" Agricoltura e bonifiche tra Mussolini e Serpieri (1928–1943)*. Milan, Italy: FrancoAngeli.

Timm Knudsen, Britta. 2011. "Thanatourism: Witnessing Difficult Pasts." *Tourist Studies* 11 (1): 55–72. http://dx.doi.org/10.1177/1468797611412064.

Trouillot, Michel-Rolph. 1995. *Silencing the Past: Power and the Production of History*. Boston, MA: Beacon Press.

Tunbridge, John E., and Gregory J. Ashworth. 1996. *Dissonant Heritage: the Management of the Past as a Resource in Conflict*. Chichester, UK: John Wiley & Sons.

UNESCO. 1979. *Report of the Rapporteur on the Third Session of the World Heritage Committee (Cairo and Luxor, 22–26 October 1979)*. CC–79/CONF.003/13. Paris: UNESCO.

Equity 8

Polestar or Pretense? International Archaeological Tourism Development in 'Less Developed Countries'

JEFFREY ADAMS

In the loosely integrated professional realm of international heritage management (IHM), rhetoric is a primary tool by which key actors—above all UNESCO and its affiliates—define, disseminate, and promote the global adoption of progressive preservation principles. It is the central means by which evolving professional values and tacit assumptions are introduced into practice, inspiring the translation of abstract ideals into concrete action via an informal, devolutionary chain linking high-level protocols to institutional missions, program strategies, project plans, and concrete measures.

Since there is little grassroots uptake of these principles in 'less developed countries' (LDC), chiefly due to competing priorities and lack of resources, interventions by UNESCO, its affiliates, and inter-governmental (e.g., the World Bank), quasi-governmental (e.g., the International Council on Monuments and Sites [ICOMOS]), and non-governmental organizations (e.g., World Monuments Fund) take on added importance in the archaeological and architectural preservation landscape. Such efforts generally incorporate, if not revolve around, a tourism component designed to ensure long-term socioeconomic sustainability. The keystone of socioeconomic sustainability, as traditionally formulated, is equity. Despite the philosophical and

DOI: 10.5876/9781607323846.c008

rhetorical centrality of the equity principle, however, there is little evidence of its real-world attainment. By reversing the deeply channeled conceptual flow from aspiration to self-congratulation, proceeding instead from outcomes to premises, I attempt to show that the unappreciated elusiveness of equity is symptomatic of a larger rhetorical overreach of the prevailing IHM paradigm.

IDEAL

The doctrine of sustainability pervades archaeological heritage management and tourism development discourse, as it does that of conservation and international economic development generally. The 1987 Brundtland Report *Our Common Future* (WCED 1987) defines sustainable development as progress that meets present needs without compromising the ability of future generations to meet their own needs. It identifies the three main pillars of sustainability as long-term environmental protection, social advancement, and economic opportunity. More succinctly, sustainability has been defined as the application of the principles of futurity, equity, and holism to the ecological, sociocultural, and economic realms (Redclift and Woodgate 1997).

On one hand, all entities within the United Nations constellation of affiliates are committed to the realization of socioeconomic parity as a matter of policy. On the other, ensuring community access to economic opportunities is at the forefront of archaeological preservation initiatives seeking financial self-sufficiency through tourism receipts. The triangular interdependency of archaeological preservation, socioeconomic development, and tourism is thus reenacted in every UNESCO-affiliated LDC preservation program and is formally articulated in documents such as the United Nations World Tourism Organization (UNWTO) 2004 *Hue Declaration on Cultural Tourism and Poverty Alleviation*, the ICOMOS *International Cultural Tourism Charter* (UNESCO 1999) and UNESCO's *World Heritage Sustainable Tourism Program Charter* (UNESCO 2008).

Through the complementary languages of sustainable development, cultural preservation, and tourism planning, then, equity has become a boilerplate objective of archaeological heritage management efforts in developing countries. The UNWTO (2004a) has defined equity as the provision of "socioeconomic benefits to all stakeholders that are fairly distributed, including stable employment and income-earning opportunities and social services to host communities, and . . . poverty alleviation." ICOMOS and the World Heritage Center use similar language to call for the economic inclusion of local communities and the poor (UNESCO 1999, 2008). Sustainable archaeological tourism development and management plans include provisions designed to ensure comprehensive stakeholder access to the fruits of tourism growth. These generally promote the culturally sensitive development of commercially viable, tourism-oriented services and amenities, such as performances, craft production, transportation, food stands, specialty shops, and guesthouses.

MIRAGE

I recently sought to discover whether the widespread invocation of equity in archaeological tourism development planning rhetoric translated into concrete results (Adams 2010). I turned first to the academic tourism research literature of recent decades, throughout which the notion of equity is consistently, if implicitly, woven. The concept underlies repeated expressions of concern for the victims of and bystanders to international tourism: from the explication of dependency theory to analyses of developing country tourism impacts and the vagaries of the tourism development life cycle, to advocacy of bottom-up, pro-poor tourism planning and local stakeholder involvement (Bandara 2001; Britton 1982; de Kadt 1979; Harrison 1992; Smith 1989). Tourism development literature reflects a spectrum of attitudes bearing on the question of equitable outcomes. These range from the cautiously optimistic (Inskeep 1991; Joshi and Rajopadhya 2007; UNWTO 2004b; Walker 2009), to the skeptical (Butler 1993; Hawkins and Mann 2007; Joppe 1996; Prentice 1993; Taylor 1995), and harshly critical (Azarya 2004; Bianchi 2004; Brohman 1996; Burns 1999; Butler 1993; de Kadt 1979; Greenwood 1989; Harrison 1992; Manyara and Jones 2007; Mowforth and Munt 1998; Tosun 2000).

Dissatisfied with the inconclusive, theoretical nature of the scholarly tourism literature, I undertook a search of archaeological heritage management publications for reliable accounts of distributional outcomes at LDC archaeological and historical heritage sites known to have been subject to international sustainable tourism development planning. I confined my study to nations conforming with the International Monetary Fund's (IMF 2012) definition of emerging and developing economies. So rare are equity-specific post-mortem analyses, I was able to find only six cases fitting my criteria, largely on the basis of anecdotal rather than rigorously quantitative grounds. That these all happen to involve World Heritage Sites—Machu Picchu (Peru), Angkor (Cambodia), Copán (Honduras), Lijiang (China), Cape Coast Castle (Ghana), and Borobudur (Indonesia)—is not surprising, since they are among the few sites for which management efforts are well documented and to which sustainable tourism principles have been consciously applied. Although some may dispute the IMF's classification of China's economy as emerging, it is worth noting that Lijiang is in Yunnan, one of the China's poorest provinces. Accounts of subsequent events at these sites gave clear indication of markedly inequitable outcomes (*for Machu Picchu*: Arellano 2007; Barby 2005; Earth Island Institute 2006; Inka Porter Project 2007; McDonnell 2006; World Heritage Committee 2005; *for Angkor*: Chapman 1998; Winter 2007; *for Copán*: Mortensen 2006; UNESCO 2004; *for Lijiang*: Crampton 1999; Li and Shao 2005; Michael 2007; Su and Teo 2009; Wang 2007; Zhao 2005; *for Cape Coast Castle*: Comer 1999; Koutra 2007; UNESCO 2004; and *for Borobudur*: Boccardi, Brooks, and Gurung 2006; Dahles 2000; Hampton 2005; Wall and Black 2004).

The dynamics, processes, and mechanisms yielding socioeconomic inequality in the six cases are unique in their specifics but stem from conditions present across the developing—and developed—world. I hold the cases therefore to be broadly representative of archaeological tourism development at LDC sites generally. Their common characteristics informed my construction of a 'Model of LDC Tourism Development Inequality' positing the global recurrence of the following processes:

Competition: The differential ability of certain actors to exploit market opportunities based upon their access to technical, financial, political, and other resources.

Dilution: The decreasing proportion of tourism benefits accruing to local populations over time as extra-local actors capture increasing shares of the tourism market.

Discrimination: The selective apportionment of access to tourism-related opportunities based on differences of class, race, ethnicity, gender, etc.

Degradation: The long-term, spatially concentrated deterioration of socio-cultural, economic, and environmental conditions, which disproportionately affect community members and the poor.

The model highlights the correlation between the shrinking relative economic status of pre-existing poor and local residents and expansion in the scale of tourism development. The notion that progressive, scale-dependent, relatively localized decline is inherent to tourism development has been raised by other researchers (Ashworth 2000; Butler 1980; Doxey 1975; Fan, Wall, and Mitchell 2008; Russo 2002). This occurs despite gains in wages, property values, and amenities because of locals' differential exposure to deteriorating physical, social, environmental, and other conditions; their shrinking claim to overall revenues due to the influx of new workers and capital; their typically small-scale and limited profit trajectory (compared to that associated with the speculative investment driving large-scale tourism infrastructure and service providers); and increasing intra-local socioeconomic polarization resulting from competition and discrimination. In sum, my research casts doubt on the possibility, let alone the past achievement of, equitable LDC tourism outcomes.

DELUSION

The methodological focus of equity rhetoric betrays a superficial appreciation of the challenge at hand, as suggested by the following proposed explanations for the disjuncture between preservation ideals and project outcomes. First, international archaeological tourism development efforts display a lack of definitional precision and corresponding inability to measure equity. Despite growing interest in the development of robust sustainability indicators among tourism researchers generally (Blake et al. 2008; Ko 2005; Choi and Sirakaya 2006; Roberts and Tribe 2008; Schianetz and Kavanagh 2008), little attention has been given to equity. In particular, there has been scant recognition of the importance of tracking the relative socioeconomic status of individual local households so as to detect intra-local divergences of wealth, including those arising between prior inhabitants and recent in-migrants.

Related to the lack of critical scrutiny given to the meaning and empirical manifestation of equity is, second, a lack of follow-up regarding the evaluation of project outcomes. This shortcoming, present throughout the development sector, will persist as long as project funding approvals remain unhinged from results-oriented performance requirements.

Third, these shortcomings mask heritage management agencies' inability to control unfolding tourism growth and the distribution of benefits. Heritage management agencies have neither the capacity nor the leverage to actively insinuate themselves into the often opaque, mixed public/private financial flows stemming from successful tourism development.

Underlying the coarseness of equity provisions in tourism planning are, fourth, simplistic assumptions about the social, cultural, economic, and political forces at play in developing countries. Sustainable management planning rhetoric is filled with idealistic, impractical measures presupposing fair and functioning civil protections, legal systems, regulatory regimes, and market environments where they are not in evidence (Burns 1999; Tosun 1998). A classic example of this is the landmark Zoning and Environmental

Management Plan for Angkor, which failed to anticipate the circumvention of planning provisions by local officials and Asian hotel operators. Rather than becoming a model of sustainable archaeological tourism, the site has become a model of uncontrolled development, unintended consequences, and socioeconomic disparity.

Central to these problematic developing country misperceptions are a series of uncritical assumptions regarding local communities. The implicit view that they are static, discrete, monolithic, or egalitarian, for example, overlooks intra-local social stratification, the fluidity of community membership, the regional in-migration of tourism opportunists, and the influence of private interests and government authorities. A pervasive, tacit belief seems to be that local individuals are inherently and appropriately suited to the management of their own heritage tourism development. As Kigongo and Reid (2007: 380) put it:

> Calls to return site management to local communities, particularly those relating to African contexts, tend to present a picture of unity of purpose as if there were a self-regulating consensus whereby all members of society could habitually identify and undertake the appropriate course of action. This is the same kind of simplistic assumption made within colonial practices of indirect rule.

A further misapprehension is that local stakeholder consultation is itself synonymous with equitable development—the notion that unambiguously representative spokespersons may be identified that can conclude and enforce binding agreements curtailing the power of established interests in favor of an underclass. In reality, the achievement of genuinely participatory decision-making during projects' early phases, where international actors ostensibly exert the greatest influence, is extremely difficult (Aas, Ladkin, and Fletcher 2005; Joppe 1996; Li 2004; Mortensen 2006; Ryan 2002; Simpson 2008; Timothy 1999; Timothy and Tosun 2003).

Finally, all of the above-mentioned errors and omissions on the parts of mostly Western international heritage tourism planners contribute to a fundamental failure to grasp the ultimate explanation for inequitable outcomes: the imperviousness of profoundly entrenched, preexisting sources of LDC inequality to outside influence (de Kadt 1979; Liu 2003; Mowforth and Munt 1998). An examination of the reproduction of inequality through the processes of competition, dilution, discrimination, and degradation across the six cases discussed earlier reveals an array of structural and systemic vectors of socioeconomic bias largely beyond the reach of well-intended international actors. By no means confined to developing countries, these include caste systems, gender roles, religious differences, social hierarchies, ethnic prejudice, clan rivalry, corruption, and social norms requiring deference to authority. Far from being an incidental outcome of flawed tourism development planning, inequality is an unavoidable source ingredient, the effect of which merely becomes amplified with escalating tourism growth. International agencies may temporarily suspend the effects of inequitable processes among select groups, but lack the mandate and (staying) power to abolish them.

REFLECTION

The ongoing, unacknowledged dysfunction of sustainable LDC archaeological tourism initiatives threatens the institutional legitimacy, professional integrity, and disciplinary vitality of international heritage management. UNESCO and its partners are not likely to fundamentally transform developing country realities, something that decades of international assistance has failed to accomplish. Whether they therefore seek remedy in enhanced means or abridged ends, further diminishing the already waning star of sustainability, depends upon their diagnosis of the base problem, a verdict linked to their rhetorical agenda.

The historical lack of organizational follow-through and critical self-examination—let alone clear, demonstrable success—calls into question the sincerity of the champions of equity. That individual heritage management professionals may genuinely desire equitability does not alter its knee-jerk deployment as a planning fixture and rhetorical flourish. Just as there exist few institutional incentives to monitor the long-term outcomes of international development projects, there are correspondingly few restraints on the loading of tourism development plans with overly ambitious objectives infused with progressive sensibilities and reinforced by early stage optimism. In the discursive incubator of these planning ideals—Western-dominated conferences, speeches, articles, etc.—the pragmatics of equity are simply assumed, its actual accomplishment treated as an afterthought. Upholding the importance of equity thus provides a cost-free way to signal conscientiousness and professionalism. The customary lip service given to equity courts distrust among host country colleagues; the evident disregard for its nonappearance amounts to a tacit endorsement of inequitable development. Yet in the grand discursive spheres of development and sustainability, the rhetoric of equity fulfills its purpose whether or not it corresponds to events on the ground.

Institutionally, the rhetoric of equity serves as a normative signpost in the field of heritage management and a justificatory index of program legitimacy within the UN bureaucracy. If the pursuit of equity is characterized by a lack of conviction, as suggested above, it is at a societal rather than a professional level. This is true because UNESCO and its affiliates operate at the munificence of member states, the contributions of which do not provide means commensurate with their essentially limitless mission. UNESCO's ethical and intellectual leadership is vitally important in and of itself, but gains prominence in inverse proportion to their financial and material resources. That UNESCO's primary utility is in painting a vision and encouraging member states to enact its realization is thus both a conscious strategy to promote the lasting self-adoption of best practices and a practical necessity in the absence of alternatives. It is this essentially suasive character, and the overheated rhetorical environment it engenders, that above all accounts for the continued circulation of operationally unrealizable aims under the sustainability umbrella. In a perpetual state of financial constraint and ethical distension, UNESCO's rhetorical posturing is itself a form of compliance with its quixotic charge.

As language designed to persuade, all rhetoric implies an agenda. Normative rhetoric encourages adherence to certain rules of conduct. UNESCO conventions are examples of what might be called 'applied' normative rhetoric in that their formulation presupposes their enforcement. In contrast to the open-ended admonishments of politicians and motivational speakers, for example, they ethically obligate signatories, requiring compliance as a condition of participation in programs such as the World Heritage List, and are widely promulgated by international heritage management professionals and organizations. This instrumentalism, I would argue, comes with its own condition: accountability. If member states are ethically obligated to comply with UNESCO recommendations, UNESCO is ethically obligated to ensure their feasibility. Answering to a reciprocal flow of information arising out of situated post hoc interpretation of project and program results, this accountability both justifies and compromises the aura of authority that is the motive force and byproduct of normative rhetoric.

Competing interpretations of the incidental vs. embedded nature of LDC archaeological tourism development inequality inform the perceived scope of the problem and thus the remediability of ideals, their articulation, and enactment. The interpretation that inequality is incidental preserves the normative status quo, implying that the formal stated equity principle is logically unimpeachable as a rhetorical device, a worthy standard reinforced, rather than undermined, by its phenomenal non-correspondence. It is only the vanity of past pronouncements, then, that require remediation.

If inequality is a project-contingent outcome, it follows that methodological rehabilitation can improve the odds of its elimination. For example, heritage management professionals could systematically refine the definition, measurement, tracking, and analysis of equity, using improved indicators over longer time spans. Rather than seeking in effect to overturn the existing host country social order, they could target specific, incremental changes to the status quo. They could also more aggressively pursue strategic partnerships with development banks and international organizations, political leaders, tourism providers, and others to seek more transparency and accountability in tourism development decision-making. More important than all of these improvements, however, is the need for the heritage management establishment to come to terms with its own limitations. Individuals are susceptible to a host of biases, including overestimation of their own abilities, favoring of information confirming their own beliefs, cultural chauvinism, wishful thinking, and the tendency to attribute the behavior of others to personal rather than situational factors. Organizations are prone to underestimate risks and overestimate benefits of future actions, and to overconcentrate on planning particulars at the expense of due consideration to historical outcomes. The adoption of independent program audits, training needs analyses, and planning innovations such as reference class forecasting might help international agencies come to grips with such ingrained mental processes and the underlying assumptions described above.

RECONCILIATION

The intractability of the underlying socioeconomic dynamics that renders so polarizing the processes of competition, dilution, discrimination, and degradation effectively forecloses the possibility of true, lasting, equitable LDC tourism development outcomes in anything but the longest term. This more pessimistic interpretation of inequality as embedded redefines the core problem as one of denial rather than operational incompetence, moving the onus beyond the tactical and strategic into the realm of rhetorical ideals. It invites the supposition that in its utopian insistence the equity principle is a red herring, holding out false hope while promoting denial about the real challenges, consequences, and larger social significance of international heritage management work. It suggests that rather than engaging in mere methodological refinement, international heritage management professionals should re-envision their role in the larger preservation cum development scheme. Of crucial importance for the future of the field as a whole, I would argue, is that our current rhetorical pretensions, not just regarding equity and sustainability but international heritage management generally, far outstrip our capabilities. When it comes to achieving the goals of human development, economic parity, social justice, and emancipation, our potency has not kept pace with our principles.

In its oft-derided 'monumentalist' past, preservation rhetoric and reality were closely matched because the goals, inspired by the 1964 *Venice Charter*, were limited, primarily technical and therefore more readily attainable. All of the early landmark projects in the modern history of international heritage management—Abu Simbel, Borobudur, Mohenjo-daro—seem naïve by contemporary standards for their unabashedly, if not exclusively, materialist bent. Still, they produced remarkable advancements in conservation science and engineering, international coordination, and project management.

In contrast, the field today seems to have entered a cul-de-sac: having proceeded inexorably down the path of definitional expansion and categorical proliferation, doctrinal refinement, inter-cultural inclusion, methodological elaboration, and philosophical re-centering from properties to people, we are running up against the limits of our own ambitions. Regarding LDC archaeological tourism development, we have embraced lofty socioeconomic goals in recognition of the value of human capital and the role of poverty in heritage neglect, only to discover that these goals are out of reach. At the same time, we have adopted tourism development as the sole viable source of long-term site management funding, only to find that it is unpredictable, unmanageable, and ultimately inequitable.

If we are to reconcile our ambitions and abilities, we must ask: to what extent should heritage managers aspire to be in the social justice business? Given the historical inability of dedicated development agencies to effect positive lasting change, do archaeologists and their fellow travelers have the knowledge, training, institutional dedication, and means for what is, in effect, social engineering? To what successful developing country track record can they point?

More particularly, regarding countries harboring fractious, competing clans, ethnic mélanges, politically- and religiously-sanctioned social hierarchies and patronage networks, for which groups and individuals is justice intended? What would it look like? How is justice perceived in countries whose axial principles are order, family, community, or spirituality, as opposed to traditional Western values such as liberty, equality, or opportunity? How important is equity *per se* as long as the majority of people enjoy a rising standard of living, however that may be defined? My research underscores that there is no single, universally applicable definition of equity. Though as an ideal it is absolute, in practice it is a contextual, relational process definable only in terms of local circumstances.

Most important of all: how can the goal of equity be realized in practice? The experience of a half-century of dedicated multilateral economic development efforts suggests that it will not be until and unless host country populations establish civic harmony, governmental accountability, the rule of law, and economic stability—at a minimum.

Perhaps as far as developing country heritage tourism development planning is concerned, we should unmoor equity from our operational portfolio, letting it remain in the ethical firmament alongside freedom, tolerance, dignity, and other supreme, unconditional, guiding values. The question remains, however: if the international heritage management community is chronically unable to deliver on its larger socioeconomic agenda, is it time to restrict our purview to more manageable feats, such as capacity building, outreach, survey, documentation, conservation, regulatory reform, and income generation? Would it be conscionable to roll back the conceptual evolution, or aspirational creep, of international heritage management in this way? More to the point: can heritage preservation in and of itself—absent its express dedication to the amelioration of larger socioeconomic pathologies—nonetheless have the power to promote lasting, endogenous, positive social and economic change?

CONCLUSION

Nobly inspired, austerely equipped, IHM agencies strive toward an ever-receding ethical summit, heedless that its apparent moral bulk hides a fragile, overhanging cornice of extravagant aims, empty claims, and unmet expectations. To enact a corrective philosophical and pragmatic retrenchment of our disciplinary ambit is neither heretical nor imprudent. Prominent representatives of both the 'expansive' and 'restrictive' schools of thought already exist. Two successful and reputable international preservation organizations, the nonprofit World Monuments Fund and private foundation the Getty Conservation Institute, concentrate their efforts on the conservation of physical fabric. The nonprofit Global Heritage Fund, on the other hand, puts tourism-oriented community economic development at the front and center of its archaeological and architectural site preservation strategy. Within the highest levels of ICOMOS, moreover, a debate has been taking place about the proper role of the heritage professional in the face of the rapid, sweeping 'democratization' of heritage: accessory to or deflector of change. The former calls for professional redefinition, to subordinate professionally defined material and aesthetic values to popularly defined social and functional values supporting community development (Araoz 2009). The latter argues the need for professional retrenchment to counter the erosion of more conservative, traditional definitions of authenticity and integrity and to more strenuously defend against the growing social acceptance of verticalization, densification, commercialization, façadism, reconstruction, and other manifestations of this depreciation (Petzet 2009).

There can be no question of abandoning the promotion of LDC social and economic advancement through the valorization and preservation of archaeological, architectural, and intangible heritage. Such is not even a question that heritage professionals are entitled to reserve the right to answer. Rather than making grandiose, unaccountable promises, however, it would be more responsible to definitively achieve modest, concrete goals in professionals' real areas of expertise. Against a historical backdrop of failed interventions, it is worth noting, after all, that the most reliably impactful forms of aid to LDC heritage management programs are things like computers, courses, and cameras—the basics.

REFERENCES

Aas, Christina, Adele Ladkin, and John Fletcher. 2005. "Stakeholder Collaboration and Heritage Management." *Annals of Tourism Research* 32 (1): 28–48. http://dx.doi .org/10.1016/j.annals.2004.04.005.

Adams, Jeffrey. 2010. "Interrogating the Equity Principle: The Rhetoric and Reality of Management Planning for Sustainable Archaeological Heritage Tourism." *Journal of Heritage Tourism* 5 (2): 103–23. http://dx.doi.org/10.1080/1743873090 3509311.

Araoz, Gustavo. 2009. *Protecting Heritage Places under the New Heritage Paradigm and Defining Limits for Change.* Discussion paper presented at the ICOMOS Advisory Committee Meeting, Valletta, Malta, October 5–10.

Arellano, Alexandra. 2007. *Choquequirao or the 'Other' Machu Picchu: Towards Sustainable Natural/Heritage Based Tourism Development.* Paper presented at the 10th US/ICOMOS International Symposium, San Francisco, California, April 18–21.

Ashworth, Gregory J. 2000. "Heritage, Identity and Places: For Tourists and Host Communities." In *Tourism and Sustainable Community Development*, ed. Greg Richards and Derek Hall, 79–98. London: Routledge.

Azarya, Victor. 2004. "Globalization and International Tourism in Developing Countries: Marginality as a Commercial Commodity." *Current Sociology* 52 (6): 949–67. http://dx.doi.org/10.1177/0011392104046617.

Bandara, Herath M. 2001. *Tourism Development Planning in Developing Countries: A Critique*. Pannipitiya, Sri Lanka: Stamford Lake.

Barby, Christian. 2005. "Peru to Save Incas' Lost City from Threat of Tourists." *The Independent*, June 4. http://www.independent.co.uk/news/world/americas/peru-to-save-incas-lost-city-from-threat-of-tourists-493025.html. Accessed July 10, 2009.

Bianchi, Raoul V. 2004. "Tourism Restructuring and the Politics of Sustainability: A Critical View from the European Periphery (the Canary Islands)." *Journal of Sustainable Tourism* 12 (6): 495–529. http://dx.doi.org/10.1080/0966958040866725I.

Blake, Adam, Jorge S. Arbache, M. Thea Sinclair, and Vladimir Teles. 2008. "Tourism and Poverty Relief." *Annals of Tourism Research* 35 (1): 107–26. http://dx.doi.org/10.1016/j.annals.2007.06.013.

Boccardi, Giovanni, Graham Brooks, and Himalchuli Gurung. 2006. *Reactive Monitoring Mission to Borobudur Temple Compounds, World Heritage Property, Indonesia (18–25 Feb. 2006)*. Bangkok: World Heritage Committee/ICOMOS.

Britton, Stephen G. 1982. "The Political Economy of Tourism in the Third World." *Annals of Tourism Research* 9 (3): 331–58. http://dx.doi.org/10.1016/0160-7383(82)90018-4.

Brohman, John. 1996. "New Directions in Tourism for Third World Development." *Annals of Tourism Research* 23 (1): 48–70. http://dx.doi.org/10.1016/0160-7383(95)00043-7.

Burns, Peter. 1999. "Paradoxes in Planning: Tourism Elitism or Brutalism?" *Annals of Tourism Research* 26 (2): 329–48. http://dx.doi.org/10.1016/S0160-7383(98)00099-1.

Butler, Richard. 1980. "The Concept of a Tourist Area Cycle of Evolution: Implications for the Management of Resources." *Canadian Geographer* 24 (1): 5–12. http://dx.doi.org/10.1111/j.1541-0064.1980.tb00970.x.

Butler, Richard. 1993. "Tourism—An Evolutionary Perspective." In *Tourism and Sustainable Development: Monitoring, Planning, Managing*, ed. James G. Nelson, Richard Butler, and Geoffrey Wall, 27–44. Waterloo, ON: University of Waterloo, Department of Geography.

Chapman, William. 1998. "'The Best Laid Schemes . . .': Land-use Planning and Historic Preservation in Cambodia." *Pacific Rim Law and Policy Journal* 7 (3): 529–54.

Choi, HwanSuk C., and Ercan Sirakaya. 2006. "Sustainability Indicators for Managing Community Tourism." *Tourism Management* 27 (6): 1274–89. http://dx.doi.org/10.1016/j.tourman.2005.05.018.

Comer, Douglas C. 1999. *Historic Cape Coast Site Analysis: Utilizing Geographical Information System (GIS) and Aerial Imagery Analysis Technology for Integrated Planning*. Redlands, CA: ESRI Corporation.

Crampton, Thomas. 1999. "Lijiang Fears Naxi Heritage is Threatened: In China, City's Fame Brings Tourists and Hassles." *New York Times*, December 11. http://www.nytimes.com/1999/12/11/news/11iht-rlijiang.t.html. Accessed June 26, 2009.

Dahles, Heidi. 2000. "Tourism, Small Enterprises and Community Development." In *Tourism and Sustainable Community Development*, ed. Greg Richards and Derek Hall, 154–69. London: Routledge.

de Kadt, Emanuel. 1979. *Tourism—Passport to Development? Perspectives on the Social and Cultural Effects of Tourism in Developing Countries*. Oxford: Oxford University Press.

Doxey, George. 1975. "A Causation Theory of Visitor—Resident Irritants: Methodology and Research Inferences." In *The Impact of Tourism: Sixth Annual Conference Proceedings of the Travel and Tourism Research Association, San Diego*, 195–98. Whitehall, MI: Travel and Tourism Research Association.

Earth Island Institute. 2006. *Sacred Site Report: Machu Picchu*. http://www.sacredland.org/index.php/machu-picchu/. Accessed November 18, 2012.

Fan, Chennan, Geoffrey Wall, and Clare J. A. Mitchell. 2008. "Creative Destruction and the Water Town of Luzhi, China." *Tourism Management* 29 (4): 648–60. http://dx.doi.org/10.1016/j.tourman.2007.07.008.

Greenwood, Davydd. 1989. "Culture by the Pound: An Anthropological Perspective on Tourism as Cultural Commoditization." In *Hosts and Guests: The Anthropology of Tourism*, 2nd ed., ed. Valene L. Smith, 171–85. Philadelphia: University of Pennsylvania Press. http://dx.doi.org/10.9783/9780812208016.169.

Hampton, Mark P. 2005. "Heritage, Local Communities, and Economic Development." *Annals of Tourism Research* 32 (3): 735–59. http://dx.doi.org/10.1016/j.annals.2004.10.010.

Harrison, David. 1992. *Tourism and the Less Developed Countries*. London: Belhaven Press.

Hawkins, Donald E., and Shaun Mann. 2007. "The World Bank's Role in Tourism Development." *Annals of Tourism Research* 34 (2): 348–63. http://dx.doi.org/10.1016/j.annals.2006.10.004.

IMF (International Monetary Fund). 2012. *World Economic Outlook Report April 2012: Growth Resuming, Dangers Remain. World Economic and Financial Surveys*. Washington, DC: International Monetary Fund.

Inka Porter Project. 2007. *Inka Porter Project—porteadores inka nan*. http://www.peruweb.org/porters/index.html. Accessed January 30, 2008.

Inskeep, Edward. 1991. *Tourism Planning: An Integrated and Sustainable Development Approach*. New York, NY: Van Nostrand Reinhold.

Joppe, Marion. 1996. "Sustainable Community Tourism Development Revisited." *Tourism Management* 17 (7): 475–79. http://dx.doi.org/10.1016/S0261-5177(96) 00065-9.

Joshi, Jharna, and Manoj Rajopadhya. 2007. *Sustainable Rural Tourism and Local Communities in Nepal.* Paper presented at the 10th US/ICOMOS International Symposium, San Francisco, CA, April 18–21.

Kigongo, Remigius, and Andrew Reid. 2007. "Local Communities, Politics, and the Management of the Kasubi Tombs, Uganda." *World Archaeology* 39 (3): 371–84. http://dx.doi.org/10.1080/00438240701563094.

Ko, Tae. 2005. "Development of a Tourism Sustainability Assessment Procedure: A Conceptual Approach." *Tourism Management* 26 (3): 431–45. http://dx.doi.org/10 .1016/j.tourman.2003.12.003.

Koutra, Christina. 2007. *Building Capacities for Tourism Development and Poverty Reduction.* Paper presented at the Fourth African Congress of the International Institute for Peace Through Tourism, Uganda, May 20–25.

Li, Fan, and Yong Shao. 2005. *The Impact of Tourism on Core Area and Buffer Zone: Heritage Management in the Old Town of Lijiang, China.* Paper presented at the ICOMOS 15th General Assembly and Scientific Symposium, Xi'an, China, October 17–21.

Li, Yiping. 2004. "Exploring Community Tourism in China: The Case of Nanshan Cultural Tourism Zone." *Journal of Sustainable Tourism* 12 (3): 175–93. http://dx.doi .org/10.1080/09669580408667232.

Liu, Zhenhua. 2003. "Sustainable Tourism Development: A Critique." *Journal of Sustainable Tourism* 11 (6): 459–75. http://dx.doi.org/10.1080/09669580308667216.

Manyara, Geoffrey, and Eleri Jones. 2007. "Community-based Tourism Enterprises Development in Kenya: An Exploration of Their Potential as Avenues of Poverty Reduction." *Journal of Sustainable Tourism* 15 (6): 628–44. http://dx.doi.org/10.2167 /jost723.0.

McDonnell, Patrick. 2006. "Machu Picchu Shows Wear of Being on Must-see List." *Los Angeles Times,* May 3, 2006. Available online at http://articles.latimes.com /2006/may/03/world/fg-machu3. Accessed November 28, 2012.

Michael, Vincent. 2007. *Weishan Heritage Valley: Pre-tourism Preservation and Conservation Planning in Yunnan, China.* Paper presented at the 10th US/ ICOMOS International Symposium, San Francisco, California, April 18–21.

Mortensen, Lena. 2006. "Structural Complexity and Social Conflict in Managing the Past at Copan, Honduras." In *Archaeology, Cultural Heritage, and the Antiquities Trade,* ed. Neil Brodie, Morag M. Kersel, Christina Luke, and Kathryn Walker Tubb, 258–69. Gainesville: University Press of Florida.

Mowforth, Martin, and Ian Munt. 1998. *Tourism and Sustainability: New Tourism in the Third World*. London: Routledge. http://dx.doi.org/10.4324/9780203437292.

Petzet, Michael. 2009. *International Principles of Preservation*. ICOMOS Monuments & Sites XX. Paris: ICOMOS.

Prentice, Richard. 1993. "Community-driven Tourism Planning and Residents' Preferences." *Tourism Management* 14 (3): 218–27. http://dx.doi.org/10.1016/0261 -5177(93)90023-E.

Redclift, Michael, and Graham Woodgate. 1997. "Sustainability and Social Construction." In *The International Handbook of Environmental Sociology*, ed. Michael Redclift and Graham Woodgate, 55–67. Cheltenham, UK: Edward Elgar. http://dx.doi.org/10.4337/9781843768593.00011.

Roberts, Sherma, and John Tribe. 2008. "Sustainability Indicators for Small Tourism Enterprises: An Exploratory Perspective." *Journal of Sustainable Tourism* 16 (5): 575–94. http://dx.doi.org/10.1080/09669580802159644.

Russo, Antonio P. 2002. "The 'Vicious Circle' of Tourism Development in Heritage Cities." *Annals of Tourism Research* 29 (1): 165–82. http://dx.doi.org/10.1016/S0160 -7383(01)00029-9.

Ryan, Chris. 2002. "Equity, Management, Power Sharing, and Sustainability: Issues of the 'New Tourism.'" *Tourism Management* 23 (1): 17–26. http://dx.doi.org/10.1016 /S0261-5177(01)00064-4.

Schianetz, Karin, and Lydia Kavanagh. 2008. "Sustainability Indicators for Tourism Destinations: A Complex Adaptive Systems Approach Using Systemic Indicator Systems." *Journal of Sustainable Tourism* 16 (6): 601–28. http://dx.doi.org/10 .1080/09669580802159651.

Simpson, Murray C. 2008. "Community Benefit Tourism Initiatives: A Conceptual Oxymoron?" *Tourism Management* 29 (1): 1–18. http://dx.doi.org/10.1016 /j.tourman.2007.06.005.

Smith, Valene L., ed. 1989. *Hosts and Guests: The Anthropology of Tourism*. 2nd ed. Philadelphia: University of Pennsylvania Press. http://dx.doi.org/10.9783 /9780812208016.

Su, Xiaobo, and Peggy Teo. 2009. *The Politics of Heritage Tourism in China: A View from Lijiang*. Oxon, UK: Routledge.

Taylor, George. 1995. "The Community Approach: Does It Really Work?" *Tourism Management* 16 (7): 487–89. http://dx.doi.org/10.1016/0261-5177(95)00078-3.

Timothy, Dallen J. 1999. "Participatory Planning: A View of Tourism in Indonesia." *Annals of Tourism Research* 26 (2): 371–91. http://dx.doi.org/10.1016/S0160-7383 (98)00104-2.

Timothy, Dallen J., and Cevat Tosun. 2003. "Appropriate Planning for Tourism in Destination Communities: Participation, Incremental Growth, and Collaboration." In *Tourism in Destination Communities*, ed. Shalini Singh, Dallen J. Timothy, and Ross Kingston Dowling, 181–204. Oxon, UK: CAB International. http://dx.doi.org/10.1079/9780851996110.0181.

Tosun, Cevat. 1998. "Roots of Unsustainable Tourism Development at the Local Level: The Case of Urgup in Turkey." *Tourism Management* 19 (6): 595–610. http://dx.doi.org/10.1016/S0261-5177(98)00068-5.

Tosun, Cevat. 2000. "Limits to Community Participation in the Tourism Development Process in Developing Countries." *Tourism Management* 21 (6): 613–33. http://dx.doi.org/10.1016/S0261-5177(00)00009-1.

UNESCO. 1999. *Eighth Draft of the International Cultural Tourism Charter, ICOMOS International Committee on Cultural Tourism*. Paris: ICOMOS.

UNESCO. 2004. *Linking Universal and Local Values: Managing a Sustainable Future for World Heritage*. World Heritage Papers 13. Paris: UNESCO.

UNESCO. 2008. *World Heritage Centre—Sustainable Tourism Programme*. Available online at http://whc.unesco.org/en/tourism. Accessed Nov. 18, 2012.

UNWTO. 2004a. *Sustainable Development of Tourism*. Available online at http://sdt.unwto.org/content/about-us-5. Accessed July 14, 2008.

UNWTO. 2004b. *Technical Seminar on Cultural Tourism and Poverty Alleviation*. Madrid, Spain: UNWTO.

Walker, Cameron J. 2009. *Heritage or Heresy: Archaeology and Culture on the Maya Riviera*. Tuscaloosa: University of Alabama Press.

Wall, Geoffrey, and Heather Black. 2004. "Global Heritage and Local Problems: Some Examples from Indonesia." *Current Issues in Tourism* 7 (4/5): 436–39. http://dx.doi.org/10.1080/13683500408667998.

Wang, Yu. 2007. "Customized Authenticity Begins at Home." *Annals of Tourism Research* 34 (3): 789–804. http://dx.doi.org/10.1016/j.annals.2007.03.008.

Winter, Tim. 2007. "Rethinking Tourism in Asia." *Annals of Tourism Research* 34 (1): 27–44. http://dx.doi.org/10.1016/j.annals.2006.06.004.

WCED (World Commission on Environment and Development). 1987. *Our Common Future*. Oxford: Oxford University Press.

World Heritage Committee. 2005. "Decision 29COM 7B.33: Historic Sanctuary of Machu Picchu (Peru)." In *Decisions of the 29th Session of the World Heritage Committee (Durban, 2005)*, ed. World Heritage Committee, 61. Paris: UNESCO.

Zhao, Zhongshu. 2005. *How to Conserve the Old Town of Lijiang and Its Setting*. Paper presented at the ICOMOS 15th General Assembly and Scientific Symposium, Xi'an, China, October 17–21.

Heritage at Risk **9**

*The Authority and Autonomy of a
Dominant Preservation Framework*

Trinidad Rico

> It seems remarkable that anything at
> all has survived from the past.
>
> —Barclay Jones

From one of the earliest dedicated studies on heritage at risk, Barclay Jones (1986: 11) in this comment invites what initially seems like empty rhetoric: is not *all* heritage 'at risk'? This is a question that informs the identification of what is, and what is not, heritage, if we consider that a necessary definition of the heritage construct is that which requires safeguarding. In recognizing the infinite magnitude of something being 'at risk' in heritage and the power that it is awarded, however, one must also consider the constructed nature of this idea. The often obscured but intentional manipulations of risk and the actors who conceptualize and define heritage typologies thereafter are less frequently examined. As a result, 'heritage at risk' acts as a rationalizing vehicle for other agendas that go unchecked, moving away from site-specific assessments of heritage values and management decisions toward generalized and commonsensical assessments. In this chapter, I aim to move away from the mystification and naturalization of risk as an innate quality of all cultural heritage to discuss the mastering of conceptual and categorical boundaries that make the

DOI: 10.5876/9781607323846.c009

'heritage at risk' discursive framework operational and successful at the local and global level.

RISK AS A RATIONALE FOR HERITAGE DISCOURSES

Jones' statement above is supported by a caveat familiar in critical heritage theory debates: the survival of some heritage places over others should not be seen as accidental or natural. The heritage record at any point in time is a product of a selective appreciation and safeguarding of meanings and values, associated with a certain perception of the past and informed by identity politics, nation-building agendas, and other factors. It is equally the result of changing patterns in the recognition of values as well as shifts in the foci and ethics of conservation as a discipline, shifts that have even been likened to 'fashion' trends (Price 2000). Yet it is also the product of a threats-based approach that mobilizes heritage discourse and sets its priorities.

The heritage preservation crusade (Lowenthal 1997) channels conservation efforts in intentional but often concealed directions by identifying and postulating heritage safeguarding priorities, a practice that also serves to gather support for the mission of conservation itself. This practice is best recognized in the emergence and proliferation of target lists of sites 'at risk,' 'endangered,' or 'in danger,' suggesting unambiguously that some places and objects are perceived to be more at risk than others. It is a suggestion widely recognized in the opening lines of most heritage safeguarding documents and policies, which invariably take endangerment as a common viewpoint: the opening statement of the UNESCO 1972 *Convention Concerning the Protection of the World Cultural and Natural Heritage* begins "*Noting* that the cultural heritage and the natural heritage are increasingly threatened with destruction (emphasis in original). This is never quantified or contextualized.

Although the bestowal of uniqueness on heritage has a long historical trajectory, a concern with the loss of past legacies can be said to have intensified since the early twentieth century. This concern should be seen as the reaction to large-scale destruction in World War I and II and the success of the Modernist movement in urban planning and architecture, which threatened to bring about excessive transformations of the built landscape. Since then, 'heritage at risk' *has* played a key role in the definition of UNESCO's mission, with heritage understood as itself a cultural refugee whose rescue could provide a panacea for post-traumatic cultural recovery and peace building efforts in the wake of widespread destruction. Naturally, early concerns for global heritage revolve around conflict-related risks, against which coordinated efforts of international organizations were mobilized (i.e., the 1954 *Hague Convention for the Protection of Cultural Property in the Event of Armed Conflict*).

But global heritage cooperation also blossomed through coordinated efforts to safeguard key historical monuments in the face of development projects and neglect. A landmark in these efforts was the request for assistance by the United Arab Republic (modern Egypt and Syria) for the safeguarding of the monuments of Nubia in 1950. Threatened with submersion in the construction of the Aswan High Dam, the ensuing thirty-year project to save these monuments, titled "Victory in Nubia," became a flagship project for UNESCO and the beginning of international cooperation in cultural heritage preservation (UNESCO 1960). After the establishment of a coherent program for international heritage preservation, other high-profile international campaigns were added to the portfolio: Florence and Venice (1970), Moenjodaro (1974), and Bamiyan (1974), representing the rapid expansion of this framework at the global scale.

The establishment of the 1972 UNESCO *Convention* also marks an early initiative to formalize the 'heritage at risk' framework. Article 11 establishes the creation of the "List of World Heritage in Danger," with the aim of highlighting properties on the World Heritage List that require assistance for their protection from a variety of threats. This model was joined in 1996 by the World Monuments Fund, which began to publish their own biannual "World Monuments Watch" list to focus global attention on particular sites and current preservation issues around the world (Calame 1998). Other lists emerged to focus on more specialized issues and agendas, such as the "Heritage at Risk Register" of English Heritage, the "Red List" of ICOM, and more recently the initiative by the Global Heritage Fund, "Saving Our Vanishing Heritage," a list of global priorities presented in correlation with levels of national economic development.

The formalization and quantification of 'heritage at risk' across the world is intimately tied to the strengthening of a heritage discourse that places risk as a central driving force. At the launching of the Nubia project, then Director-General of UNESCO, Vittorini Veronese, wrote that "treasures of universal value are entitled to universal protection" (quoted in Chamberlin 1979: 178), invoking a relationship of heritage to cultural rights that is uncompromising without further examination of the values represented by this qualification. Decades later, Linda Marchisotto of the World Monuments Fund took the popular perception of universal significance to a new level, writing that "our cultural heritage is as important to our survival as the air we breathe and the water we drink. It too is endangered" (Marchisotto 1990: 5). This statement is representative of a practice of using and abusing the rhetoric of catastrophism and danger in order to garner political and financial support for heritage projects. I have discussed elsewhere the significant role that a concern for catastrophes, more specifically natural disasters, has had in the mobilization and unification of heritage affairs under the 'heritage at risk' model (Rico 2014). It is a framework that focuses inordinately on the quantification of threats rather than a contextual analysis of culturally specific understandings of the risk and consequences, and the effects of its identification on specific forms of heritage.

The focus on risk has become central to the professional discourse and public understanding of the field with little, if any, critical deconstruction, likely the product of blurring boundaries between the language of fundraising and that of heritage preservation as an intellectual discourse. As a result, the frequency and assertiveness with which 'heritage at risk' is mobilized in institutional discourses and the proliferation of aforementioned lists would suggest that it is a well understood category. Consequently, there have been numerous efforts by organizations to quantify the types and extent of risks as they affect heritage places, as well as to define more precisely the relationship between threats and vulnerabilities for cultural heritage within this framework. But there are inherent weaknesses of using 'risk' objectively, as a point of departure for condition assessments and setting priorities for heritage management.

For example, the ICOMOS (2005) report *Threats to World Heritage Sites 1994–2004* aimed to quantify and qualify threats to World Heritage properties. This report uses information presented by State Parties themselves as well as that supplied by ICOMOS *Missions and Evaluation Reports* to monitor the condition of World Heritage Sites carried out between 1994 and 2004, and it builds substantially on the qualitative data included in the Heritage @ Risk series (i.e., Bumbaru et al. 2000). Other than addressing the problematic nature of relying on data provided by State Parties themselves, the report acknowledges some of the limitations to this approach, considering the challenges associated with the identification and assessment of threats. The major issue reported by the author is the lack of agreed definitions of what constitutes a major threat. The use of threat as a typology cannot be considered an objective framework and the author admits, for example, that the degrees of intensity of different threats were difficult to assess (ICOMOS 2005: 8). In addition, several sub-types of threats can be linked to each other in a spiral of cause and effect, resulting in the use of parameters that are hard to establish with certainty. Yet, despite the use of a weak framework, the report surprisingly concludes that threats are indeed increasing as hypothesized (ICOMOS 2005: 20).

This position reveals a trend to identify threats "from a strict preservation-based perspective without political considerations" (Bumbaru et al. 2000: 9). However, the diverse contexts in which the construction and destruction of heritage takes place at the global level would suggest that the determination of risk should only be seen as a politically constructed process informed by an epistemological position about the creation and circulation of risk indicators. The 'heritage at risk' framework is then presented as a universal rationale for preservation, defined exclusively within a geography of threat.

THE (DE)CONSTRUCTION OF HERITAGE AT RISK

The contours of the 'heritage at risk' framework are more volatile and open to manipulation than may be initially perceived. These are contingent on the establishment of a coherent matrix of factors, including many of the rhetorical devices discussed in this volume, which come together to coordinate convenient discursive boundaries that enable the deployment of risk as a commonsensical verdict. As it was briefly observed in the above ICOMOS (2005) report, the absence of an articulated scale when speaking of 'heritage at risk' makes it difficult to use comparatively. Therefore, it may not be challenged or supported adequately, obscuring political transactions that become attached to heritage condition assessments (Meskell 2014). As a result, the ability of risk to be debated as a subjective perception that is relevant to local, national, international, and especially cultural contexts is unquestionably crippled.

The discussion that is missing in heritage theory and method addresses the use of specific timeframes (when is it 'at risk'?), specific spatial boundaries (what is 'at risk'?), and defined standards for permissible changes (how 'at risk' is it?), factors that tacitly demarcate and manage the scope of heritage concerns but fail to be articulated. These are variables that are currently constructed in such a way that allows the production of a standardized working scale, enabling global comparisons of risk among otherwise disparate heritage places and hence the determination of priorities. As a result, the construction of 'heritage at risk' may be easily manipulated. Emerging critical discussions about the foundations of the use of risk as a keystone in heritage (Harrison 2013, 2015) and ethnographic approaches that reveal the way this qualifier is mobilized in decision making (Meskell 2014) are instrumental to this debate.

This critical position argues that to speak of an 'unprecedented scale'—as the issue of risk is often framed—is at best an informed guess. A lack of specificity of scale is widespread in heritage assessment methodologies that promote the application of a universal formula for 'heritage at risk.' Another recent initiative demonstrates the strength of this formulaic approach in action. In 2010, the Global Heritage Fund produced the report "Saving Our Vanishing Heritage: Safeguarding Cultural Heritage Sites in the Developing World" with the aim of identifying and quantifying endangered sites and their threats, as well as defining priorities and counteracting the ongoing destruction of sites. The report assesses the condition of over 500 sites globally, using different levels of threat to identify four different types of sites: 'Destroyed,' 'Rescue Needed,' 'At Risk,' and 'Stable,' with a separate list of twelve 'Sites on the Verge.' However apparently detailed, it fails to justify the creation of such a complex system of categorization, an exercise that, it suggests, is left to the experts summoned for this purpose. The chain of expertise is further mystified by relying on previously identified sites at risk, borrowed from the "List of World Heritage in Danger" of UNESCO, the ICOMOS Heritage @ Risk publications, and the "World Monuments Watch," an amalgam of data that loses the context of its creation as it is remixed and removed from its point of production. Despite a debatable lack of robust data, the report claims to demonstrate "*a clear need* for global action to protect and preserve the most significant and endangered cultural heritage sites" (Global Heritage Fund 2010: 7, my emphasis), a conclusion that exemplifies the widespread lack of interest in tackling the complexity and sophistication of the variables that compose 'heritage at risk,' focusing instead on the naturalization of an agreed upon formula in order to justify access to and urgency in preservation projects.

To further emphasize the need for establishing contextually informed 'heritage at risk' agendas, there is strong ethnographically informed evidence to demonstrate that ill-discerning designations of heritage as being 'at risk' may result in undesirable destruction of heritage value itself. A frequently cited example is the preservation of the Ise Shrine in Japan that involves a complete rebuilding every twenty years following a thirteen-hundred-year-old reconstruction tradition, the *Shikinen Sengu* (Adams 1998). Continuing this debate, the work of Denis Byrne (1995) in the preservation of Thai Buddhist *stupa* stresses the significance of assessing decay based on a standard of heritage authenticity that is grounded on indigenous values of materiality: in this case, Buddha's final lesson on impermanence. As this perception privileges abandonment, decay, and impoverishment, it demands a unique process of maintenance and restoration of material culture (Byrne 1995: 274–75). Anna Karlström (2005, and Chapter 2 in this volume) extends this discussion to heritage in Laos, considering the concept of preservation as an active process of materialization (cf. Buchli 2002: 14–15). She explores further the notion of impermanence and the value of decay in consideration of circular time in Buddhism and how this affects the construction of integrity.

It is in the context of these findings that dominant heritage preservation and restoration approaches applied to divergent heritage values result in devastating destruction. It is clear that a misled perception of risk forms the basis for turning heritage preservation into a potentially destructive force. An uncritical deployment of heritage practices is a concern that has been marginally noted in these disciplines (Palumbo 2003; Stovel 1998). The ethnographically informed research of Byrne and Karlström also stresses the importance of situating the production of knowledge that defines 'heritage at risk' within existing perceptions of time and space, pointing particularly to the importance of examining the channels of expertise involved.

Risk Assessment

Risk assessment is a key component of the field of conservation, which developed formally in the 1920s and 1930s with the aim of understanding and managing change and decay (Oddy 1992). Earlier concerns with the mechanisms of deterioration had been focused on identifying and quantifying different forms of change, but in the context of the Enlightenment in the nineteenth century a scientific awakening took place within conservation, giving shape to a new conservation philosophy that rejected notions of deterioration as an inevitable process (Ward 1986). This attitude went as far as sustaining that all change is undesirable, and by definition, constitutes decay. Risk of undesirable change has therefore been a motivation behind the development of museum conservation condition assessments, as well as disaster planning (Hunter 1994), cost-benefit analysis models (Ashley-Smith 1999), and quantitative approaches to weathering (Brimblecombe, Grossi, and Harris 2006). More recently, risk maps in site management have been used as a more streamlined and economical way of maintaining and conserving architectural and archaeological features, with improvements in technology enabling more precise connections between environmental threats in specific spaces (Accardo et al. 2003). The technocratic turn in the communication and standardization of documentation of 'heritage at risk' has only intensified in the past few decades and persists as a vehicle for expert hegemony.

While 'heritage at risk' as a framework enjoys uncritical circulation through risk assessment methodologies at all levels and the institutional models already mentioned, a more nuanced deconstruction of what makes up 'heritage at risk' as a formula of global application demonstrates the true complexity of this rhetorical device in action. It can be argued that the only way to quantitatively estimate risk is through the consideration of threats and vulnerabilities as understood in risk management (see Wisner 2003). Risk assessment models ask that these factors be established first in order to circulate the state of risk as uncontested knowledge. Threats have been extensively described in heritage conservation theory and management, and include phenomena ranging from relative humidity to issues internal to conservation management itself, constituting the part of risk management that has been better tackled by the literature and practice of conservation. However, the least debated variable of the risk formula—the degree of vulnerability—responds to the essentialist concern that asks what, exactly, is at risk in 'heritage at risk.' The answer to this question is tightly associated with debates around the creation and maintenance of authenticity and integrity, which brings particular relevance to the discussions that Byrne (1995) and Karlström (2005) have initiated. These refer to two widely contrasting philosophies that have been at odds with each other since early debates in the field of conservation and are worth revisiting now.

One of these philosophies, established by Eugène-Emmanuel Viollet-le-Duc (1858–1868), promoted the value of the original state of monuments, sanctioning any later additions and alterations to maintain or improve a building's image in a way that followed the wishes of the owner (Sitwell and Staniforth 1998). The aims of restoration in the early 1900s were defined as the achievement of a unity of style (Locke 1904). A competing philosophy developed by John Ruskin (1849) embraced destruction as part of the life-history of buildings and objects, espousing the equality of all layers of history and disapproving the restoration practices of Viollet-le-Duc (1858–1868). In Ruskin's view, restoration was ultimately unattainable and equivalent to destruction, describing as he did the dominant nineteenth-century practice as one that created a feeble and lifeless forgery (Morris 1877). Ruskin considered authenticity to lie in the age-value of monuments, what David Lowenthal calls the "wear and tear [that] adorn antiquity" (Lowenthal 1985: 152), recognizing the historical, scientific, and archaeological value of artifacts that depart from a museological stasis. The tension between these philosophies continues to resurface today when the existence of a heritage 'aura' (Benjamin 1992) is debated as inherent or as the product of discursive practices (Shanks 1998) and perceptions of the past (Holtorf and Schadla-Hall 1999; Holtorf 2001).

What is most significant in this discussion is that any kind of change is difficult to ascertain with objectivity, coherence, and consensus. A subjective tolerance to change is needed and preferred, thanks to the contextualization of values and recognition of the co-existence of multiple values in heritage. In accordance with this position, heritage may be at once 'at risk' and 'not at risk,' depending on which values are taken into consideration as being vulnerable, and how these are affected by specific threats. As discussed above, the changing context in which material death and decay is perceived and valued culturally should be a key informant of the 'at risk' condition, a scale that always resists standardization. Therefore, as heritage places and objects enter and exit a state of 'at risk,' questions about the authority and agendas of the experts involved in the practice of categorization come center stage, as a 'heritage at risk' global narrative is determined and promoted worldwide.

THE EXCLUSIONARY POLITICS OF HERITAGE AT RISK

Much useful data on the process of inclusion and exclusion of specific heritage sites into a risk category is inaccessible, due to its unspoken rationale, but also related to the strong de-politicization of the process as it is presented by global heritage organizations responsible for these categorizations (Meskell 2014). Discussions of this practice can therefore rely on processes of inscription and removal of heritage into the respective lists, which are very visible. For a long time, the idea of removing a heritage site from the UNESCO World Heritage List was both a theoretical possibility and a regulatory threat that came as a caveat to every successful nomination to the List. In 2010, the site of Zabid in Yemen was threatened with removal due to perceived architectural violations by residents, who used stone cement instead of *yagur* (traditional red stone), a practice that heritage experts considered negligent (UNESCO 2000). In the same year, there was an initiative to 'shame' the Historic Areas of Istanbul into the UNESCO "List of World Heritage in Danger," the sub-list that showcases World Heritage Sites in a state of risk, due to the proposed construction of the Golden Horn Subway Connection and the anticipated damage to surrounding historic fabric, stirring local and international controversy as development was interpreted to be neglect (Head 2010).

However, only twice has the UNESCO World Heritage Committee gone so far as to de-list a site. In 2007, the Sultanate of Oman's Arabian Onyx Sanctuary became the first site to be removed from the List, by request of the government of Oman itself, who decided to decrease the size of the site by 90 percent after oil had been found within its boundaries (UNESCO 2007). In 2009, the World Heritage Site of Dresden Elbe Valley in Germany was removed from the List after construction plans for the Waldschlösschen Bridge proceeded, affecting the core area of the cultural landscape and requiring a redescription of its boundaries in order to preserve its significance and integrity (UNESCO 2009). These cases suggest that a closer look needs to be taken at how risk as a category is manipulated to mobilize heritage in and out of a state of heightened urgency.

The manipulation of risk is a framework that is only now beginning to be debated as a key construct of modernity in the perception and management of heritage. A recent study by Meskell (2014) addresses the way that states of conservation are attached to other political and economic agendas and alliances, revealing the way that this category is mobilized for other purposes. Harrison (2013) has recently argued that a sense of uncertainty, vulnerability, or risk informs the relationship of heritage and modernity as a philosophical and political concept. Heritage stands in an uneasy relationship with time, haunted by the idea of decline or decay, while recognizing that progress and obsolescence are inevitable:

> the ambiguity of modernity's relationship with the past produces what appear to be opposing sentiments in the desire to be unshackled from the past, whilst simultaneously fetishising and conserving fragments of it. This ambiguity is expressed and partially reconciled through the modern concept of 'risk.' (2013: 26)

Harrison's argument builds on the work of anthropologist Mary Douglas, whose discussions on risk and threat are explored in relation to modernity, as a product of perceptions of vulnerability in the context of globalization, whose uses "fit the tool of the task of building a culture that supports a modern industrial society" (Douglas 1992: 15). Douglas' (1966) problematization of the risk construct and management is associated with a transgression of boundaries and the idea of being 'out of place.' As Harrison (2013) points out, this transgression is associated with anomalies within classificatory systems, treated with distrust as potential sources of social disorder and threat.

Beck (1992, 2002) has framed this anxiety within discussions of a 'risk society,' in which dangers are perceived as an inherent quality of the experience of modernity and the result of its preoccupation with the future. Beck (1992: 21) defines risk as:

> a systematic way of dealing with hazards and insecurities induced and introduced by modernisation itself. Risks . . . are consequences which relate to the threatening force of modernisation and to its globalization of doubt.

In Beck's view, risk constitutes an attempt to colonize the future, used to control the future consequences of human action (Beck 2002). However, he questions our ability to make decisions under conditions of manufactured uncertainty and whether global risks can ever be shared. The manufacture of uncertainty is a process underscored by the questionable quantification of risks (Beck 2002: 40) and our inability to calculate their probability, which Lakoff (2007: 7) argues is exemplary of a new social world in which technical expertise cannot calculate and manage the risks it generates.

As I have discussed throughout this chapter, the inherent 'uncertainty about uncertainties' does not prevent the expert voice in heritage preservation and management from promoting and launching a technology of expertise that claims to be able to understand, identify, and manage the risk factor in heritage constructs. However, discussions of risk beyond the realm of heritage debates highlight the significance of establishing a common ground of shared values in order to form risk through a selection of dangers and its actors. The work of Douglas and Wildavsky (1982) brings to the forefront the process of risk formation, arguing that ranking dangers—a requirement of risk assessment—demands prior agreement on criteria, while stressing that acceptability of a given level of risk is a political question, two issues that I wish to underscore in this chapter. A selective risk awareness toward the environment with which we interact demands the establishment of a rationale for weighing in on possibilities, where irreversible risks cause the greatest reactions, overwhelming other considerations. In heritage preservation, undesirable irreversible change is more than just a possibility, it is seen as inevitability. In fact, facing an inability to tolerate any rate of destruction of heritage, this discourse must take into account not what is probable or improbable, but what is most feared (Ewald 2002), departing from the assumption that the event will happen (Lakoff 2007: 253), as change (conceptual, contextual, or physical) is fluid and unstoppable.

Of extreme relevance to a field that is intrinsically and increasingly reliant on the delimitation of multiple and co-existing values, Douglas and Wildavsky (1982: 8) further note that "common values lead to common fears," summarizing succinctly the grounds on which 'heritage at risk' as a framework is set on a global value system. The complexity of the risk-driven framework compels a departure from the idea that risk is a collective construct, stressing instead that "when risks are objectively ascertainable, it follows that the gap between the expert and the lay public ought to be closed in only one direction—towards the opinion of the expert" (Douglas and Wildavsky 1982: 193). As I have discussed through different institutional approaches at work, risk is calculated and defined by a range of 'experts' who produce statistics and data that make risk calculable and hence manageable. Integral to this process is the identification and classification of threats and vulnerabilities, with an increasing trust in experts and abstract expert systems over local forms of knowledge

(Giddens 1991: 29–32, quoted in Harrison 2013: 27). Experts may then rely on seemingly disparate types of events that fit into the framework (Lakoff 2007), as suggested by the frequent reliance on a discourse that equates a loss of heritage with a loss of a human future. This is a characteristic of the rhetoric of catastrophe that predominates in the dominant heritage discourse.

CONCLUSION: BEYOND AN EXTINCTION FRAMEWORK

This chapter questions the validity of 'heritage at risk' as a polarizing force in the definition of preservation urgencies, but also of heritage itself. In discussing 'heritage at risk' as a construction and rhetorical unit of key significance in the philosophies and methodologies of cultural heritage preservation, I argue that risk should be seen as a tool that is at the center of the manipulation of discursive boundaries in heritage management and conservation. I argue that a reliance on risk conveniently destroys the relevance of these boundaries, whose articulation is much needed for the adequate contextualization of heritage constructs and the politics therein. For this purpose, I describe the construction of 'heritage at risk' within the existing construction and mobilization of authority in cultural heritage preservation and the role that it has as an established instrument of rationalization for the dominant politics of identification and construction of cultural heritage.

This critique aligns with a post-colonial promotion of an understanding that decay is not universally rejected, that linear time is not universally perceived, and that the materiality of heritage is not universally valued (see Karlström in this volume). It questions the fate and validity of heritage that is not considered to be 'at risk,' calling for an investment in situating the tools, methodologies, and actors involved in this type of assessment and the contexts in which they gain validity. The pivotal role that the expert has in determining and measuring risk has not been addressed in heritage and preservation management, and hence this chapter stresses the significance of situating the critical debates on heritage discourse within the production of heritage constructs and the expert technologies that are promoted in discourse and practice. As Douglas (1992: 15) has so succinctly revealed, the idea of risk appears to have been custom made for the purposes of modernity—its universalizing terminology, abstractness, power of condensation, scientificity, and connection with objective analysis. In many ways, these resonate with the characteristics of a universalizing heritage construct and its operation through global networks of experts and their methods of evaluation. We need to examine more closely any resistance to expert verdicts that assigns risk to heritage spaces and objects.

Or perhaps we should be asking whether there is any mechanism in heritage management and discourse that would be able to capture the expression of such a counternarrative.

REFERENCES

Accardo, Giorgio, Antonella Altieri, Carlo Cacace, Elisabetta Giani, and Annamaria Giovagnoli. 2003. "Risk Map: A Project to Aid Decision-Making in the Protection, Preservation and Conservation of Italian Cultural Heritage." In *Conservation Science 2002: Papers from the Conference Held in Edinburgh, Scotland, 22–24 May 2002*, ed. Joyce H. Townsend, Katherine Eremin, and Annemie Adriaens, 44–49. London: Archetype Publications.

Adams, Cassandra. 1998. "Japan's Ise Shrine and Its Thirteen-Hundred-Year-Old Reconstruction Tradition." *Journal of Architectural Education* 52 (1): 49–60. http://dx.doi.org/10.1111/j.1531-314X.1998.tb00255.x.

Ashley-Smith, Jonathan. 1999. *Risk Assessment for Object Conservation*. Oxford: Butterworth-Heinemann.

Beck, Ulrich. 1992. *Risk Society: Towards a New Modernity*. London: Sage.

Beck, Ulrich. 2002. "The Terrorist Threat: World Risk Society Revisited." *Theory, Culture & Society* 19 (4): 39–55. http://dx.doi.org/10.1177/0263276402019004050.

Benjamin, Walter. (Original work published 1936) 1992. *Illuminations*. London: Fontana.

Brimblecombe, Peter, Carlotta M. Grossi, and Ian Harris. 2006. "Climate Change Critical to Cultural Heritage." In *Heritage, Weathering and Conservation, Vol 1: Proceedings of the International Conference on Heritage, Weathering and Conservation, HWC–2006, 21–24 June 2006, Madrid, Spain*, ed. Rafael Fort, Monica Alvarez de Buergo, Miguel Gomez-Heras, and Carmen Vazquez-Calvo, 387–93. London: Taylor & Francis. http://dx.doi.org/10.1007/978-3-540-95991-5_20.

Buchli, Victor. 2002. *The Material Culture Reader*. Oxford: Berg.

Bumbaru, Dinu, Michael Petzet, Marilyn Truscott, and John Ziesemer, eds. 2000. *Heritage at Risk: ICOMOS World Report 2000 on Monuments and Sites in Danger*. Munich: K.G. Saur.

Byrne, Denis. 1995. "Buddhist *Stupa* and Thai Social Practice." *World Archaeology* 27 (2): 266–81. http://dx.doi.org/10.1080/00438243.1995.9980307.

Calame, Jon. 1998. "World Monuments Watch 1996–97: Lessons from the First Cycle." *Journal of Architectural Conservation* 4 (2): 54–61. http://dx.doi.org/10.1080/13556207.1998.10785216.

Chamberlin, Eric Russell. 1979. *Preserving the Past*. London: J. M. Dent & Sons Ltd.

Douglas, Mary. 1992. *Risk and Blame: Essays in Cultural Theory*. London: Routledge. http://dx.doi.org/10.4324/9780203430866.

Douglas, Mary. 1966. *Purity and Danger: An Analysis of Concepts of Pollution and Taboo*. London: Routledge.

Douglas, Mary, and Aaron Wildavsky. 1982. *Risk and Culture: An Essay on the Selection of Technical and Environmental Dangers*. Berkeley: University of California Press.

Ewald, François. 2002. "The Return of Descartes's Malicious Demon: An Outline of the Philosophy of Precaution." In *Embracing Risk, the Changing Culture of Insurance and Responsibility*, ed. Tom Baker and Jonathan Simon, 273–301. Chicago, IL: University of Chicago Press.

Giddens, Anthony. 1991. *Modernity and Self-Identity: Self and the Late Modern Age*. Cambridge, UK: Polity Press.

Global Heritage Fund. 2010. "Saving Our Vanishing Heritage: Safeguarding Endangered Cultural Heritage Sites in the Developing World." http://global heritagefund.org/vanishing. Accessed December 10, 2010.

Harrison, Rodney. 2013. *Heritage: Critical Approaches*. London: Routledge. http://dx.doi.org/10.1093/oxfordhb/9780199602001.013.021.

Harrison, Rodney. 2015. "World Heritage Listing and the Globalization of the Endangerment Sensibility." In *Endangerment, Biodiversity and Culture*, ed. Fernando Vidal and Nelia Dias, 195–217. London: Routledge.

Head, Jonathan. 2010. "Istanbul's UNESCO World Heritage Status under Threat." *BBC News Europe*. http://www.bbc.co.uk/news/world-europe-11095638. Accessed July 2, 2011.

Holtorf, Cornelius. 2001. "Is the Past a Non-renewable Resource?" In *Destruction and Conservation of Cultural Property*, ed. Robert Layton, Julian Thomas, and Peter Stone, 286–97. London: Routledge.

Holtorf, Cornelius, and Tim Schadla-Hall. 1999. "Age as Artefact: On Archaeological Authenticity." *European Journal of Archaeology* 2 (2): 229–47. http://dx.doi.org/10.1179/eja.1999.2.2.229.

Hunter, John E. 1994. "Museum Disaster Preparedness Planning." In *Care of Collections*, ed. Simon J. Knell, 246–61. London: Routledge.

ICOMOS. 2005. *Threats to World Heritage Sites 1994–2004: An Analysis*. Paris: ICOMOS.

Jones, Barclay G., ed. 1986. *Protecting Historic Architecture and Museum Collections from Natural Disasters*. Stoneham, MA: Butterworths.

Karlström, Anna. 2005. "Spiritual Materiality: Heritage Preservation in a Buddhist World?" *Journal of Social Archaeology* 5 (3): 338–55. http://dx.doi.org/10.1177/14696 05305057571.

Lakoff, Andrew. 2007. "Preparing for the Next Emergency." *Public Culture* 19 (2): 247–71. http://dx.doi.org/10.1215/08992363-2006-035.

Locke, William John. 1904. "The Sixth International Congress of Architects, 1904, Madrid." *The Architectural Journal, Being the Journal of the Royal Institute of British Architects (RIBA)* 6 (3): 343–46.

Lowenthal, David. 1985. *The Past is Foreign Country*. Cambridge: Cambridge University Press.

Lowenthal, David. 1997. *The Heritage Crusade and the Spoils of History*. London: Viking.

Marchisotto, Linda. 1990. "Saving Our Past: A Race Against Time." In *Saving Our Past: A Race Against Time: 1965–1990—25th Anniversary World Monuments Fund*, ed. World Monuments Fund, 5. New York, NY: World Monuments Fund.

Meskell, Lynn. 2014. "States of Conservation: Protection, Politics, and Pacting within UNESCO's World Heritage Committee." *Anthropological Quarterly* 87 (1): 217–43. http://dx.doi.org/10.1353/anq.2014.0009.

Morris, W. 1877. "The Principles of the Society (for the Protection of Ancient Buildings) as Set Forth upon its Foundation." *Builder* 35 (25 August): 41–43.

Oddy, Andrew. 1992. *The Art of the Conservator*. London: British Museum Press.

Palumbo, Gaetano. 2003. "Threats and Challenges to the Archaeological Heritage in the Mediterranean." In *Management Planning for Archaeological Sites: An Interdisciplinary Workshop Organized by the Getty Conservation Institute*, ed. Jean Marie Teutonico and Gaetano Palumbo, 3–12. Los Angeles, CA: Getty Conservation Institute.

Price, Clifford. 2000. "Following Fashion: The Ethics of Archaeological Conservation." In *Cultural Resource Management in Contemporary Society: Perspective on Managing and Presenting the Past*, ed. Francis P. McManamon and Alf Hatton, 213–30. London: Routledge.

Rico, Trinidad. 2014. "The Limits of a 'Heritage at Risk' Framework: The Construction of Post-disaster Cultural Heritage in Banda Aceh." *Journal of Social Archaeology* 14 (2): 157–76. http://dx.doi.org/10.1177/1469605314527192.

Ruskin, John. 1849. *The Seven Lamps of Architecture*. 4th ed. London: Smith Elder.

Shanks, Michael. 1998. "The Life of an Artefact in an Interpretive Archaeology." *Fennos Candia Archaeologica* 15: 15–20.

Sitwell, Christine, and Sarah Staniforth, eds. 1998. *Studies in the History of Painting Restoration*. London: Archetype Publications and The National Trust.

Stovel, Herb. 1998. *Risk Preparedness: A Management Manual for World Cultural Heritage*. Rome, Italy: ICCROM.

UNESCO. 1960. "Campagne internationale pour la sauvegarde des monuments de la Nubie/ International campaign to save the monuments of Nubia." *Museum* 13 (2): 65–66.

UNESCO. 2000. "World Heritage Committee Adds Three Sites to the List of World Heritage in Danger." *UNESCO World Heritage Center—News.* Available online at http://whc.unesco.org/en/news/167. Accessed July 2, 2011.

UNESCO. 2007. "Oman's Arabian Oryx Sanctuary: First Site Ever to be Deleted from UNESCO's World Heritage List." *UNESCO World Heritage Center—News.* Available online at http://whc.unesco.org/en/news/362. Accessed July 2, 2011.

UNESCO. 2009. "Dresden Is Deleted from UNESCO's World Heritage List." *UNESCO World Heritage Center—News.* Available online at http://whc.unesco .org/en/news/522. Accessed July 2, 2011.

Viollet-le-Duc, Eugène-Emmanuel. 1858–68. *Dictionnaire raisonné de l'architecture française du XIe au XVIe siècle 1858–68*, Volume 8. Paris: B. Bance.

Ward, Philip R. 1986. *The Nature of Conservation: A Race against Time.* Marina del Rey, CA: Getty Conservation Institute.

Wisner, Ben. 2003. *At Risk: Natural Hazards, People's Vulnerability and Disasters.* London: Routledge.

Heritage Discourse 10

*The Creation, Evolution, and Destruction
of Authorized Heritage Discourses within
British Cultural Resource Management*

Malcolm A. Cooper

There is a growing literature in the general field of cultural studies exploring the social, intellectual, and political processes by which systems of heritage management are created and maintained, and how in turn these determine what is regarded as heritage and why. Recently brought together under the term *heritage studies* (Carman and Sorenson 2009: 11–28), there are a number of common, and frequently bipolar, dimensions of study such as: national and local; expert and non-expert; univocal and multivocal; exclusion and inclusion; and communities as receivers and creators of heritage. The intellectual explorations presented here fall into Kellner's (1989: vii–xi) approach of *getting the story crooked*, that is, seeking to *get under* the everyday systems and 'common-sense' activities to understand how they have become common sense, how certain discourses become dominant at particular times and places, and what governance structures and processes support the construction and operation of dominant discourse. By 'discourse,' I mean the process and mechanisms by which language is used to achieve particular outcomes and through which one community of interest gains and maintains a privileged position over others through establishing 'common-sense' statements that frequently become implicit and unquestioned within specific social situations.

DOI: 10.5876/9781607323846.c010

The purpose of this chapter is to explore the concept of heritage discourse in relation to cultural resource management (CRM) in Britain and to seek to take a nuanced view of how competing discourses are created and challenged by drawing on day-to-day experiences of operating within such a framework. This chapter follows from earlier research, which has sought to understand the everyday work of CRM within one or more theoretical frameworks that look at discourse and society with a cultural studies framework (Cooper 2005, 2008, 2010b). Underlying these studies has been an interest in how discourse and particular narratives and phrases are developed and used to question and challenge activities and decisions by CRM organizations and individuals. In particular it is evident that these change over time as they seek to gain or increase their purchase by linking a specific (and often case-based) narrative to broader political or social narratives.

AUTHORIZED HERITAGE DISCOURSES

One of the most commonly used perspectives for understanding the work of cultural resource managers in recent years has been Laurajane Smith's concept of an 'Authorized Heritage Discourse' (AHD, see Smith 2006: 29–34). Growing out of post-modern and, in particular, post-colonial perspectives that focused on indigenous peoples, this model has been increasingly applied more generally to the relationship between local community and governmental and/ or professional discourses. The operation of an AHD is not a passive process leading to the identification and protection of entities of *self-evident* historic importance. Instead, an AHD is implicated in an active process of both creating and legitimizing the significance of specific entities—and by implication negating the creation and legitimization of others. Under such a perspective, the AHD is created and used by public policymakers to "govern or regulate the expression of social or cultural identity" (Smith 2004: 2). In her work, Smith has also explored the concept of the 'technology of government' (cf. Rose and Miller 1992), which she sees as providing the mechanisms by which beliefs and discourse are operationalized on a day-to-day basis (Smith 2004: 11). Armed with this philosophy and methodology, and frequently using discourse analysis, Smith and other researchers such as Emma Waterton (2010) have explored in detail how privileged heritage discourses come into being and are maintained. The work on AHDs has been important in focusing attention onto the many philosophical structures and arguments which underlie the 'common-sense' practice of heritage management in the late twentieth and early twenty-first centuries. There has, however, been a tendency within this work to assume that government and the heritage organizations which carry out government's bidding in the heritage management field (i.e., applying the legislation and policy responsibilities which fall on government as a result of the enactment of heritage legislation and adoption of policy) do so in a consistent and straightforward manner and that this can be understood by reference solely to consideration of legislation and policy. Waterton's study is of particular interest as it illustrates the sheer variability of understanding, approach, and consistency that can be seen in a large state heritage agency.

THE INVOLVEMENT OF THE STATE

The area for study in this chapter is that relating to regulatory mechanisms as applied to the protection and management of entities comprising the historic environment in Britain. This involves a process of designation (such as the 'listing' of buildings and the 'scheduling' of ancient monuments) and the subsequent operation of a consents process by which proposed works are assessed in terms of any potential adverse impacts, with inappropriate works amended or refused. In Britain a two-tier system has developed, with certain consents regimes operated at a local level by local planning authorities and others at a national level by state heritage bodies such as English Heritage (England), Historic Scotland (Scotland), and Cadw (Wales).[1] To a great degree, those operating at a national and local level undertake an identical process—identifying the location and significance of site/building, assessing the impact of proposed works on its significance, reaching a view on the acceptability or otherwise of the proposals, and deciding whether or not to grant consent (albeit they are sometimes working within differing legislative and policy frameworks).

However, when undertaking this type of regulatory work, it is apparent that the actual process of decision making involves far more than the seemingly mechanical and objective process just described. This results from the evident fact that the decision making process is not independent of the society (and the organization) within which it takes place and that a range of influences, some more visible than others, are at play at any time. These might involve, for example, political issues and media pressure. These not only affect the broader structures such as legislation and policy in the medium to long-term, but they also affect the day-to-day decisions on specific cases. Institutions such as government and local authorities often have complex political currents flowing through them. These are both open to influence from without and, in turn, can influence within. Once the historic environment became a formal responsibility of government, so it became open to influences operating within and on governmental structures at a national and local level.

It is worth pausing here to reflect that a key characteristic of the twentieth and early twenty-first centuries in Britain has been the acceptance that *the* appropriate approach for defining and managing the historic environment is through the adoption of appropriate *government* legislative powers and related mechanisms. That this was not always an accepted belief can be seen in the difficult passage of heritage legislation through Parliament between 1870 and 1882, when the first ancient monument legislation was adopted (Champion 1996: 38–41). The principle of national government involvement in heritage management is still regularly challenged in Britain today.

An example here might be helpful. A key principle in Britain for over a century has been that certain historic buildings and monuments are of such significance that they should be taken into government care and looked after 'for the benefit of the Nation.' Over the past century and a quarter the application of this principle has led to the creation of significant *property-in-care* portfolios held on behalf of government by English Heritage, Historic Scotland, and Cadw. These portfolios include sites such as Stonehenge, Edinburgh Castle, and Caerleon Roman Amphitheatre. However, one of the weaknesses of the heritage legislation in Britain, embodied into the 1882 *Ancient Monuments Protection Act* and remaining to this day, is that while the state takes over the day-to-day control of the site, the site-ownership remains with the landowner, thereby allowing the sale and purchase of such sites by this landowner. This has led to cases where sites have been sold and subsequent owners have sought to take back control of 'their' sites and monuments. Recent high profile cases include that of Rowallan Castle in East Ayrshire, Scotland, where a public local inquiry spent some time exploring the intentions of the legislation in this regard, and where the owner/applicants sought to discredit Historic Scotland's management of the site as part of their approach to persuade Scottish Ministers to surrender guardianship of the castle.[2] There is certainly a strong view in some quarters that the state should relinquish a number of such properties, unsurprisingly perhaps where such sites have become (or are perceived to have the potential to become) significant income generators.

It is in cases such as these that we see most clearly the operation of competing discourses and in particular where rhetorical devices—i.e., persuasive grammatical constructions that have emotional or common-sense appeal—are used in the press and elsewhere to establish 'persuasive' arguments. One common phrase used in such arguments is 'letting private owners take the burden of running and maintaining the site from the state.' This is a charged phrase in that it does not attempt to reflect the relevant heritage legislation or policy or the fact that the state may have committed significant levels of funding and other resource to the site, but instead seeks to link to recent arguments about political philosophy and public service. It seeks to influence consideration of the specific case by exploiting the prevalent rhetoric of the reduction of central government control and state expenditure which has become a feature of neo-liberalist government philosophies adopted by recent administrations in the United Kingdom (see McLaughlin, Osborne, and Ferlie 2002; Harvey 2005). While at face value, this might appear persuasive at a time of pressure on pub-lic finances, like many rhetorical devices it does not bear scrutiny insofar as the *relief of this burden* may well be accompanied by the removal of public access and possible sale (effectively taking advantage of the large amount of public funds already invested in the conservation and management of such sites for personal gain). Yet many politicians and members of the public are persuaded by the apparent common-sense arguments contained in such rhetoric, and when looking at competing discourse, it is often such rhetorical devices that form a crucial weapon in the armories (see Billig 1996; Fairclough 1989).

When investigating the use of rhetoric in relation to the CRM process in Britain, it is important to note that rhetoric does not always operate on the system as a whole but is frequently focused on one or more of the elements that comprises the system, and exhibits a particular character relating to the specific process being challenged. Before we go further, we need then to look briefly at the common elements that comprise a CRM system—that is, the technology of government.

THE TECHNOLOGY OF GOVERNMENT

To begin the process of exploring the technology of government applied to CRM in Britain, we need go no further than Gerard Baldwin Brown's (1905) book, *The Care of Ancient Monuments*. Despite being over a century old (and perhaps best remembered as leading to the creation of the Royal Commission on the Ancient and Historical Monuments for Scotland, Wales and England), this book remains a succinct and masterful analysis of the key elements of an effective heritage protection system as a whole. It certainly contributed to the momentum for new and far stronger ancient monument legislation in 1913 and led also to a far more sophisticated infrastructure and increased funding for heritage.

Baldwin Brown undertook a detailed and comprehensive analysis of heritage legislation across Europe (which forms part two of the book). He provided a

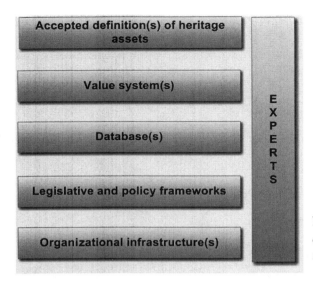

FIGURE 10.1. *Components of a cultural resource management system.*

definition of 'monuments,' looking at issues such as the value-systems being applied and where there needed to be an age cutoff in terms of the very recent, and he set out arguments for why such monuments should be preserved. He went on to look at the various agencies that might become involved from private societies (both national and local), official and semi-official agencies and museums (we would understand these being arms-length or stated-sponsored bodies), and national and local legislation. He identified the importance of inventorization and publication and also dealt with the issues of ownership of artifacts, control of excavation, and the particularly thorny issue of monument restoration, all of which remain issues to this day.

Drawing on this and later discussions, Figure 10.1 sets out the key elements of a CRM system. To work effectively, the basic building blocks are: an accepted definition of heritage assets; systems for recognizing and quantifying their value or significance; accessible databases of information to allow the sites and the boundaries of their protection to be identified; a legislative and policy framework that controls certain types of activities in relation to the heritage asset and introduces some form of consents process (and a scheme of punishment for activities that do not follow it); an organizational infrastructure with specific roles and responsibilities identified for particular elements of this structure; and experts who occupy the organizational infrastructure and are responsible for developing and maintaining the dynamics of the system.

Behind these key areas in the model of course sits two additional considerations. The first is political and public support, and the second is the availability of funding. Without these, the system will underperform or will wither and die irrespective of whether the other elements exist. However, it is important to stress that in reality the structures and processes identified in Figure 10.1 are far more interwoven and dynamic than this diagram might suggest. Also, while each appears non-problematical, in fact each area embodies a history and a wide range of decisions, assumptions, and issues that frequently provide the basis for rhetorical attack both from within and without the discipline or profession. Baldwin Brown recognized this issue in *The Care of Ancient Monuments*. In the section headed *Quis Custodiet Ipsos Custodes: The Function of Public Opinion*, he acknowledges the importance of public opinion:

> public opinion prepares the way for legislation, and no Acts for the defence of monuments can be passed, and no funds voted for the proper carrying out of these Acts, unless there be in the background in the mind of the people a certain force of intelligent belief in the need for agency of the kind . . . speakers and writers have insisted that the movement must carry the public with it, or it will have no real staying-power. (Baldwin Brown 1905: 31)

It is perhaps public opinion that has become increasingly important and powerful in the intervening period, and which is frequently the target of rhetoric.

HERITAGE ASSETS, THEIR VALUE, AND DATABASES

As we have already seen, prior to the early 1880s in Britain, government intervention was not deemed acceptable. When the 1882 *Ancient Monuments Protection Act* came forward, the type of entities that were seen as legitimate for protection under the Act were exceptionally limited in scope, focusing mainly on prehistoric monuments. Over the intervening period, we have seen though a very significant expansion in the numbers of entities being identified as worthy of protection as 'heritage assets.' The scope was broadened, being expanded to include, among others, industrial heritage, historic urban and rural landscapes, marine heritage, twentieth century architecture, and intangible heritage.

The very definition of an entity as a heritage asset carries with it some sense of 'otherness' and, through this, a recognition (or construction) of value. We have seen much work on the development and refinement of value systems in relation to heritage assets, particularly in recent years. In the early days of the

Government Inspectorates (i.e., the Government departments entrusted with carrying out national heritage responsibilities), it was not unusual for the official files of historic properties-in-care to contain little in the way of description or assessment of value, this being presumably self-evident and occurring at a time when the expert was unlikely to be challenged. However, against the background of the increasing desire for accountability and an increased likelihood of challenge, we have seen the development of increasingly sophisticated systems for assessing significance often based on the application of, or assessment against, specific criteria. This has worked both in the discipline itself in terms of seeking to assess and calculate the potential of sites within wider academic research design(s) and outside the discipline in terms of providing explicit justification for recognition as a heritage asset and for assessing its significance in a clear and robust manner.

Looking therefore at the identification of monuments and the application of value-systems, how might competing discourses and rhetoric function? A particularly well documented area relates to industrial heritage and, in particular, nineteenth century urban working class housing. Among others, Alan Mayne (1993) has explored how in San Francisco, Birmingham, and Sydney, the key way of ensuring public and political support for demolition was to create a one-to-one identification between such housing and the phrase 'slum,' the latter being frequently used as a labeling device in the late nineteenth and early twentieth centuries. Once any group of buildings had been so labeled, the link to high levels of social deprivation, disease, distress, disorder, and disaffection was established as non-problematic, and demolition then became a common-sense proposition (Mayne 1993; Mayne and Murray 2001). While the focus of Mayne's study was the clearance and improvement programs of the late nineteenth and early twentieth centuries, the same process of labeling of buildings as slums continues to be prevalent today. In addition to the use of the rhetoric relating to slums, we have seen the appearance of a further narrative, that industrial remains were representative of both exploitation and past failure. Again, the intention here was to create a gradient of public opinion where, by supporting preservation of such buildings and sites, one was either supporting past exploitation or was seeking to preserve reminders of failures that, by implication, would adversely impact on an area and its desired regeneration (see Cooper 2005).

A second example that also attracts significant levels of rhetoric involves twentieth century and, in particular, post-War buildings as potential heritage assets worthy of protection. For many, heritage equates with sites such as mystical stone circles or burial mounds, ruined abbeys, or perhaps the quaint stone or timber-built vernacular houses using traditional and local material. In such cases, there is a commonly held view that equates historic importance with aesthetics, one which is commonly reinforced by the media. It is perhaps unsurprising therefore that the listing of, for example, Bicknell and Hamilton's concrete brutalist signal box at Birmingham New Street Station led to surprise in many quarters:

> It is also a first-rate essay in Brutalism, the deployment of heavy, roughly textured concrete masses to achieve dour sculptural effects. It looks vaguely like part of a coastal defence system. Such buildings are viewed nowadays with more affection than they used to be, but the New Street signal-box is never going to fit most definitions of beauty. The best one could say is, perhaps, that it is proudly and unapologetically itself. (Miller 2003: np)

Birmingham has also seen a recent debate over John Madin's 1974 Central Library. English Heritage proposed the building for listing as a significant example of post-War architecture, but the City Council drummed up significant levels of public support for its demolition. HRH Prince Charles—already famous for using the term 'carbuncle' to refer to the proposed extension to the National Gallery in Trafalgar Square, London in a speech in 1984—has been quoted as saying "it was an incinerator more suitable for burning books than keeping them" (Foster 2005: 77).[3]

Moving northwards to Scotland, Edinburgh City Council and Historic Scotland have recently published a list of key post-War buildings for Edinburgh. A sympathetic article by the journalist Tim Cornwell (2011) recognized the challenge being faced by the two organizations, "The knee-jerk reaction to the buildings presented here is to ask how these concrete and glass constructions can ever be rated worth preserving." For those involved in the statutory designation process, the protection of post-War buildings arguably is and will remain the most challenging area of activity (cf. Cooper 2010a).

The use of rhetoric to challenge the assessment of significance is not of course solely related to industrial and modern heritage. More recently, issues around sustainability have offered opportunities for new rhetoric to be developed, in which the historic environment is seen as in opposition to 'sensible' environmental concerns. In Edinburgh New Town—a World Heritage site with a high concentration of listed buildings—there is persistent pressure to introduce energy efficiency measures such as window replacement, solar panels, and other measures using the rhetoric that 'this is good for the environment.' There is a sense of irony here in that it would seem entirely reasonable to argue that the preservation of existing buildings (rather than demolition and replacement) is already highly sustainable, but it is not unusual to see (dubious) sustainability arguments being used to garner public support for unsympathetic changes. If we take an extract from an article in one of Scotland's main newspapers, *The Scotsman*, as an example:[4]

> Rising fuel costs and environmental concerns have forced councillors to consider lifting a ban on double glazed windows in Edinburgh's most historic buildings. Hundreds of residents in and around the New Town are currently prevented from replacing their draughty old windows, because of fears that double glazing would change the appearance of their properties.

We are seeing here the creation of the common-sense argument in support of the case for double-glazing using a number of elisions and rhetorical devices. In Table 10.1 the rhetoric has been broken down into specific parts in order to consider it in more detail. By doing this, it becomes clear that what appears at first sight a common-sense and persuasive argument for allowing double-glazing in listed buildings in the World Heritage Site is in fact an artifact of argument construction that uses a combination of charged language, unsubstantiated statements, and omissions to create this effect.

When cases such as this are investigated, the number of residents usually proves to be in a *very* small minority (with the pressure coming in fact from double-glazing companies), and the cause of drafts is not a flaw in the design of windows but a lack of regular maintenance and repair. An entirely realistic alternative is therefore to retain and repair the 'draughty old windows'—it is cheaper, more sustainable, and will allow the status (and value) of the buildings to be retained. However, one senses that journalists and newspaper editors would not find an article that identified agreements between owners and conservationists (and a lack of any controversy) to be as interesting for their readers.

More sophisticated (but equally spurious) arguments are used with regularity to take advantage of the concerns with climate change and energy efficiency, supported by carefully selected 'scientific' figures that support the desired outcome. Alan Tierney (2010: np) neatly summarized the problem and the vulnerability of historic buildings to rhetoric based on sustainability arguments:

> historic buildings come out very badly in energy assessments—largely because of flawed assumptions and a lack of accurate data. That's not even half the story, though. The really big problem with energy assessments is that they only take account of energy 'in use'—basically what is needed for heating and lighting. No account is taken of the energy required to put the building up in the

TABLE 10.1 Edinburgh New Town and double glazing

Element of argument	Omitted information
1 Edinburgh New Town has historic buildings.	The majority of these are listed at a very high grade and lie within conservation areas and within a UNESCO World Heritage site. Nonetheless the implication of proposed replacement of windows on historic importance and therefore on the New Town's listed and World Heritage status is not given.
2 Historic buildings in the New Town have drafty and old windows.	Here the writer is seeking to make an equivalence between 'old' and 'draughty'. However this is not in reality demonstrated, the number of drafty windows is not given, and the scale and explanation for the draft is absent.
3 Hundreds of residents wish to replace their windows.	It is not clear how many residents wish to replace their windows, what source is being used, what percentage of the overall population of the New Town they represent, and whether there is a balancing issue with the broader public interest rather than considering just the residents themselves.
4 These residents are being prevented by other people's fears.	It is not clear who the 'fear' belongs to—although by implication these fears do not belong to the residents wishing to replace the windows. The context of this statement and lack of explanation implies that the 'fear' is not well grounded.
5 The common-sense concern about energy efficiency and sustainability means that such windows should be replaced with double glazing.	Alternatives to the proposed solution of replacement with double-glazing are not given. There is also an assumption that double glazing will deliver the sought-after improvements in a sustainable manner. The implication of a change to double-glazing in terms of the adverse impact of such changes on the desirability and value of the property is also not given.
6 The combination of residents' wishes and energy efficiency issues is forcing councillors to consider changing their views.	There is no counter argument being presented for councillors to consider. Therefore under the weight of consideration councillors are being forced to change their policy.
7 It is therefore reasonable that councillors should consider giving permission for double-glazed windows in historic buildings in the New Town.	Is it reasonable and responsible for councillors to allow double glazing in response to residents' wishes and the broader energy efficiency and climate change agenda?

first place: its embodied energy (EE). The EE of a building is the total energy required to construct it—to obtain the raw materials, process and manufacture them as necessary, transport them to site, and put them together.

. . . So what does all this mean? Well, as American architect Carl Elefante put it, 'the greenest building is the one that's already built.' In other words, careful and sensitive upgrading of existing buildings is much more sustainable than replacing them. What is more, because historic buildings are so far ahead of modern buildings in embodied energy, they shouldn't need to meet the same exacting standards for energy-in-use to justify their sustainability.

Yet all of the signs are that government, both nationally and locally, regularly fall prey to such 'common-sense' sustainability arguments being put forward by elements of the building industry who would prospect from a relaxation of policies of protection for historic buildings.

LEGISLATION, POLICY, AND ARCHAEOLOGICAL ORGANIZATIONS

Where organizations or individuals cannot discredit the historic entity itself, rhetorical devices are also commonly used to seek to establish highly critical common-sense positions into other elements of the CRM system. A common form of attack is to portray legislation and policy as heavy handed and no longer fit-for-purpose, and that it is being applied by self-interested experts against the broader public interest (e.g., Geoghegan 2012).

In terms of the rhetoric of self-interest, at a recent public local inquiry, where Historic Scotland was opposing the proposed restoration of a historic property in their care, one argument used by the appellants was that Historic Scotland's approach was 'SPABish.' By this, the appellants meant that Historic Scotland was seeking to apply outdated principles, as the Society for the Protection of Ancient Buildings (SPAB) was founded in the nineteenth century. Therefore, the common-sense argument was that as these principles were over a hundred years old, they were very much 'out of date'—even though SPAB still exists and pursues these principles today. Further, Historic Scotland noticed and drew to the attention of the Planning Inspector hearing the case that earlier in their evidence, the appellants had placed great stress on the assessment of good architecture relating to its 'firmness, commodity, and delight.' Under cross-examination, the appellants' witness was reluctant or unable to identify where this phrase came from and was 'helped' by Historic Scotland's barrister. The quote is attributed to the Roman architect, engineer, and author Vitruvius who was writing in the first century B.C.!

If you can't discredit the legislation and policy, however, it has become increasingly common to seek to discredit the organizations and their staff. This fits in with a broader rhetoric against public servants that has become popular in the media and in Parliament in recent years. By way of example here, English Heritage has pursued a strong policy of objecting to tall buildings in London where they affect the setting of World Heritage Sites in the city. In 2001, this led the then mayor of London, Ken Livingstone, in an extraordinary outburst, to accuse English Heritage of being 'the Taliban of British architecture' and of causing more damage to London than the Luftwaffe (Sudjic 2001). In Scotland, Historic Scotland is persistently referred to as 'Hysteric Scotland' and 'the abominable no-men' in a long-term campaign to discredit their regulatory activities. The organization has also been accused of being Hannoverian by one owner seeking to link his case to the Scottish nationalist agenda in a high-profile proposed scheme for restoration of a historic castle. Hannoverian, in this context, seeks to portray the decision as 'English' against a desire by the 'Scottish,' thereby playing into the historical events of the Jacobite Revolution where there was competition for the throne between the Stuart and Hannoverian dynasties. There is also the regular usage of the terms 'bureaucrat' and 'Sir Humphries' as forms of abuse, again seeking to conjure up visions of inefficiency and self-interest (as was promoted by the British television comedy series *Yes Minister*).

It is worth bearing in mind here that bodies such as English Heritage and Historic Scotland are applying legislation and policies which *belong to government* (rather than themselves), and which are adopted after significant levels of public consultation and Ministerial involvement. Yet this fact is frequently ignored by the media and the public, and it is sometimes ignored by the politicians themselves who perhaps see greater political advantage in attacking their own civil servants and legislation than defending them. Similarly, the legislative systems and the civil servants applying them are accountable insofar as the decisions reached can be tested at public local inquiry, through complaints systems and through the Government Ombudsman. Yet the issue with any regulatory system is that if the decisions reached are not liked, they become highly vulnerable to attack using alternative discourses and challenging rhetorical devices. While on the face of it, the use of such terminology can appear both amusing and superficial, once picked up by the media these can and do lead to significant reputational damage and adverse shifts in public opinion. This, in turn, can lead to the loss of political and financial support, even where the criticisms underlying the rhetoric are partial or misplaced (see Sparrow 2000, 2008).

CHALLENGES FROM WITHIN

Before concluding, I want to look briefly at the idea of the AHD itself. There is a temptation in the CRM literature to portray the AHD as both monolithic and static. There is frequently also an underlying assumption that legislation and policy can be made equivalent with particular day-to-day actions in a deterministic fashion. That is to say, once an AHD is in place, individual actors are constrained to act in an identical manner, leading to consistency of approach and outcome over time and place. Ironically, such determinism fits more comfortably within a modernist perspective rather than a post-modern philosophical perspective that most writings on AHD adopt. This is perhaps best evidenced by the *lack* of research and publication on the *practice* of heritage management on a day-to-day basis. Instead, there is a repeated focus on the adoption (and wording) of legislation and policy. Indeed, in seeking to explore the 'practice' of heritage management at conferences and through publication, I have been accused of 'looking for theory in what is purely the practical business of heritage management' and 'doing dirty laundry in public.'

The reality is, however, far from a picture of a monolithic discourse at play. As we have seen, discourses, and the mechanisms that embody them, are subject to challenge from without—through political pressure, through the media, and in some cases through the courts. But perhaps more importantly, dominant discourses are also challenged from within—this may happen within disciplines and professions (or within specific sectors of these), within specific organizations, and in some cases even *within* individual departments within organizations. Whatever the original intentions, individuals and groups responsible for implementing legislation and policy on a day-to-day basis can, and do, influence both when and how legislation and policy is applied. Internal regulation mechanisms within organizations and monitoring by external bodies such as the Ombudsman or Parliamentary committees seek to reduce this variability. However, the point to be made here is that an AHD should not be regarded as monolithic and static, but instead as a highly fluid and dynamic web of competing discourses in a highly energized and tensioned relationship (Cooper 2013).

Another example here might be helpful. Bodies such as English Heritage, Historic Scotland, and Cadw are likely to employ staff who come from a variety of different disciplines. Among others, these might include archaeologists, architectural historians, landscape historians, architects, and planners. Each group will have been trained within their own discipline and inculcated with its particular history and principles. Inevitably, this means that in certain types of case, there may be significant differences in view and approach in different groups. In both England and Scotland, for example, the very significant differences of views within and between the state organizations on the acceptability or otherwise of castle restoration seem to reflect the training and background of the individuals and groups involved—at times almost irrespective of the actual legislation and policy. In a recent paper discussing the history of castle and towerhouse restoration in Scotland, Diane Watters (2011: 172) wrote:

> By the end of the twentieth century the ideological and heritage debate concerning the pros and cons of castle restoration was quickly gathering force. In 2001, a government heritage policy document, *The Conservation of Architectural Ancient Monuments in Scotland: Guidance on Principles*, written by Richard Fawcett, was published by Historic Scotland. It set down clearly and uncompromisingly the current state policy on conservation and the restoration of monuments for reuse, emphasizing the resurgence of the prestige of SPAB orthodoxy among some within Historic Scotland, in striking contrast to the flexibility once possible under Walker's regime.

One wonders about the intentions of this paper, and its charged statement is certainly worthy of a more detailed rhetorical analysis than is possible here. Suffice it to say, the author does not acknowledge that the document referred to applied to *ancient monuments*, where the philosophy underlying the legislation and policy has always been to *preserve as found* (but where adaptive re-use schemes have continued to be allowed where the alternative is the loss of the structure), whereas David Walker dealt with *listed buildings*, where the philosophy is to seek to keep buildings in sympathetic use.

Despite appearances to the contrary, establishing a position on specific pieces of casework is frequently a negotiated process within organizations or within the heritage sector, seeking to resolve competing discourses. In the same way that an Authorized Heritage Discourse comes under pressure on a daily basis from without the heritage sector, *the same applies internally*, leading to common issues in terms of maintaining consistency of approach across time and geographical area.

CONCLUSIONS

For those involved in CRM, to be successful it is necessary for there to be accepted definitions of heritage assets, effective value-systems, accessible databases, appropriate organizational infrastructures and, above all, well-trained and knowledgeable professionals. However, as Gerard Baldwin Brown recognized in 1905, these are not sufficient, and public support is also crucial for any activity relying on government-based systems of legislation, policy, and funding. Public support is hard-won and easily lost for regulatory bodies, particularly in a world where a story of the 'little person' or the local community fighting against a 'faceless bureaucratic machine' is likely to attract significant media interest.

While it is tempting to see the world of CRM as a story of a monolithic and unchanging Authorized Heritage Discourse, with legislation and policy being applied repetitively and consistently week-after-week, the reality is far from this. The AHD is itself constantly under attack both internally and externally and renews itself on a daily basis. A key weapon for those wanting to reduce the impact of the AHD is the use of rhetoric as part of growing public and political support for their own discourse, and the power of the alternative discourse becomes more powerful if specific arguments can be aligned with broader discourses. Hence, we see sustainability, neoliberalism, and general market economics being used to influence not only day-to-day decisions but also the broader frameworks within which decisions are taken (Cooper 2010b). This is not, however, to be regarded as exceptional or quirky. It is the very stuff of regulation in the twenty-first century, and if we wish CRM to continue providing an effective basis for protecting and promoting our historic environment, we would do well to spend more time as a discipline studying and improving our engagement with the theory and practice of discourse and rhetoric and also to undertake far more research on the *practice* of heritage management.

NOTES

1. On April 1, 2015, English Heritage was split into two separate organizations. The statutory, regulatory, and grant-aid functions are now carried out by the newly named Historic England, while their historic properties-in-care are now managed by a new charitable trust that retained the name English Heritage. In Scotland, on October 1, 2015, Historic Scotland and the Royal Commission on the Ancient and Historical Monuments of Scotland will merge into a single organization named Historic Environment Scotland.

2. See http://www.historic-scotland.gov.uk/rowallan-pli-chap1and2-2.pdf, accessed June 18, 2012.

3. See HRH The Prince of Wales 1984, speech to the Royal Institute of British Architects, available online at http://www.princeofwales.gov.uk/media/speeches /speech-hrh-the-prince-of-wales-the-150th-anniversary-of-the-royal-institute-of, accessed 18 June 2012; also http://www.scribd.com/doc/17563341/Birmingham-Central

-Library-Should-it-Stay-or-Should-it-Go for more information on the debate about its preservation or demolition, accessed June 18, 2012.

4. *The Scotsman Newspaper*, 3 September 2008. Available online at http://www .scotsman.com/news/scotland/top-stories/city-u-turn-over-double-glazing-ban-in -the-frame-1-1272088, accessed April 27, 2014.

REFERENCES

Baldwin Brown, Gerard. 1905. *The Care of Ancient Monuments*. Cambridge: Cambridge University Press.

Billig, Michael. 1996. *Arguing and Thinking: A Rhetorical Approach to Social Psychology*. Cambridge: Cambridge University Press.

Carman, John, and Marie Louise S. Sorenson. 2009. "Heritage Studies: An Outline." In *Heritage Studies: Methods and Approaches*, ed. Marie Louise S. Sorenson and John Carman, 11–28. London: Routledge.

Champion, Timothy. 1996. "Protecting the Monuments: Archaeological Legislation from the 1882 Act to PPG 16." In *Preserving the Past: The Rise of Heritage in Modern Britain*, ed. Michael Hunter, 38–56. Stroud, UK: Alan Sutton.

Cooper, Malcolm A. 2005. "Exploring Gaskell's Legacy: Competing Constructions of the Industrial Historic Environment in England's North West." In *Industrial Archaeology: Future Directions*, ed. Eleanor Casella and James Symonds, 155–73. New York, NY: Springer. http://dx.doi.org/10.1007/0-387-22831-4_8.

Cooper, Malcolm A. 2008. "This Is Not a Monument: Rhetorical Destruction and the Social Context of Cultural Resource Management." *Public Archaeology* 7 (1): 17–30. http://dx.doi.org/10.1179/175355308X305997.

Cooper, Malcolm A. 2010a. "Future? What Future." In *Scotland: Building for the Future Transactions*, ed. Malcolm Cooper and Deborah Mays, 74–83. Edinburgh: Historic Scotland.

Cooper, Malcolm A. 2010b. "Protecting our Past: Political Philosophy, Regulation and Heritage Management in England and Scotland." *Historic Environment* 1 (2): 143–59. http://dx.doi.org/10.1179/175675010X12817059865961.

Cooper, Malcolm A. 2013. "Competition and the Development of Authorised Heritage Discourses in a Re-Emergent Scottish Nation." In *Training and Practice for Modern Day Archaeologists*, ed. John Jamieson and James Eogan, 87–104. New York, NY: Springer. http://dx.doi.org/10.1007/978-1-4614-5529-5_6.

Cornwell, Tim. 2011. *Modern Need Not Mean Monstrous, The Scotsman Newspaper*, 19 May 2011. http://www.scotsman.com/news/tim-cornwell-modern-need-not-mean -monstrous-1-1649163. Accessed April 27, 2014.

Fairclough, Norman. 1989. *Language and Power*. London: Longman.

Foster, Andy. 2005. *Birmingham*. New Haven, CT: Yale University Press.

Geoghegan, John. 2012. "Cabinet Singles Out Planning Systems as 'Blockages to Growth.'" *Planning Magazine*, February 29, 2012.

Harvey, David. 2005. *A Brief History of Neoliberalism*. Oxford: Oxford University Press.

Kellner, Hans. 1989. *Language and Historical Representation*. Madison: University of Wisconsin Press.

Mayne, Alan. 1993. *The Imagined Slum*. Leicester, UK: Leicester University Press.

Mayne, Alan, and Tim Murray, eds. 2001. *The Archaeology of Urban Landscapes: Explorations in Slumlands*. Cambridge: Cambridge University Press.

McLaughlin, Kathleen, Stephen P. Osborne, and Ewan Ferlie. 2002. *New Public Management: Current Trends and Future Prospects*. London: Routledge.

Miller, Keith. 2003. "Making the Grade: Birmingham New Street Signal Box." *The Telegraph*, August 2. http://www.telegraph.co.uk/property/3315674/Making-the -grade-Birmingham-New-Street-signal-box.html. Accessed April 27, 2014.

Rose, Nikolas, and Peter Miller. 1992. "Political Power Beyond the State: Problematics of Government." *British Journal of Sociology* 43 (2): 173–205. http:// dx.doi.org/10.2307/591464.

Smith, Laurajane. 2004. *Archaeological Theory and the Politics of Cultural Heritage*. London: Routledge. http://dx.doi.org/10.4324/9780203307991.

Smith, Laurajane. 2006. *Uses of Heritage*. London: Routledge.

Sparrow, Malcolm K. 2000. *The Regulatory Craft*. Washington, DC: Brookings Institution Press.

Sparrow, Malcolm K. 2008. *The Character of Harms*. Cambridge: Cambridge University Press.

Sudjic, Dean. 2001. "A Thoroughly Modernizing Mayor." *The Observer*, July 8. http:// www.theguardian.com/education/2001/jul/08/arts.highereducation. Accessed April 27, 2014.

Tierney, Alan. 2010. "Sustainability and Historic Buildings." *Country Life*, September 28. http://www.countrylife.co.uk/articles/sustainability-and-historic-buildings -20898. Accessed April 27, 2014.

Waterton, Emma. 2010. *Politics, Policy, and the Discourses of Heritage in Britain*. Basingstoke, UK: Palgrave Macmillan. http://dx.doi.org/10.1057/9780230292383.

Watters, Diane. 2011. "Castle Reoccupation in the Twentieth Century." In *Scotland's Castle Culture*, ed. Audrey Dakin, Miles Glendinning, and Aonghus MacKechnie, 143–72. Edinburgh: John Donald.

Intangible Heritage **11**

What Brain Dead Persons Can Tell Us
about (Intangible) Cultural Heritage

Klaus Zehbe

Richard Rorty's (1989) pragmatic philosophy of language asserts that no world exists separately from how people describe the world. My approach to the rhetoric and redescription of cultural heritage builds from this philosophy, and I use Rorty's notion of redescription to draw attention to *processes* of change in cultural heritage. Central to my argument is the claim proposed by several contributors in this volume (chapters by Adams, Rico, Cooper, and Baird) that experts, or rather expert communities, provide the vocabularies and standards for describing the world.

Using Ludwik Fleck's (1981) sociological theory of knowledge, I track the work of expert communities in developing the concept of 'intangible heritage' by showing how a particular heritage vocabulary or 'thought style' (Fleck's term) evolved historically alongside the institutionalization of expert communities in the framework of UNESCO's standard setting instruments. Smith (2006: 11) has saliently critiqued institutionalized "power and knowledge claims of technical and aesthetic experts" in the field of heritage in her concept of the 'Authorized Heritage Discourse' (AHD).

Taking an ironist's stance—a stance that acknowledges both the contingency of vocabularies to describe the world as well as the contingency of my own positioning toward such vocabularies (cf. Rorty 1989:

DOI: 10.5876/9781607323846.c011

73–95)—my approach to 'intangible cultural heritage' temporarily unbinds the concept from "final vocabularies" (Rorty 1989: 73) entrenched in the AHD. Rather than attempting a redescription of intangible heritage vocabularies from the ground up (i.e., through the presentation of fresh data from fieldwork), I use rhetoric and redescription as a heuristic strategy to expand heritage vocabularies. Particularly, I tactically exploit the redescriptive capacity of rhetorical devices, here metaphor and allegory, for creating new vocabularies. My ultimate aim is to tap into the creative, future-oriented potentials of heritage proposed by this volume (see Chapter 1). In order to do this, I examine the concept of 'intangible heritage' ironically through the concept of 'brain death.'

BRAIN DEATH AS A RHETORICAL DEVICE

My strategic use of the concept of 'brain death' as an allegory or extended metaphor for intangible heritage addresses three conceptual aims. First, the concept of 'brain death' allows a concise exploration of the work of expert communities in constituting heritage vocabularies, which I undertake through Fleck's (1981) sociological theory of 'thought styles' and 'thought collectives.'

Second, by linking the medically and ethically contested concept of 'brain death' to intangible heritage, I wish to denaturalize understandings of intangible cultural heritage as *living* heritage (cf. UNESCO 2014). Concomitant to the notion of living heritage are the ideas that it is embodied (cf. Logan 2007: 33; Ruggles and Silverman 2009) or that it is carried by people (cf. UNESCO 2007). Drawing on the bioethical deliberations of the Japanese philosopher Masahiro Morioka (1989) on brain death, I hold that neither brain death nor intangible heritage can be *found in* or *carried by* a human body as a methodical proxy for the person. Rather, these concepts unfold in and through the relations of people.

Third, brain death as a trope for intangible cultural heritage renders a wealth of new information about the relationships of people with regard to intangible cultural heritage, particularly on account of the tensions and ambiguities surrounding brain death as a phenomenon. The allegory of brain death, qualified as a 'thought style,' thus offers a detailed, sociologically and historically reflected approach to the concept of 'intangible cultural heritage,' which in turn opens up a different theoretical perspective on the very concept of 'heritage.'

Brain Death as a Thought Style

What may literally appear as an oxymoron, does provide a useful starting point by shifting the perspective of the argument. In the following, I am not concerned with the state of a brain that thinks, but with those who think about the state of the brain. That is, I distinguish between the speculative physiological condition of a dead brain and the medical concept of 'brain death' in the framework of Fleck's sociology of knowledge. By analogy, my present epistemological discussion is not about properties of 'intangible heritage' and inducing theories about the ontological status of this type of heritage, but about those who describe properties of heritage as scientific facts and on what kind of basis.

The Scientific Fact of Death

Fleck (1981) in his sociological theory of knowledge proposes that scientific facts are constructed by experts from the mutual influence of concepts at a given time in history. He further holds that the relationships of concepts share a particular stylistic bond, which determines what is possible for the experts to think and take as a fact. Fleck (1981: 9) calls this stylistic bond a 'thought style.' Experts so joined by a stylistic bond are a 'thought collective,' which is the carrier of the thought style (1981: 39). In order to characterize the thought style of 'brain death', I shall map out the medical facts about death.

From today's medical knowledge, prolonged failure of heartbeat and breathing will irreversibly disintegrate all biological systems of the human organism and will lead to the inevitable decomposition of the body (Müller 2011: 3). Irreversible cardiac arrest and permanent ceasing of respiration thus cause death. Coldness, stiffness (*rigor mortis*), and livid skin color (*livor mortis*) are perceivable signs of the disintegration of the various systems of the organism and considered reliable signs that death has occurred. Prior to 1952, cardiac death and brain death happened simultaneously or shortly after another. The first successful use of the cardio-pulmonary-bypass or heart-lung-machine in 1952, however, marked a turning point in the definition of death.

While the heartbeat is not controlled by the brain, breathing is, and severe damage to the brain can lead to the cessation of all spontaneous breathing, resulting in cardiac death. However, with the use of the cardio-pulmonary-bypass the heart and lung functions of persons with brain damage can be stabilized for an extended time. Through the heart-lung-machine, a distinction between persons with brain damage became historically observable: in 1959, the French neurologists Pierre Mollaret and Michel Goulon noted people with brain damage who were extremely unresponsive to neural stimuli. They described these people to be in a state beyond coma, or *coma dépassé* (Mollaret and Goulon 1959, cited in The President's Council on Bioethics 2008: 3).

The Ad Hoc Committee of the Harvard Medical School to Examine the Definition of Brain Death (1968) took further advances in intensive medical care provision as its cue to examine Mollaret and Goulon's state of extreme coma. Confronted with practical, legal, and ethical issues for hospital staff (e.g., people with irreversible coma blocking beds in intensive care units, and removing organs from comatose patients for transplantation) the Committee redescribed Mollaret and Goulon's state of extreme coma as 'brain death.' For the Committee, "An organ, brain or otherwise, that no longer functions and has no possibility of functioning again is for all practical purposes dead" (1968: 85). In order to assess the state of 'brain death', the Committee developed criteria (1968: 85–86) by which it defines how to practically ascertain the state of a "*permanently* nonfunctioning" brain: a person with a permanently nonfunctioning brain shall no longer respond to intense nerve or pain stimuli, nor show reflexes, spontaneous movement, or spontaneous breathing. Absence of brain waves in electroencephalography is proposed as a final confirmatory test. For Morioka (1989: 12), the absence of brainwaves in electroencephalography in particular "is considered evidence that the cerebrum, which governs the ability to think and have emotions, is not working."

Physicians infer from this irreversible state of coma that the 'person'—as the locus of memory, thought, and feeling—has ceased to exist, i.e., that the person is deceased. Consequently, 'brain death' is defined as a new category of death (Ad Hoc Committee of the Harvard Medical School to Examine the Definition of Brain Death 1968: 85). However, a person fallen into the state of brain death in intensive medical care does not exhibit the perceivable signs of death (i.e., cardiac arrest, cessation of respiration, coldness, *livor mortis*, or *rigor mortis*).

THE THOUGHT STYLE OF BRAIN DEATH

While the condition of brain death is contested on both medical and ethical grounds (cf. Müller 2011: 4–6; The President's Council on Bioethics 2008: 38–45), especially regarding the question of what makes the human body an integrated system, the above description of the condition of brain death offers processes that can be used to illustrate Fleck's sociological theory of thought styles. In *Genesis and Development of a Scientific Fact*, Fleck (1981) describes four stages by which a thought style develops:

Original Observation of the Phenomenon

First, a state of extreme coma becomes observable through a combination of advances in medical practice and technology, particularly the first successful use of the heart-lung-machine in 1952. Mollaret and Goulon (1959) describe the phenomenon as a *coma dépassé*, i.e., a previously known state (*coma*) to which a qualification (*dépassé*) is added to indicate the unknown conditions beyond the state of coma. At this initial stage, observation is still imprecise and the phenomenon not clearly framed (cf. Fleck 1981: 94–95).

Subsequent Stylization of the Phenomenon

Second, after a stage of further inquiry and clarification, the medical concept of 'brain death' is formulated to address recurring questions that arise from the clinical phenomenon of "individuals whose heart continues to beat but whose brain is irreversibly damaged" (Ad Hoc Committee of the Harvard Medical School to Examine the Definition of Brain Death 1968: 85). The concept of 'brain death' both describes and standardizes various experiences according to an accepted pattern and state of knowledge. Fleck, using an architectural metaphor, calls these patterns 'thought styles' (1981: 9).

According to Fleck (1981: 19), thought styles are in principle incomplete and depend on the discovery of new features for their development. He cautions that for any concept formulated within a thought style "the current concept does not constitute the logically or essentially only possible solution" (1981: 22). These concepts—while incomplete—emerge only "through organized cooperative research, supported by popular knowledge and continuing over several generations," and further, "Many very solidly established scientific facts are undeniably linked, in their development, to prescientific, somewhat hazy, related proto-ideas or pre-ideas, even though such links cannot be substantiated" (1981: 22–23). Nevertheless, these proto-ideas form associations with the concept, which can become in the course of the concept's historical development active associations, i.e., dominant and generally determining for the concept, or remain passive and secondary until some new feature is discovered (1981: 10).

The scientific fact of 'brain death' can be understood in Fleck's theory as an expression of a particular medical thought style that combined the proto-ideas of biological death resulting from cardiac death with a psychological concept of the brain as the locus of the individual's memory, thought, and emotion. The thought style further organizes different phenomena in advanced medical care—such as unresponsiveness to stimuli, lack of reflexes, and absence of spontaneous movement and spontaneous breathing—into a coherent pattern: 'brain death' (Ad Hoc Committee of the Harvard Medical School to Examine the Definition of Brain Death 1968: 85–86). Through this standardization or stylization the condition of brain death is established as a scientific fact (Fleck 1981: 83). But, it is important to note that for Fleck a 'scientific fact' is only valid "in a particular thought style, in a particular thought collective" (1981: 39). Fleck hereby emphasizes that scientific facts have no validity outside of the vocabularies that led to their construction (cf. Fleck 1981: 1). Here Fleck's idea of thought styles and his emphasis on communication in the construction of facts bears close resemblance to Rorty's notion of vocabularies to describe the world and Rorty's philosophical claim that "only sentences can be true, and that human beings make truths by making languages in which to phrase sentences" (Rorty 1989: 9).

COLLECTIVE CARRIERS OF THE PHENOMENON

Third, the concept of 'brain death' is formulated by a group of specifically trained experts who exchange thoughts about practices and knowledge in their field of expertise. Fleck calls such groups of people 'thought collectives' (1981: 39). By way of example, the Ad Hoc Committee of the Harvard Medical School to Examine the Definition of Brain Death (1968: 85) was composed of thirteen members: ten medical doctors, one law specialist, one theologian, and one historian of science. People in the thought collective work to develop practices and ideas in line with the accepted methods and epistemologies of their respective field of expertise, i.e., within their respective accepted thought style. The thought collective thus becomes the "'carrier' for the historical development of any given field of thought, as well as for the given stock of knowledge and level of culture," i.e., for its particular thought style (Fleck 1981: 39). In the present example of brain death, the thought collective is largely made up from physicians and their field of thought revolves around advanced medical care in hospitals. How these experts address questions in relation to brain dead persons in intensive care characterizes the 'style' of their thought style.

INEVITABLE INSTITUTIONALIZATION OF THE PHENOMENON

Fourth, the concept of 'brain death' addresses and regulates concomitant questions in the wider social sphere such as the allocation of limited resources for intensive medical care treatment, at which point the heart-lung-machine should be turned off, and at which point organs may be removed from comatose patients for transplantation. These questions arise from the very specialized practices of those experts that originally produced the phenomenon.

Thus, the condition of brain death can only come into existence through highly specialized practices of experts who have similar training as those experts who defined the concept of 'brain death' in the first place. Only these specially trained experts have the medical tools and skills to diagnose the condition. Consequently, the phenomenon almost exclusively falls into the cognizance and responsibility of these experts.

THE THOUGHT STYLE OF INTANGIBLE CULTURAL HERITAGE

Fleck's theory of knowledge, as shown through the example of brain death, aids in understanding how experts construct scientific facts and how, from these facts, they create vocabularies for describing the world. Turning now to intangible heritage, I suggest that Fleck's theory provides a sociologically and historically finer-grained analysis for the genesis of the concept of 'intangible cultural heritage' in UNESCO's 2003 *Convention for the Safeguarding of the Intangible Cultural Heritage* (hereafter 2003 *Convention*) than UNESCO's own extensive documentation of the *Convention*'s genesis. In addition to UNESCO's (2012) documentation, several publications comment on concepts and developments at various stages of the process (cf. Seeger 2001; Seitel 2001; Hafstein 2007; Aikawa-Faure 2009; Blake 2009). In sum, these provide insight into the historical development of a particular thought collective and its thought style. The four development phases identified previously in the discussion of brain death, i.e., original observation, subsequent stylization, collective carriers, and inevitable institutionalization, will be revisited in the course of the argument.

INITIAL FRAMES OF OBSERVATION: PROTO-IDEAS OF INTANGIBLE CULTURAL HERITAGE

The development of the concept of 'intangible cultural heritage' rests on several proto-ideas about heritage. An etymological interpretation of the term 'heritage' offers an approach to lay open such proto-ideas. From these proto-ideas, later shifts in the meaning of 'heritage' can be evaluated. The *Oxford English Dictionary* (*OED Online* 2012a) defines heritage as that "which has been or may be inherited; any property, and esp. land, which devolves by right of inheritance" (*OED Online* 2012a, s.v. "heritage"). The etymology of the English word goes back to the Latin *heres* (heir). For the purpose of identifying significant layers of meaning, it is useful to shed some light on the framework in which *heres* as well as *heredium* (that which has been or may be inherited) appear as categories.

In Roman civil law, based on the Law of the Twelve Tablets, the legal term *suus heres* (one's own or proper heir) denotes the legitimate successor of the head of the family (*paterfamilias*). The term *heredium* presupposes in Roman legal thought a link between the legitimate succession of offspring within a family and the transference of property and duties. Such duties typically included the maintenance of the family grave (*sepulchrum familiare*) and worship of the *sacra familiaria*, i.e., the protective family deities or deified ancestors (Kaser 1971: 98).

In Roman thought 'heritage' is a totality, which has both material and immaterial dimensions. The material part of the *heredium* is the family's land, which is retained whole through primogeniture. The family grave on the property testifies to the sole heir's rightful claim to land. The Roman *heredium* thus ensures the future economic and legal viability of family property. The immaterial dimension included the duty of the successors to worship the family ancestors. This was done to guarantee the continued well being of the family. The Roman concept of 'heritage' thus primarily aimed at the continuity of family life and family property, notions that hold particular resonance with UNESCO's interventions in the field of heritage.

Subsequent Stylization: Con-Fusion of Monument, Territory, and Nation

In later Europe, many dimensions of the Roman *heredium* were lost. The proto-idea of family graves as material heritage became dominant on account of two particular historic moments in European history. As a consequence of these developments, 'heritage' came to signify almost exclusively the monuments and the landed property of the social and political elites (cf. *OED Online* 2012a, s.v. "heritage").

Lowenthal (1997: 63–68) in his book *The Heritage Crusade and the Spoils of History* identifies the French Revolution as one important moment, where "public possession [of chateaux and cathedrals, archives and antiquities, paintings and royal tombs] soon raised these relics from reminders of aristocratic rule to emblems of an inclusive national saga" (1997: 63). The other moment he sees in the gradual devolution of hereditary property of landed elites into collective or state property in Great Britain at the end of the nineteenth and beginning of the twentieth centuries (1997: 64–68). For Lowenthal, both processes contributed significantly to national 'heritage' movements. In Britain, this movement led in 1877 to the foundation of the Society for the Protection of Ancient Buildings (SPAB), a society that focuses on architectural conservation.

Lowenthal's description of the origins of the SPAB can be interpreted in Fleck's theory as the historic stylization of the concept of 'heritage' in a particular thought style by a thought collective that accumulated expertise in material or architectural heritage. Smith's (2006: 17–21) reflection on these historic processes also suggests a specific thought style and thought collective in cultural heritage. The AHD combines the notion of 'heritage' as a territory-based monument with a community of experts specially trained or skilled for the care of such monuments. The AHD thus takes—in the words of Smith (2006: 11)—"its cue from the grand narratives of nation and class on the one hand, and technical expertise and aesthetic judgement on the other."

While these processes and notions inform the current concept of 'heritage' in the AHD, it is the institutionalization of heritage experts in UNESCO's framework of standard setting instruments that originally shaped and still significantly shapes the concept of 'intangible cultural heritage.' UNESCO's success in the field of international heritage conservation, spearheaded by the 1972 *Convention Concerning the Protection of the World Cultural and Natural Heritage,* firmly established UNESCO's heritage interventions within the framework of international policy coordination. This institutionalization, as I shall demonstrate in the following, is largely responsible for the stylization of the concept of 'intangible cultural heritage' in terms of a particular historically contingent thought style about heritage.

COLLECTIVE CARRIERS: HERITAGE WANTED—DEAD OR ALIVE

Lowenthal (1997: ix) observes that "All at once heritage is everywhere—in the news, in the movies, in the marketplace." While he asserts that "heritage is as old as humanity" (1997: 1), he makes out—at the time of writing—a particular 'cult' or 'heritage crusade,' which "ravage[s] the past in the very act of revering it" (1997: xii). Interestingly, Lowenthal's remarks on the ubiquity of 'heritage' coincide more or less with the appearance of the following definition for 'heritage' in the 1993 draft additions to the OED: "Characterized by or pertaining to the preservation or exploitation of local and national features of historical, cultural or scenic interest, esp. as tourist attractions" (*OED Online* 2012a, s.v. "heritage"). In the same year, UNESCO reoriented its activities in the area of 'intangible culture' and renamed its program "Intangible Cultural Heritage" (UNESCO

1993). Concurrent with this new perspective, UNESCO convened from 1995 to 1999 eight regional seminars to evaluate the 1989 *Recommendation on the Safeguarding of Traditional Culture and Folklore* (hereafter 1989 *Recommendation*). While all eight seminars stressed the need to safeguard traditional culture and folklore, the regional seminars for Latin America and the Caribbean (Mexico City, 1997), Africa (Accra, 1999), and the Pacific (Noumea, 1999) objected to the use of the term 'folklore' for traditional practices and knowledge on account of the term's felt pejorative connotations (cf. Seeger 2001: 39–41).

The recommendations of the regional seminars mark a particular moment in the historic deployment of the term 'heritage' in the field of traditional practices and knowledge, which coincided with a more general concern or need for 'heritage' at the time—both tangible and intangible, dead and alive. At the same time, the recommendations mark a turn away from the concept of folklore as the "traditional beliefs, legends, and customs, current among the common people" (*OED Online* 2012b, s.v. "folklore"), toward a particular thought style about practices and knowledge as 'heritage' that aspires to be on a par with Western notions of material heritage (cf. Seeger 2001: 223). Combined with UNESCO's other concurrent activities, this led to the development of the 2003 *Convention* (for an account of UNESCO's activities from a perspective close to UNESCO, see Aikawa-Faure 2009).

Institutionalization: The Thought Style
of Intangible Cultural Heritage

In the preliminary discussions for the 2003 *Convention*, the anthropologist and folklorist Peter Seitel (2001: 8) specifies that:

> operationally, one systematically comprehends tradition as living people: those identified by their fellow community members as knowledgeable; those who can specify what is good and bad in particular instances of traditional processes, what is old and new, central and peripheral. It is people who answer the myriad of questions that can be conceived about a given set of practices and perform those practices and innovate on them.

For Seitel, human practice can be reconstructed by ethnographic methods. Core assumptions of ethnographic methods are, on the one hand, that people are embedded in communities with locally specific behavior and meanings, and, on the other, that traditions can be reconstructed by asking authoritative individuals questions about specific practices or things, prioritizing the individual's account of these practices and things.

The notion of authoritative individuals echoes the Roman concept of *aucto-ritas*, i.e., authority in the sense of the social attestation of exemplary character, specialist knowledge, public leadership as well as including the notion of authorship. All of these attributes seem important in the context of the 2003 *Convention* since such attributes link the authoritative individual and her or his knowledge and practices back to the community, which recognizes the individual as authoritative.

Janet Blake (2009), who worked on legal aspects of the 2003 *Convention*, emphasizes that the community has a special status in the *Convention*, due to the *Convention's* different articulation of 'safeguarding' compared to previous UNESCO instruments for the 'protection' of cultural heritage. While the concept of safeguarding does build on the 1989 *Recommendation*, the 2003 *Convention* takes a significant departure by presenting safeguarding as "fostering the conditions within which it [the intangible cultural heritage] can continue to be created, maintained and transmitted" (Blake 2009: 51). She continues:

> Since the community is the essential context for this, it must imply the continued capability of the cultural communities themselves to practise and transmit their ICH [intangible cultural heritage]. Hence, the community is placed at the centre of this Convention rather than the heritage itself and the safeguarding of ICH must take into account the wider human, social and cultural contexts in which the enactment of ICH occurs. (2009: 51)

Nevertheless, legal frameworks seem ill equipped to deal with such a focus on community, as legal systems historically emphasize individuals. Blake (2009: 53) elaborates that in international legal discourse the

> classical theoretical position is that some 'individual' rights (such as the enjoyment of culture) presuppose the existence of a community of individuals and the underlying assumption is that the rights of groups are taken care of automatically by protecting individuals' rights. Moreover, individuals do not exist *in abstracto* but, in reality, are defined by their membership of certain (cultural, ethnic, linguistic, etc.) groups.

It becomes apparent from Blake's comments on the 2003 *Convention* that the concept of 'intangible cultural heritage' has a methodological tendency toward objectifying human practices and expressions (for further discussion see also Hafstein 2007: 93–95). In effect, this tendency naturalizes specific assumptions about intangible cultural heritage, most notably that the living body is the *locus* of performance of and knowledge about intangible cultural heritage. The living individual as *locus* of rights and inalienable properties is both a historically contingent concept and one that is crucial to international legal discourse, such as that found within UNESCO's standard setting instruments. The concept of 'intangible cultural heritage'—as put forward by the 2003 *Convention*—rather than being a corrective or a challenge to the AHD (cf. Smith and Akagawa 2009: 3), I see to be part of the same authorizing processes.

BEYOND THE AHD: THE REDESCRIPTIVE POTENTIAL OF METAPHOR

Like Mollaret and Goulon's initial observation of a state 'beyond coma,' the relational character of 'intangible cultural heritage' does not easily fit into the institutionalized thought style of 'heritage' as something that could be ascribed to living or dead entities. While arguably a different matter, the allegory of 'brain death' unfolds a redescriptive potential by dislocating notions of the individual as carrier and displacing the living body as the locus of knowledge and performance of 'intangible cultural heritage.' Morioka's (1989) bioethical deliberations on persons affected by brain death highlights the contested and ambiguous nature of 'brain death' as a phenomenon that emerges in the space between discursive oppositions such as inside/outside, living/dead, or individual/group. The phenomenon of brain death, rather than being a fact, should be considered as a field that unfolds in and through the different interactions of people in relation to the phenomenon.

Brain Death as a Social Field

Morioka (1989: 3) begins his book *Brain Dead Person* (*Nōshi no Hito*) by noting that most theories about 'brain death' look at the phenomenon from a physician's perspective. This illustrates Fleck's theory of thought styles, in that the phenomenon of 'brain death' is predominantly described by a particular thought collective that has historically developed alongside medical advances (cf. Morioka 1989: 11). Morioka, however, questions the assumption that the phenomenon of brain death is adequately described through a doctor's perspective alone. For him, the phenomenon of brain death cannot be understood from the assumed "existence of a dead brain" (1989: 6), but has to be seen from the various social processes that unfold and revolve around the person who has entered the 'state of brain death.' Importantly, brain death unfolds for Morioka as an encounter of different living people with different relationships to the brain dead person (1989: 13).

He describes significant elements in these relationships on four levels (1989: 5–6, 32–38). There are usually three categories of people who directly encounter the brain dead person in an intensive care unit: "doctors who perform the resuscitation of the brain, nurses who care for the patient, and the family that watches the patient from outside the ICU (Intensive Care Unit)" (1989: 5). On a fourth level, administrative hospital staff and health insurance managers usually do not encounter brain dead persons directly; however, they, too, deal with brain dead persons, though on a more abstract level.

Morioka (1989: 13) proposes that the phenomenon of brain death changes according to the various positions and roles of people surrounding the brain dead person. For doctors, the concept of brain death is framed by medical and technical questions about the inner state of the person's brain. For nurses in the intensive care unit, the brain dead person is foremost a human body that requires care. For the family, the brain dead person "is the irreplaceable person with whom they have lived until recently . . . with whom they have shared their lives and history" (1989: 6). For hospital managers and health insurance representatives, the brain dead person causes costs and ties up staff, equipment, and resources simply by occupying a bed in an intensive care unit (1989: 32–38).

Focusing in particular on the family's experience encountering a person who does not exhibit the perceivable signs of death, i.e., stiffness, lividness, coldness, cessation of breathing and heartbeat, Morioka proposes that the family members do not face an inner state of the person's brain, nor his or her body, but a "'person' who has entered the state of brain death" (Morioka 1989: 6). On account of these different experiences for each party concerned, Morioka (1989: 9) elaborates:

'Brain death' is not found in the brain of a 'person whose brain ceased functioning,' but in the realm of human relationships surrounding this person. What we should consider is 'the realm of brain death,' or 'brain death as a field.' In other words, the essence of 'brain death' can be found in the relationship between people. The 'brain death' viewed by the doctor, when he/she looks inside the brain of a 'person whose brain ceased functioning,' should be no more than one aspect of 'brain death.'

INTERPRETING THE METAPHOR: WHAT BRAIN DEAD PERSONS CAN TELL US ABOUT (INTANGIBLE) CULTURAL HERITAGE

What, then, does brain death tell us about heritage? Examined through Fleck's sociological theory of knowledge, neither 'brain death' nor 'intangible cultural heritage' can be theorized as ontological entities independent of their historic contexts and the people who maintain intellectual exchanges on the respective topics.

The true epistemic potential of the metaphor, however, unfolds in Morioka's argument that the perception of 'brain death' changes depending on what kind of interactions people have in relation to the phenomenon. I warrant that similar changes occur in the perception of heritage, particularly in UNESCO's concept of 'World Heritage,' depending on whether one interacts with 'heritage' phenomena as a scholar, manager, resident, or diplomat. Similar to the 'brain dead person' who does not show signs of death, 'heritage'—either 'dead'/ tangible or 'alive'/intangible—does not exhibit signs of its heritage status. The signs of heritage are ascribed by highly specialized thought collectives or 'epistemic communities' (cf. Haas 1992). It is the work of these institutionalized communities of experts that significantly informs Smith's AHD. Looking ironically at heritage through the allegory of 'brain death,' epistemic communities in the AHD resemble doctors who tend to find objects—dead brains—once certain criteria are fulfilled. Morioka cautions in his analysis of the phenomenon of 'brain death' that dead brains are not all there is to find. Consequently, he urges that more attention be paid to the sphere of people's relationships in the field of 'brain death.'

Building from the work of Morioka, Fleck, and Smith, I emphasize that there is no such thing as 'heritage,' but an open number of intersecting and mutable (cf. Fleck 1981: 12) social relationships that generate different scientific facts and different thought styles for different people on different levels. Borrowing from Charles Fourier's (1841) utopian theory of community, I describe these intersecting relationships as a vortex (*tourbillon*), i.e., a relatively stable collective entity over time whose elements enter into constantly changing relationships with one another. Rather than championing chaos, I see here one of the greatest social and creative potentials of heritage.

The here proposed redescription of 'heritage' as a vortex of intersecting, inherently incomplete, mutable relationships on various levels opens a theoretical perspective on heritage that doesn't construct it as an "exclusionary practice" (Olwig 1999: 370), but as an open, multi-sited and multi-voiced communicative process. Communicating about heritage in such a way offers potentials for creating new social vocabularies by tactically confronting and juxtaposing the vocabularies of different stakeholders.

In rhetoric, the juxtaposition of two distinct vocabularies constitutes a metaphor. On a meta-practical level, I have tried to demonstrate the redescriptive potential of metaphor by doing exactly that: tactically confronting the vocabulary of 'intangible cultural heritage' with a different vocabulary in the allegory of 'brain death.' Here emerges the outline of a strategy, which uses metaphor—and by extension rhetoric—to expand social vocabularies and to play out the creative and future-oriented potentials of heritage proposed by this volume.

REFERENCES

Ad Hoc Committee of the Harvard Medical School to Examine the Definition of Brain Death. 1968. "A Definition of Irreversible Coma." *Journal of the American Medical Association* 205 (6): 85–88.

Aikawa-Faure, Noriko. 2009. "From the Proclamation of Masterpieces to the 'Convention for the Safeguarding of Intangible Cultural Heritage." In *Intangible Heritage*, ed. Laurajane Smith and Natsuko Akagawa, 13–44. New York, NY: Routledge.

Blake, Janet. 2009. "UNESCO's 2003 Convention on Intangible Cultural Heritage: The Implications of Community Involvement in 'Safeguarding.'" In *Intangible Heritage*, ed. Laurajane Smith and Natsuko Akagawa, 45–73. New York, NY: Routledge.

Fleck, Ludwik. 1981. *Genesis and Development of a Scientific Fact.* Trans. Fred Bradley and Thaddeus J. Trenn. Chicago, IL: University of Chicago Press.

Fourier, Charles. 1841. *Théorie des Quatre Mouvements et des Destinées Générales.* [The Complete Works of Charles Fourier. Vol 1. Theory of the Four Movements and General Destinies]. vol. 1. Œuvres Complèts de Charles Fourier. Paris: Imprimerie Duverger.

Haas, Peter M. 1992. "Epistemic Communities and International Policy Coordination." *International Organization* 46 (1): 1–35. http://dx.doi.org/10.1017/S0020818300001442.

Hafstein, Valdimar Tr. 2007. "Claiming Culture: Intangible Heritage Inc., Folklore©, Traditional Knowledge™." In *Prädikat "Heritage": Wertschöpfungen aus kulturellen Ressourcen* ["Heritage" Rating: Adding Value from Cultural Resources], ed. Dorothee Hemme, Markus Tauschek, and Regina Bendix, 75–100. Berlin: Lit.

Kaser, Max. 1971. *Das römische Privatrecht. Abschnitt 1. Das altrömische, das vorklassische und das klassische Recht* [Roman Private Law, Section 1: The Old Roman, Preclassic and Classic Law]. Munich: C.H. Beck.

Logan, William S. 2007. "Closing Pandora's Box: Human Rights Conundrums in Cultural Heritage Protection." In *Cultural Heritage and Human Rights*, ed. Helaine Silverman and D. Fairchild Ruggles, 33–52. New York, NY: Springer. http://dx.doi.org/10.1007/978-0-387-71313-7_2.

Lowenthal, David. 1997. *The Heritage Crusade and the Spoils of History.* Harmondsworth, UK: Viking.

Mollaret, Pierre, and Maurice Goulon. 1959. "Le Coma Dépassé." *Revue Neurologique* 101 (1): 3–15.

Morioka, Masahiro. 1989. *Nōshi no Hito* [Brain Dead Person]. Tokyo: Hozokan. http://www.lifestudies.org/braindeadperson00.html. Accessed April 24, 2014.

Müller, Sabine. 2011. "Wie tot sind Hirntote? [How Dead are the Brain Dead?]." *Aus Politik und Zeitgeschichte* 2011 (20–21): 3–9.

OED Online. 2012a. "Heritage, n." Oxford: Oxford University Press. http://www.oed.com/view/Entry/86230. Accessed November 30, 2012.

OED Online. 2012b. "Folklore, n." Oxford: Oxford University Press. http://www.oed.com/view/Entry/72546?redirectedFrom=folklore&. Accessed November 30, 2012.

Olwig, Karen Fog. 1999. "The Burden of Heritage: Claiming a Place for West Indian Culture." *American Ethnologist* 26 (2): 370–88. http://dx.doi.org/10.1525/ae.1999.26.2.370.

Rorty, Richard. 1989. *Contingency, Irony, and Solidarity.* Cambridge: Cambridge University Press. http://dx.doi.org/10.1017/CBO9780511804397.

Ruggles, D. Fairchild, and Helaine Silverman, eds. 2009. *Intangible Heritage Embodied.* New York, NY: Springer.

Seeger, Anthony. 2001. "Summary Report on the Regional Seminars." In *Safeguarding Traditional Culture: A Global Assessment,* edited by Peter Seitel, 36–41. Washington, DC: Smithsonian Institution, Center for Folk Life and Cultural Heritage.

Seitel, Peter. 2001. "Proposed Terminology for Intangible Cultural Heritage: Toward Anthropological and Folkloristic Common Sense in a Global Era." http://www.unesco.org/culture/ich/doc/src/05297-EN.pdf. Accessed April 24, 2014.

Smith, Laurajane. 2006. *Uses of Heritage.* London: Routledge.

Smith, Laurajane, and Natsuko Akagawa, eds. 2009. *Intangible Heritage.* London: Routledge.

The President's Council on Bioethics. 2008. *Controversies in the Determination of Death.* Washington, DC: The President's Council on Bioethics.

UNESCO. 1993. *International Consultation On New Perspectives For UNESCO's Programme: The Intangible Cultural Heritage.* Paris: UNESCO. http://unesdoc.unesco.org/images/0014/001432/143226eo.pdf. Accessed April 24, 2014.

UNESCO. 2007. *Guidelines for the Establishment of National "Living Human Treasures" Systems.* Paris: UNESCO. http://www.unesco.org/culture/ich/doc/src/00031-EN.pdf. Accessed April 24, 2014.

UNESCO. 2012. *Meetings on Intangible Cultural Heritage (Co-)organized by UNESCO.* http://www.unesco.org/culture/ich/index.php?lg=en&pg=00015. Accessed April 24, 2014.

UNESCO. 2014. *Intangible Cultural Heritage.* Paris: UNESCO. http://en.unesco.org/themes/intangible-cultural-heritage. Accessed April 24, 2014.

Memory 12

Towards the Reclamation of a Vital Concept

GABRIEL MOSHENSKA

> You keep using that word.
> I do not think it means what you think it means.
>
> —INIGO MONTOYA

For the past twenty years, the concept of memory has embedded itself in the humanities. From cultural studies it spread to various parts of history, anthropology, human geography, and beyond, and like any invasive species, it killed off a great deal of the native biodiversity. Now it is firmly rooted inside heritage studies, and this is what I want to take a closer look at: to see what this means and what those of us working at the heritage/memory interface can do about it.

To begin, it is important to clarify that memory is not an inherently bad concept. Memory is a vast and fascinating field of study that transcends disciplinary boundaries and enriches our understanding of, and engagement with, the world and its population. Memory brings together neurochemistry, cultural history, psychology, sociology, archaeology, and brain surgery—or at least it could in theory. In practice, most memory work remains isolated within specific disciplines, and this isolation precludes the kinds of collaborative scholarship that could not only increase our understanding of memory, but also correct many of the conceptual and methodological weaknesses that have crept into the field.

DOI: 10.5876/9781607323846.c012

The greatest problem in memory studies is the word *memory*—or more precisely, the huge range of different and often highly specific concepts that it is used to signify. This hyperinflation of memory terminology has, as I will show, created considerable concern among memory scholars, as it makes it difficult, if not impossible, to reconcile different fields of study or even to conduct comparative research. This problem has been particularly severe in the humanities, where there is much less terminological rigor and far less expectation for research to be cumulative. In other words, if it reads well you'll probably get away with it. And for some time now, we have been getting away with it.

This chapter is a polemic, albeit a structured and (hopefully) coherent one. It is born of my frustration and dissatisfaction with the use and abuse of the term *memory* within heritage studies; with the facile methodologies and self-consciously clever word-games that it often substitutes for analysis and critique; and with the theoretical framework that has been created around it. However, I am not arguing for the destruction of memory studies—far from it. Memory offers a view into some of the most fascinating aspects of human existence, of the ways in which we understand the creation and evolution of cultures, and much, much more. Memory is a breathtakingly exciting field to work within and to contemplate. The problem is that we have allowed our rhetoric to grow to a monstrous size, and that we—again, I speak for those of us working across memory and heritage studies—now need to tame it.

The aim of this chapter is to outline the problem as I see it and to suggest some possible solutions. Other disciplines such as history and anthropology have begun to push back the memory tide, and there is something to be learned from those efforts. However, I don't want to throw out the baby with the bathwater: there is a great deal that memory studies can offer to heritage studies, and I want to suggest some ways that these positive outcomes can be achieved, principally through a more rigorous, cautious, and restricted use of terminology when discussing memory—and more importantly, when *not* discussing memory. In particular, I want to focus on language that emphasizes the much-neglected role of agency in memory: those who remember, and those who choose to commemorate. This chapter draws on my doctoral research that I carried out on the archaeology and memory of the Second World War in Britain (Moshenska 2009, 2010).

BACKGROUND

To understand the origins of the memory problem (perhaps I should capitalize it for effect—the Memory Problem—or even The Memory Problem), it is worth looking at the development of memory studies and, in particular, the widely contested concepts of individual memory and collective memory and how the two have been understood to interrelate. The full history of memory studies is beyond the scope of this chapter, but for good discussions, see Olick and Robbins (1998), Winter (2000), and Roediger and Wertsch (2008). As Klein (2000) has noted, the history of memory studies has tended to be written from within the discipline in "virtually Whiggish" or teleological terms, a common characteristic of disciplinary histories: "most popular genealogies of our current memory discourse begin in the nineteenth century and piece together a lineage descending through Freud and Halbwachs and into our current texts" (Klein 2000: 132). Other scholars claimed as ancestors of the modern discipline include Henri Bergson (1988), Aby Warburg and Walter Benjamin, and more recently Pierre Nora (1989) and Yosef Yerushalmi (1982). The most significant conceptual leap came with Halbwachs's (1992) study of what has come to be called 'collective memory': a concept that has formed the foundation of memory studies into the present (Halbwachs 1992; Nora 1989).

Halbwachs, a student of Bergson and Emile Durkheim, defined collective memory as the shared narratives of the past created by groups, cultures, or nations to define and interpret collectively experienced events. Halbwachs asserted that collective memory, while formed from shared experiences, was able to reshape individuals' own memories through influence and enculturation. Successive models of collective memories have maintained Halbwachs' key idea that individual and collective memories are inextricably intertwined, while a lively debate has endured questioning the exact nature of this relationship. Halbwachs, as a devout Durkheimian reacting against the dominant themes of early twentieth century psychology, tended toward an extreme anti-individualist viewpoint that individual memory was entirely determined by the culturally dominant collective memory. Critics of this work have asserted that, in Halbwachs' model, "the individual [is] a sort of automaton, passively obeying the interiorised collective will" (Fentress and Wickham 1992: ix). In fact, this is a slight mischaracterization: Halbwachs recognized the existence of individual memory but argued that the actual recall of these memories was most often stimulated by collective commemorative practices (Green 2004: 38).

Nonetheless, at the basis of the current memory boom is the idea that collective memory—whatever its relationship to individual memory, although this is usually ignored—offers insights into processes and practices of group identity creation, contested pasts, cultural hegemony, and resistance. It is this tantalizing sense of political relevance, of memory as counter-history and counter-hegemony, that has attracted so many politically engaged scholars, some (though by no means all) looking for opportunities to conduct relatively non-arduous, non-rigorous, feel-good research. It is this warm, albeit largely imagined sense of political engagement that links memory studies so strongly to heritage studies; in both cases, the study of the traces of the past as they are encountered and operationalized in the present create opportunities for socio-politically relevant scholarship, but in practice this potential is rarely achieved. Instead, scholarly engagements with the political dimensions of heritage and memory are usually reduced to tokenistic assertions of critical theoretical propriety, as the historian of memory Alon Confino (1997: 1387) has noted (in, I imagine, a somewhat exasperated tone):

> The often-made contention that the past is constructed not as fact but as myth
> to serve the interest of a particular community may still sound radical to some,
> but it cannot (and should not) stupefy most historians.

This well-meaning but increasingly stale air of intellectual radicalism underpins a great deal of work in both memory and heritage studies. In perpetuating this pattern, practitioners risk losing sight of the true breadth and exciting potential of memory as a field of study and practice.

This is not to say that the politicization of the rhetoric of memory is an inherently bad thing. On the contrary, the potential of memory studies to inspire productive political rhetoric is one of its most exciting aspects. Thus, alongside my desire for a more academically rigorous field of memory work within and alongside heritage studies, I regard the weak assertions of political relevance for academic memory studies to be a missed opportunity. One example of intellectual practice that engages with memory in meaningful and productive ways is the discourse around the acknowledgment and representation of the crimes of the Nazis in post-1945 Germany. In this problematic environment the rhetoric of memory became a socially transformative force in the hands of public intellectuals, artists, writers, and curators. The extraordinary phenomenon of the 'counter-monument' movement in the 1980s and 1990s illustrated how the rhetoric inherent in traditional monumental architecture could be subverted and channeled into radical and challenging memorial devices within society and space. Public scandals and high-profile legal cases have emerged from representations of the Second World War and the Holocaust in books, documentaries, museum exhibits, artworks, and memorials in several European countries since 1945. These include the 'Aubrac affair' in 1990s France around the contested commemoration of the wartime French Resistance, and the publication of Binjamin Wilkomirski's fabricated Holocaust memoirs in 1995 (Suleiman 2006). In light of the obvious capacity of the rhetoric of memory to inspire radical debate about the past in the public sphere, the dilution and weakening of the concept within academic memory studies is all the more frustrating, leading to growing concern among some scholars in the field.

THE PROBLEM

There is a growing sense within history, anthropology, and beyond that the concept of memory has become bloated and all-consuming and risks becoming practically worthless as an analytical concept capable of being studied in any meaningful way. The clearest evidence for this lies in the use of the word memory as a vague rhetorical device distinct from any logically useful sense of the term. It is not my intention in writing this chapter to criticize specific scholars or point fingers at particularly egregious examples of the use and abuse of the rhetoric of memory in heritage studies. The problem is widespread enough that examples can be found easily, not least by web searches for terms such as 'heritage and memory,' 'historical memory,' 'material memory,' 'landscape memory,' 'destruction of memory,' 'archival memory,' and similar.

Memory has become the most predatory synonym since, I would argue, the term heritage came into widespread use in the 1980s. Thus, David Lowenthal could state as late as 1996 that, alongside heritage, "History, tradition, memory, myth, and memoir variously join us with what has passed" (Lowenthal 1996: 3). Today, terms like tradition and myth are routinely subsumed within memory, to the detriment of their distinctive specialist fields of study, as Klein (2000: 128) has noted:

> For years, specialists have dealt with such well-known phenomena as oral history, autobiography, and commemorative rituals without ever pasting them together into something called *memory*. Where we once spoke of folk history or popular history or oral history or public history or even myth we now employ memory as a metahistorical category that subsumes all these various terms. (emphasis in original)

I would add to this list of disciplines at risk of being swallowed (if not in whole, then at least in part) by memory studies: folklore studies, cultural history, history-from-below, subaltern studies, ethnic studies, historical anthropology, and of course heritage studies. Memory is used to refer to a bewildering number of things including (*inter alia*): data, literature, archives, knowledge, impressions of the past, traditions, old things, stories, myths and legends, popular histories, memes, souvenirs, places, monuments, and so on. A word that means so much can signify no one thing accurately.

It is important to point out that I am in no way opposed to interdisciplinarity: rather I am concerned that in many cases scholars of 'memory studies' are striding confidently into fields with methodologies and existing states-of-the-art and ethical standards of which they are unwittingly and carelessly ignorant. The sense that memory is a woolly, vague, and all-encompassing concept has encouraged woolly, vague research. If the same word is used to talk about different things, then it is extremely difficult to have any meaningful conversations at all.

The important ongoing debates about the relationship between individual and collective memory cited earlier have largely been ignored within heritage studies, where the term memory is almost always used as shorthand for collective memory (e.g., Fentress and Wickham 1992; Green 2004). This raises a number of problems, not least the conflation of terminology between individual and collective memory, as Bourke (2004: 473) among others has noted:

> it is never wise to borrow a term from psychology and preface it with the word 'collective.' Amongst the dangers in using the metaphor of 'memory' to refer to commemorative sites or shared narratives of the past is the fact that it threatens to elide problems of causality. After all, individuals 'remember,' 'repress,' 'forget' and 'are traumatized,' not societies.

The concept of trauma that Bourke highlights is a particularly popular theme within memory studies (which has little time for happy memories), and ties in to what Kansteiner (2002: 179) has noted to be a widespread "metaphorical use of psychological and neurological terminology, which misrepresents the social dynamics of collective memory as an effect and extension of individual, autobiographical memory." He further notes that "The concept of trauma, as well as the concept of repression, neither captures nor illuminates the forces that contribute to the making and unmaking of collective memories" (2002: 187). In other words, the weak rhetoric of memory—'memory' imagined or stretched beyond what it has traditionally and widely been taken to signify—elides the operations of social, political, and economic dominance that actually shape popular understandings of the past—and also the agency that underlies these processes.

This argument and others like it help to clarify the area of study where memory studies has taken deepest root and some of the problems that this raises. In brief, a great deal of memory work—but by no means all—focuses on *representations* of the past within specific temporal and spatial contexts (Kansteiner 2002: 179). In this sense, it closely resembles a great deal of problematically weak work taking place within heritage studies. As a teacher, a conference organizer, a journal editor, a book editor, and a peer-reviewer, I have encountered a considerable amount of work within heritage studies that amounts to roughly the same thing: an individual's personal reflections on a representation of the past—a memorial, a film, a heritage site—that they feel is flawed or biased in some way. In too many cases, pieces of writing of this kind, many of which would constitute strong starting points for a research project or a more in-depth analysis, are regarded by their authors as valid and coherent research in themselves.

Within memory studies, as within heritage studies, this examination of representations of the past, particularly of controversial or painful pasts, has often been characterized by underdeveloped, impressionistic research methodologies and a general lack of rigor. Unlike oral history with its emphasis on interviews, ethnography with its experiential fieldwork, or documentary history with its basis in archives, memory studies has no methodology of its own and has tended to borrow—often without a full understanding—the tools of other disciplines. Thus, ethnographies of memory tend to be suspiciously brief and superficial, and a considerable number of text-based studies are based on re-interpretations of secondary sources. It is particularly interesting how few studies that assert their concern with 'memory' take any interest at all in collecting and archiving individual reminiscences. In contrast, much of what purports to be memory studies is in fact a general humanities-lite critique of narratives and representations of the past. As Kansteiner (2002) has pointed out, a great deal of work of this kind in memory studies (and also, I would argue, within heritage studies) has tended to ignore the fact that these representations of the past have audiences and that without an appreciation of their responses and their agency, any study of representations is extremely limited.

This unwillingness to acknowledge agency is characteristic of analyses of representations of the past in both memory and heritage studies, and I would argue that it is particularly problematic when applied not only to the audiences for these representations, but to their creators as well. Too much writing in memory and heritage treats 'representations' and 'narratives' as naturally occurring phenomena sparked by a pervading environment of cultural and political hegemony. In memory, as in heritage, this is a profoundly disempowering situation and one that is reinforced not only by the concepts spreading from memory studies but by the vague and passive-sounding language in which they are most often couched. In response, I would like to assert a different perspective and propose a new approach to memory in heritage studies, one that seeks out the creators of narratives, and asserts that 'Authorized

Heritage Discourses' (Smith 2006), as often as not, have authors whose individual agency should not be ignored.

PUTTING AGENCY BACK INTO MEMORY

My solution to the problems that memory and memory rhetoric have wrought within heritage studies is simple: to change the way we talk about memory and, in particular, to all but eliminate the use of the word 'memory.' In its place, I want to encourage the use of more specific, active terms such as 'remember' and 'commemorate' that describe actual processes and encourage analysis that focuses on agency and context.

Egyptologist Jan Assmann is one of a few leading scholars who have tried to extract usable, useful ideas from the morass of memory studies. Assmann (1995) first distinguished 'communicative' and 'cultural' memory: the first being the sense of the past created through everyday conversations, popular culture, recollections, and informal acts of commemoration. Cultural memory, in Assmann's formulation, refers to the narratives of the past that form the self-identity of nations, cultures, and other groups who curate and guard them. While it would be problematic to suggest that communicative and cultural memory can be considered in isolation from one another (something that Assmann does not do), his work does encourage us to consider the different scales that so-called collective memory can operate at. In terms of the authorship of memory narratives, it is important to consider the 'communicative'—the small scale, intersubjective level where narratives are formed, reformed, and propagated by informal conversation and contact within small, face-to-face communities. Building on this recognition of the different scales of collective memory, Kansteiner (2002: 180) proposes an even more partitioned approach that draws on methods from reception studies and distinguishes between

> the intellectual and cultural traditions that frame all our representations of the past, the memory makers who selectively adopt and manipulate these traditions, and the memory consumers who use, ignore, or transform such artifacts according to their own interests.

My own proposed model for approaching memory phenomena draws on both of these as well as the work of other distinguished scholars (e.g., Ashplant, Dawson, and Roper 2000; Winter 2000). In brief, it recognizes three distinct processes in what is commonly called memory, a more generative rhetoric of memory that addresses and builds upon observable phenomena:

(1) The creation of narratives within small groups through a variety of processes including individual remembering and storytelling.

(2) The use of media, events, literature, education, propaganda, and other cultural, political, and intellectual processes to promote and amplify specific narratives. These include most formal acts of commemoration.

(3) Pitting opposed narratives against one another, most often in the public sphere: this includes many of the most controversial aspects of heritage such as debates around genocide representation and genocide denial, often on national and international scales.

As these points demonstrate, it is possible to discuss the concepts such as representations of the past and narratives of the past that most commonly link heritage studies and memory studies, creating a more productive memory rhetoric grounded in specificity and the critical study of memory phenomena. More importantly, emphasizing terms such as 'remembering,' 'commemoration,' and others reminds us to look beyond the surface of these complicated processes at the tangled webs of agency, power, and influence that they conceal. To truly understand what is commonly called memory, it is insufficient to deal (as so many do) in trite generalizations and sweeping statements about the 'memory' of an entire nation or culture or to treat memory itself as something imbued with agency.

If heritage/memory researchers can put the more intellectually vacuous outgrowths of memory studies firmly back in their box, then we can hopefully begin to undo some of the damage that this sort of thinking has wrought within heritage studies and continue to promote the study of representations of the past as a critical, analytical field worthy of our attention and endeavor.

REFERENCES

Ashplant, Timothy, Graham Dawson, and Michael Roper. 2000. "The Politics of War Memory and Commemoration: Contexts, Structures and Dynamics." In *The Politics of War Memory and Commemoration*, ed. Timothy Ashplant, Graham Dawson, and Michael Roper, 3–85. London: Routledge.

Assmann, Jan. 1995. "Collective Memory and Cultural Identity." *New German Critique* 65: 125–33. http://dx.doi.org/10.2307/488538.

Bergson, Henri. 1988. *Matter and Memory*. New York, NY: Zone Books.

Bourke, Joanna. 2004. "Introduction: 'Remembering' War." *Journal of Contemporary History* 39 (4): 473–85. http://dx.doi.org/10.1177/0022009404046750.

Confino, Alon. 1997. "Collective Memory and Cultural History: Problems of Method." *American Historical Review* 102 (5): 1386–403. http://dx.doi.org/10 .2307/2171069.

Fentress, James, and Chris Wickham. 1992. *Social Memory*. Oxford: Blackwell.

Green, Anna. 2004. "Individual Remembering and 'Collective Memory': Theoretical Presuppositions and Contemporary Debates." *Oral History* 32 (2): 35–44.

Halbwachs, Maurice. (Original work published 1925) 1992. *On Collective Memory*. Chicago, IL: University of Chicago Press.

Kansteiner, Wulf. 2002. "Finding Meaning in Memory: A Methodological Critique of Collective Memory Studies." *History and Theory* 41 (2): 179–97. http://dx.doi .org/10.1111/0018-2656.00198.

Klein, Kerwin Lee. 2000. "On the Emergence of Memory in Historical Discourse." *Representations* 69 (1): 127–50. http://dx.doi.org/10.1525/rep.2000.69.1.01p0064y.

Lowenthal, David. 1996. *The Heritage Crusade and the Spoils of History*. Cambridge: Cambridge University Press.

Moshenska, Gabriel. 2009. *Archaeology, Material Culture, and Memory of the Second World War*. PhD dissertation, Institute of Archaeology, University College London.

Moshenska, Gabriel. 2010. "Working with Memory in the Archaeology of Modern Conflict." *Cambridge Archaeological Journal* 20 (1): 33–48. http://dx.doi.org/10.1017 /S095977431000003X.

Nora, Pierre. 1989. "Between Memory and History: Les Lieux de Mémoire." *Representations* 26 (1): 7–24. http://dx.doi.org/10.1525/rep.1989.26.1.99p0274v.

Olick, Jeffrey K., and Joyce Robbins. 1998. "Social Memory Studies: From 'Collective Memory' to the Historical Sociology of Mnemonic Practices." *Annual Review of Sociology* 24 (1): 105–40. http://dx.doi.org/10.1146/annurev.soc.24.1.105.

Roediger, Henry L., and James V. Wertsch. 2008. "Creating a New Discipline of Memory Studies." *Memory Studies* 1 (1): 9–22. http://dx.doi.org/10.1177/175069 8007083884.

Smith, Laurajane. 2006. *Uses of Heritage*. London: Routledge.

Suleiman, Susan R. 2006. *Crises of Memory and the Second World War*. Cambridge, MA: Harvard University Press.

Winter, Jay. 2000. "The Generation of Memory: Reflections on the 'Memory Boom' in Contemporary Historical Studies." *Bulletin of the German Historical Institute* 27: 69–92.

Yerushalmi, Yosef H. 1982. *Zakhor: Jewish History and Jewish Memory*. Seattle: University of Washington Press.

Natural Heritage **13**

Heritage Ecologies and the Rhetoric of Nature

MELISSA F. BAIRD

Because this is how an empire is claimed
not just with stakes in a stolen land,
but with words grown over palates,
with strength of tongue as well as strength of hand.

—OWEN SHEERS

In June 2012, world leaders, scientists, NGOs, environmentalists, indigenous peoples, and other interested
people convened in Brazil for the United Nations
Conference on Sustainable Development. Known as
'Rio+20,' the Conference marked the twentieth anniversary of the historic Earth Summit, where nations
signed the legally binding *Convention on Biological
Diversity* (CBD), a guiding document in natural heritage policy and research. The CBD was one of the first
environmental initiatives to champion and recognize
indigenous cultural heritage and intellectual property. Interestingly, that same year, the World Heritage
Committee created the cultural landscape designation,
in part to address divisions between cultural and natural
heritage. Building on the momentum and taking direction from the Earth Summit, Rio+20 focused discussions around the 'three pillars' of sustainable development: economic development, social development, and
environmental protections. Although Rio+20 served as

DOI: 10.5876/9781607323846.c013

a platform of innovative thinking around sustainable development, attention to heritage and culture were noticeably absent in discussions. In fact, the Final Rio Document, a focused product outlining sustainability and development goals, was criticized by the International Work Group for Indigenous Affairs (IWGIA) for not addressing culture.[1]

I am not surprised that heritage was not explicit in conversations, as I have found that cultural and natural heritage are often not identified within sustainable development or conservation approaches. This underestimation of the importance of heritage in conservation initiatives is significant. Heritage engages a global network of experts who are leading voices in conservation, preservation, and policy matters and are sanctioned by the nation-state as well as by international governing bodies (e.g., UNESCO, ICOMOS, IUCN, the World Bank, and so on). As key power holders, experts testify and provide opinions in land rights and native title claims, bioprospecting contracts, biotechnology patents, water rights and sacred sites claims, ecosystem inventories, and cultural and natural heritage nominations to the World Heritage list. For example, the UNESCO World Heritage Committee's recent acceptance of Tanzania's request to excise part of the Selous Game Reserve to allow for uranium mining brings into sharp relief the centrality of heritage experts in development negotiations. Mapping out the nuances and contexts of just how governments, environmentalists, heritage experts, and other decision makers draw on the rhetoric of nature (or not) is part of the work that we must do.

This chapter examines how the rhetoric of nature is embedded within heritage ecologies, defined here as a set of relationships within environmental and heritage practices that engages with and mediates our ideas of nature. In this brief discussion, I cannot present a complete analysis of the nature/culture or social/ecological divide (but see, e.g., Escobar 1996, 1998; Macnaghten and Urry 1998; Soper 1995). Instead, I follow Kathryn Lafrenz Samuels' claim that heritage be recognized as a "kind of rhetoric" (Chapter 1). Lafrenz Samuels' call is timely, especially for teasing out where ideas of nature (or wilderness, sustainability, and conservation, for that matter) are embedded in heritage practices. In the final section, I imagine how the rhetoric of nature can be also an emancipatory discourse and/or deployed in ways that reshape conceptions of heritage. I ask if counter-hegemonic alternatives can provide nuance and specificity as a way for stakeholders to intervene or mobilize discourse into agency or resistance.

HERITAGE ECOLOGIES AND THE RHETORIC OF NATURE

Natural (and environmental) and cultural heritage are conceptual categories that carry enormous influence and are invoked at the local and international levels to influence and provide political legitimacy to cultural and environmental policy. Understanding how these concepts are conceived and deployed in heritage practices and tracing their political and legal implications is due. The epistemologies of nature, namely the multiple theories and methods that are brought to bear in interpreting the natural and cultural worlds, are legacies of Enlightenment thinking that conceptually separated out human experience from nature (see Baird 2009 for discussion). The nature/culture paradigm has deep roots in Western models of time and space and is tied to historical formations and colonial practices. Although scholars have sought to unsettle this limited and largely Eurocentric view of the world (Haraway 1991; Latour 1993; Ingold 2000; Strathern 2004; de la Cadena 2010), challenges remain. Recent ethnographic studies have gone a long way in correcting this bias to show how the divide is situated in practice (see Baird 2009; Helmreich 2009; Meskell 2012). These studies provide insights into ongoing and sometimes contentious debates over the role of culture in conservation and development (Agrawal and Redford 2009; Curran et al. 2009; Inglis and Bone 2006; Kopnina 2012; Redford and Sanderson 2000; Schwartzman, Nepstad, and Moreira 2000; Terborgh 2000). They show how, in many ways, communities are framed as either key drivers in environmental impacts (Oates 1999) or central to conservation approaches (Hughes 2005; Van Damme, Sibongile, and Meskell 2009). No matter the position one takes, how we frame our ideas of nature and culture do have significant and far-reaching consequences for stakeholders. In other words, rhetoric matters.

In World Heritage contexts, I have argued that ideas of heritage are largely determined through the agendas and recommendations of Western experts, international heritage agencies, and the nation-state and reframed to fit specific World Heritage values (Baird 2009). Meaning, experts often rely on specific visions that are largely environmental, aesthetic, and material. This is not specific to World Heritage; as in other contexts, such as nature reserves or parks, outsider interests often shape ideas of what is natural (and what is not). Dan Brockington (2002), for example, showed how 'indigenous' pastoral herders of the Tanzania's Mkomazi Game Reserve were evicted from their land, the result of lobbying by powerful international conservation NGOs who sought to establish a wildlife sanctuary. In the Tanzania example, what 'experts' imagined was natural had lived consequences for the pastoral herders.

The paradox is that a suite of unintended consequences are introduced once communities are removed. Latour (2004: 170), in thinking about the politics of nature around the protection of African elephants posited, "you want to save the elephants . . . by having them graze separately from cows? . . . but how are you going to get an opinion from the Maasai who have been cut off from the cows, and from the cows deprived of elephants who clear the brush?" These tensions and the contested space of social nature calls attention to the need to examine and make explicit the concepts we use. How do stakeholders and agencies deploy ideas of nature (or landscapes) in their conceptualizations of heritage?

To answer these questions, we must map out how the rhetoric of nature is taken up in practice and around conceptions of heritage. This is not easy to do, as heritage ecologies engage a suite of stakeholders, from individuals working for local or national heritage organizations, to governments, industries, nongovernmental or grassroots organizations, and international heritage bodies. Locating heritage within this field of power and, more specifically, how it articulates with environmental decisions and strategies, is challenging but particularly salient for heritage scholars and activists. How does the rhetoric of nature infuse languages and practices? How do these tropes gain traction? Where did they originate and how are they reproduced? Ultimately, this approach seeks to make explicit the ways that institutions draw on the rhetoric of nature to sanction what gets studied, protected, and privileged.

How does the rhetoric of nature (or Nature) gain currency in how we make sense and construct knowledge about the world? Environmental historian William Cronon (1992) would say that it was as simple as telling stories. Ideas of nature are used as framing devices to order and reorder, select or obscure, and promote or demote elements of the natural world and our place within it. In the case of World Heritage, for example, "nature phenomena or areas of exceptional natural beauty and aesthetic importance"[2] derive from ideas of what constitutes the heritage inventory. Rhetorical strategies are used to describe nature or wilderness as a refuge, sanctuary, or setting for political reform and to influence and seduce, shape and inform our management practices. Yet, such competing ideas of nature/culture often collide, as Julie Cruikshank (2005) showed in her ethnographic study of the Saint Elias Mountains (now part of a transboundary UNESCO World Heritage site between Canada and the United States). In that case, early explorers, scientists, and environmental activists (including John Muir) transposed their ideas of Nature (sublime, inanimate, a resource) onto the landscape. These early contested visions of 'Nature' are presently built into legal agreements, policies, and practices that govern and direct how the Park is managed today. As Paul Lane noted (this volume), the stakes for descendent communities are high.

Although Cronon's thesis is useful in understanding the power of the stories we tell and how environmental policies articulate with narratives, I think there is much more at stake. If we agree, as Laurajane Smith (2006: 4) argued, a "dominant Western discourse" surrounds heritage practices, then how does rhetoric privilege certain values and ideas of nature or the past? I suggest that ideas of nature are taken up and refashioned in ways that efface the complicated histories: what seems natural or organic is in fact imagined and constructed. More importantly, *how* these ideas are used in heritage legislation or protection has consequences, as shown in the examples where outsiders (e.g., archaeologists, heritage managers, NGOs, environmentalists) call upon their authority or obligation to steward and protect. The possessive nature of heritage practices is significant and tied up with imperial expansions and intellectual progress, and resounds today in contemporary ideas and applications of conservation and stewardship (Baird 2009). These visions gain even more currency when they converge with ideas of race, power, and identity.

NATURE/CULTURE/HERITAGE

What are the cultural politics of nature and making place? As yet this question remains unresolved, but a number of ethnographic studies of natural areas map out and made clear competing claims and tensions (Breglia 2006; Cruikshank 2005; Igoe 2004; Fontein 2006; Meskell 2012; Neumann 1998; West 2006). In post-apartheid South Africa, for example, ideologies of *terra nullius* converged with biodiversity and sustainability initiatives in Kruger National Park, examining how "natural ecologies supplanted peopled histories and . . . social urgencies" and resulting in what Lynn Meskell (2012: 204) has described as ecological apartheid. Such conservation strategies are not only known in Africa, but have also displaced communities worldwide as a way to 'protect nature' (Cernea and Schmidt-Soltau 2006; Igoe 2004).

I found that negotiating identity was central to the creation of the first World Heritage cultural landscape, Tongariro National Park in Aotearoa/New Zealand (for discussion see Baird 2009, 2013). In 1990, Tongariro was listed as a Natural World Heritage property, and in 1993, the Park became the first World Heritage cultural landscape. I traced the logic of institutional and expert knowledge to show how the ecological integrity and scientific, aesthetic, and conservation values of the Park were promoted and worked in ways that reframed Maori peoples' complex and multifaceted relationships to landscapes in relationship to the 'natural' world. Much of this relates to the structure of park management, as managers follow the *National Parks Act* that I argued naturalized the ecological and natural values of the Park. But it also relates to the history of colonization and how early settlers failed to fully grasp Maori systems of knowledge about and responsibilities to the land, instead viewing New Zealand as a wilderness—"a landscape devoid of geographical meaning inhabited by people without history" (Marr, Hodge, and White 2001: 4; see also Ruru 2004, 2008). In the process of renaming, settlers transposed a 'European value system' onto the lands, which violated Maori peoples' customary land rights and laws (Tapsell 1997: 332).

The separation of nature/culture is evident in how the Park became a World Heritage property. The cultural heritage was presented in such a way that it was subordinate to the natural values of the Park. In the process of making heritage, Maori cultural systems *taonga* and *wahi tapu* were renamed as heritage resources and realigned to fit with outsiders' ideas of nature and wilderness. Ideas of landscapes, originating with ICOMOS and IUCN and adopted by the World Heritage Committee, were used to develop the World Heritage nominations. Heritage managers reframed Maori knowledge practices and cultural traditions as heritage resources and promoted them for their aesthetic, scenic, and natural values.

And this renaming speaks to a larger issue: cultural landscape designations, in many ways, expand the heritage inventory by creating new typologies and constructions of place. In the case of the World Heritage cultural landscapes, for example, the inventory includes songs, oral traditions, memories, Dreaming tracks, languages, knowledge systems, archaeological sites, historic buildings, rock art, ecosystems, flora and fauna, geological formations, wetlands, and karsts, among others. This expanded view positions heritage managers as experts and spokespersons along the full heritage continuum, in some cases outside of their expertise, training, or qualifications. In many contexts, heritage managers may not have the skills, training, or cultural competence to work with some types of heritage included within the cultural landscapes inventory. Indigenous landscapes, for example, often include sacred sites, oral traditions, songs, and other sensitive material that, in many cases, should not be identified or discussed by outsiders.

The rhetoric of nature, sustainability, and conservation gain traction and align with political ideologies, development projects, and environmental legislation and reposition stakeholders physically apart from their lands and far from their political and spiritual systems of authority. The conservation ethics and call for stewardship resounds in the common sense via the rhetorical devices and practices that are naturalized and even imposed on non-Western nations. Heritage, as a social construct, operates in ways that are mainly invisible and unquestioned. In many cases, biodiversity models of threatened resources act as proxies and inform the language of cultural diversity initiatives. As Meskell (2012: 30) warned, "prioritizing ecological and climatic risk . . . has displaced cultural heritage and its immediate stakeholders." Thus, the limited focus on environmental or ecological crises reframes cultural heritage into something less important, or worse, as something detrimental to environmental protections. Sustainability, in this model, views cultures as threats and as something to be mediated. The challenge is to tease out how these conservation tropes inform management decisions and practices, articulate the production of scientific knowledge, or are built into legal frameworks.

THE SOCIAL NATURE OF HERITAGE

How exactly do states, NGOs, tourism organizations, local communities, corporations and other decision-makers shape, deploy, and broker ideas of natural heritage? The World Bank, for instance, recognizes the importance of natural heritage in their capacity building efforts, and developed policy guidelines and evaluative criteria, as well as encourages partnerships with international agencies such as IUCN, ICCROM, and ICOMOS (Stone and Wright 2007). At the same time, the World Bank does not have a clearly defined human rights policy or agenda (Sarfaty 2012). The notion that such a powerful institution, which assesses environmental and cultural heritage, also lends money and expertise to "governments that have committed gross and systemic human rights violations" (2012: 2) calls attention to fractions within this institution. Alternatively, the World Commission on Protected Areas (WCPA) of the IUCN also informs heritage policies and practices. The rhetoric of investments and capacity building are part of a larger aim of making natural and protected areas economically viable. The planning and protection of protected areas is an admirable goal, which becomes somewhat murky when infused with other stakeholder's interests from industry. UNESCO and other heritage advisory bodies are engaging with industry actors and multinational corporations (e.g., mining) to mediate issues of development and environmental impacts. The 'rhetoric' of sustainability infuses these discussions and is deployed in ways that obscures motivations.

The challenge is to wade through many contradictory and conflicting approaches to see how the rhetoric of nature articulates with theory and practice. The CBD, discussed earlier, is highly influential in heritage legislation

(Posey 2001). Taken together, we see how varied approaches and understandings are woven into policymaking, policy documents, and the results of negotiations, lobbying, and national interests, among others. Take, for example, the International Council of Mining and Metals (ICMM), a cohort of extractive industry executives and actors engaged in sustainable resource development. Since 2010, ICMM has worked closely with IUCN and other groups to develop documents to outline best practices. The 2012 document on World Heritage and mining not only calls attention to the conflicts and issues with mining heritage, but also strategically positions mining interests within the discussion (ICMM 2012).

An important area of concern is how the rhetoric of nature is taken up by multinational corporations and biotechnology, medical, energy, and extractive industries (Anderson 2012; Ballard and Banks 2003; Buscher and Wolmer 2007; Greene 2004; Hayden 2003; Halvaksz 2008; Kapelus 2002; Macintyre and Foale 2004; O'Faircheallaigh 2008; Reddy 2006; Ronayne 2008). Global mining industry Rio Tinto Ltd.'s recently published resource guide, *Why Cultural Heritage Matters* (Bradshaw et al. 2011), presents its vision for conduct and the protection of cultural heritage and the environment. The guide has been promoted by academic institutions, international governing bodies, and individuals as an example of best practices. The question remains whether or not these efforts are a genuine attempt to take responsibility and develop a cultural strategy or constitute a type of 'greenwashing' that superficially addresses communities' concerns. Whatever the case, these relationships need to be made clear, particularly the role of experts in negotiations (cf. Welker, Partridge, and Hardin 2011).

In thinking through the social nature of heritage, I envision an approach that is broad and deep and rooted in an awareness of why nature matters. The impulse to critique, I argue, obstructs ways in which we can create new lexicons of ideas and practices. How can we move beyond critique to think about the work that heritage does? It is true that the rhetoric of nature engages identity politics, whether discussing the identity of powerful global institutions or environmental NGOs. Yet at the same time, narrow thinking divorced from how heritage is also engaged in other contexts limits what we can say or do. How can the rhetoric of nature be used to reshape our conceptions of heritage? One way to do so is to redirect and highlight why the rhetoric of nature matters to institutions and decision makers and make this distinction explicit. A potential area could be within heritage and biotechnology and bioprospecting. The global market for biotechnology engages heritage practitioners as scientists and experts who engage with the rhetoric of nature by naming and renaming plants and resources. A counterhegemonic approach would traverse the space by recognizing counternarratives and challenging assumptions. Sita Reddy (2006) showed how this is possible in the context of traditional medical knowledge (TMK) in South Asia. In this case, making explicit the assumptions embedded in outsiders' conceptions of TMK had an 'emancipatory potential' by reshaping power relations and challenging the status quo. Challenging rhetoric may be the key to asserting rights and act as a way to legitimize and validate rights. Mi'kmaq scholar Marie Battiste (2008: 503) urged scholars to adopt research practices that "enable Indigenous nations, peoples, and communities to exercise control over information relating to their knowledge and heritage." In this statement, Battiste calls attention to how the rhetoric of nature can be reframed as an emancipatory discourse by creating space within our models that encourage stakeholders to define their categories of relevance related to lands. The (re)appropriation of ideas of nature, culture, sustainability, or conservation work in ways that ensure sensitivity and respect for traditional protocols and custodial responsibilities.

WITH STRENGTH OF TONGUE AS WELL AS STRENGTH OF HAND

As the epigraph of this chapter serves to illustrate, power rests with those who control the story; "empire(s) are claimed" as Sheers (2000: 22) states, "not just with stakes in a stolen land but with words grown over palates, with strength of tongue as well as strength of hand." Sheers' poem exemplifies the practices that are legitimized by narratives that control, exclude, or deny; they work to secure the storyteller's claims and, as Sheers intimates, are a colonial act. Here, the rhetoric of nature works in similar ways, meaning it shapes our ideas and understandings of heritage and has lived consequences.

Heritage ecologies should be part of this conversation. Engaging stakeholders and decision-makers, scientific experts and heritage practitioners, heritage ecologies encapsulate the dynamic and evolving nature of heritage practices. Understanding how the rhetoric of nature intersects with sustainable development initiatives or land-use policies, for instance, can provide insights to research and policy and may hold practical benefits to understanding the dynamics of heritage. As framing devices, the rhetoric of nature infuses our discourse and practices and mediates how heritage is understood. One challenge is, in an era of climate change and global warming, that we do not seek to lessen environmental protections. At the same time, the privileging of nature over culture may actually lessen protections by severing the deep cultural connections to place that we may not fully understand. Moving beyond binaries and breaking down barriers—conceptual, political, and structural—is vital for recasting nature/culture into a counter-hegemonic approach.

How is the rhetoric of nature circulated and produced? Our understandings of heritage encompass a series of values and assumptions that are neither neutral nor objective. Tropes of nature and conservation abound in heritage contexts and influence laws, policies, and practices. Our ideas of heritage can be viewed as interlocking frameworks that inform and extend. Value is assigned and negotiated through relationships and actions, and ideas of what constitutes the heritage inventory are constantly negotiated and reimagined. Therefore, it is critical that heritage scholars trace the logic of nature, wilderness, and sustainability within their work and understand in what ways they shape current policies and practices. Recognizing that heritage is being called upon to do the work of environmental protections, it behooves us to understand how it is historically and socially constructed. It is not enough to critique the flow of knowledge, but instead to grasp how it gains immediacy and relevancy, how it is used in crafting legislation, and ultimately, how it gains traction on the ground.

ACKNOWLEDGMENTS

My deepest appreciation to the editors, Kathryn Lafrenz Samuels and Trinidad Rico, for their commitment and vision that is enabling new understandings of heritage. This chapter was developed while a postdoctoral scholar at the Stanford Archaeology Center and Woods Institute for the Environment. Thank you also to Lynn Meskell for her unfailing support and encouragement.

NOTE

1. http://www.uncsd2012.org/index.php?page=view&nr=1258&type=230&menu=39, accessed 15 November 2012.

2. http://whc.unesco.org/en/criteria/, accessed 22 April 2015.

REFERENCES

Agrawal, Arun, and Kent Redford. 2009. "Conservation and Displacement: An Overview." *Conservation & Society* 7 (1): 1–10. http://dx.doi.org/10.4103/0972-4923.54790.

Anderson, Jane E. 2012. "On Resolution: Intellectual Property and Indigenous Knowledge Disputes." *Landscapes of Violence* 2 (1): 1–14.

Baird, Melissa F. 2009. *The Politics of Place: Heritage, Identity, and the Epistemologies of Cultural Landscapes*. Doctoral dissertation, Department of Anthropology, University of Oregon, Eugene. University Microfilms International, Ann Arbor, MI.

Baird, Melissa F. 2013. "'The Breath of the Mountain is My Heart': Indigenous Cultural Landscapes and the Politics of Heritage." *International Journal of Heritage Studies* 19 (4): 327–40. http://dx.doi.org/10.1080/13527258.2012.663781.

Ballard, Chris, and Glenn Banks. 2003. "Resource Wars: The Anthropology of Mining." *Annual Review of Anthropology* 32 (1): 287–313. http://dx.doi.org/10.1146/annurev.anthro.32.061002.093116.

Battiste, Marie A. 2008. "Research Ethics for Protecting Indigenous Knowledge and Heritage: Institutional and Researcher Responsibilities." In *Handbook of Critical and Indigenous Methodologies*, ed. Norman K. Denzin, Yvonna S. Lincoln, and Linda Tuhiwai Smith, 497–510. Los Angeles, CA: Sage. http://dx.doi.org/10.4135/9781483385686.n25.

Bradshaw, Elizabeth, Katie Bryant, Tamar Cohen, David Brereton, Julie Kim, Kirsty Gillespie, and Ian Lilley. 2011. *Why Cultural Heritage Matters: A Resource Guide for Integrating Cultural Heritage Management Into Communities Work at Rio Tinto*. Melbourne: Rio Tinto. http://www.riotinto.com/documents/reportspublications/rio_tinto_cultural_heritage_guide.pdf. Accessed April 25, 2014.

Breglia, Lisa. 2006. *Monumental Ambivalence: The Politics of Heritage*. Austin: University of Texas Press.

Brockington, Dan. 2002. *Fortress Conservation: The Preservation of the Mkomazi Game Reserve, Tanzania*. Bloomington: Indiana University Press.

Buscher, Bram, and William Wolmer. 2007. "Introduction: The Politics of Engagement between Biodiversity Conservation and the Social Sciences." *Conservation & Society* 5 (1): 1–21.

Cernea, Michael M., and Kai Schmidt-Soltau. 2006. "Poverty Risks and National Parks: Policy Issues in Conservation and Resettlement." *World Development* 34 (10): 1808–30. http://dx.doi.org/10.1016/j.worlddev.2006.02.008.

Cronon, William. 1992. "A Place for Stories: Nature, History, and Narrative." *Journal of American History* 78 (4): 1347–76. http://dx.doi.org/10.2307/2079346.

Cruikshank, Julie. 2005. *Do Glaciers Listen? Local Knowledge, Colonial Encounters, and Social Imagination*. Vancouver: University of British Columbia Press.

Curran, Bryan, Terry Sunderland, Fiona Maisels, John Oates, Stella Asaha, Michael Balinga, Louis Defo, Andrew Dunn, Paul Telfer, Leonard Usongo, et al. 2009. "Are Central Africa's Protected Areas Displacing Hundreds of Thousands of Rural Poor?" *Conservation & Society* 7 (1): 30–45. http://dx.doi.org/10.4103/0972-4923.54795.

de la Cadena, Marisol. 2010. "Indigenous Cosmopolitics in the Andes: Conceptual Reflections Beyond 'Politics.'" *Cultural Anthropology* 25 (2): 334–70. http://dx.doi .org/10.1111/j.1548-1360.2010.01061.x.

Escobar, Arturo. 1996. "Construction Nature: Elements for a Post-Structuralist Political Ecology." *Futures* 28 (4): 325–43. http://dx.doi.org/10.1016/0016-3287 (96)00011-0.

Escobar, Arturo. 1998. "Whose Knowledge, Whose Nature? Biodiversity, Conservation, and the Political Ecology of Social Movements." *Journal of Political Ecology* 5 (1): 53–82.

Fontein, Joost. 2006. *The Silence of Great Zimbabwe: Contested Landscapes and the Power of Heritage.* London: University College London Press.

Greene, Shane. 2004. "Indigenous People Incorporated? Culture as Politics, Culture as Property in Pharmaceutical Bioprospecting." *Current Anthropology* 45 (2): 211–37. http://dx.doi.org/10.1086/381047.

Halvaksz, Jamon Alex. 2008. "Whose Closure? Appearances, Temporality, and Mineral Extraction in Papua New Guinea." *Journal of the Royal Anthropological Institute* 14 (1): 21–37. http://dx.doi.org/10.1111/j.1467-9655.2007.00476.x.

Haraway, Donna Jeanne. 1991. *Simians, Cyborgs, and Women: The Reinvention of Nature.* New York, NY: Routledge.

Hayden, Cori. 2003. *When Nature Goes Public: The Making and Unmaking of Bioprospecting in Mexico.* Princeton, NJ: Princeton University Press.

Helmreich, Stefan. 2009. *Alien Ocean: Anthropological Voyages in Microbial Seas.* Berkeley: University of California Press.

Hughes, David McDermott. 2005. "Third Nature: Making Space and Time in the Great Limpopo Conservation Area." *Cultural Anthropology* 20 (2): 157–84. http:// dx.doi.org/10.1525/can.2005.20.2.157.

ICMM (International Council on Mining and Metals). 2012. *Identifying Potential Overlap between Extractive Industries (Mining, Oil and Gas) and Natural World Heritage Sites.* http://www.icmm.com/document/6950. Accessed March 25, 2014.

Igoe, Jim. 2004. *Conservation and Globalization: A Study of the National Parks and Indigenous Communities from East Africa to South Dakota.* Belmont, CA: Thomson/ Wadsworth.

Inglis, David, and John Bone. 2006. "Boundary Maintenance, Border Crossing and the Nature/Culture Divide." *European Journal of Social Theory* 9 (2): 272–87. http:// dx.doi.org/10.1177/1368431006064188.

Ingold, Tim. 2000. *The Perception of the Environment: Essays on Livelihood, Dwelling, and Skill.* London: Routledge. http://dx.doi.org/10.4324/9780203466025.

Kapelus, Paul. 2002. "Mining, Corporate Social Responsibility and the 'Community': The Case of Rio Tinto, Richards Bay Minerals, and the Mbonambi." *Journal of Business Ethics* 39 (3): 275–96. http://dx.doi.org/10.1023/A:1016570929359.

Kopnina, Helen. 2012. "Toward Conservational Anthropology: Addressing Anthropocentric Bias in Anthropology." *Dialectical Anthropology* 36 (1–2): 127–46. http://dx.doi.org/10.1007/s10624-012-9265-y.

Latour, Bruno. 1993. *We Have Never Been Modern*. Cambridge, MA: Harvard University Press.

Latour, Bruno. 2004. *Politics of Nature: How to Bring the Sciences into Democracy*. Cambridge, MA: Harvard University Press.

Macintyre, Martha, and Simon Foale. 2004. "Politicized Ecology: Local Responses to Mining in Papua New Guinea." *Oceania* 74 (3): 231–51.

Macnaghten, Phil, and John Urry. 1998. *Contested Natures*. Thousand Oaks, CA: Sage Publications.

Marr, Cathy, Robin Hodge, and Ben White. 2001. *Crown Laws, Policies, and Practices in Relation to Flora and Fauna, 1840–1912*. Wellington, NZ: Waitangi Tribunal Publication.

Meskell, Lynn. 2012. *The Nature of Heritage: The New South Africa*. London: Wiley-Blackwell.

Neumann, Roderick P. 1998. *Imposing Wilderness: Struggles over Livelihood and Nature Preservation in Africa*. Berkeley: University of California Press.

O'Faircheallaigh, Ciaran. 2008. "Negotiating Cultural Heritage? Aboriginal–Mining Company Agreements in Australia." *Development and Change* 39 (1): 25–51. http://dx.doi.org/10.1111/j.1467-7660.2008.00467.x.

Oates, John F. 1999. *Myth and Reality in the Rain Forest: How Conservation Strategies are Failing in West Africa*. Berkeley: University of California Press.

Posey, Darrell A. 2001. "Intellectual Property Rights and the Sacred Balance: Some Spiritual Consequences from the Commercialization of Traditional Resources." In *Indigenous Traditions and Ecology: The Interbeing of Cosmology and Community*, ed. John A. Grim, 3–23. Cambridge, MA: Publications of the Center for the Study of World Religions, Harvard Divinity School.

Reddy, Sita. 2006. "Making Heritage Legible: Who Owns Traditional Medical Knowledge?" *International Journal of Cultural Property* 13 (2): 161–88. http://dx.doi.org/10.1017/S0940739106060115.

Redford, Kent H., and Steven E. Sanderson. 2000. "Extracting Humans from Nature." *Conservation Biology* 14 (5): 1362–64. http://dx.doi.org/10.1046/j.1523-1739.2000.00135.x.

Ronayne, Maggie. 2008. "Commitment, Objectivity and Accountability to Communities: Priorities for 21st-Century Archaeology." *Conservation and Management of Archaeological Sites* 10 (4): 367–81. http://dx.doi.org/10.1179/1350503 08X12513845914589.

Ruru, Jacinta. 2004. "Indigenous Peoples' Ownership and Management of Mountains: The Aotearoa/New Zealand Experience." *Indigenous Law Journal* 3: 111–37.

Ruru, Jacinta. 2008. "A Māori Right to Own and Manage National Parks?" *Journal of South Pacific Law* 12 (1): 105–10.

Sarfaty, Galit. 2012. *Values in Translation: Human Rights and the Culture of the World Bank.* Stanford, CA: Stanford University Press.

Schwartzman, Stephan, Daniel Nepstad, and Adriana Moreira. 2000. "Arguing Tropical Forest Conservation: People versus Parks." *Conservation Biology* 14 (5): 1370–74. http://dx.doi.org/10.1046/j.1523-1739.2000.00227.x.

Sheers, Owen. 2000. *The Blue Book.* Bridgend, Wales: Seren.

Smith, Laurajane. 2006. *Uses of Heritage.* London: Routledge.

Soper, Kate. 1995. *What is Nature? Culture Politics and the Non-Human.* Oxford: Blackwell.

Stone, Diane, and Christopher Wright. 2007. *The World Bank and Governance: A Decade of Reform and Reaction.* London: Routledge.

Strathern, Marilyn. 2004. *Partial Connections.* Walnut Creek, CA: AltaMira Press.

Tapsell, Paul. 1997. "The Flight of Pareraututu: An Investigation of *Taonga* from a Tribal Perspective." *Journal of the Polynesian Society* 106: 323–74.

Terborgh, John. 2000. "The Fate of Tropical Forests: A Matter of Stewardship." *Conservation Biology* 14 (5): 1358–61. http://dx.doi.org/10.1046/j.1523-1739.2000 .00136.x.

Van Damme, Masuku, Lynette Sibongile, and Lynn Meskell. 2009. "Producing Conservation and Community in South Africa." *Ethics, Place and Environment* 12 (1): 69–89. http://dx.doi.org/10.1080/13668790902753088.

Welker, Marina, Damani J. Partridge, and Rebecca Hardin. 2011. "Corporate Lives: New Perspectives on the Social Life of the Corporate Form: An Introduction to Supplement 3." *Current Anthropology* 52 (S3): S3–16. http://dx.doi.org/10.1086 /657907.

West, Paige. 2006. *Conservation is Our Government Now: The Politics of Ecology in Papua New Guinea.* Durham, NC: Duke University Press. http://dx.doi.org/10.1215 /9780822388067.

Place 14

*Cochiti Pueblo, Core Values, and
Authorized Heritage Discourse*

ROBERT PREUCEL AND REGIS PECOS

In 1965, the US Army Corps of Engineers began construction of a massive dam on the Cochiti Pueblo land
grant in northern New Mexico (Figure 14.1). Completed
ten years later at a cost of $94.4 million, Cochiti Dam
contains the Rio Grande river and provides flood and
sediment control for the city of Albuquerque (US
Army Corps of Engineers 1985: 11). The Army Corps
defines the project as significant for three reasons: it
is an outstanding example of an earth filled embank-
ment (the largest structure of its kind in New Mexico
and the tenth largest in the world), it completes the
flood control program of the Middle Rio Grande, and
it provides unique recreational facilities (West 1971:
188). However, the dam came at a great human price.
The dam profoundly transformed the lifeways of the
people of Cochiti Pueblo by compromising their traditional agricultural activities, destroying their ancestral
homes and burial grounds, and disrupting their sacred
religious practices. It threatened their sense of place.

In this chapter, we consider some of the key challenges Cochiti Pueblo has faced in the last forty years
in response to the building of Cochiti Dam. These
challenges throw into sharp relief the ways in which
Cochiti people conceptualize themselves and their
future. Indeed, they demonstrate the skills of Cochiti
leadership and the power of traditional knowledge

DOI: 10.5876/9781607323846.c014

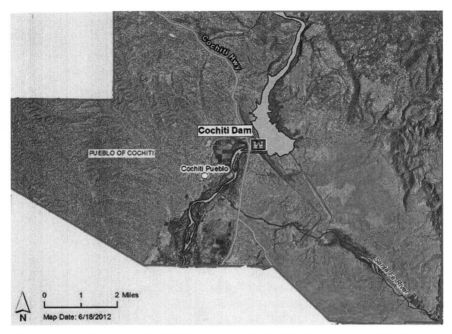

FIGURE 14.1. *Location of Cochiti Dam within Cochiti Pueblo (courtesy of US Army Corps of Engineers).*

in assuring cultural survival. Cochiti Pueblo's responses to these challenges reveal the very impossibility of separating out concepts like 'place,' 'heritage,' and 'cultural resource' for many Native American tribes and Indigenous communities worldwide. Although these terms are part of the dominant heritage discourse and are used by Cochiti people for strategic purposes, they fail to express the core values of what it means to be *of Cochiti*. The Cochiti people are clear that they, and not the federal government, are responsible for their own destiny.

The Cochiti example sheds considerable light on the complex interrelations of people, place, and heritage. It indicates that people make places through social practices, both material and discursive, and that these practices conjoin people and things in specific locations at particular times for distinctive purposes. Following Laurajane Smith (2006), it is possible to argue that there is no such thing as heritage in the abstract, rather it must be conceived as multi-layered discourse about the proper relationships between a people's past, present, and future. This moral discourse encompasses not only about how we talk about the meanings of the past, but it is also about the social institutions and technical practices we create for structuring our ongoing relationships with the past. The Cochiti case study demonstrates some of the ways tribal governments and federal institutions, in this case Cochiti Pueblo and the US Army Corps, have co-constructed and sometimes transformed each other through debate and dialogue.

ON PLACE AND PLACEMAKING

Place is a term widely used in contemporary cultural anthropology, human geography, sociology, and urban planning (e.g., Feld and Basso 1996; Gieryn 2000; Soja 1996; Tuan 1977). It is often contrasted with space, where space is considered to be objective and abstract and place is regarded as subjective and phenomenological. Yi Fu Tuan (1977: 6), for example, argues that places come into being when humans assign value to previously undifferentiated space. Henri Lefebvre (1991: 38–39) notes that 'socialized space' can be broken down into spatial practice (the daily routines of a society), the representation of space (conceptualized space of architects and planners), and representational space (space as lived through its associated images and symbols). Similarly, Edward Soja (1996) holds that space must be understood as simultaneously real and imagined because it always represents a link between the physical and the cultural.

Placemaking can be defined as the social practices associated with the public inscription of collective memories (Preucel and Matero 2008: 84). Because the making of place is an inherently political process, certain places may be incorporated into sanctioned views of the social imaginary. Places of resistance, such as battlefields, may be sanitized and depoliticized as they are incorporated into specific narratives emphasizing the continuity of past and present. Alternatively, they may be recuperated and used to deny continuity as a means of challenging the dominant social order. Placemaking is thus a technology of reordering reality, and its success depends upon the degree to which this refashioning generates habitual action.

Placelessness, by contrast, can be seen as "the casual eradication of distinctive places and the making of standardized landscapes that results from an insensitivity to the significance of place" (Relph 1976). It can be associated with 'supermodernity' and the increasing use of temporary spaces such as hospitals, airports, and shopping malls (Augé 1995). It often produces a condition of anomie or disorientation. The control of place is a central strategy of the colonial process. It is exemplified when a people are forcibly removed from their homeland and relocated to new places, not of their own choosing. In the American Southwest, the 'long walk' of the Navajo from Fort Defiance in Arizona to Fort Sumner in New Mexico is a classic example (Denetdale 2007).

Placemaking is deeply implicated in contemporary heritage discourse. For example, the idea of universal or world heritage identifies places, usually defined as monuments, groups of buildings, or sites, which are of such universal significance to all of humankind that they are to be preserved for the benefit of future generations. This view is embodied in the preamble of the UNESCO 1972 *Convention Concerning the Protection of the World Cultural and Natural Heritage*. Similarly, the idea of national heritage or patrimony specifies that there are places of national significance associated with important people, historic events, or aesthetic values that warrant preservation on behalf of a citizenry. English Heritage, for example, holds that "England's historic environment helps define our national identity. It helps shape how we think about ourselves and how other people see us. It is the mix of old and new, our interest in our past and our confidence in the future which defines our nation today" (English Heritage et al. 2007: 2). Here, heritage is used as a technology to give social values material permanence and thus ensure the continuity of contemporary social forms and institutions.

Not all places that are memorialized carry positive values. Lynn Meskell (2002) has coined the term 'negative heritage' to refer to places that become the repository of traumatic memory in the collective imaginary. She gives as examples Auschwitz, Hiroshima, and District Six. For her, such places can be memorialized by means of monuments that may serve both as reminders of the past and lessons for the future. In this context, heritage occupies a positive and culturally elevated position. However, she cautions that "we should recognize that not all individuals, groups or nations share those views, or have the luxury of affluence to indulge these desires" and that "we uncritically hold that heritage, specifically 'world heritage,' must be a good thing and thus find it difficult to comprehend groups who support counter claims, whether for the reasons of a religious, moral, economic, or political nature" (2002: 558).

Laurajane Smith (2006; see also Waterton, Smith, and Campbell 2006) has offered a valuable critique of heritage from the perspective of discourse analysis. She interrogates claims for universal heritage and identifies them as part of 'Authorized Heritage Discourse' (AHD). According to her, this discourse "takes its cue from the grand narratives of Western national and elite class experiences, and reinforces the idea of innate cultural value tied to time depth, monumentality, expert knowledge and aesthetics" (Smith 2006: 299).

What counts as heritage is thus intimately bound up with the legitimization of political power. She also notes that authorized discourse establishes a series of social relationships linking the expert, heritage site, and visitor where the expert is the sanctioned mediator of the visitor experience (2006: 34). The effect of AHD is to naturalize and make seem inevitable certain cultural values and narratives about nation and nationhood (2006: 4).

The central trope of AHD is the concept of preserving the past for the future according to professional standards of the heritage industry. This rhetoric effectively controls how people challenge and rewrite the dominant interpretations of the past. Yet, there always exists alongside AHD a range of these alternative discourses and practices embodied by specific interest groups. Some of these discourses may challenge the authority of the dominant professional discourse. Others may draw language and strategies from AHD and put them to their own uses. But, in either case, these alternative discourses are not reducible to the dominant discourse. Heritage is thus an ongoing process of negotiating social meanings and practices that are linked to political identity and self-determination.

The greatest challenge to AHD has come from alternative discourses, especially the activism of Indigenous peoples around the world (Smith 2006: 36). Smith suggests that although this discourse is sometimes framed in the context of repatriation and reburial, it involves more than a debate over ownership. It is about human rights. More specifically, it is about the right to define yourself and the community to which you belong. Indigenous scholars have accordingly critiqued archaeologists, anthropologists, historians, and museum curators for their neglect of contemporary Indigenous agency and politics (2006: 276). They have also challenged the universalizing tendencies of the World Heritage Convention for failing to incorporate culturally relevant concepts of heritage. They have questioned the focus on the material (artifacts, monuments) at the expense of the immaterial and intangible forms of heritage (language, dance, songs). We now turn to how the construction of Cochiti Dam has impacted heritage discourse for the Army Corps and Cochiti Pueblo.

COCHITI PUEBLO

Cochiti Pueblo is the northernmost of the seven Keresan speaking pueblos in New Mexico. It is located approximately 30 miles southwest of Santa Fe. The Pueblo has a total population of 1,727 people (2010 Census). There are 607 community members living in the pueblo, including some who became residents through marriage (Cochiti Pueblo 2009: 9). The majority of the community, at 26 percent of the population, is in the 25–44 year-old range, with the second highest group in the 45–65 age range at 22 percent (2009: 8). While Keres is the traditional language, English is the primary language used by most people in their everyday lives. Spanish is also spoken by some of the elders, especially those 65 or older, who constitute 17 percent of the population (2009: 12).

Cochiti maintains 54,000 acres of reservation land located on either side of the Rio Grande. The principal land use includes farming, livestock, recreational, economic development, and agricultural and residential construction. Cochiti manages the Town of Cochiti Lake containing 568 residents living on land leased from the Pueblo (2010 Census). It also manages the Robert Trent Jones Golf Course, one of the highest ranked pueblo golf courses in the state. Cochiti works closely with the federal agencies controlling lands abutting the reservation and has established joint land management agreements with the Bureau of Land Management for Kasha-Katuwe Tent Rocks National Monument (Pinel and Pecos 2012) and with the US Army Corps of Engineers for Cochiti Dam (Matlock 2008).

Cochiti, like other Native American communities, exists in a sovereign space defined in part by its political relationships with a series of foreign colonizing powers. For Cochiti, these relationships began in 1598 with the founding of the Spanish colony of New Mexico. Cochiti and the other pueblos asserted their sovereignty during the famous Pueblo Revolt of 1680 (Knaut 1995). These relationships continue up to the present day with the US federal government and the Bureau of Indian Affairs. In the last thirty years, the Cochiti Tribal Council has adroitly navigated a number of cultural and economic challenges that have threatened their way of life and created sharp tensions within their community. The most important of these have been associated with the building of Cochiti Dam.

COCHITI DAM

To fully understand the impact of the construction of Cochiti Dam, it is necessary to understand Cochiti's traditional land use practices. The lands south of White Rock canyon are part of Cochiti's ancestral homeland. They contain ancestral villages, sacred shrines, agricultural fields, wild plant gathering areas, and hunting grounds. Prior to the construction of the dam, many families maintained *ranchitos* (field houses) in this area so that they could tend their corn, beans, squash, chile, and melons (Benjamin, Pecos, and Romero

1996: 117). This is the time when individual families, or groups of relatives, would live together, and children would be taught skills of hunting small game, farming, and food preparation. In the fall, the families would return to the pueblo with their crops and hold their harvest ceremonies. This annual cycle, living in the fields in the summer and returning to the pueblo in the fall, constituted the very rhythm of Cochiti life.

The Middle Rio Grande Conservancy District was created in 1925 to manage irrigation agriculture and control flooding in the Albuquerque Basin. Of special concern were the lands of Cochiti Pueblo, Santo Domingo Pueblo, San Felipe Pueblo, Santa Ana Pueblo, and Isleta Pueblo that together accounted for 18 percent of the total acreage and required Congressional approval for inclusion and taxation (Clark 1987: 209). The nature of the Conservancy District's consultation with the tribes is not clear. There were protests on the grounds that Indian rights were not sufficiently protected (1987: 209–10). The Conservancy began its assessment in the Cochiti district located just south of White Rock canyon. This area was a natural location for a dam since it is where the river emerges from a constrained channel. The Conservancy District completed a diversion dam about three miles north of Cochiti and included a major canal on each side of the river (Lange 1979: 368). However, the initial construction project was hurried and few of the ditches were cemented (Clark 1987: 212). Sediment built up in the main riverbed and wild plants began to encroach. In 1941, the levees failed to contain a major flood that inundated communities throughout the Rio Grande valley, including parts of downtown Albuquerque (Middleton 2002: 54).

In 1956, the US Senate Committee on Public Works requested the Army Corps to make a study (West 1971: 179). The report, issued in 1960, recommended the construction of a new dam halfway between the old dam and Cochiti Pueblo. This dam was to be considerably larger than the old dam and linked to the creation of the Town of Cochiti Lake and economic development under the management of Great Western Cities Inc. The debate over the dam and housing development split the pueblo into two factions (Pecos 2007). Some people advocated taking advantage of the development opportunities, while others opposed them on traditional grounds. After considerable internal turmoil and the federal government's threat of seizure under eminent domain, the Tribal Council finally agreed to support the dam and town in order to benefit from the promised economic opportunities.

In 1969, Cochiti signed a 99-year lease with Great Western Cities, Inc. for the development of 6,500 acres of property into a recreational city of 50,000 persons (Pinel 1988). This included recreational facilities such as a golf course

Figure 14.2. *View of Cochiti Pueblo from Cochiti Dam (courtesy of US Army Corps of Engineers).*

and marina. This venture was one of the first times that a private development corporation invested on reservation lands (Pecos 2007: 643). However, the venture was short lived. In 1985, the corporation declared bankruptcy and the Cochiti Community Development Corporation is now managing the Town of Cochiti Lake.

In 1975, the Army Corps completed Cochiti Dam and Reservoir (Figure 14.2). However, two issues quickly came to the fore. First, in the process of constructing the spillway the Army Corps destroyed one of Cochiti's most sacred shrines (Pinel 1988). Joseph Suina, a Tribal Council member, states, "This was one of our sacred sites, not just to Cochiti, but to other pueblos. They blamed Cochiti when it was destroyed. Even today some still blame us" (Matlock 2009). Cochiti people took this action to be a breech of faith since they had been given assurances by the Army Corps that the shrine would be left inviolate. Second, water seepage began to flood the traditional fields east of the pueblo compromising the growing of traditional crops. Cochiti immediately filed a report and the Army Corps installed a 17-acre drainage system several years later, but it proved to be ineffective (Pinel 1988). In 1987, 550 of the 800 acres of tribal irrigated farmland were flooded so badly that farming was impossible (Pinel 1988). Cochiti was forced to file a lawsuit in 1985 against the Army Corps to seek remediation.

The relations between the Army Corps and Cochiti became badly strained. In Congressional testimony, Cochiti pointed out that, although a significant amount of ecosystem research has been conducted in the area, little comprehensive analysis had been conducted regarding how the Dam's operations might impact Pueblo resources. They drew attention to the fact that the Army Corps is required to protect Cochiti natural and cultural assets as part of its Native American Trust responsibilities. Their testimony was persuasive because it combined a factual argument (the Army Corps was negligent in consultation) with moral one (the loss of traditional ancestral farming lands threatened Pueblo livelihood and religion). In 1992, Cochiti received a $12 million settlement, half of which was spent on developing a new drainage system (Pinel 1988).

In 2000, there was a widespread drought in the north central Rio Grande district. As a result, the District Engineer began to hold monthly meetings with the Pueblo Governor. These meetings proved to be very beneficial in establishing a respectful relationship. They came to fruition in 2003 when the Army Corps held a reconciliation ceremony near the location where Cochiti's religious site was destroyed. The entire Cochiti community attended, and the District Engineer publically apologized for the damage the government caused and committed to a future of collaboration. In 2004, the Army Corps and Cochiti initiated a series of studies intended to characterize the interactions of Cochiti Dam and Lake with Tribal resources. These included water quality studies, sediment studies, biological studies, cultural studies, economic impact studies, information management and mapping, independent technical reviews, supervision, and management. In 2008, Cochiti Pueblo signed an historic agreement with the Army Corps to participate in the overall management of the Cochiti Lake area (Matlock 2008). This cooperative agreement was the first of its kind in the state.

The cultural impacts of the dam have been far reaching. Willie Martin, a Tribal Council member, explained, "Cochiti people are taught to give to and protect the land so that they in turn will be protected. They are now powerless to fulfill a sacred responsibility, and without farming have no way to teach this responsibility to their children" (Pinel 1988: 26). Here, he is articulating the core values of reciprocity and balance central to Cochiti life. He continues to describe its impact on ceremonial life. "The dam has cut the pueblo off from the canyon where its ancestors lived, and has destroyed and flooded shrines. Not all the land was farmed at the time the seepage began; but the dam has torn the fabric of the community from the loom" (Pinel 1988: 26-27).

COCHITI DAM ARCHAEOLOGY

The construction of Cochiti Dam required archaeological mitigation under federal law. However, the schedule of the work required that it be carried out under salvage laws rather than cultural resource management laws (Broilo and Biella 1977: 3). Under salvage laws, land modification projects receive the highest priority. This contrasts with cultural resource management laws where consideration of archaeological resources is part of the project planning phases. In practice, this meant that there was no opportunity to redirect the project due to the significance of the archaeological resources. From 1962 to 1976, three agencies oversaw different aspects of the archaeological survey and excavation: the Museum of New Mexico, the National Park Service, and the University of New Mexico (Mathien 2004: 100–108).

In 1962, the Museum of New Mexico conducted salvage archaeology within the proposed dam construction area. Alfred E. Dittert, Charlie Steen, and Albert H. Schroeder began survey work (Lange 1968: 314). Charles Lange directed the Cochiti Dam Archaeological Salvage project (Lange 1968). He and his team excavated three sites, the Red Snake Hill site (LA 6461), the North Bank site (LA 6462), and the Alfred Herrera site (LA 6455). A total of thirteen burials were recovered from the North Bank site and sixty-four from the Alfred Herrera site (Heglar 1968). Additional survey was carried out during 1963, 1964, and 1965 by Lange, Stanley Bussey, and Stewart Peckham (Lange 1968: 318). David Snow conducted a series of archaeological surveys under Lange's direction. These surveys focused on the areas leased by the California City Development Company (Snow 1970a) and the Great Western United Corporation (Snow 1970b), as well as the Tetilla Peak Recreation Area (Snow 1973). These surveys revealed an occupation sequence from the Archaic to the Historic periods and included campsites, field houses, and agricultural fields. Snow (1971) then began a series of test excavations during the 1964–1966 field seasons. In 1966, Polly Schaafsma (1975) conducted a rock art survey of the Cochiti Reservoir district.

In 1974, the National Park Service granted a contract to the Office of Contract Archaeology at the University of New Mexico to perform an archaeological assessment of the Cochiti Reservoir and Flood Pool (Broilo and Biella 1977: 5). This involved baseline studies of the environmental setting (geology, ecology, faunal resources, paleoclimate, water supply) and an overview of the cultural resources (past research, methodology, survey, and significance) (Biella and Chapman 1977). In 1975, a second phase was initiated that involved developing and completing a program of mitigation for the adversely affected resources in the permanent pool of Cochiti Reservoir and conducting an intensive survey of the flood control pool of the reservoir (Chapman and Biella 1977). In 1976, a third phase involved mitigation of adversely affected resources in the flood control pool of Cochiti Reservoir (Biella 1979; Biella and Chapman 1979).

The National Park Service also sponsored archaeology and survey in the area of the flood pool as it extended into Bandelier National Monument. In 1974, Ron Ice, Don Fiero, and Dan Leniham conducted a preliminary survey to relocate sites identified on previous surveys (Mathien 2004: 107). This was followed up by a more detailed survey by Bruce Anderson, Don Fiero, and George West. The Park Service then developed a mitigation plan to excavate eight sites in the permanent flood pool and another fifteen within the potential flood pool area (Hubbell and Traylor 1982).

Although archaeology was required under salvage laws, it was conducted with limited consideration of the views and perspectives of the Cochiti people. The majority of the projects did not reach out to Cochiti Pueblo and thus failed to take into consideration the cultural and religious impacts of this research. For example, the Cochiti Dam archaeologists excavated burials and associated grave goods now curated at the Maxwell Museum of Anthropology. In addition, archaeologists removed the stone lion from the shrine of the stone lions on Potrero de los Idoles, bundled it in a mattress, and helicoptered it to the Maxwell Museum. These actions had serious cultural repercussions for the Cochiti people. As Pecos (2007: 645) has written, "one of the most emotional periods in our history was watching our ancestors torn from their resting places, removed during excavation. The places of worship were dynamited, destroyed, and desecrated by the construction. The traditional homelands were destroyed." In retrospect, Pecos was surprised that there was not greater protest from the pueblo against the salvage archaeology. He suggests that it was allowed to go forward because of an overwhelming sense of hopelessness that the Pueblo could not win this fight against the government, especially when it followed on the heels of such an ugly internal fight about the building of the dam in the first place.

Cochiti Pueblo has worked assiduously to heal these wounds through dialogue with the relevant institutions and the implementation of new repatriation legislation. For example, prior to the passage of the *Native American Graves*

Protection and Repatriation Act (NAGPRA), Cochiti successfully petitioned the Maxwell Museum to return the stone lion back to its shrine. The most difficult task, however, was the repatriation of their ancestors and associated grave goods removed during the Cochiti Dam excavations. Under NAGPRA, Cochiti has repatriated 223 ancestors and associated grave goods. The Pueblo knew that it was their moral responsibility to bring them home. But they also knew that it would revive internal conflict because the Pueblo has no formal procedures for reburying the dead. As Pecos explains, "There is no process. To rebury them without direct engagement was itself deeply troubling internally. No one knew what to do. The discussion was itself taboo. It epitomizes the depth of internal conflict with repatriation to varying degrees. Unequivocally, no one would take the position to celebrate the return. However, it immediately turns to conflict because the how was deeply problematic." The Pueblo, therefore, authorized the Army Corp to conduct the reburial in an undisclosed location on Cochiti land. Because of their negative experiences with archaeology, Cochiti now requires that all archaeological work to be approved by the Tribal Council and conducted in close consultation with the Pueblo.

COCHITI LANGUAGE REVITALIZATION

The dam not only disrupted traditional agriculture, it also disrupted the very rhythm of Cochiti life. With the loss of the agricultural lands, there was no opportunity to teach children the core values associated with farming traditional crops. Increasingly, people moved away from the village and took up residence in suburbs created by US Department of Housing and Urban Development (HUD) housing. This pattern of neolocal residence broke up the traditional multigenerational way of life and led to many households with no elders on hand to instruct the children. More and more intermarriage between Cochiti and non-Cochiti people took place. The cumulative effects of these interrelated developments led to a sharp decline in proficiency in the Cochiti language among the Cochiti youth.

In 1992, because of the threat that this trend posed to Cochiti culture, the Cochiti Pueblo Tribal Council created the Cochiti Indian Education Committee and the Cochiti Education Task Force to address this problem. The council unanimously agreed to establish language revitalization as the community's first priority (Benjamin, Pecos, and Romero 1996; Pecos and Blum-Martinez 2001: 77). They began by evaluating the community's resources, activities, programs, and history. This set the stage for a discussion of the impacts of these programs on the use of native language. Many of the committee members were in their thirties or forties and had lived through the controversies associated with the dam. Some people, who initially felt personally responsible for language loss, came to appreciate the broader forces of assimilation (Pecos and Blum-Martinez 2001: 77).

In 1993, Cochiti conducted three community-wide surveys to determine the status of the Cochiti language (2001: 78). Each of the surveys targeted a specific cohort of speakers and highlighted a different speech context. The first survey focused on the use of Keres by the elderly in public settings. A second survey focused on the use of the language by parents in the home. A third survey addressed the use of the language among older children and adolescents in school and extracurricular activities. The results of the survey revealed that most tribal members thirty-five years of age and older were fluent speakers. However, it also revealed that the younger the person, the less likely he or she spoke or understood the language. The Pueblo identified this situation as a serious problem for the pueblo's future because its governance and ceremonies are conducted exclusively in the Cochiti language.

As a result, the Cochiti Tribal council passed a resolution to establish the Cochiti Keres Language Revitalization Program in 1995 (Herrera 2008). It employed twelve teachers and served between seventy and ninety children. Over the years, approximately forty-five community members, who are fluent or intermediately fluent, have received training to teach Keres in a classroom setting. In 2001, the tribe also created the Pueblo de Cochiti Language Nest, with the assistance of an Administration for Native Americans grant (Herrera 2008). The Language Nest is a place where childcare is provided for Cochiti children who are six months to three years old. This language nest is modeled after the language nests in the Maori communities of New Zealand.

In 2014, Cochiti established the Keres Children's Learning Center as a not-for-profit educational organization to support Cochiti Pueblo children and families in maintaining, strengthening, and revitalizing their heritage language. The mission of the Learning Center is to create a linguistically and culturally rich learning environment that supports the fundamental principles and core values of native life that are essential in the socialization of Cochiti Pueblo children. It is providing a quality preschool program for children ages three to six years old, using teaching practices that include Keres language immersion and holistic approaches grounded in the Montessori Method. The Learning Center is committed to providing an environment in which children hear Keres spoken naturally throughout all Center activities, learn through culturally appropriate activities reflective of traditional practices, and become well prepared for future schooling.

Cochiti linguistic self-determination is a matter of cultural survival. As Suina (2004: 299–300) has put it, the Pueblos must maintain sole authority over their language programs so that they can ensure their responsibilities to future generations. This value also requires that federal and state governments adopt Pueblo-specific parameters on Native language instruction in schools. "It is the language that carries the nature and character of who we are and how we related to one another, and to Mother Earth, and to all the things we experience in life. Once we've lost that, we have lost everything" (Cochiti councilman, quoted in Suina 2004: 300).

COCHITI/ARMY CORPS COURSES

In the past five years, Cochiti Pueblo and the Army Corps have worked hard to build a new relationship based upon trust and mutual understanding. Towards this end, Cochiti Pueblo and the Army Corps, Albuquerque District sponsored two courses on Cochiti Pueblo Perspectives on Cultural Preservation and Natural Resources Management in 2010 and 2011. The first of these was held from April 19–22, 2010, and the second from April 25–28, 2011. Each of these courses allowed approximately twenty managers from across the Army Corps and various partner agencies to learn about Cochiti Pueblo in an immersion experience.

Cochiti elders, administrators, and families also participated in these courses. Numerous activities were offered to educate the participants about Cochiti life, past and present. Suina spoke at length about the importance of the Keres language to pueblo life. He explained that all government functions and the majority of their cultural practices are performed in Keres and, for this reason, they have developed programs dedicated to teaching the language to their children. Pecos gave a presentation on Cochiti core values (Figure 14.3). He drew attention to the common goal, shared by all parents Native and non-Native, of building a better world for future generations. He provided a historical overview of the impositions on Indian culture that were instituted by Federal Indian law. He also emphasized that during this current period of self-determination, Cochiti needed to come together or face self-termination. Preucel led a tour of Hanat Kotyiti, the ancestral village occupied by Cochiti people immediately after the Pueblo Revolt of 1680. He emphasized the importance of Cochiti's history of resistance to foreign control and the collaborative research that he and Cochiti are pursuing, which has involved a dozen Cochiti high school students (Preucel 2000). The highlight of the course, however, was the 'home stay,' when course participants spent the night with a Cochiti family.

FIGURE 14.3. *Regis Pecos teaching Cochiti core values to the Cochiti/Army Corps course participants in 2011.*

This program had very positive impact on the Army Corps participants. During the farewell dinner held on the final night, each participant shared what he or she had learned from the program. Karen Downey, the operations manager at John Martin Reservoir and Dam in Colorado explained,

> The biggest impact on me had to be the telling of the Cochiti history leading up to the interaction with the government. To hear how dealings with the Army Corps disrupted the lives of the Cochiti people and nearly destroyed an entire culture with roots in the ancient past was very disturbing to me. The Cochiti peoples' passionate recounting of their love of family and ancestors, sacred beliefs and connection to their native lands intertwined with their core values made me understand the important things that I should treasure in my own life. (Skopeck 2011: 4)

Mary C. Anderson, a regulatory project manager in Detroit District, said the part of the training that had the biggest impact on her was focusing on core values versus individual gain, as well as developing open listening skills. She stated, "Now, at work, I will be more open to hearing what the applicant, violator, consultant or agent has to say and get the full story behind a project (Skopeck 2011: 4).

CONCLUDING THOUGHTS

The ability to control and define the experience of 'being in place' is central to a community's social, cultural, and political identity (Smith 2006: 290). Increasingly, Indigenous peoples worldwide have adopted aspects of AHD to assert control of their homelands and exercise their sovereign rights. No longer is the discourse of heritage the sole domain of Western specialists, such as archaeologists, historians, and lawyers. Indigenous leaders are expanding this discourse by forcing Western institutions to consider alternative characterizations of heritage, many of which are based on traditional or core values. These values are grounded not in the idea of ownership where transactions are completed and done with, but rather in notions of reciprocity where ongoing relationships of obligation bind together people and place into a moral landscape.

The Cochiti case demonstrates the effectiveness of their core values discourse both within the community and to outsiders. Within the pueblo, Cochiti elders are teaching their children the inseparable nature of material (agriculture, shrines, ancestral villages) and immaterial heritage (language, songs, dances). When, for example, a Cochiti person visits a place once inhabited by their ancestors (an archaeological site), the appropriate behavior is to say a prayer in the Cochiti language and make an offering to acknowledge their ancestors and to explain why they have come to disturb their peace. This act establishes a transcendent relationship between contemporary Cochiti people and their ancestors that crosses time and space. Pecos (2012) has developed a core values paradigm as part of the Leadership Institute at the Santa Fe Indian School. The central question he poses his students is "how will future generations speak of us? Will they honor us or disown us by what we did in our time that defined their inheritance? Will they speak of us in the same way that we speak and honor Our Forefathers like those who sacrificed their lives in the Pueblo Revolt?"

Cochiti leaders are also instructing federal agencies, like the Army Corps, about their core values that center on the well-being of their children and the perpetuation of their community. They are articulating how the loss of traditional farming lands due to the construction of Cochiti Dam has impacted agriculture, the very fabric of Cochiti life. This meant that children could not be instructed properly in the centrality of the growth of corn, beans, and melons to Cochiti ritual practice. The loss of access to ancestral sites and shrines threatens people's abilities to make offerings to their ancestors or instruct children in the events that occurred at those sites. This instruction, which is given in the Cochiti language, is an example of place-based learning and crucial to how the Cochiti language is kept alive. The core values discourse, which builds on common human experiences of family and parenthood, is proving to be extremely effective as is indicated by the thoughtful statements given by the Army Corps participants in the Cochiti/Army Corps workshops.

As traumatic as the Cochiti Dam experience was, Cochiti does not consider it 'negative heritage.' It is seen as a legacy of the Cochiti leaders who secured concessions from the Army Corps in exchange for allowing its construction and who fought for remediation for failures in the dam operation. It is also seen as an opportunity for the future. Cochiti leaders have begun the process of rehabilitating their relationships with Army Corps based upon shared values of trust and mutual understanding. This new rapport has led to an innovative joint management program of the dam. In 2012, Cochiti Pueblo received a grant from the First Nations Development Institute's Native Agriculture and Food Systems Initiative for the Cochiti Youth Enterprise (CYE). CYE believes one way to empower youth is through the reinvigoration of farming and traditions of healthy food. Cochiti's success is due, in part, to their community's skills at combining elements of AHD with traditional core values for Cochiti purposes.

ACKNOWLEDGMENTS

We would like to acknowledge the teachers and students of Cochiti Pueblo Language programs who are so dedicated and committed to ensuring the continuance of the Cochiti language. We also thank Lt. Col. Jason Williams (US Army Corps of Engineers, Albuquerque District), Ron Kneebone (Tribal Liason, US Army Corps of Engineers), and Mark Rosaker (Cochiti Lake Project Manager, US Army Corps of Engineers).

REFERENCES

Augé, Marc. 1995. *Non-Places: Introduction to the Anthropology of Supermodernity.* London: Verso.

Benjamin, R. R., Regis Pecos, and Mary Eunice Romero. 1996. "Language Revitalization Efforts in the Pueblo de Cochiti: Becoming 'Literate' in an Oral Society." In *Indigenous Literacies in the Americans: Language Planning from the Bottom Up*, ed. Nancy H. Hornberger, 115–36. New York, NY: Mouton de Gruyter.

Biella, Jan V., ed. 1979. *Archaeological Investigations in Cochiti Reservoir, New Mexico, Volume 3: 1976–1977 Field Seasons.* Albuquerque: University of New Mexico, Office of Contract Archaeology.

Biella, Jan V., and Richard C. Chapman, eds. 1977. *Archaeological Investigations in Cochiti Reservoir, New Mexico, Volume 1: A Survey of Regional Variability.* Albuquerque: University of New Mexico, Office of Contract Archaeology.

Biella, Jan V., and Richard C. Chapman, eds. 1979. *Archaeological Investigations in Cochiti Reservoir, New Mexico, Volume 4: Adaptive Change in the Northern Rio Grande Valley.* Albuquerque: University of New Mexico, Office of Contract Archaeology.

Broilo, Frank J., and Jan V. Biella. 1977. "The Cochiti Reservoir Archaeological Project." In *Archaeological Investigations in Cochiti Reservoir, New Mexico, Volume 1: A Survey of Regional Variability*, ed. Jan V. Biella and Richard C. Chapman, 3–5. Albuquerque: University of New Mexico, Office of Contract Archaeology.

Chapman, Richard C., and Jan V. Biella, eds. 1977. *Archaeological Investigations in Cochiti Reservoir, New Mexico, Volume 2: Excavation and Analysis, 1975 Season.* Albuquerque: University of New Mexico, Office of Contract Archaeology.

Clark, Ira G. 1987. *Water in New Mexico: A History of Its Management and Use.* Albuquerque: University of New Mexico Press.

Cochiti Pueblo. 2009. *Community Health Profile 2009.* Cochiti Pueblo, NM: Cochiti Pueblo.

Denetdale, Jennifer Nez. 2007. *Reclaiming Diné History: The Legacies of Navajo Chief Manuelito and Juanita.* Tucson: University of Arizona Press.

English Heritage, the National Trust, Heritage Lottery Fund, the Historic Houses Association, and Heritage Link. 2007. *Valuing our Heritage: The Case for Future Investment in the Historic Environment.* London: English Heritage.

Feld, Steven, and Keith H. Basso, eds. 1996. *Senses of Place.* Santa Fe, NM: School of American Research Press.

Gieryn, Thomas F. 2000. "A Space for Place in Sociology." *Annual Review of Sociology* 26 (1): 463–96. http://dx.doi.org/10.1146/annurev.soc.26.1.463.

Heglar, Rodger. 1968. "Human Skeletal Remains." In *The Cochiti Dam Archaeological Salvage Project, Part 1: Report on the 1963 Season*, ed. Charles Lange, 262–304. Museum of New Mexico Research Records No. 6. Santa Fe: Museum of New Mexico Press.

Herrera, Joanie. 2008. "Speak Keres. Then, Now, Forever: An Analysis and Comparison of Native Language Revitalization Efforts among Adult Learners." *Ronald E. McNair and Research Opportunity Scholar Journal* 6: 127–38.

Hubbell, Lyndi, and Diane Traylor, eds. 1982. *Bandelier: Excavations in the Flood Pool of Cochiti Lake, New Mexico.* Santa Fe, NM: Southwest Cultural Resources Center, National Park Service.

Knaut, Andrew L. 1995. *The Pueblo Revolt of 1680: Conquest and Resistance in Seventeenth-Century New Mexico.* Norman: University of Oklahoma Press.

Lange, Charles H., ed. 1968. *The Cochiti Dam Archaeological Salvage Project, Part 1: Report on the 1963 Season. Museum of New Mexico Research Records No. 6.* Santa Fe: Museum of New Mexico Press.

Lange, Charles H. 1979. "Cochiti Pueblo." In *Handbook of the North American Indian, Volume 9,* ed. Alfonso Ortiz, 366–78. Washington, DC: Smithsonian Institution.

Lefebvre, Henri. 1991. *The Production of Space.* Trans. Donald Nicholson-Smith. Oxford: Blackwell Press.

Mathien, Joan. 2004. "History of Archaeological Investigations on the Pajarito Plateau." In *Archaeology of Bandelier National Monument: Village Formation on the Pajarito Plateau, New Mexico,* ed. Timothy A. Kohler, 69–116. Albuquerque: University of New Mexico Press.

Matlock, Staci. 2008. "Cochiti Pueblo to Help Manage Lake: Cooperative Agreement between U. S. Army Corps, Native Americans first in N.M." *Santa Fe New Mexican,* June 23.

Matlock, Staci. 2009. "Rio Grande Voices: Culture Interrupted." *Santa Fe New Mexican,* July 5.

Meskell, Lynn. 2002. "Negative Heritage and Past Mastering in Archaeology." *Anthropological Quarterly* 75 (3): 557–74. http://dx.doi.org/10.1353/anq.2002.0050.

Middleton, Beth. 2002. *Flood Pulsing in Wetlands: Restoring the Natural Hydrological Balance.* New York, NY: John Wiley and Sons.

Pecos, Regis. 2007. "The History of Cochiti Lake from the Pueblo Perspective." *Natural Resources Journal* 47: 639–53.

Pecos, Regis. 2012. "Where We Have Been, Where We Are, Where We Are Going: Our Core Values Paradigm." Powerpoint presentation, Leadership Institute at the Santa Fe Indian School, Santa Fe.

Pecos, Regis, and Rebecca Blum-Martinez. 2001. "The Key to Cultural Survival: Language Planning and Revitalization in the Pueblo of Cochiti." In *The Green Book of Language Revitalization in Practice,* ed. Leanne Hinton and Ken Hale, 75–85. San Diego, CA: Academic Press. http://dx.doi.org/10.1163/9789004 261723_008.

Pinel, Sandra L. 1988. "Stopping the Flood of Damages from Cochiti Dam." *Cultural Survival Quarterly* 12 (2): 25–29.

Pinel, Sandra L., and Jacob Pecos. 2012. "Generating Co-management at Kasha Katuwe Tent Rocks National Monument, New Mexico." *Environmental Management* 49 (3): 593–604. http://dx.doi.org/10.1007/s00267-012-9814-9.

Preucel, Robert W. 2000. "Living on the Mesa: Hanat Kotyiti, a Post-revolt Cochiti Community in the Northern Rio Grande." *Expedition* 42: 8–17.

Preucel, Robert W., and Frank G. Matero. 2008. "Placemaking on the Northern Rio Grande: A View from Kuaua Pueblo." In *Archaeologies of Placemaking: Monuments, Memories, and Engagement in Native North America*, ed. Patricia Rubertone, 81–99. Walnut Creek, CA: Left Coast Press.

Relph, Edward. 1976. *Place and Placelessness*. London: Pion.

Schaafsma, Polly. 1975. *Rock Art in the Cochiti Reservoir District. Museum of New Mexico Papers in Anthropology no. 16.* Santa Fe: Museum of New Mexico Press.

Skopeck, Kristen. 2011. "Cultural Immersion Course Promotes Introspection." *Rip Rap: US Army Corps of Engineers Albuquerque District* 23 (6): 2–4.

Smith, Laurajane. 2006. *Uses of Heritage*. London: Routledge.

Snow, David H. 1970a. *An Inventory of the Archaeological Sites on Lands Leased by the California City Development Company, Cochiti Pueblo Grant, Sandoval County, New Mexico.* Laboratory of Anthropology Notes No. 80C. Santa Fe: Museum of New Mexico.

Snow, David H. 1970b. *An Inventory of the Archaeological Sites on Lands Leased by the Great Western United Corporation: 1970 Season.* Laboratory of Anthropology Notes No. 80B. Santa Fe: Museum of New Mexico.

Snow, David H. 1971. "Excavations at Cochiti Dam, New Mexico: 1964–1966 Seasons." Manuscript on file. Santa Fe: Museum of New Mexico.

Snow, David H. 1973. *A Preliminary Report of Archaeological Survey: The Tetilla Peak Recreation Area Access Road, 1972–1973.* Laboratory of Anthropology Notes No. 80A. Santa Fe: Museum of New Mexico.

Soja, Edward. 1996. *Thirdspace: Journeys to Los Angeles and Other Real-and-Imagined Places*. Oxford: Blackwell.

Suina, Joseph H. 2004. "Native Language Teachers in a Struggle for Language and Cultural Survival." *Anthropology & Education Quarterly* 35 (3): 281–302. http://dx.doi.org/10.1525/aeq.2004.35.3.281.

Tuan, Yi-Fu. 1977. *Space and Place: The Perspective of Experience*. Minneapolis: University of Minnesota Press.

US Army Corps of Engineers. 1985. *Water Resources Development in New Mexico*. Dallas, TX: US Army Corps of Engineers, Southwestern Division.

Waterton, Emma, Laurajane Smith, and Gary Campbell. 2006. "The Utility of Discourse Analysis to Heritage Studies: The Burra Charter and Social Inclusion." *International Journal of Heritage Studies* 12 (4): 339–55. http://dx.doi.org/10.1080 /13527250600727000.

West, Richard L. 1971. "Cochiti—A Key Water Resource Development for New Mexico." In *Proceedings of the Sixteenth Annual Water Conference, March 25–26, 1971*, 179–97. Las Cruces: Water Research Institute, New Mexico State University.

*Heritage Rights and the Rhetoric of
Reality in Pre-Revolution Tunisia*

Kathryn Lafrenz Samuels

The imaginary, simply as such, is
neither unreal nor real.

—R. G. Collingwood

About a half hour outside the Tunisian capital, Tunis,
lies the Roman archaeological site of Uthina (Oudhna
in Arabic). The site is not particularly remarkable as
far as Roman sites in North Africa go, but it bears
a colorful relationship to Tunisia's political past in
the modern era. Variously a French farmstead and a
munitions storage—then a rubble pile thanks to the
accidental explosion of said munitions—the site bore
the vicissitudes of French colonial homage to the
Roman empire. Roman ruins provided a letters pat-
ent for French interests in North Africa, whose decay
evidenced a country in decay, a land of *terra nullius*
(Lafrenz Samuels 2012).

These same ruins provided the backdrop for elabo-
rate parties in the late 1980s and early 1990s. Tunisian
elite arrived to Roman-themed dinners where the
prime minister and Tunisian technocrati dined alongside ambassadors and foreign financiers from Roman-
style plates. Amidst the clinking of silverware, the
rush and lull of conversation perhaps revolved around
garnering officials' support and attracting international
funding to develop the site for tourism. Hamed Karoui,

DOI: 10.5876/9781607323846.c015

the Prime Minister, organized and chaired a *conseil des ministres restraint* (special ministerial council) in 1992 to establish an archaeological park at Oudhna and initiate a plan for development. The project was placed under the protection of now deposed President Zine El Abidine Ben Ali, who contributed a significant amount of funding as well (Ben Hassen, Golvin, and Maurin 1998; Ben Hassen and Massy 1998).

The dinners reveal an imaginative engagement with the Roman heritage of Oudhna, pointing beyond the site in constructing particular imaginaries of Tunisia and its links to the international community. In one respect, the goal of the dinners—to raise awareness about the site and promote its development for tourism—worked to imagine the global face of Tunisia: a long history of integration with the Mediterranean and Europe, enmeshed in a network of empire, and steeped in the western tradition and its democratic values. Tunisia was viewed as one of the most 'liberal' Arab states and an ally in fighting terrorism. The site of Oudhna provided Tunisia the material substance for presenting this face to foreign tourists.

Yet Tunisia's face at this time was a highly groomed and managed one for the global stage. The simulated Roman dinners and campaign for site development also worked through patronage networks of *clientélisme*—where the best economic opportunities were had by the President's family and his entourage—and Tunisian strategies of tourism development managed visitors and their perceptions of Tunisia through the selective construction of specific tourism routes and experiences. This was a country where foreign embassy officials thrilled at the rare chances for meeting with the Tunisian administration, so infrequently did the government grant an audience. Many international development projects spoke of 'opening up' Tunisia's economy and political process. The site of Oudhna offered one such opening, through the global economic integration and cultural exchanges involved in cultural tourism. Oudhna was one of the primary sites targeted by the Tunisia Cultural Heritage Project (TCHP), a World Bank financed project aimed at fostering economic growth and reducing poverty. The specific mechanism for doing so was 'capacity building': strengthening Tunisia's heritage infrastructure to develop cultural tourism.

Human rights are treated as a bedrock institution for modern democracies, but human rights abuses were endemic to Tunisian democratic practice under the tight *de facto* one-party authoritarian control of Ben Ali's regime. Forms of oppression included the widening disparities in wealth due to *clientélisme* networks, violent suppression of political opposition (especially Islamic political parties), and its police-state (*mukhabarat*) nature—police were increased when Ben Ali took office, from 20,000 to 80,000 in ten years (Anderson 1995; Angrist 1999; Bellin 1994, 2000; Durac and Cavatorta 2009; Entelis 2005; Hazbun 2007; King 2003; Murphy 1999, 2001). In the field, I was frequently informed that at least one in ten people on the street were secret police (which is about right given the population size), and in Tunis, the ratio was said to be even lower. The paranoia of many of my colleagues and informants was palpable.

The repressive nature of Tunisian democracy under Ben Ali was a function of neoliberal policies encouraged by the international community through development programs that used economic reform to effect political reform. But because these economic reforms in Tunisia instead deepened political repression, creating the environment for systemic human rights abuses, this raised a paradox that has been called Tunisia's 'façade democracy' (Durac and Cavatorta 2009: 15; Entelis 2005: 549; Sadiki 2002a, 2002b; Willis 2002). To speak of a façade democracy assumes a veneer of democratic practice—an inclusive, tolerant, liberal, and transparent exterior—when 'in reality,' unmasked, Tunisian political society was anything but.

Instead, I suggest the case of Tunisian democracy showcases the global diversity of democratic practice and, more importantly, highlights the antithetical interests of neoliberalism and human rights. I demonstrate how a 'rhetoric of reality' dissolves the apparent paradox of Tunisia's façade democracy, allowing national and international actors to co-produce Tunisian democracy through development projects such as the TCHP. Central to this 'rhetoric of reality' were technologies of imagination that channeled the social imaginary of what was and what was possible. This eclipsing of imaginative capacity provided fertile soil for the systemic human rights abuses of Ben Ali's regime. In response, redescribing human rights in terms of imaginative capacity offers a fuller account of rights in pre-Revolution Tunisia and suggests productive ways forward in developing the concept of heritage rights.

CAPACITY BUILDING AND HERITAGE CAPABILITIES

The site of Oudhna was selected for the TCHP in a dovetailing of interests between the Tunisian state and the World Bank. Oudhna offered the ideal location for building Tunisia as a destination for cultural tourism, located only thirty miles from Tunis and capable of pulling tourists away from their usual beach haunts. A fairly typical Roman site, it contains a good assortment of the kinds of monumental architecture that visually impress tourists:

an amphitheater, capitol, baths, villa, cisterns, all located at the end of an aqueduct under active and laborious restoration that courses along the main road leading to the site.

For the World Bank, the site offered the opportunity for developing a model management plan that was to be used as a management template for archaeological sites throughout Tunisia. At the same time, the Middle East and North Africa (MENA) region was held up by the World Bank as the model region for developing heritage for economic growth and poverty reduction (Cernea 2001). A Russian doll of modeling and future applications, the site of Oudhna therefore carried great significance to development planners for demonstrating the potential of heritage development.

The TCHP marks an ambitious scaling-up from previous MENA heritage projects planned by the World Bank, which had previously focused on single sites or cities. The TCHP adopted a sector-wide approach, taking on the whole framework of how heritage was dealt with and managed within a single country, in order to 'build capacity.' 'Capacity building' means institutional strengthening, which in the context of the Tunisian heritage sector meant targeting national policies and legal frameworks, strengthening the heritage agencies through new recruitment, training, and reorganization (e.g., increasing cooperation between the Department of Tourism and the Department of Culture), encouraging local participation, preparing archaeological sites and monuments for tourism, marking out tourism routes, and attracting private industry to build hotels and other tourism facilities.

Multilateral development banks like the World Bank have remarkable agility at incorporating critiques to fashion new development approaches. The 'capacity building' language of development banks grew out of the human capabilities approach (also called human development approach) originally introduced by Amartya Sen (1993, 1999) and Martha Nussbaum (1997, 2006, 2011) as an alternative to standard development theories and international human rights regimes. As Nussbaum describes, development models typically measure quality of life based on Gross Domestic Product (GDP), but numerous countries (like Tunisia) have shown increasing GDP at the same time that economic inequalities and social disparities deepened. This meant that, except for a small sub-set of elites, the everyday experience of most citizens was one of declining fortunes. A capabilities approach sought to correct the way economic development was conceived, instead focusing on comparative quality-of-life assessments premised on social justice, asking questions like "What are people actually able to do and be?" "What opportunities are available to them?" and "What does a life worthy of human dignity require?" (Nussbaum 2011: x,

18, 32). The approach has had increasing impact on development agencies and international actors, the most visible being the Human Development Reports published annually since 1990 through the United Nations Development Programme (UNDP) and regional spin-offs such as the *Arab Human Development Report*.

A capabilities approach also supplements standard human rights accounts by offering a cohesive philosophical framework for thinking through human rights, paying particular attention to human dignity, government, and duties and responsibilities. At the same time, it critiques the distinction made in human rights circles between first-generation (political and civil) and second-generation (economic and social) rights, arguing that political and civil rights have social and economic roots (Nussbaum 2011: 62–68). This is an important point because heritage, in addressing social and economic roots, has a more significant role to play in human rights than might be recognized under conventional human rights regimes (Lafrenz Samuels 2010).

A human capabilities approach has been put forward by Lynn Meskell (2010) and Ian Hodder (2010) as a useful framework for thinking through heritage rights. Meskell (2010) suggests that heritage rights come into play with the destruction of heritage resources or their appropriation, which "patently deforms human capabilities and well-being . . . and does damage for multiple generations" (2010: 844) and furthermore inhibits a group's "ability to flourish" (2010: 845). In another sense, Hodder (2010: 872–73) speaks of a 'heritage capability' that might support other dimensions of well-being, e.g., "to be employed, to have good health, to think, feel, imagine," and is a concept that "allows us to examine whether people are in practice able to participate in sites, objects, identities in such a way as to fulfill their capabilities."

I argue that one core capability identified by Nussbaum (2006, 2011)—imagination—holds particular purchase for a conception of heritage rights. Heritage enables individual and social imaginaries regarding what is possible and offers an endowment of cultural resources to draw from in composing "opportunities to choose and act" (Nussbaum 2011: 20). Tunisia under the Ben Ali administration experienced a growing economy at the same time that social and economic inequalities deepened. In general, human capabilities were eclipsed. A 'rhetoric of reality' was co-constructed by the Tunisian state and international development community: international efforts to effect political reform in Tunisia took the form of development projects (e.g., the TCHP), which the Ben Ali administration used to construct a highly managed visage of democracy and liberalism for an international audience while simultaneously retrenching its own power.

FAÇADE DEMOCRACY

Globalization (*al-awlamah*) in the Arab world is a patchy and heterogeneous phenomenon, best understood as being a suite of social practices, discourses, and processes limited to specific channels and trajectories of social relations. A principal channel is international finance, which provides funds contingent upon economic reforms built around liberalization and 'opening up' the country's economy (El-Said and Harrigan 2006: 444–45; Haneef 2002). The Tunisian version of 'opening up'—*infitah* (Hazbun 2007: 12; Richards and Waterbury 2008: 233)—was a selective and highly managed 'openness,' revealing the creative strategies through which the Ben Ali administration negotiated its relations with the international community. Such strategies are concentrated in its supposedly 'paradoxical' governance techniques and the promotion of cultural tourism. Cultural tourism was a point of intersection between national and international interests: it was the new hope for growing Tunisia's economy, representing 10 percent of GDP in the year preceding the 2011 Revolution (UNWTO 2010), at the same time that tourism development was pursued by international organizations and foreign governments as a means to 'open up' the country politically.

The apparent contradictions of Ben Ali's administration played on inconsistencies present in neoliberal governance itself, which bear a public face of openness, accountability, transparency, and inclusiveness, even as it seeks to extend control. Exploiting such contradictions allowed a repressive regime like Ben Ali's to flourish under the banner of democratization. In matters of economics and governance, Tunisia had long been applauded as the 'good student' or 'success story' of democracy promotion, liberalization, and IMF (International Monetary Fund) reforms. Ben Ali's administration adopted international expertise and advice and was presented as having a healthy, robust economy. According to World Bank measurements, poverty in Tunisia dropped from 20 percent in 1980, to less than 10 percent five years later, further down to 4.1 percent in 2000 (Blin 2009: 149 and 155, citing figures from World Bank 1995 and Ayadi, Matoussi, and Victoria-Feser 2001). However, poverty statistics for Tunisia are notoriously difficult to confirm, even fanciful, especially in grossly underestimating rural poverty (World Bank and the Islamic Development Bank 2005: 25–26). The adoption of neoliberal economic tenets and decline in poverty appear correlated during periods of structural adjustment from 1987 to 1994 and from 1995 to 2005. However, as Blin (2009) and Harrigan and El-Said (2009) have shown, Tunisia achieved economic growth *in spite of* World Bank reforms.

While Tunisia was held up by international organizations as a model of state reform, it continued its deliberalization policies, becoming more repressive and authoritarian in governance. Ben Ali and his administration found creative solutions for exploiting the illiberal nature of neoliberal development. An example is instructive here. Economic reforms espoused by the World Bank and other international lenders sought to move responsibility for social welfare out of state administration and into civil society. Tunisia complied with this dutifully. The provision of social welfare was moved out of the governmental administration and 'privatized' to the person of the President himself. Ben Ali established the National Solidarity Fund (*Fonds National de Solidarité*), also known as the '26:26' after the number of the bank account to which donations were made. The Fund was a personal account of Ben Ali, to which Tunisians were expected to make donations on certain days during the year, and which provided housing, water, electricity, healthcare, and education to low-income families. While the President was rarely pictured in public, these projects were highly publicized, with photos of the President in the midst of projects funded by the 26:26 fund. Instituting social welfare in Tunisia as the personal prerogative of the President reinforced traditional *clientélisme* relationships of patronage in place since the Ottoman empire, within which taxes played an integral role (Angrist 1999; Ben Romdhane 2006; Blin 2009; Cassarino 2004; Hibou 2004, 2005, 2006). Recall too that Ben Ali had contributed significant funds to developing the Oudhna site.

CHANNELING SOCIAL IMAGINARIES

With the TCHP project, Ben Ali's administration similarly undertook a creative reinterpretation of international prescriptions for neoliberal development. The international community saw strengthening of the heritage sector as a means to 'open up' Tunisia through tourism—through the physical presence of foreigners and also through international channels of finance investing in Tunisia's tourism industry—which the Ben Ali administration adapted through its selective and highly managed *infitah* strategy. As an example, this *infitah* strategy can be seen in its preparation of the Uthina site for tourists, a site steeped in the colonial and postcolonial turns of Tunisian history.

Benedict Anderson (1983) argued that the nation was an 'imagined community' because community members will "never know most of their fellow-members, meet them, or even hear of them, yet in the minds of each lives the image of their communion" (1983: 6). The question then was how this connection was imagined—through what means this connection was forged—and initially, Anderson pointed to script languages and the printing press as the primary means for building a national 'imagined community.' However, Thongchai Winichakul (1994: 15–16) criticized Anderson's account for presenting nation-states as a political community born from some kind of novel idea, rather than from the historic conditions of colonial and post-colonial rule. Anderson therefore came back with a triumvirate of institutions—the census, the map, and the museum—that "profoundly shaped the way in which the colonial state imagined its dominion—the nature of the human beings it ruled, the geography of its domain, and the legitimacy of its ancestry" (Anderson 1991: 163–64). In many postcolonial territories the census, map, and museum bore a greater legacy to national imaginations than the script languages and printing press of his earlier analysis.

Under the TCHP, the work at Oudhna continued this legacy of post-colonial state-building to strengthen the Ben Ali administration. This was achieved in part through a 'museumizing imagination' (Anderson 1991: 178) that constructed a selective and highly managed visual landscape for visiting tourists, sweeping out of sight the vestiges of colonial control and increasing inequalities under Ben Ali's regime. The entire landscape surrounding the site was rezoned and cleared of any residences visible from the viewshed ('cone visual') seen from atop the capitol. A number of land swaps were undertaken and groups of houses from the nearest town of Farch El Annabi were removed. The area surrounding the site was taken to be part of the site's charm and value, as an 'exceptional natural environment' that calls out for its development "as a landscape preserved almost in its ancient state" (Republique Tunisienne 2007: 15). To further create the impression of an ancient place, cars would not be allowed into the site and only native plants were to be used in the landscaping. The entrance to the site was completely reworked to allow a direct approach facing the Capitol upon entering the protected area of the site. The colonial farmhouse built on top of the Capitol (Figure 15.1) was removed, and a compound of farmhouses and storage buildings currently surrounding the Capitol and blocking this new entrance were to be demolished. At the same time, project documents present a situation of *terra nullius*. The landscape surrounding Dougga was presented as de-peopled and untouched: "Oudhna is a site 'virgin in itself and around it' ('*vierge sur lui-meme et autour de lui*')." The World Bank project documents describe the surrounding environment as "un-discovered and un-exploited" (World Bank 2001b: 39). In addition to extending the boundary of the site to include more protected land, a buffer zone was also created.

The material remains of Oudhna provided a medium through which political relations could be imagined—the "imagined linkage" (Anderson 1983:

Figure 15.1. *Colonial farmhouse built on top of the Capitol at Uthina (Oudhna), shortly before demolition (photo by the author).*

33)—under the Ben Ali regime. The specific plans set forth by his administration accomplished several things. It extended control over the site beyond the boundaries to encompass the entire viewshed, thereby better managing tourists' perceptions. It also tidied away out of sight the deepening inequalities of Ben Ali's regime visible in the poverty of Farch El Annabi, as well as constructing a national past sanitized of colonial rule and influences. This museumizing landscape approach, involving the clearing and preservation of the visual landscape around the city, was adopted as a new strategy for site planning and management. It was also a principal component of Oudhna's 'model' site plan to be replicated elsewhere across Tunisia (and as a component of the TCHP, elsewhere throughout the world via the World Bank), using logics of model building and replicability that further channeled and constrained capabilities.

Other imaginaries were at work too, oriented around the logic of international development that rose from the ashes of colonialism. Following Charles Taylor (2004), a social imaginary can be articulated by looking to that which makes shared practices possible or realizable. Therefore, we might turn to the medium of development documents and their shared genre, representing highly technical products that construct specific outlooks and possibilities through detailed social restructuring. Annelise Riles (2006: 2) has written about the materiality of documents as the "paradigmatic artifacts of modern knowledge practices." Development documents are so effective as a medium for social imaginaries that development plans become real to themselves, constructing an internal coherence that appeals to reality as a rhetorical device. I call this strategy a 'rhetoric of reality.'

While the gap between development plans and outcomes has frequently been criticized, anthropologists (e.g., Ferguson 1990) have highlighted the work this gap performs in keeping development expertise in business. Examining the social imaginary built with development documents takes this production of expertise seriously and asks what shared practices become possible or realizable on account of this expertise. Rather than emphasize the lack of coherence between development plans with what is happening 'on the ground'—which reproduces the logic of debt and credit that drives development—being attentive to the 'rhetoric of reality' in play within these documents is offered here as a way to redescribe the work that development documents perform. It aligns 'real' with 'imaginary,' fact with fiction (cf. Poovey 2008), within the same frame of analysis to emphasize the persuasive character of development plans, particularly in channeling specific visions of what is possible or realizable—in short, channeling specific social imaginaries. By doing so, the 'rhetoric of reality' in development documents eclipses capacities for alternative imaginaries.

The TCHP's project documents (World Bank 2001a, 2001b, 2001c, 2001d) employ several strategies that solidify the world of their making. Bullet points outline project goals, with verbs in command form or lacking agents of execution. Statements are made authoritatively, and the government of Tunisia is presented as the receiver of knowledge, only recently gaining awareness or interest in developing its heritage for tourism, and whose citizens and communities should be made aware as well. Striking are the many references to existing and future documents and record-keeping, so that the purpose of the project becomes the production of more paper-based products, which construct reality through an intertextual authority of repetition and citation. Projects become synonymous with the documents: for example, the government of Tunisia is required to submit their training and recruitment program to the World Bank (World Bank 2001d: 5).

The stated objective of the project is to assist the Tunisian government in sustainable heritage management. What outcomes the plans do forecast are long-term and vague ("contribute to a change in the image of the country, leading to greater awareness of cultural identity"), self-referential ("leading to . . . sustainable cultural heritage management"), or already borne out by analysis of Tunisia's experience in heritage tourism ("an increase of foreign currency and yield per tourist") (World Bank 2001c: 3).

The documents also repeatedly refer to the 'modest' economic benefits expected, drastically scaling back project expectations. For example, an escape clause at the end of the Project Information Document states:

> It is important to note that the new approach will represent major changes that may not be observable in the short term. Long-term sustainability is also a function of decentralization requiring a change, which may be resisted by research specialists in the culture field. The short term impact of the project, even if successful, thus may be modest, limited to demonstrating the value of greater community involvement, tourism promotion, and site and management conservation (World Bank 2001c: 8–9, repeated in World Bank 2001b: 20).

This transfers blame, should the project not meet intended outcomes, to Tunisian heritage managers who are presented as a 'possible controversial aspect' of the project: "The conversion of INA [Institute National d'Archéologie et d'Art] to INP [Institut National du Patrimoine] has generated resistance from the INP archaeologists, some of whom resist modern management practices involving shared decision making and an emphasis on site usage through tourism promotion. The project objectives may intensify these reactions" (World Bank 2001b: 22). By circumscribing expectations, the documents find firmer footing in presenting the plans as realistic. Furthermore, working with material heritage—material that is parlayed as being further back on the scale of progressive development—lowers the hurdle for demonstrating progress. That is, minimal effort is required for performing progress, given the backdrop of antiquity.

Taylor's (2004) imaginary, focusing as it does on how norms and shared practices are made realizable, aligns in shared purpose with the 'reality' constructed by development projects and their planning documents. Indeed, Taylor (2004: 50) was careful to point out that his social imaginary was tied to the West, to "the way we collectively imagine . . . our social life in the contemporary Western world." Over the centuries this imaginary, which saw itself as the bearer of civilization (in no small part drawing on its Roman heritage), was transformed into a supranational order defined by democratic rule and human rights (2004: 179).

CONCLUSION

Developing heritage presents unique opportunities for the international development industry, and the 'rhetoric of reality' nurtured in development plans. Comaroff and Comaroff (1992) have famously written of an 'historical imagination,' the specificity of which lies in its attention to the constructedness of reality itself: "how realities become real, how essences become essential, how materialities materialize" (1992: 20). Therefore, we might presume that projects seeking to 'reclaim' or 'enhance' (*mise en valeur*) the past are engaging most directly with this constructedness of reality. The past offers a wide playing field of possibilities that may be drawn on in supporting or confronting various national or transnational imaginaries, the apparent paradoxes of Tunisian rule vis-à-vis the international community, while simultaneously constraining alternative imaginaries.

The alternative social imaginaries that do manage to assert themselves within the context of repression are less assertive and presumptuous in what can be made realizable or collectively shared. Seeing borders that cannot be transcended, these imaginaries nevertheless frequent distant horizons composed of an optative space and time (cf. Crapanzano 2004: 14). In Tunisia, archaeological sites like Oudhna offered such a horizon, building capabilities for imagination through the unique capabilities offered by heritage resources. One self-styled radical, also a heritage manager, offered pointed observations on the authoritarian regime under which Tunisians lived. On the topic of heritage sites he told me, "sites should be playgrounds for the imagination. They should give people the chance to imagine the different lives that people lived there, the alternatives. But it doesn't matter whether this corresponds to history, just to let their imagination run free, that's what sites need to be."

The imaginative capacities enabled by cultural heritage support individuals and communities in imagining other possibilities and other futures, such as those pursued by the people of Tunisia in the Revolution that began in late 2010, early 2011. As the history of activities at the site of Oudhna suggests, the social and economic basis of heritage resources had direct bearing on political and civil rights in Tunisia and their abuse under the Ben Ali regime by channeling certain capabilities and imaginaries and eclipsing others. The intricate dance between the international community and Ben Ali's administration within neoliberal development schemes implicate both as co-producers of Tunisian democracy, with its widening social inequalities and social repression that would boil over in the frustrations of Tunisia's unemployed youth. It is not likely just a coincidence that a new World Bank tourism development project has been initiated in the same region comprising the hometown of Mohamed Bouazizi, who initiated the Revolution through his act of self-immolation.

Finally, I suggest that we can look to imaginative capacity as a key mechanism for redescription in the study and management of cultural heritage. Given the role of imagination in a capabilities approach to human rights, this draws the project of redescription into the emerging field of heritage rights.

REFERENCES

Anderson, Benedict. 1983. *Imagined Communities: Reflections on the Origin and Spread of Nationalism*. London: Verso.

Anderson, Benedict. 1991. *Imagined Communities: Reflections on the Origin and Spread of Nationalism*. Revised ed. London: Verso.

Anderson, Lisa. 1995. "North Africa: The Limits of Liberalization." *Current History* 94 (591): 167–71.

Angrist, Michele P. 1999. "The Expression of Political Dissent in the Middle East: Turkish Democratization and Authoritarian Continuity in Tunisia." *Comparative Studies in Society and History* 41 (4): 730–57. http://dx.doi.org/10.1017/S0010417599003114.

Ayadi, Mohamed, Mohamed S. Matoussi, and Maria-Pia Victoria-Feser. 2001. "Putting Robust Statistical Methods into Practice: Poverty Analysis in Tunisia." *Swiss Journal of Economics and Statistics* 3 (14): 463–82.

Bellin, Eva. 1994. "The Politics of Profit in Tunisia: Utility of the Rentier Paradigm?" *World Development* 22 (3): 427–36. http://dx.doi.org/10.1016/0305-750X(94)90133-3.

Bellin, Eva. 2000. "Contingent Democrats: Industrialists, Labor, and Democratization in Late-developing Countries." *World Politics* 52 (2): 175–205. http://dx.doi.org/10.1017/S0043887100002598.

Ben Hassen, Habib, Jean-Claude Golvin, and Louis Maurin. 1998. "La ville: Recherches anciennes et présentation d'ensemble." In *Oudhna (Uthina): La redécouverte d'un ville antique de Tunisie*, ed. Habib Ben Hassen and Louis Maurin, 21–35. Tunis, Tunisia: INP/Ausonius.

Ben Hassen, Habib, and J.-L. Massy. 1998. "Introduction: Un project d'évaluation et de mise en valeur du site d'Oudhna. Les reserches de 1993 à 1996." In *Oudhna (Uthina): La redécouverte d'un ville antique de Tunisie*, ed. Habib Ben Hassen and Louis Maurin, 11–17. Tunis, Tunisia: INP/Ausonius.

Ben Romdhane, Mahmoud. 2006. "Social Policy and Development in Tunisia since Independence: A Political Analysis." In *Social Policy in the Middle East: Political, Economic, and Gender Dynamics*, ed. Massoud Karshenas and Valentine

Moghadem, 31–77. London: Palgrave/United Nations Research Institute for Social Development (UNRISD).

Blin, Myriam. 2009. "Structural Reform and the Political Economy of Poverty Reduction in Tunisia: What Role for Civil Society?" In *Economic Liberalisation, Social Capital and Islamic Welfare Provision*, ed. Jane Harrigan and Hamed El-Said, 145–75. Basingstoke, UK: Palgrave Macmillan.

Cassarino, Jean-Pierre. 2004. "Participatory Development and Liberal Reforms in Tunisia: The Gradual Incorporation of *Some* Economic Networks." In *Networks of Privilege in the Middle East: The Politics of Economic Reform Revisited*, ed. Steven Heydermann, 223–42. New York, NY: Palgrave.

Cernea, Michael M. 2001. *Cultural Heritage and Development: A Framework for Action in the Middle East and North Africa*. Washington, DC: World Bank.

Collingwood, Robin G. 1946. *The Idea of History*. Oxford: Clarendon Press.

Comaroff, John L., and Jean Comaroff. 1992. *Ethnography and the Historical Imagination*. Boulder, CO: Westview Press.

Crapanzano, Vincent. 2004. *Imaginative Horizons: An Essay in Literary-Philosophical Anthropology*. Chicago, IL: University of Chicago Press.

Durac, Vincent, and Francesco Cavatorta. 2009. "Strengthening Authoritarian Rule through Democracy Promotion? Examining the Paradox of the US and EU Security Strategies: The Case of Bin Ali's Tunisia." *British Journal of Middle Eastern Studies* 36 (1): 3–19. http://dx.doi.org/10.1080/13530190902749523.

El-Said, Hamed, and Jane Harrigan. 2006. "Globalization, International Finance, and Political Islam in the Arab World." *Middle East Journal* 60 (3): 444–66.

Entelis, John P. 2005. "The Democratic Imperative vs. the Authoritarian Impulse: The Maghrib State Between Transition and Terrorism." *Middle East Journal* 59 (4): 537–58.

Ferguson, James. 1990. *Anti-Politics Machine: 'Development,' Depoliticization, and Bureaucratic Power in Lesotho*. Minneapolis: University of Minnesota Press.

Haneef, Mohamed A. 2002. "Economic Development, Globalization, and Muslim Countries." *Studies in Contemporary Islam* 4 (1): 27–51.

Harrigan, Jane, and Hamed El-Said. 2009. *Economic Liberalisation, Social Capital, and Islamic Welfare Provision*. Basingstoke, UK: Palgrave Macmillan. http://dx.doi.org/10.1057/9781137001580.

Hazbun, Waleed. 2007. "Images of Openness, Spaces of Control: The Politics of Tourism Development in Tunisia." *Arab Studies Journal* 15/16: 10–35.

Hibou, Béatrice. 2004. "Fiscal Trajectories in Morocco and Tunisia." In *Networks of Privilege in the Middle East: The Politics of Economic Reform Revisited*, ed. Steven Heydermann, 201–22. New York, NY: Palgrave.

Hibou, Béatrice. 2005. "The Privatization of the State: North Africa in Comparative Perspective." In *The Dynamics of States: The Formation and Crises of State Domination*, ed. Klaus Schlichte, 71–96. Aldershot, UK: Ashgate.

Hibou, Béatrice. 2006. "Domination and Control in Tunisia: Economic Levers for the Exercise of Authoritarian Power." *Review of African Political Economy* 33 (108): 185–206. http://dx.doi.org/10.1080/03056240600842628.

Hodder, Ian. 2010. "Cultural Heritage Rights: From Ownership and Descent to Justice and Well-being." *Anthropological Quarterly* 83 (4): 861–82. http://dx.doi.org/10.1353/anq.2010.0025.

King, Stephen J. 2003. *Liberalization Against Democracy: The Local Politics of Economic Reform in Tunisia*. Bloomington: Indiana University Press.

Lafrenz Samuels, Kathryn. 2010. *Mobilizing Heritage in the Maghrib: Rights, Development, and Transnational Archaeologies*. PhD dissertation, Department of Anthropology, Stanford University, Stanford, CA.

Lafrenz Samuels, Kathryn. 2012. "Roman Archaeology and the Making of Heritage Citizens in Tunisia." In *Making Roman Places: Past and Present*, ed. Darian Totten and Kathryn Lafrenz Samuels, 159–70. Portsmouth, RI: Journal of Roman Archaeology Supplement Series.

Meskell, Lynn. 2010. "Human Rights and Heritage Ethics." *Anthropological Quarterly* 83 (4): 839–59. http://dx.doi.org/10.1353/anq.2010.0023.

Murphy, Emma C. 1999. *Economic and Political Change in Tunisia: From Bourguiba to Ben Ali*. Basingstoke, UK: Macmillan. http://dx.doi.org/10.1057/9780333983584.

Murphy, Emma C. 2001. "The State and the Private Sector in North Africa: Seeking Specificity." *Mediterranean Politics* 6 (2): 1–28. http://dx.doi.org/10.1080/713604511.

Nussbaum, Martha C. 1997. "Capabilities and Human Rights." *Fordham Law Review* 66: 273–300.

Nussbaum, Martha C. 2006. *Frontiers of Justice: Disability, Nationality, Species Membership*. Cambridge, MA: Belknap Press.

Nussbaum, Martha C. 2011. *Creating Capabilities: The Human Development Approach*. Cambridge, MA: Harvard University Press. http://dx.doi.org/10.4159/harvard.9780674061200.

Poovey, Mary. 2008. *Genres of the Credit Economy: Mediating Value in Eighteenth- and Nineteenth-Century Britain*. Chicago, IL: University of Chicago Press. http://dx.doi.org/10.7208/chicago/9780226675213.001.0001.

Republique Tunisienne, Ministère de la Culture et de la Sauvegarde du Patrimoine. 2007. *Étude d'aménagement du site archéologique d'Oudhna: Phase 4B—Projet definitif du plan de protection*. Tunis, Tunisia: Ministère de la Culture et de la Sauvegarde du Patrimoine.

Richards, Alan, and John Waterbury. 2008. *A Political Economy of the Middle East*. 3rd ed. Boulder, CO: Westview Press.

Riles, Annelise. 2006. "Introduction: In Response." In *Documents: Artifacts of Modern Knowledge*, ed. Annelise Riles, 1–40. Ann Arbor: The University of Michigan Press.

Sadiki, Larbi. 2002a. "Bin Ali's Tunisia: Democracy by Non-democratic Means." *British Journal of Middle Eastern Studies* 29 (1): 57–78. http://dx.doi.org/10.1080/13530190220124061.

Sadiki, Larbi. 2002b. "Political Liberalization in Bin Ali's Tunisia: Façade Democracy." *Democratization* 9 (4): 122–41. http://dx.doi.org/10.1080/714000286.

Sen, Amartya. 1993. "Capability and Well-being." In *The Quality of Life*, ed. Martha Nussbaum and Amartya Sen, 30–53. Oxford: Oxford University Press. http://dx.doi.org/10.1093/0198287976.003.0003.

Sen, Amartya. 1999. *Development as Freedom*. New York, NY: Anchor Books.

Taylor, Charles. 2004. *Modern Social Imaginaries*. Durham, NC: Duke University Press.

UNWTO. 2010. *Tourism Factbook: Tunisia Basic Indicators*. Madrid, Spain: UNWTO.

Willis, Michael J. 2002. "Political Parties in the Maghrib: The Illusion of Significance?" *Journal of North African Studies* 7 (2): 1–22. http://dx.doi.org/10.1080/13629380208718463.

Winichakul, Thongchai. 1994. *Siam Mapped: A History of the Geo-Body of a Nation*. Honolulu: University of Hawai'i Press.

World Bank. 1995. *Tunisia: Poverty Alleviation: Preserving Progress While Preparing for the Future*. Washington, DC: World Bank.

World Bank. 2001a. *Tunisia Cultural Heritage Project: Project Agreement (7059-TUN)*. Washington, DC: World Bank.

World Bank. 2001b. *Tunisia Cultural Heritage Project: Project Appraisal Document (20413-TUN)*. Washington, DC: World Bank.

World Bank. 2001c. *Tunisia Cultural Heritage Project: Project Information Document (PID6985)*. Washington, DC: World Bank.

World Bank. 2001d. *Tunisia Cultural Heritage Project: Loan Agreement (7059-TUN)*. Washington, DC: World Bank.

World Bank and the Islamic Development Bank. 2005. *Tunisia: Understanding Successful Socioeconomic Development: A Joint World Bank-Islamic Development Bank Evaluation of Assistance*. Washington, DC: World Bank and Islamic Development Bank.

*Primordial Conservationists, Environmental
Sustainability, and the Rhetoric of Pastoralist
Cultural Heritage in East Africa*

Paul J. Lane

Over the past few decades, especially following publication of the Brundtland Report *Our Common Future*
(WCED 1987) and the 1992 United Nations Conference on Environment and Development in Rio de
Janeiro (also known as the 'Earth summit'), the concept of 'sustainability' has entered the public sphere and
mainstream policy agendas (Dixon and Fallon 1989;
Myers and Macnaghten 1998). While the antiquity
of the concept is much older (Mitcham 1995), today
the term is widely used by international agencies (such
as the United Nations), government bodies, national
and international non-governmental organizations
(NGOs), and local communities in both the developed
'North' and the less developed countries that constitute
the global 'South.' Central to the use of the concept of
sustainability by all these bodies is the emphasis placed
on the desirability of balancing short-term gains
against longer term conservation goals, whether these
refer to natural or cultural resources. Yet, as one might
expect, there are competing definitions of sustainability,
especially when the term is linked with 'development'
(e.g., Nygren 1998; Redclift 2005), and this is reflected
in the different rhetorical strategies employed.

In the context of sub-Saharan Africa, one of the
main areas in which the concept is deployed is in wildlife and biodiversity conservation (e.g., Davies 2012). In

DOI: 10.5876/9781607323846.c016

particular, in the years since the Earth summit, there has been a shift away from the 'top down' approaches and philosophies of 'fortress conservation' that lay behind the creation of national parks and game reserves across sub-Saharan Africa (e.g., Brockington 2002). In their place, 'bottom up' initiatives such as Community Conservation, Community Based Natural Resource Management, or Integrated Conservation and Development Projects have come to be the norm. These approaches are founded on the principle "that conservation goals should be pursued by strategies that emphasize the role of local residents in decision-making about natural resources" (Adams and Hulme 2001: 13). As part of these changes in approach, and in common with development projects more generally (Sillitoe, Bicker, and Pottier 2002), there has been a revaluation of local or 'indigenous' knowledge (IK) systems. Whereas in the past, these were either simply ignored or actively denigrated (especially in older studies), incorporation of local knowledge on how to use and manage natural resources has become a central feature of new approaches to biodiversity conservation.

This chapter explores elements of the rhetoric involved in promoting IK as the epitome of sustainable practice, and particularly the manner in which an idealized and essentially timeless heritage is mobilized by external actors and indigenous communities alike as material testimony to the long-term survival of East Africa's wildlife and biodiversity hotspots both in the past and in the future. In so doing, my aim is to highlight some of the paradoxes inherent to such arguments before discussing other contrasting imaginaries. Since in East Africa the greater majority of National Parks and Wildlife Reserves are located in areas immediately adjacent to lands used by pastoralists, and in many cases were created from former pastoralist rangelands from which these communities were evicted, I focus here on the diverse constructs of pastoralist heritage found in different contexts and across different media.

THE RHETORIC OF PASTORALIST HERITAGE AS SUSTAINABLE PRACTICE

Following the arguments presented by Classical authors such as Aristotle (*The Art of Rhetoric*) and Cicero (*De Oratore*), rhetorical analysis often begins with consideration of the five 'canons,' or fundamental sets of relationships, that provide a template for structuring the association of ideas used to develop a particular persuasive argument (Leach 2002: 213–17). These are invention, arrangement, style, memory, and delivery. While strict adherence to these can be criticized for resulting in rather formulaic arguments and deliveries, they nonetheless can serve as useful heuristic devices for analyzing a particular discourse, especially where this 'discourse' comprises not just words but a combination of both written and spoken texts, images, material culture, and bodily practices. Accordingly, the following analysis is structured around these five canons, so as to explore how notions of 'pastoralist heritage' are used to support the rhetoric that sustainable development needs to be founded on the principles of indigenous knowledge and practice. Brief definitions of each of the canons, taken from the online resource[1] *Silva Rhetoricae: The Forest of Rhetoric* developed by Gideon O. Burton (2007) are offered, followed by a discussion of the specific imagery, contexts, and rhetorical tropes that relate to this canon.

More specifically, a combination of 'resources' are used and analyzed here. First and foremost of these are several 'sites' in southern Kenya and northern Tanzania specifically marketed as places of pastoralist heritage, typically referred to as 'cultural villages' or *manyattas*, that were visited at different times between 2008 and 2010. Analysis of these focuses on the nature of the visitor's experience, the range of activities used to constitute a 'genuine' experience of pastoralist heritage, and the texts and images that promote and explain these locales for tourists. In addition, the analysis draws on images and texts used by different actors within the mainstream tourist industry to simultaneously promote the experience of pastoralist heritage to tourists and to appropriate the rhetoric of sustainability for their own ends. Analysis of these focuses on the manner in which text and image serve to reinforce each other. The content of a selection of websites produced by pastoralist community groups and national and regional NGOs, as well as travel blogs written by tourists since 2004, are also examined with a focus on how and in what context notions of 'heritage' and 'sustainability' are juxtaposed. All of these websites were last accessed in June 2012 when this research was completed, and the cited URLs were valid at that time. As of April 2015, however, some of these were no longer current.

INVENTION

> Invention concerns finding something to say
> (its name derives from the Latin *invenire*, 'to find').
>
> —GIDEON O. BURTON (2007)

Africa » Tanzania » North » Arusha March 26th 2007
More than two hundred years ago the Maasai arrived *and have since lived in harmony with the land* in their traditional way of life.[2]

Rhetorical invention typically involves a combination of 'commonplaces' and 'special' categories of relationships, which are known collectively as *topoi* or 'topics of invention.' The term 'commonplaces' refers to the kind of generalized, open-ended, and ambiguous abstractions that often make up 'taken for granted' arguments about the world, and which frequently entail the identification of an antecedent and its consequence. They are also often couched in the present tense as if they embody "truths held to be permanent" (Myers and Macnaghten 1998: 338). In their analysis of a range of different policy and popular literature on the idea of environmental sustainability, Myers and Macnaghten (1998: 338) found that there were four recurrent central meanings of 'sustainability,' namely 'equity,' 'futurity,' 'quality of life,' and 'environment,' with each associated with a set of distinct commonplaces.

In some cases these cross-cut one another. The promotion of IK and its inclusion in conservation and development planning is a clear example of the emphasis that a sustainability rhetoric places on equity, for instance, but it also has clear association with maintaining particular environmental conditions as a means to secure a better quality of life. It should come as no surprise, therefore, that an important trend in recent decades has been the increasing number of Maasai and other regional pastoralist groups who now self-identify themselves as 'indigenous.' This process began in the mid-1990s, as illustrated in Tanzania by the creation of a broad network of ethnically based Pastoralist and Indigenous NGOs, whose members invoke the experiences of indigenous peoples around the world so as to contextualize their own struggles and identities (Igoe 2006; Hodgson 2009). Prior to the 1990s 'indigenous' was not "an identity category that . . . made a great deal of sense in the region" (Igoe 2006: 400–401), when pastoralists were politically, economically, and socially marginalized by both national governments and the wider sedentary sections of East African society. Today, however, while such groups may still remain marginalized, 'being indigenous' is no longer necessarily a handicap since being possessors of indigenous knowledge is regarded as an asset. Thus, pastoralist communities now commonly present themselves via websites and their promotional literature as having had the foresight to retain their indigenous knowledge and, as a consequence, should now be lauded as the true guardians of East Africa's future (Table 16.1).

As is clear from Table 16.1, as well as the four narrative tropes of sustainability identified by Myers and Macnaghten (1998), an additional trope now deployed by pastoralist communities and reproduced by others is the notion of 'heritage.' More specifically, the argument is made that pastoralists have a long tradition of 'acting sustainably' (e.g., nos. 1 and 2, Table 16.1) and in ways that enhanced biodiversity, making them appear as the logical choice as custodians

TABLE 16.1 Rhetorical uses of tradition and heritage taken from a selection of Maasai NGO websites; all accessed June 2012.

Extract (emphasis added)	Source and Topic
(1) *We Maasai have lived in harmony within the rich ecosystems of East Africa for centuries.* In the balance our ancestors found with the natural environment, people shared the land with elephants, giraffes, rhinoceros, and other majestic wildlife. *We see ourselves as custodians of the land*, which to us is a sacred living entity. The land contains our history; it is the keeper of our memories and culture, and protector of our forefathers' bones.	Maasai Environmental Resource Coalition http://www.maasaierc.org/maasailegacy.html On living in harmony with nature.
(2) The *Maasai people have always been known to live in harmony with the natural environment.* Even though this is still the case to a large extent, today's way of life and way of co-existing with the living environment is rapidly changing.	Walking with Maasai http://www.walkingwithmaasai.org/eco-tourism Eco-tourism initiative.
(3) The Maasai are *one of the last remaining indigenous tribal communities* in East Africa. Although *we have managed to keep most of our traditions and culture, our way of life is on the verge of change.* Influences from the outside world, along with natural disasters such as drought, are quickly changing our way of life.	Maasai Association http://www.maasai-association.org/mcc/mission.html One of the stated objectives of their Maasai Cultural Heritage Center is to 'Inspire the Maasai to preserve and share indigenous knowledge'.
(4) *The world increasingly relies on many traditional communities like the Maasai to protect the ecological treasures* that exist within the land that they own. But the incredible wilderness and wildlife of Africa's grasslands and the famous culture of the Maasai people *both face daunting threats to their long-term survival.*	Maasai Wilderness Conservation Trust http://www.maasaitrust.org/maasai-conservation.html Mission statement; the MWCT funds and operates programs that promote sustainable economic benefits from conserving this ecosystem.
(5) Education . . . appears to provide the *best opportunity for the modernized world to learn from the Maasai* community about aspects of Maasai culture, such as *strategies for living sustainably.*	Maasai Community Partnership Project http://maasaicpp.org/current-programs/maasai-education-research-and-conservation-institute/ On the role of its Maasai Education, Research and Conservation Institute.
(6) The *Maasai community has managed to overcome the strong currents of the Western cultural influence* but now it is being faced by a lot of cultural erosion threats, cultural dispossessions, cultural and natural resources piracy.	Maasai Cultural Heritage http://nice-amahoro.com/index.php?page=maasai-cultural-heritage From profile and concept paper on Nature and Intercultural Expeditions (NICE) website.

of these environments and natural resources for future generations. However, these 'traditions' are now under threat from external forces of modernization (e.g., nos. 2, 3 and 6, Table 16.1), requiring active support of the work of these NGOs. This will not only benefit the local Maasai communities, but also has the potential to offer lessons and insights for the global community and especially the 'modernized world' (e.g., nos. 4 and 5, Table 16.1).

Arrangement

Concerns how one orders speech or writing. In ancient rhetorics, arrangement referred solely to the order to be observed in an oration, but the term has broadened to include all considerations of the ordering of discourse, especially on a large scale.
—Gideon O. Burton (2007)

After overnight camping close to the shores of Lake Natron, we will take you to the Maasai village where you will meet and have tea *with our Maasai family.* You'll be able to ask questions about their life (through a translator), take pictures of their home (and with permission individually, the tribal members) and get a 'taster' of what daily life is like *in an authentic and very remote Maasai community.*[3]

As East Africa's pastoralist communities have recast themselves as custodians of the land and are being recast by others as archetypal primordial conservationists, their material heritage has also become a signifier of that knowledge. The manner in which images of Maasai or other pastoralists are framed by the tourist industry to promote their own products plays a critical role in this. There are several readily identifiable visual 'genres'—such as images of young warriors jumping vertically during dance, or of them tending herds of livestock. Such images are often placed in proximity to pictures of wildlife and/or savannah landscapes, and so work to naturalize Maasai (and by default other pastoralists) by making them seem to be at one with, and a part of, the elements of the natural world (Galaty 2002). Perhaps the most iconic (Salazar 2009: 55) are the images that depict a lone young male pastoralist standing on one leg supporting his weight on a long, narrow-bladed metal spear, around which his other leg is twined.[4] He stares out across a verdant landscape of low acacia trees and bushy scrub that stretches away to an uninterrupted horizon. The young man in this archetypal image is almost always dressed in a checked, red *shuka* (a toga-like garment), typically worn today by Maasai and Samburu men. Often, the pattern and texture of light and colors suggest it is either dawn or sunset, and wild animals may dot the plain across which the young man gazes. By visually constructing an association between verdant landscapes, abundant wildlife, and young males, the suggestion is raised that perhaps the latter are as skilled in maintaining ecological balance as they are at maintaining their own physical poise.

From this we are also encouraged to infer that this is achieved *less* as a result of the ecological mutualism that has evolved between pastoralist practices, their livestock, vegetation succession, and wildlife (see, e.g., Muchiru, Western, and Reid 2008), and more as a consequence of the maintenance of a *pastoralist heritage* that is marked materially by the wearing of a *shuka*, the use of a spear, the sporting of headdresses and ear decorations, and the braiding of hair among young men. The inclusion of cultural centers and other forms of preserving and celebrating this distinctive pastoralist cultural heritage has thus become an almost obligatory aspect of the mission statements of pastoralist NGOs and the external bodies they work with (see below).

STYLE

> Concerns the artful expression of ideas . . . From a rhetorical perspective style . . . names how ideas are embodied in language and customized to communicative contexts.
>
> —GIDEON O. BURTON (2007)

Who knows how long we stayed looking. Who knows what year it was when we were there. Who knows if it will ever change. It was tremendously moving; OK, it was put on for the tourists, but it *felt amazingly authentic*. It was exactly the dances as they're described by the early European colonists; the dogs asleep in the small shadows were the same dogs; the flies . . . were the same flies, the smell of earth and wood smoke and age was the smell that has always been there.[5]

The images and rhetoric of pastoralist communities as primordial custodians of the land that are used to promote wildlife tourism are of course archetypes, which hide more than they reveal about the nature of pastoralist societies and the circumstances in which many find themselves today. Yet these images, or closely similar ones, not only pervade Western popular depictions of the state of pastoralism in Africa today but also lie at the heart of dominant perceptions and representations of the most enduring of relationships between pastoralists and the environments they inhabit. In particular, the visual association with a land of plenty and a healthy sustainable ecosystem constructs pastoralists as being a part of 'nature.' In so doing, this imagery robs pastoralists of their history. Thus, for instance, the fact that the creation of the various National Parks and Game Reserves that now host the wildlife tourists wish to see resulted in the expulsion of pastoralists, and other human communities, from these very same landscapes is generally left unstated. Moreover, the material culture this imagery and the pastoralist communities themselves project as being 'traditional' is in fact of entirely modern origin—"customary animal skins have been replaced by polyester tartan blankets produced in Pakistan"; "beads used in ornaments . . . come from the Czech republic"; and "the traditional knives are . . . imported from China" and have sharper and smaller blades than those used in the past (Salazar 2009: 61). Such historical details are overlooked by the majority of tourists, who only wish to imagine that they are encountering 'traditional Africa.' One blog even went so far as to invoke a shared (and entirely erroneous) history with the Romans:

> He wore the traditional orange red *shuka*, knotted at his shoulder like a Roman toga (the Romans once occupied North Africa, where the Masai originally lived, and it is thought that the *shuka* as well as the Masai *panga*, which resembles the short Roman fighting sword, and even their sandals, were copied from the Romans).[6]

The constant reproduction of these images, which are widely circulated within the region as well as outside the continent, also serves to create a distinction between pastoralists and other communities and ethnicities who, or so the sub-text goes, by abandoning their own 'traditional' dress, housing styles, and crafts have seemingly succumbed to Westernization and the ills associated with globalization. At the same time, the preference for images of Maasai over other communities, and of citizens in 'traditional dress' rather than 'Western' or 'Modern African' clothing, reduces the cultural complexity of East Africa to a single, pre-modern ideal (Akama 2002).

DELIVERY
> Originally referred to oral rhetoric at use in a public context, but can be viewed more broadly as that aspect of rhetoric that concerns the public presentation of discourse, oral or written.
> —GIDEON O. BURTON (2007)

Goals for 2012 and beyond
> The cultural *heritage center will make it possible to preserve* and celebrate *Maasai cultural heritage*, and inspire the community to preserve . . . indigenous knowledge for generations to come.[7]

As tourism has intensified in East Africa, so increasingly more pastoralist groups have been drawn into the market economy and into performing and portraying aspects of their 'traditions,' 'indigenous knowledge,' and 'heritage' (these terms are rendered here in quotes since they can all be open to different interpretations and uses, and their particular meaning varies from context to context). Simultaneously, more and more aspects of pastoralist (especially 'Maasai') 'tradition,' 'indigenous knowledge,' and 'heritage' have been appropriated by non-pastoralist communities as part of their own marketing strategies. Thus, for example, hotels and lodges in or close to national parks often claim to be modeled along the lines of a 'traditional Maasai *manyatta*'—although their resemblance to actual *manyatta* goes well beyond the bounds of poetic license and is often coupled with references to the 'glamour and luxury' of a bygone, colonial era (Table 16.2, no. 3) that would have been unlike anything found in a pastoralist settlement. In one case (Table 16.2, no. 5) the hotel in

TABLE 16.2 Extracts from selected websites promoting tourist hotels and lodges in southern Kenya and northern Tanzania. All accessed June 2012, unless specified.

Content (emphasis added)	Source and Notes
(1) E Unoto Retreat *resembles an authentic Tanzanian Maasai village* and has been designed to blend with the natural surroundings. The lodge was also constructed incorporating traditional Maasai methods and with environmental awareness.	http://www.maasaivillage.com/; home page
(2) Mara Serena Safari Lodge: *Styled to echo the circular motif of a traditional Maasai manyatta*, the lodge blends international sophistication with raw African beauty.	http://www.serenahotels.com// serenamara/default-en.html; home page and room description page.
(3) Ngorongoro Crater Lodge, *inspired in design by African architecture*, the Maasai Manyatta, is a magnificent return to the elegance of the traveling colonial nobility, a bygone era.	http://www.africantravel.com/hotels -lodges/tanzania/he-northern-circuit /ngorongoro-crater-lodge/.
(4) Mara Sopa Lodge has been *sympathetically built in traditional Maasai style* and its location provides ample opportunity for game viewing within the park.	http://www.sunsetafricasafaris.com /Safari_Camps_And_Lodges_In_ Masai_Mara_National_Reserve.htm
(5) Sarova Mara Game Camp *keeps alive the tradition of the Maa speaking people* in the Isokon Maasai Cultural Village . . . a true showcase of Maasai Culture. This unique display and interactive edutainment presentation *allows you to immerse yourself in one of earth's oldest cultures.*	http://www.sarovahotels.com /incentives/incentive_mara.php

Figure 16.1. *Roadside sign for a cultural* manyatta *on the outskirts of Namanga, southern Kenya (photo by the author, 2009).*

question even claims to be responsible for 'keeping alive' Maasai heritage and tradition through its cultural village.

Quite understandably, the region's pastoralist communities have tapped into this rhetoric for their own goals, and a great many pastoralist communities now run their own 'traditional *manyatta*,' and as the quote above suggests, there seems to be an implication that the protection of cultural heritage *requires* a heritage center—rather than this being a consequence of continuities in practice. The last two decades in particular have witnessed a veritable explosion in the number of 'cultural villages' (Figure 16.1) where pastoralist communities encourage tourists to visit and learn about their culture (see Table 16.3). A number of those in southern Kenya and northern Tanzania, in particular, were established by prominent, educated members of the local community who either hold white collar jobs elsewhere in the region, or have recently retired from such positions. These individuals are typically motivated by a desire to 'bring development to their community' by providing a source of income generation and employment.

Various aid agencies and NGOs have also promoted 'heritage tourism' as a means of income generation. The Dutch overseas agency Stichting Nederlandse Vrijwilligers (SNV) was particularly active in this regard in Tanzania

TABLE 16.3 Selected extracts from a variety of local, regional, and international organizations aimed at promoting Maasai cultural tourism and sustainable development; all accessed June 2012.

Extract (emphasis added)	Source and Topic
Mission and Projects: Ensure the survival of the Maasai people by *preserving our cultural heritage, supporting sustainable socio-economic development* within our communities, and protecting traditional land rights and political representation so that we can determine our own future on our own lands.	Mission statement, Maasai Environmental Resource Coalition, available at http://www.maasaierc.org/missionandprojects.html
About Us: Twala Cultural Manyatta is a community project initiated by local women to *preserve the rich cultural and historic heritage* of the local Maasai people. This ecotourism facility is constructed using local and traditional materials.	Twala Cultural Manyatta brochure, available at http://www.baboonsrus.com/resources/PDF_Twala_Manyatta.pdf
KENYA: Maasai Cultural Village: Working with the Maasai community, a new form of cultural village will be *designed and built to support the traditional Maasai culture* but taking them successfully into the future.	Project plan, Arts based interdisciplinary projects, Graduate School of Education, University of Melbourne, available at http://www.education.unimelb.edu.au/eldi/elc/unesco/culturalvillages/kenya3.html
Kitumusote Maasai Cultural Safari: "The Kitumusote Maasai Cultural Safari was developed by Kitumusote members with the *goal of creating long-term sustainable income* for the organization whilst sharing various aspects of Maasai daily life, customs, and traditions."	Kitumusote community-based NGO homepage, available at http://www.kitumusote.org/projects/kitumusote_maasai_cultual_safari
Safari with us and support the development of the Loita Maasai: Visit our land and share in our hospitality. *Enjoy our unique and pristine environment.* Visit the forest of the lost child and consult our Laibons and spiritual leaders. Enjoy a retreat and feast in the meat camps organized by Maasai morans. Recuperate and experience the healing effect of the natural herbs.	Ilkerin Loita Integrated Development Programme homepage, on opportunities for eco-tourism and cultural safari opportunities, available at http://ilkerinloita.org/ecotourism.php

during the last fifteen years or so, resulting in the creation of a Cultural Tourism Programme (CTP) and the establishment and financing of some twenty-eight cultural tourism enterprises in collaboration with the Ministry of Natural Resources and Tourism and the Tanzania Tourist Board.[8] Of the twenty-eight separate schemes, five explicitly offer an opportunity to visit a Maasai *manyatta* (Ilkurot, Engrauka, Longido, Oldonyo Sambu, and Osotowa), while one other (Monduli Juu) offers the chance to meet a traditional Maasai healer.

Whereas SNV claims that the idea for CTP developed from the 'bottom up' after being approached in 1994 by a group of young Maasai who wished to develop cultural tourism in their area, Salazar (2012: 14) is more skeptical. He points in particular to the long tradition of SNV in promoting cultural tourism in developing countries and that once SNV withdrew in 2001 (in line with its philosophy of setting up sustainable and self-governing enterprises), the program began to falter quite rapidly (2012: 15).

There have been similar ventures in Kenya. For example, in 1996 the Kenya Wildlife Service began to promote conservation partnerships with Maasai communities living around the boundaries of Amboseli National Park in the south of the country (Ritsma and Ongaro 2002: 130). This resulted in the creation of at least seven cultural *manyattas* on different group ranches, and since 2000, the African Wildlife Foundation have worked with representatives of these. One outcome of this has been the creation of a new association—the Association for Cultural Centres in the Amboseli Ecosystem—in an effort to coordinate their activities and help them provide better management so as to enhance both visitor experience and deliver the conservation goals that underpinned their creation in the first place (2002: 134).

In appearance, many (but by no means all) of these cultural *manyattas* resemble the kind of pastoralist settlements that dot the landscape around the margins of the most popular National Parks in the region, and in many cases their primary function is as a place of routine settlement for a pastoralist kin group. For the occupants of these settlements, 'cultural tourism' is just one of several economic and subsistence activities they perform. The basic form of these is thus fairly similar from place to place—a sub-circular enclosure created from cut thorn-scrub, encompassing a series of dung, mud, and wattle sub-rectangular houses with rounded corners that are arranged in a circle around a central cattle byre and perhaps smaller livestock pens for sheep and goats (Figure 16.2). As 'living settlements,' this also helps convey a sense of authenticity that is not matched at other similar 'cultural villages' deliberately created by external parties such as tourist lodges or development-oriented NGOs.

There is considerable variability in terms of the kinds of activities on offer. Typical activities include an opportunity to go inside a house (Figure 16.3), watch *moran* (members of the warrior age-set) make fire by rubbing sticks together, or in their full regalia, as well as observing and even participating in various dances (such as the 'Lion Dance' performed by *moran*), listen to women singing the 'wedding song,' and to purchase curios.

There is also considerable variation in how and why such cultural villages were established and in how they are managed. In the Maasai Mara area

FIGURE 16.2. *Women lined up to welcome visitors at Oldoinyo-Orok 'Maasai cultural village,' Namanga, Kenya (photo by the author, 2009).*

of southwest Kenya, for example, there are at least twenty-seven cultural villages on the Narok side of the Masai Mara Reserve. Many of these were established by tour operators or hotels and lodges in the area, and a common complaint of the communities involved has long been that the tour operators and/or the mini-bus drivers and non-local guides demanded a significant share of their 'gate fees' as a reward for bringing the tourists. In 2008, a UK-based NGO, Tribal-Voice, worked with these communities to establish their own tourism association so as to break free from this kind of exploitation.[9] While such initiatives may well mean that more of the tourist income reaches the intended recipients, and may even result in a better quality of tourist experience (e.g., Table 16.4, no. 2), these cultural villages are no less artificial than those set up by lodges and tour operators, and efforts to remove or hide the material traces of 'modernity' are just as common (Ritsma and Ongaro 2002; Salazar 2009, 2012). The occupants of several of these newly created *manyattas*, especially those around Amboseli, are also often in conflict with the wildlife authorities and human-wildlife conflicts have by no means gone away—neither of which, in and of themselves, lend much credence to the claim that pastoralists have always lived

FIGURE 16.3. *Inside a Maasai house at Oldoinyo-Orok 'Maasai cultural village,' Namanga, Kenya (photo by the author, 2009).*

in harmony with wild animals. Perhaps most critically, the establishment of cultural *manyattas* has encouraged a greater permanency of residence than would typically be the case for a normal residential unit practicing subsistence pastoralism. Paradoxically, this may have consequences ultimately for the ecological relationships that *have* helped enhance biodiversity since this results not from sedentary occupation of the land, as is becoming the norm around 'cultural *manyattas*,' but from regular settlement abandonment and mobility (see, e.g., Stelfox 1986; Augustine 2003; Muchiru, Western, and Reid 2008; Lane 2011, and references therein).

MEMORY

The canon of Memory . . . suggests that one consider the psychological aspects of preparing to communicate and the performance of communicating itself, especially in an oral or impromptu setting. Typically Memory has to do only with the orator, but invites consideration of how the audience will retain things in mind.
—GIDEON O. BURTON (2007)

Helping the Maasai by visiting the community of Lenkisem: *Your chance to help a Maasai community* is NOW possible by visiting Lenkisem, a community located only 25 km from Amboseli National Park, you will be able to interact with the local community—*one of the few places untouched by the so-called globalization*—exchanging thoughts and visions and, when/if needed, provide them with the necessary tools for self-development.[10]

The saturation of the tourist experience with the kinds of associations discussed above generates a self-repeating circuit of culture (Figure 16.4), whereby representations draw tourists in and staged encounters reinforce initial perceptions. As they reflect and report on their own experiences, tourists re-state these same stereotypes—at times marveling at how genuine their encounters were, at others regretting how much tourism has changed things from how they once were. Countless online comments capture these dual sentiments (Table 16.4). In common with visitors to these kinds of cultural heritage settings in other parts of the world, concerns about the authenticity of the setting, and so also the experience of the visitor, are prominent.

Aspects of pastoralist culture and heritage have been used to promote tourism in East Africa since the early decades of the twentieth century (Akama 2002; Bruner 2002; Galaty 2002; Salazar 2009). Staged 'Maasai' dances, performed almost exclusively by young men dressed as *moran*, are

TABLE 16.4 Selected examples from personal blogs and press reports on Maasai heritage (with emphasis added).

---

(1) Maasai—Oct 29, 2004:

"We made the long haul back from the Central Serengeti to Arusha today . . .We had been planning to visit a Maasai . . . boma, or family village, on the way back, but after arriving at the first designated village, we changed our minds because it was so crowded with tourists . . . After much debate, we ended up stopping at the third village (*it was further away* and the least popular of the three). Fortunately, *we were the only outsiders there.*"

http://www.thirteenmonths.com/tz04_maasai.htm; accessed October 2007, June 2012.

(2) May 1, 2012:

"We visited the Masai Mara National Park this week. It was a real highlight of our trip. On the way . . . we visited a Masai Village. We did visit a village in Tanzania but it was a commercialised village and wasn't functional . . . The village near the National Park was functional . . . people actually lived there. *It was a more authentic experience.*"

http://blog.mikeandamy.com.au/2012/01/05/masai-village-kenya/; accessed June 2012.

(3) A Visit to Maasai Bomas—December 2002, p. 2:

"Once we arrived at Baraka's boma we were formally greeted and ushered into one of the huts. The only light was from the partially obscured doorway so once inside it took a few moments for our eyes to adjust. *It was like stepping back 300 years.*"

http://www.themcdonalds.ca/africasites/MasaiBomas/masaibomas2.html; accessed September 2007, June 2012.

(4) October 31 2009: US Actor Edward Norton runs NYC Marathon tomorrow for Maasai cause.

". . . it's because people like the Maasai actually in *resisting the draw for modern life* left their landscape largely intact for these animals to live in."

http://faraitoday.com/2009/10/31/u-s-actor-edward-norton-runs-nyc-marathon -tomorrow-for-maasai-cause/; accessed June 2012.

---

common features at many such hotels and lodges, as well as at other types of venue. Recent analyses of some examples have emphasized that while these may be formally similar, variations in the context and relations of their production shape how tourists read them and interpret their own experience as an 'authentic' engagement with 'real Africa' (Bruner and Kirshenblatt-Gimblett 1994; Bruner 2001).

These visual cultural representations are used most frequently by the tourist industry and so can perhaps be explained as just another example of the extent to which many kinds of tourism are driven by a hedonistic search for the exotic. Nonetheless, the same visual tropes also feature on official websites for Kenya[11] and Tanzania.[12] As Fürsich and Robins (2004: 138) have argued, less

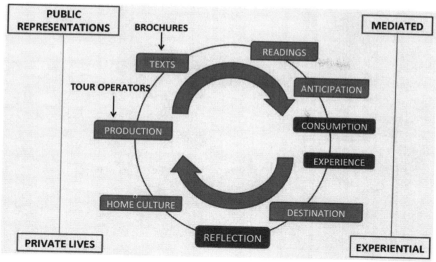

FIGURE 16.4. *The tourist's 'Circuit of Culture' (after Norton 1996: 360).*

developed countries that "create the concept of a tourist nation by contrasting pristine nature and a sanitized, nostalgic past against contemporary life run the risk of undermining the national goal of modernization."

CONCLUSION—TRAPPED IN THE PAST?

Many contemporary pastoralist communities now position themselves as the traditional custodians of East Africa's wildlife and as having a 'heritage' of ecological stewardship. The promotion of certain practices and selected elements of their material world at 'cultural *manyattas*' and 'cultural heritage centers' as signifiers of this tradition is part of this strategy which, as discussed above, is typically accomplished through the use of a visual and textual rhetoric that has long been in place to promote regional wildlife tourism. As a consequence, to the outside world at least, East Africa's pastoralists are commonly seen not just as resilient guardians of their own traditions and heritage but of the entire region's claim to be authentically African.

It is noteworthy, however, given the ubiquity of images that cast East Africa's pastoralists as living in harmony with nature since time immemorial, that two other sets of popular visual cultural representations of these same communities also circulate within the public sphere. At first sight these seem to be the antithesis of those discussed above. There is, for example, a range of

FIGURE 16.5. *Txteagle's advertisement for mobile crowdsourcing (reproduced by kind permission of Txteagle).*[13]

visual tropes that juxtapose pastoralists (and once again, usually, young Maasai males) and overt symbols of Western modernity, typically although not exclusively as part of a strategy of product placement. The countless photographs and postcards showing *moran* cycling across a savanna landscape is a common example.[14] More recently, mobile phone companies, such as Safaricom[15] (one of the first mobile network providers in the region) have played on a similar contrast between tradition and modernity, and others have been quick to follow this lead (Figure 16.5).[16] In all such images, the viewer is invited to marvel at the traditional pastoralist's adaptability but equally critically, their *cultural resilience*. New technologies may be embraced—even happily, as the smiling faces suggest—but tradition, the fundamental core of society, remains secure.

What is obscured by this juxtaposition of apparent material symbols of 'modernity' and 'tradition' is that of all of East Africa's ethnicities, it is the Maasai and other pastoralists whose identities have been most commoditized while simultaneously the dynamism of their societies is constantly being denied. As outlined here, East Africa's pastoralist communities have 'bought into' this traditional/modern dichotomy, and so in their own practice are in danger of reproducing an essentialized view of culture as a static given (Galaty 2002: 347). This is unfortunate since the constant re-statement of contemporary pastoralist practices as 'traditional,' far from conveying a notion of sustainability, as now intended by pastoralists and conservationists alike, also encourages a belief that the region's pastoralists are *reluctant to change*. By adhering to their cultural 'heritage,' East Africa's pastoralists have thus often been portrayed as being irrevocably wedded to livestock accumulation. This, it has been argued, results inevitably in 'overstocking' which, in turn, becomes a primary cause of rangeland deterioration and soil erosion. Such negative ideas concerning the ecological consequences of pastoralist heritage—the so-called 'tragedy of the commons'—certainly underlie many past and even current narratives of regional drought, landscape degradation, and famine (see Fratkin 1997). Like the rhetoric that positions pastoralists as traditional conservationists, these narratives and images have been in circulation at least since the turn of the twentieth century when an outbreak of rinderpest, a fatal cattle disease, combined with widespread epidemics and land appropriation by European settlers, decimated pastoralist communities (Homewood and Rodgers 1987). Although the specifics may have changed, this rhetoric remains familiar today through its use by numerous international relief agencies and NGOs in their promotional literature for specific development programs (e.g., Oxfam 2008)[17] and in fundraising campaigns and media reports launched in response to regional humanitarian emergencies.[18]

Significantly, perhaps, instead of smiling young men gazing over the verdant bush, the more archetypal of these images, though equally gendered, usually depict an emaciated woman making her way across a dry, barren landscape. She has children in tow and the wind has whipped up the dust which swirls around her and her wards. While she may be wearing 'traditional' dress and beaded ornaments which readily identify her as a member of an African pastoralist society, her clothes are frequently ragged, her hair drab and dust-covered, her jewelry seemingly more a burden than a source of pride. What little vegetation can be seen is leafless or withered; the bright sunlight harsh and relentless. Here, the rhetoric is redolent of a lack of resources, environmental collapse, hardship, and acute vulnerability to the vagaries of climatic and environmental change. It is an image much used by NGOs, international relief agencies, and the Western media to generate their own source of dollars for redistribution, in this case as 'aid' rather than as an earned income. There is also perhaps a greater sense of immediacy and appeal to the emotions and senses in these images and less of a timeless quality. *But*, there is also often an absence—a lack of any discursive visual referents to the historically contingent causes of drought and the social, economic, and political drivers of famine. In the absence of any historical context, outsiders are left to ponder whether part of the heritage of pastoralists, and especially women, is also to remain the passive victims of these processes and events. Unable to break free of tradition, this rhetoric suggests, pastoralists are ultimately the architects of their own demise.

In summary, in common with other communities around the world that have been drawn into similar cultural tourism ventures, East Africa's pastoralists seem to be caught in a double bind by prevailing rhetoric that hinges on the contrasting and even contradictory notions and expectations of 'authenticity' held by the various actors involved (for further discussion see, e.g., Wang 1999; Cole 2007; Cohen 2010; and Theodossopoulos 2013, among many others). On the one hand, placing 'time' into sustainability discourse through the invocation of 'heritage' certainly makes perfect sense, since the very notion of sustainability requires a temporal perspective. As Stump (2010) notes, for any practice to be regarded as sustainable there needs to be some temporal scale against which its efficacy can be judged. Beneficial consequences of this have included the creation of novel income generating opportunities (although the income received does not always reach the pastoralists themselves), heightened international concern over the plight of pastoralist communities and the negative consequences of older 'fortress' approaches to wildlife conservation, and increased access to the resources offered by development-oriented NGOs and especially those with a global reach. However, by laying claim to a heritage as conservationists, Maasai and other pastoralist communities, no doubt unwittingly, also help create and sustain a modernist/anti-modernist dichotomy, which builds on well-established narrative tropes and is signaled by the apparent deliberate retention of a specific material and visual culture. This may work effectively for certain external audiences, especially foreign tourists. However, by encouraging a greater permanence of settlement around the 'cultural *manyattas*' used to showcase this 'traditional heritage,' Maasai and other pastoralists may in fact be putting at risk the very ecological resilience of the landscapes this rhetoric is intended to help protect.

This is because the ecologically beneficial consequences for local biodiversity of a pastoralist presence in East Africa's semi-arid landscapes is dependent on structured patterns of mobility and regular settlement abandonment over many centuries, not the kind of long-term sedentism that heritage tourism, like national policies and development agencies before them, is now encouraging.

In other words, sustainability in these environments is less about maintaining a status quo and more about being able to respond to and shape the direction of change. From this perspective, by denying change and reproducing a static image of 'tradition' as symbolized by the superficial retention of a specific material 'heritage,' East Africa's pastoralist communities may in fact be undermining the qualities of their own resilience while also detracting attention from the changed contexts (e.g., Homewood, Kristjanson, and Trench 2009) in which they now have to seek their livelihoods. Consequently, far from promoting an image of stasis and continuity, pastoralists and conservationists alike may wish to consider how to create a new rhetoric of sustainability based on concepts of adaptive change and cultural dynamism so as to avoid some of the pitfalls associated with their current heritage rhetoric, as discussed here.

ACKNOWLEDGMENTS

I would like to thank the editors for inviting me to contribute to this volume, to present an early draft at the 2011 Theoretical Archaeology group (TAG) conference at the University of Birmingham, and for their exceptional patience during the finalization of this chapter. Earlier versions were presented at the African Studies Association UK 2008 biennial conference, University of Lancaster, and the 2011 African Archaeology Research Day, Institute of Archaeology, University of London. I am grateful to the participants in the sessions where these ideas were presented, for their comments. Elements of the field research on which this chapter is based was conducted under the auspices of the European Union funded Marie Curie Excellence Grant project "Historical Ecologies of East African Landscapes" (MEXT-CT-2006-042704), hosted by the University of York. Thanks are also due to Zoe Cormack and Elizabeth Deane who assisted with some of the background research on cultural *manyattas* in Tanzania and Kenya and to the British Institute in Eastern Africa for logistical support.

NOTES

1. http://rhetoric.byu.edu, accessed May 2012.

2. http://www.travelblog.org/Africa/Tanzania/North/Arusha/blog-142170.html, accessed May 2008, June 2012, emphasis added.

3. http://peacematunda.org/tourism/maasai-cultural, accessed June 2012, emphasis added.

4. For variations on this theme see, e.g., the following websites (accessed June 2012): http://mulengetours.com/nature-and-local-communities-adventures-9-day-tour/; http://tripwow.tripadvisor.com/slideshow-photo/a-masai-moran-viewing-the-plains -masai-mara-national-reserve-kenya.html?sid=71609814&fid=upload_13300831655- tpfilo2aw-22965; http://www.flickr.com/photos/78449184@N00/3030125094/; http:// www.facebook.com/pages/C3Co-Cooperation-Collaboration-Community/198895341 272?sk=app_132295096816940.

5. http://www.igougo.com/travelcontent/journalEntryFreeForm.aspx?JournalID =36648&entryID=17695&Mode=4, accessed October 2011, emphasis added.

6. http://davidlansing.com/category/africa/kenya/maasai-mara/, accessed June 2012.

7. http://www.maasai-association.org/projects.html, accessed June 2012, emphasis added.

8. http://www.tanzaniaculturaltourism.com, accessed May 2012.

9. http://www.tribal-voice.co.uk/projects.html, accessed June 2012.

10. http://lenkisem.wordpress.com, accessed June 2012, emphasis added.

11. See http://www.tourism.go.ke/ministry.nsf/pages/cultural_tourism; accessed June 2012.

12. See http://www.tanzania.go.tz/ministriesf.html, accessed June 2012.

13. http://cdn.thenextweb.com/files/2011/04/cellphone_africa-520x362.jpg.

14. Examples include those on the following websites (accessed June 2012): http://travel.nationalgeographic.com/travel/countries/your-biking-photos/; http://www.allposters.com/-st/Bicycle-Posters_c19670_p8_.htm;

15. See, for example, http://www.textually.org/textually/archives/2007/03/015381.htm, accessed June 2012.

16. See, for example, http://www.globalenvision.org/2011/10/20/how-technology-changing-world-and-allowing-you-change-it-too; http://www.nitibhan.com/2012/04/mobile-phones-social-media-and-maasai.html; http://www.oxfamblogs.org/eastafrica/?p=3615; http://www.altalang.com/beyond-words/2009/02/18/beyond-txt-crowdsourcing-with-txteagle/, accessed June 2012.

17. Available at http://www.oxfam.org/policy/bp116-pastoralism-climate-change-0808.

18. For the 2011–2012 famine and regional drought, e.g., http://www.cafod.org.uk/news/emergencies-updates/east-africa-drought-2011-07-07/east-africa-q-a-2012-06-01; http://www.theatlantic.com/infocus/2011/07/famine-in-east-africa/100115/; http://www.washingtonpost.com/world/africa/somalis-walk-for-days-as-famine-pushes-war-racked-nation-deeper-into-abyss/2011/08/25/gIQATpOEgJ_story.html; http://www.virgin.com/people-and-planet/blog/east-africa-food-crisis (all accessed June 2012).

REFERENCES

Adams, William M., and David Hulme. 2001. "Conservation and Community: Changing Narratives, Policies, and Practices in African Conservation." In *African Wildlife and Livelihoods: The Promise and Performance of Community Conservation*, ed. David Hulme and Marshall Murphree, 9–23. Oxford: James Currey.

Akama, John. 2002. "The Creation of the Maasai Image and Tourism Development in Kenya." In *Cultural Tourism in Africa: Strategies for the New Millennium*, ed. John S. Akama and Patricia Sterry, 43–53. Arnhem, Netherlands: Association for Tourism and Leisure Education.

Augustine, David J. 2003. "Long-Term, Livestock Mediated Redistribution of Nitrogen and Phosphorus in an East African Savanna." *Journal of Applied Ecology* 40 (1): 137–49. http://dx.doi.org/10.1046/j.1365-2664.2003.00778.x.

Brockington, Daniel. 2002. *Fortress Conservation: The Preservation of the Mkomazi Game Reserve, Tanzania.* Oxford: James Currey.

Bruner, Edward M. 2001. "The Maasai and the Lion King: Authenticity, Nationalism, and Globalization in African Tourism." *American Ethnologist* 28 (4): 881–908. http://dx.doi.org/10.1525/ae.2001.28.4.881.

Bruner, Edward M. 2002. "The Representation of African Pastoralists: A Commentary." *Visual Anthropology* 15 (3/4): 387–92. http://dx.doi.org/10.1080/08949460213912.

Bruner, Edward M., and Barbara Kirshenblatt-Gimblett. 1994. "Maasai on the Lawn: Tourist Realism in East Africa." *Cultural Anthropology* 9 (4): 435–70. http://dx.doi.org/10.1525/can.1994.9.4.02a00010.

Burton, Gideon O. 2007. *Silva Rhetoricae: The Forest of Rhetoric.* Available online at http://rhetoric.byu.edu.

Cohen, Erik. 2010. "Tourism, Leisure and Authenticity." *Tourism Recreation Research* 35 (1): 67–73. http://dx.doi.org/10.1080/02508281.2010.11081620.

Cole, Stroma. 2007. "Beyond Authenticity and Commodification." *Annals of Tourism Research* 34 (4): 943–60. http://dx.doi.org/10.1016/j.annals.2007.05.004.

Davies, Jonathan, ed. 2012. *Conservation and Sustainable Development: Linking Practice and Policy in Eastern Africa.* London: Earthscan.

Dixon, John A., and Louise A. Fallon. 1989. "The Concept of Sustainability: Origins, Extensions, and Usefulness for Policy." *Society & Natural Resources* 2 (1): 73–84. http://dx.doi.org/10.1080/08941928909380675.

Fratkin, Elliot. 1997. "Pastoralism: Governance and Development Issues." *Annual Review of Anthropology* 26 (1): 235–61. http://dx.doi.org/10.1146/annurev.anthro.26.1.235.

Fürsich, Elfriede, and Melinda B. Robins. 2004. "Visiting Africa: Constructions of Nation and Identity on Travel Websites." *Journal of Asian and African Studies* 39 (1/2): 133–52. http://dx.doi.org/10.1177/0021909604048255.

Galaty, John G. 2002. "How Visual Figures Speak: Narrative Inventions of 'The Pastoralist' in East Africa." *Visual Anthropology* 15 (3/4): 347–67. http://dx.doi.org/10.1080/08949460213910.

Hodgson, Dorothy L. 2009. "Becoming Indigenous in Africa." *African Studies Review* 52 (3): 1–32. http://dx.doi.org/10.1353/arw.0.0302.

Homewood, Katherine, Patricia Kristjanson, and Pippa Trench, eds. 2009. *Staying Maasai?: Livelihoods, Conservation, and Development in East African Rangelands.* London: Springer. http://dx.doi.org/10.1007/978-0-387-87492-0.

Homewood, Katherine M., and W. Alan Rodgers. 1987. "Pastoralism, Conservation, and the Overgrazing Controversy." In *Conservation in Africa: People, Policies, and Practice*, ed. David M. Anderson and Richard H. Grove, 111–28. Cambridge: Cambridge University Press.

Igoe, James. 2006. "Becoming Indigenous Peoples: Difference, Inequality, and the Globalization of East African Identity Politics." *African Affairs* 105 (420): 399–420. http://dx.doi.org/10.1093/afraf/adi127.

Lane, Paul J. 2011. "An Outline of the Later Holocene Archaeology and Precolonial History of the Ewaso Basin, Kenya." In *Conserving Wildlife in African Landscapes: Kenya's Ewaso Ecosystem*, ed. Nicholas Georgiadis, 11–30. Smithsonian Contributions to Zoology 632. http://dx.doi.org/10.5479/si.00810282.632.11.

Leach, Joan. 2002. "Rhetorical Analysis." In *Qualitative Researching With Text, Image and Sound: A Practical Handbook*, ed. Martin W. Bauer and George Gaskell, 207–26. London: Sage.

Mitcham, Carl. 1995. "The Concept of Sustainable Development: Its Origins and Ambivalence." *Technology in Society* 17 (3): 311–26. http://dx.doi.org/10.1016/0160-791X(95)00008-F.

Muchiru, Andrew N., David J. Western, and Robin S. Reid. 2008. "The Role of Abandoned Pastoral Settlements in the Dynamics of African Large Herbivore Communities." *Journal of Arid Environments* 72 (6): 940–52. http://dx.doi.org/10.1016/j.jaridenv.2007.11.012.

Myers, Greg, and Phil Macnaghten. 1998. "Rhetorics of Environmental Sustainability: Commonplaces and Places." *Environment & Planning A* 30 (2): 333–53. http://dx.doi.org/10.1068/a300333.

Norton, Andrew. 1996. "Experiencing Nature: The Reproduction of Environmental Discourse Through Safari Tourism in East Africa." *Geoforum* 27 (3): 355–73. http://dx.doi.org/10.1016/S0016-7185(96)00021-8.

Nygren, Anja. 1998. "Environment as Discourse: Searching for Sustainable Development." *Environmental Values* 7 (2): 201–22. http://dx.doi.org/10.3197/096327198129341546.

Oxfam. 2008. *Survival of the Fittest: Pastoralism and Climate Change in East Africa.* Oxfam Briefing Paper 116. Oxford: Oxfam.

Redclift, Michael. 2005. "Sustainable Development (1987–2005): An Oxymoron

Comes of Age." *Sustainable Development* 13 (4): 212–27. http://dx.doi.org/10.1002
/sd.281.

Ritsma, Nanda, and Stephen Ongaro. 2002. "The Commoditisation and
Commercialisation of the Maasai Culture: Will Cultural *Manyattas* Withstand
the 21st Century?" In *Cultural Tourism in Africa: Strategies for the New Millennium*,
ed. John S. Akama and Patricia Sterry, 127–36. Arnhem, Netherlands: Association
for Tourism and Leisure Education.

Salazar, Noel B. 2009. "Imaged or Imagined? Cultural Representations and the
'Tourismification' of Peoples and Places." *Cahier d'Études africaines* 49 (1/2): 49–71.

Salazar, Noel B. 2012. "Community-Based Cultural Tourism: Issues, Threats, and
Opportunities." *Journal of Sustainable Tourism* 20 (1): 9–22. http://dx.doi.org/10.108
0/09669582.2011.596279.

Sillitoe, Paul, Alan Bicker, and Johan Pottier, eds. 2002. *Participating in Development:
Approaches to Indigenous Knowledge*. ASA Monographs 39. London: Routledge.
http://dx.doi.org/10.4324/9780203428603.

Stelfox, J. Brad. 1986. "Effects of Livestock Enclosures (Bomas) on the Vegetation of
the Athi Plains, Kenya." *African Journal of Ecology* 24 (1): 41–45. http://dx.doi.org
/10.1111/j.1365-2028.1986.tb00340.x.

Stump, Daryl. 2010. "Ancient and Backward or Long-Lived and Sustainable: The
Role of the Past in Developmental Debates in Eastern Africa." *World Development*
38 (9): 1251–62. http://dx.doi.org/10.1016/j.worlddev.2010.02.007.

Theodossopoulos, Dimitrios. 2013. "Laying Claim to Authenticity: Five
Anthropological Dilemmas." *Anthropological Quarterly* 86 (2): 337–60. http://
dx.doi.org/10.1353/anq.2013.0032.

Wang, Ning. 1999. "Rethinking Authenticity in Tourism Experience." *Annals of
Tourism Research* 26 (2): 349–70. http://dx.doi.org/10.1016/S0160-7383(98)00103-0.

WCED (World Commission on Environment and Development). 1987. *Our
Common Future—The Brundtland Report*. Oxford: Oxford University Press/
WCED.

After Words **17**

A De-dichotomization in Heritage Discourse

TRINIDAD RICO

As a book project that was born in the conference rooms of two sessions separated by the Atlantic Ocean in late 2011, it was perhaps surprising to hear iterations of the same question opening the discussion section on both occasions: *what is the way forward, then?*

The question refers to the aims that we had outlined in the abstracts and introductions to these sessions: to contribute to the ongoing process of disarming and redescribing rhetorical devices in circulation that give validity and power to established and dominant heritage discourses. More specifically, this volume and the sessions that inspired it aim to address the narrow and increasingly empty usage of certain heritage vocabularies. These established usages are seen to prevent the potential for these vocabularies to inspire a diversity of meanings and perspectives outside of the dominant discourse, as described by Kathryn Lafrenz Samuels in the introduction to this volume. Hence, contributors to this volume do not simply aim to decommission selected rhetorical terms, but to question, expand, and un-define the meanings firmly embedded in these commonly and widely circulated terms.

Questioning the way forward from these exercises in redescription, as some of our audience members did, suggested hopefully that we had been successful at disenfranchising the established authority of rhetorical

DOI: 10.5876/9781607323846.c017

devices that have become common currency. But it is a line of enquiry that also reflects a familiar anxiety associated with the de-authorization of the expert production of knowledge as it was posed by postprocessual debates in archaeology, a "decline of ideology" in the face of a plurality of meanings (Hodder 1999: 179). In the process of revisiting established terminologies used in heritage studies and practice, and situating debates within increasingly shifting and complex contexts, these redescriptions could be interpreted as systematically invalidating and revoking all possible future directions by eliminating attempts at creating manageable working definitions for each one of these concepts. But we would argue that this is a misinterpretation of the aims and outcomes of the debates that this volume proposes.

These debates do not aim to stall further dialogue, but rather to recognize the epistemological cycles that embrace a heritage vocabulary that is, or rather should be, constantly in flux. This fluidity is not naturally occurring in the normative framework of heritage in which these vocabularies play a key role. But it is achieved through the promotion of debates that embrace using contextual points of departure and promote a high frequency of further redescriptions, a process that asks that boundaries and best practice be sidelined in favor of acknowledging transitions of meaning in time and place. The call for redescription therefore recognizes that heritage debates are taking place and understood in this moment in time. Therefore, rather than stalling, we hope to be charting the way forward by inviting further description, recentralization and re-appropriation of terms in more productive ways and in less polarized grounds. The way forward is in all directions and at once, and this is why the authors of these chapters embark in a series of redescriptions of some of the fundamentals of heritage discourse and practice that is not the first, and will not be the last of its kind.

It is necessary to clarify that this volume is not by any means representative of the full range of the heritage rhetoric that is currently put to use. In fact, many of the discussions elaborated here summon other key concepts of significance in the heritage vocabulary that are also in need of redescription, but were not included in this project. Moreover, in organizing the volume into different rhetorical terms for discussion, we are faced with a key issue of epistemological logistics. We come to the realization that it is not possible to discuss each rhetorical device as a stand-alone debate, as it is evident that these terms are deeply interconnected within heritage discourse and practice. Terms rely on each other for validity and act as points of reference to each other, in such a way that their discussion in isolation only highlights their artificiality as units of discussion, pointing out the degree to which they have become naturalized constructs. There is not one chapter in this volume that does not require the support of other widely circulated concepts for 'scaffolding' its argument.

THE SHIFTING SANDS OF HERITAGE VOCABULARY

One of the levels of complexity that is highlighted throughout the discussions in these chapters is the way that each rhetorical device shifts within itself and in relation to other debates. Among the questions that this can raise are: what is the point of departure to ascertain heritage truths? What kind of conceptual and ideological scaffolding is required in order to create and use heritage rhetorical devices that appear to be self-sustaining? These questions point to ongoing debates that aim to expose the ways in which the heritage discourse and practice have been naturalized, by situating it in non-universal contexts geographically and chronologically. It is not surprising to see existing and new discursive relationships reinforced throughout these discussions, as coherence within the heritage discourse is possible through—and constitutes strong evidence of—the degree to which heritage vocabularies are self-referential. For example, this had been discussed by Smith (2006: 11–12) as a key characteristic of the Authorized Heritage Discourse in its construction of a material reality for itself that enables the assumption of an innate value and meaning for heritage. As Smith further explains, this process results in the obscuring of multivocality and the promotion of particular forms of expertise that may mediate the meaning and nature of these heritage vocabularies.

At the risk of over simplifying the nuanced discussions taking place in each one of these chapters, a quick glance through the construction of each term and the debates that problematize their redescription makes evident myriad examples of interconnectivity within heritage vocabularies, exemplifying the extent to which each must rely, explain, or refer to other established heritage terms, many of which are featured in this volume. Although each chapter is focused on a unique debate, it could be argued that none of these terms can effectively be self-referential. In this way, for example, Anna Karlström's debate on authenticity (Chapter 2) frequently refers to perceptions of destruction, a discussion central to Trinidad Rico's chapter on heritage at risk (Chapter 9), which in turn benefits greatly from following and running alongside Karlström's engagement with the materialistic, performative, and constructivist approaches to authenticity. This is not the only set of relationships visible throughout these discussions, nor the most evident one. Malcolm Cooper's (Chapter 10) discussion of heritage discourse also relates to discussions of destruction, and his dialogue also relies extensively on an ongoing circulation of the concepts of universality, values, materiality, and significance, basic fundamental units in the promotion and operation of a heritage discourse that are touched on by many of the discussions in this volume.

Moving on, Alexander Bauer's (Chapter 5) discussion of cultural property refers to debates surrounding the existence and application of heritage rights, a rich rhetorical ground discussed here by Lafrenz Samuels (Chapter 15). Cecilia Rodéhn's (Chapter 6) redescription addressing the definition and use of the term democratization informs part of the debate in Jeffrey Adams' (Chapter 8) discussion of equity, as they both aim to further complicate the circumstances of the construction and operation of these terms. Sigrid Van der Auwera's contribution (Chapter 3) on civil society also relies extensively on conceptions of democracy, but key to this discussion is the construction of cultural diversity, joining Alicia McGill (Chapter 4), who invites further complexity to the commonly circulated idea of communities, considering in particular issues of identity and its sustainability. Paul Lane's (Chapter 16) exploration of sustainability is based on the fundamental sets of relationships that structure rhetoric, exploring manifestations of the rhetoric of equity, nature, indigeneity, and memory, as well as engaging with authenticity, and stewardship.

Moreover, Van der Auwera also proposes a discussion of the operation of a civil society in consideration of the existence of difficult heritage communities, a term whose validity and usage is the object of Joshua Samuels' (Chapter 7) discussion of difficult heritage. Melissa Baird's (Chapter 13) explorations of the rhetoric of nature in cultural heritage refer to the concepts of stakeholder, stewardship, and place, the latter addressed by Robert Preucel and Regis Pecos' redescription (Chapter 14), which, in turn, includes reference to the circulation of intangible heritage knowledge as naturally inseparable from material culture. Addressing this term in more detail, Klaus Zehbe's (Chapter 11) problematization of the idea and authority of intangible heritage points out the need for more explicit ways in which professionals construct heritage facts, highlighting the significance of examining more closely the role and agency of forms of expertise. Expertise is a rhetorical device that is not explicitly addressed as a chapter in this volume but underlies many, if not all, the discussions taking place. The same could be said of the rhetorical manipulations of time as a construct that is foundational to the idea and authority of heritage discourses, and whereas Rico's chapter tangentially discusses it in this volume, it remains a term in dire need of further description and redescription.

In pointing out advertently or inadvertently the interconnection of these terms, the array of debates taking place in these chapters aims to de-authorize the simplified unproblematized contexts in which these terms are often put to work. They demonstrate that the challenge is greater than initially perceived, as the rhetorical terms discussed in this volume may have independent validity within the cultural contexts in which they now operate, illuminating clearly the problem of establishing valid discursive boundaries at the global and local levels and from different disciplinary standpoints. Discussions in this volume point out the ways in which, although historically not grounded in localized constructs, some rhetorical terms may be used strategically and willingly vernacularized in unique ways to adapt to local institutions and meanings (cf. Merry 2006).

How groups use rhetoric to conceptualize themselves and their future is effectively demonstrated in the case studies discussed by Preucel and Pecos, as well as Lane, who present ways in which rhetorical terms that were initially imposed are now used strategically to ensure cultural survival. These strategic deployments highlight the complexity of the context in which these terms are debated, deconstructed, and even disarmed. They demonstrate that it is not a task as simple as denying these rhetorical terms validity, as they may have already taken root and been put to use in vernacularized ways. For example, as the AHD and subaltern discourses work together, it may become more difficult and artificial to separate them, pointing out a second level of complexity expressed in these debates—that is, a necessity to break away from the dichotomous thinking that has also been established in the positivist framework of the AHD, but also *about* the AHD.

HERITAGE BINARIES AND THE FUTURE OF DICHOTOMIZATION

The heritage discipline is plagued with dichotomies, as earlier calls for de-Westernization of the discipline resulted in what can now be perceived to be Orientalist notions of categorization. The emphasis on a divisive polarization has occurred equally to homogenize or destabilize the hegemony of the AHD. For example, in discussing the emergence of the idea of heritage, John Merryman (1986) has referred to "two ways of thinking about cultural property," a duality represented by cultural internationalism and cultural nationalism, originating in an eighteenth-century dispute about the respective merits of particularism and cosmopolitanism (Gillman 2010), but failing to consider how this would relate to the origins and establishment of non-AHD heritage traditions (Byrne 1991).

Locating heritage constructs in the context of Eastern vs. Western territories is a classic example of this challenge, as it is a practice that has drawn territorial boundaries that persist and become themselves common currency in heritage discourse and practice (see, for example, an early debate in Wei and Aass 1989). Karlström questions in this volume the robustness of these ideological territories, as well as other mapping exercises that aim to empower an 'us vs. them' platform for discussion. Likewise, Rodéhn aims to demonstrate the problematic effects of constructing a 'present,' 'past,' and 'future' as anything but a lived experience. Furthermore, while Bauer questions the usefulness of tried binaries surrounding a dichotomy of nationalism vs. internationalism, Cooper takes this point home by reminding us that heritage studies has been firmly located within a plethora of these type of binaries: national vs. local; expert vs. non-expert; univocal vs. multivocal, etc., in order to point out that heritage discourse and practice is not in fact monolithic and unchanging.

In a different approach to perceived dualities, a relatively recent debate of tangible and intangible heritage identified irreconcilable differences and presented this interrelationship as one having questionable sustainability. In this argument, Baillie and Chippindale (2007) question the incorporation of intangible heritage into existing heritage frameworks, rejecting the intersection of these categories, as they argued that to redefine heritage is to "lose the special defining character of the heritage as being concerned with physical remains" (2007: 176). Aligning their argument firmly within the AHD, they suggest that an inclusionary category would be "diffuse, unnecessary and analytically of no proven utility." In sharp contrast and resisting this statement, arguments in this volume encourage a view of dichotomization that is more transparently attached to agents and agendas, in order to reveal socially constructed categories put to use through expert knowledge. Moreover, they question our own authority in the exercise of categorization.

Moving beyond binaries is crucial for a redirection of the heritage work toward more counterhegemonic approaches, a view promoted by Baird in the conclusions to her chapter. Both Lane and Rodéhn independently propose the significance of nesting these vocabularies in temporal perspectives, to break away from dichotomous trends. And it is with this aim in mind that these chapters address heritage vocabularies inseparably from their historiography but avoid the promotion of consistency in categories used throughout the rise and development of these concepts over time. Authors consider how contextually these terms are operated in practice or, like Adams suggests, attached to local circumstances. The struggle is then to avoid locating arguments as being *anti-* or *pro*-AHD, in consideration of heritage practices that result from conveniently symbiotic approaches that originate from an appropriation of heritage vocabularies.

The caveat that follows, then, is that the chapters in this book reclaim selected terms, but only temporarily. It could be said that these terms are borrowed. The interconnectivity between rhetorical devices and current efforts to further shake the grounds on which they are constructed demonstrate that the use and further circulation of these terms can only advance toward further complexity. Inspired by postprocessual debates that were similarly accused of stalling dialogue, this volume embraces a non-dichotomous thinking much like the one proposed for archaeology when the field faced similar binary-oriented obstacles. Ian Hodder (1999: 200) encourages thinking in terms of "both/and" rather than "either/or," and acknowledging networks and flows rather than boundaries. It is a conversation across boundaries (Appiah 2006) espoused by cosmopolitans, who in this case examine practices of heritage construction and identity mediation that resist basic dualisms, such as national/international, and domestic/foreign (Meskell 2009).

Hence, in order to respond to requests to define a 'way forward,' discussions in this volume suggest a variety of ways that align with an embrace of reflexivity, contextuality, interactivity, and multivocality in order to create a continual process of interpretation and re-interpretation (Hodder 1999). Gabriel Moshenska (Chapter 12) calls for a taming of 'hyperinflated' meanings, arguing that agency needs to be put back into the empty rhetoric of memory in order to make the term meaningful. Likewise, McGill hopes that agency is made explicit, but in this case, in articulations of cultural diversity through education so that it may enable forms of resistance to heritage ideologies. The call for transparency in the creation and articulation of rhetorical terms also becomes clear in Zehbe's conclusions, which stress the ways that thought styles as proposed and articulated by experts exist and co-exist for heritage. Samuels also stresses throughout his chapter the importance of developing an awareness of how the choice of specific terms affects methodological approaches and interpretations. And Lane discusses competing definitions that operate as the breeding ground for different rhetorical strategies, enabling the articulation of modes of resistance and negotiations. There is, therefore, no single approach to critically engage with the rhetorical uses of heritage.

In the age of themed disciplinary handbooks and encyclopedic-styled volumes that present key concepts, offering definitions for use in heritage and other cultural studies, discussions in this volume aim to demonstrate that there is no point of reference to give definitions the authority that they are made to have. The variety of approaches to redescription stresses the fact that the way forward is, indeed, less chartered territory.

REFERENCES

Appiah, Kwame Anthony. 2006. *Cosmopolitanism: Ethics in a World of Strangers.* New York, NY: W.W. Norton.

Baillie, Britt, and Christopher Chippindale. 2007. "Tangible-Intangible Cultural Heritage: A Sustainable Dichotomy? The 7th Annual Cambridge Heritage Seminar, 13 May 2006. McDonald Institute for Archaeological Research, University of Cambridge, UK." *Conservation and Management of Archaeological Sites* 8: 174–76.

Byrne, Denis. 1991. "Western Hegemony in Archaeological Heritage Management." *History and Anthropology* 5 (2): 269–76. http://dx.doi.org/10.1080/02757206.1991.99 60815.

Gillman, Derek. 2010. *The Idea of Cultural Heritage.* Cambridge: Cambridge University Press.

Hodder, Ian. 1999. *The Archaeological Process: An Introduction.* Oxford: Blackwell.

Merry, Sally E. 2006. "Transnational Human Rights and Local Activism: Mapping the Middle." *American Anthropologist* 108 (1): 38–51. http://dx.doi.org/10.1525/aa .2006.108.1.38.

Merryman, John H. 1986. "Two Ways of Thinking about Cultural Property." *American Journal of International Law* 80 (4): 831–53. http://dx.doi.org/10.2307 /2202065.

Meskell, Lynn, ed. 2009. *Cosmopolitan Archaeologies.* Durham, NC: Duke University Press. http://dx.doi.org/10.1215/9780822392422.

Smith, Laurajane. 2006. *Uses of Heritage.* London: Routledge.

Wei, Chen, and Andreas Aass. 1989. "Heritage Conservation: East and West." *ICOMOS Information* 3: 3–8.

JEFFREY ADAMS is a heritage management scholar and instructional design consultant interested in the practical and theoretical dimensions of global heritage use who holds a Ph.D. from the University of Minnesota and master's degree from the University of Hawaii. His research has focused on archaeological heritage tourism development, heritage management theory, and underwater treasure salvage policy. Among his recent publications is a book chapter entitled "The Role of Underwater Archaeology in Framing and Facilitating the Chinese National Strategic Agenda" in the volume *Cultural Heritage Politics in China* (2013).

MELISSA F. BAIRD is Assistant Professor of Anthropology, Heritage and Environmental Policy at Michigan Tech University. As an environmental anthropologist, Melissa's research examines the nature of global heritage and environmental politics in non-Western contexts. Her work centers on the ecological, political, and social impacts of resource extraction and traces how multinational corporations, the State, private sector, heritage experts, and other decision makers draw on the rhetoric of heritage, rights, and sustainability in environmental decisions and management.

ALEXANDER A. BAUER is an archaeologist whose research foci are the archaeology of the Near East and Eurasia, ancient trade, archaeological method and theory, archaeological ethics, and cultural heritage law and policy. He is currently Associate Professor of Anthropology at Queens College and the Graduate Center of the City University of

New York and, since 2005, has served as the Editor (in Chief) of the *International Journal of Cultural Property*, an interdisciplinary journal on cultural heritage law and policy. He is also the co-editor of *New Directions in Museum Ethics* (2012) with Janet Marstine and Chelsea Haines.

MALCOLM A. COOPER is Honorary Research Fellow in the School of History, Classics and Archaeology at the University of Edinburgh, researching Gerard Baldwin Brown and the Conservation Movement in Britain. Prior to this, he was the Chief Inspector at Historic Scotland, having previously held a number of senior positions with English Heritage. He is a Fellow of the Society of Antiquaries of London and the Society of Antiquaries of Scotland, and an Honorary Fellow of the Royal Incorporation of Architects in Scotland. He is a member of the Chartered Institute of Management, the Institute of Historic Building Conservation, and the Institute for Archaeologists.

ANNA KARLSTRÖM is Lecturer in Heritage Studies at Uppsala University, Department of Art History. Her research examines 'heritagization' processes, relations between heritage and the sacred, contemporary perspectives on archaeology, and Southeast Asian and Australian indigeneity. Her Ph.D. thesis resulted in the book *Preserving Impermanence: The Creation of Heritage in Vientiane, Laos* (2009).

KATHRYN LAFRENZ SAMUELS is Assistant Professor of Anthropology at the University of Maryland whose research examines cultural heritage in the transnational sphere in the ambit of international economic development, democracy building, human rights, and global climate change. She is co-editor of *Cultures of Contact: Archaeology, Ethics, and Globalization* (2007) with Sebastian De Vivo and Darian Totten, and *Making Roman Places: Past and Present* (2012) with Darian Totten.

PAUL J. LANE is Professor of Global Archaeology at Uppsala University and Honorary Research Fellow in the School of Geography, Archaeology, and Environmental Studies, University of the Witwatersrand. His research interests include the transition to farming in eastern and southern Africa, landscape historical ecology, the archaeology of pastoralism, the archaeological manifestations of enslavement, and the role of ethnographic analogy in archaeological interpretation. He is co-editor of the 2013 *Oxford Handbook of African Archaeology*.

ALICIA EBBITT MCGILL is Assistant Professor in the Department of History at North Carolina State University, where she contributes to the graduate program in Public History. Her research in Belize focuses on how constructions of heritage are promoted through public venues (e.g. tourism, education, archaeological practice) and shape the cultural production of young citizens, including how messages about the past are interpreted and negotiated by teachers and youths as they navigate contemporary racial and ethnic politics.

GABRIEL MOSHENSKA is Lecturer in Public Archaeology at University College London, Institute of Archaeology. His research interests include the history of archaeology, material cultures of childhood, the archaeology of the Second World War, Egyptian mummies in European cultural history, and the early reception of Milton's theological writings.

REGIS PECOS is Co-Director of the Santa Fe Indian School Leadership Institute and Chief of Staff to the New Mexico Speaker of the House. He received his undergraduate degree in History from Princeton University, where he recently finished a term as Trustee for the University, and completed his graduate work at the University of California at Berkeley. He served as both Lt. Governor and Governor and is a lifetime member of the Tribal Council at Cochiti Pueblo. Regis served for sixteen years as Executive Director of the New Mexico Office of Indian Affairs under four administrations.

ROBERT PREUCEL is Director of the Haffenreffer Museum of Anthropology and Professor of Anthropology at Brown University. Trained as an anthropological archaeologist, he is particularly interested in the relationships of archaeology and society. His fieldwork projects include the archaeology of a utopian community in Massachusetts (the Brook Farm Project) and a post Pueblo Revolt community in New Mexico (the Kotyiti Research Project).

TRINIDAD RICO is Assistant Professor of Anthropology at Texas A&M Qatar. She holds a Ph.D. in Anthropology from Stanford University and an M.A. in Principles of Conservation from University College London. Her broad research interests include critical heritage theory, the construction of risk and expertise, and the mobilization of Islamic values in cultural heritage. She is co-editor of *Cultural Heritage in the Arabian Peninsula: Debates, Discourses, and Practices* (2014) with Karen Exell. Her forthcoming book is *Constructing Destruction: Heritage Narratives of the Tsunami City*.

CECILIA RODÉHN is Postdoctoral Researcher and Senior Lecturer at the Centre for Gender Research at Uppsala University, Sweden. She received her doctoral degree in Museum Studies from the University of Kwazulu-Natal South Africa, focusing on the transition of South African museum from apartheid to democracy. Rodéhn has also taught master courses in museum and heritage studies at Uppsala University. Her main research interest concerns issues related to democratization of heritage as well as museum education.

JOSHUA SAMUELS is Clinical Assistant Professor at The Catholic University of America. He earned his Ph.D. in 2013 from Stanford University, where he conducted an archaeology of land reform in Sicily under Fascism, and an M.Sc. in Archaeomaterials from the University of Sheffield in 2004. His current research interests include spatial analysis, archaeological approaches to the recent past, heritage ethics, and post-conflict reconstruction.

SIGRID VAN DER AUWERA works as Postdoctoral Researcher at the University of Antwerp and the KULeuven. In 2012, she earned her Ph.D. on the protection of cultural property in the event of armed conflict. Currently, her research mainly focuses on international heritage policies (UNESCO, Council of Europe), socio-economic impacts of heritage, and civil society involvement in the field of heritage.

KLAUS ZEHBE worked as a research assistant at the UNESCO Chair in Heritage Studies at Brandenburgische Technische Universität Cottbus, Germany, before taking up his current position as a lecturer in the Department of Education Studies at Technische Universität Dortmund, Germany. He is a doctoral candidate at Freie Universität Berlin, writing on education processes in traditional Japanese performing arts. His research interests include theories of culture and heritage as well as the anthropology of education and performance.

Maasai Mara, cultural villages in, 270–71
Machu Picchu, 131
Madin, John, Birmingham Central Library, 171
Mafia, and Fascist land reform, 115
Malinowski, Bronislaw, 14
mandalas, creation of, 38–*39*
manyattas, 261, *278*; tourism and, 267–73
Maori, 233; cultural landscapes, 211–12
Marchisotto, Linda, on endangered cultural heritage, 149–50
marginalized groups, and democracy, 101, *102*
market nations, antiquities trafficking, 88
Martin, Willie, 229
material heritage, 188
material past, 31; ritual performance and empowerment of objects, 34–35
Maxwell Museum of Anthropology, 231
Maya, 65; in Belize, 69, 71–72, 75
medicine, brain death in, 184–87
memory, 20, 55, 197–98, 224, 291; collective, 199–200; individual and collective, 202–3; processes of, 204–5; rhetoric of, 273–75; use of term, 201–2
memory studies, 199, 202–3; agency, 203–4
MENA. *See* Middle East and North Africa region
merit-making, in Laotian Buddhism, 32, 40
Merryman, John Henry, 289; on cultural internationalism and nationalism, 82, 84–85
Meskell, Lynn, 247
Metropolitan Museum of Art (New York), 81; and Italy, 81, 89–90
Middle East and North Africa (MENA) region, World Bank development, 246
Middle Rio Grande Conservancy District, 227
mining, 208, 214
Ministry of Culture (Sicily), 90
Ministry of Information and Culture Heritage Department (Laos), 33–34, 35
Ministry of Natural Resources and Tourism (Tanzania), 269
Ministry of Tourism (Belize), 73–74
Minneapolis Institute of Arts, 90
Missions and Evaluation Reports (ICOMOS), 150
Mkomazi Game Reserve, pastoralists on, 209–10

"Model of LDC Tourism Development Inequality," 132
modernity, 117; heritage and, 156, 276; and tradition, 276–78
Mohenjo-daro, 138
monuments, 86, 200
moral rights legislation, 85
Morgantina, 81
Morioka, Masahiro, 182; *Brain Dead Person*, 192–93
Mostar Bridge (Bosnia-Herzegovina), rebuilding, 57
murals, destruction of, 32
Museum of Fine Arts (Boston), 81
Museum of New Mexico, Cochiti Dam and Reservoir, 230
museums, 51, 90; collecting, 81–82, 83; democratization of, 17, 95, 97, 99–100, 101–2, 104; purpose of, 98–99
mutualism, ecological, 265

NAGPRA. *See* Native American Graves Protection and Repatriation Act
Nara Document (ICOMOS), 29–30
National Cultural Policy (Belize), 73
national identity, 66; enculturation into, 68, 69–70
nationalism, 55, 105; cultural, 55, 66–67, 84, 88–89; heritage and, 188–89; and imagined communities, 14, 69–70; vs. internationalism, 82–83, 289, 290
National Library (Iraq), 54
National Museum (Iraq), looting, 54
National Museum of Florence, 90
National Museum of Naples, 90
National Parks Act (New Zealand), 212
National Park Service, Cochiti Dam and Reservoir, 230–31
National Social Research Organization (Belize), 69
National Solidarity Fund (*Fonds National de Solidarité*; 26:26), 249
nation-building, 68; imagined community of, 69–70
nation-states, as political community, 250
Native American Graves Protection and Repatriation Act (NAGPRA), 86, 87, 89, 91, 231–32
Native American Trust, 229

social structure, inequality in, 134–35
Social Studies Bowl (Belize), 75
Society for American Archaeology, *Code of Ethics*, 87
Society for the Preservation of Afghan's Cultural Heritage (SPACH), 56
Society for the Protection of Ancient Buildings (SPAB), 174, 189
source nations, 85
South Africa, 112, 211; museum practice in, 97, 101–2
South Asia, traditional medical knowledge, 215
Southeast Asia, popular religion in, 9, 31–32
SPAB. *See* Society for the Protection of Ancient Buildings
space, socialized, 223
SPACH. *See* Society for the Preservation of Afghan's Cultural Heritage
spiritual power: maintenance of, 36–37, 41–42
staff, heritage organizations, 176–77
stakeholders, 288; environmental preservation, 212–13; heritage ecologies, 210–11
state, in heritage management, 165–67
State Board of Antiquities and Heritage (Iraq), 57
statues, spiritual power of, 41–42
Steen, Charlie, 230
Stefano, Michele di, 120
stewardship, 14, 87, 288; environmental, 212–13
Stichting Nederlandse Vrijwilligers (SNV), heritage tourism, 268–70
stone lion, Cochiti, 231
storytelling, rhetoric of nature, 210
students, as cultural agents, 74
stupas, care for, 39, *40*, 42, 152
style, rhetoric of, 265–66
Suina, Joseph, 228, 234
sustainability, 9, 208, 211, 213, 269(table), 278, 288; archaeological tourism, 130–32; heritage, 262–63; heritage management, 252–53; socioeconomic, 129–30; wildlife and biodiversity conservation, 259–60; of World Heritage sites, 171–72
sustainable management, 133–34
Switzerland, antiquities trafficking, 88
symbolism, Fascist Sicilian, *121–22*

Taliban, Bamiyan Buddhas and, 82, 85
Tanzania, 208, 262; cultural tourism in, 269–70; pastoralists in, 209–10, 261; tourism in, 267(table), 274–75
TCHP. *See* Tunisia Cultural Heritage Project
teachers: in Belize, 69, 70; as cultural agents, 74–75
temples: care for, 39–40; restoration of, 32–34, *39–41*
terra nullius, 211, 243, 250
territorialization, 55
Tetilla Peak Recreation Area, 230
Thailand, 31, 152
Theravada Buddhism, 34
thought style, 15; brain death as, 182–83, 184–87
threats, 154; identifying, 150–51
Threats to World Heritage Sites 1994–2004 (ICOMOS), 150
Tibetan Buddhism, sand *mandalas* in, 38–38
Tilapia Fest (Crooked Tree), 75
time: heritage and, 156; scholarly construction of, 97–98
Tito, Josip Broz, death of, 55
TMK. *See* traditional medical knowledge
Tokeley-Parry, Jonathan, 88
Tongariro National Park, 211–12
tour guides, education in, 73–74
tourism, 17, 135; authenticity and, 30–31; in Belize, 72, 73–74; cultural, 248, 268–74; East African pastoralists and, 261, 264–73; heritage, 268–70; local economy and, 132–33; reconciliation, 137–39; slow, 119–20; sustainable archaeological, 130–32; in Tunisia, 243–44, 245–46, 254–55
tourism industry, images in, 9, 275–76
tradition, 190; and modernity, 276–78
traditional medical knowledge (TMK), 215
tragedy of the commons, 277
Training Modules in Tourism, 73
trauma, concept of, 202
tree trunk, as empowered object, 35–*36*
Tribal-Voice, 271
True, Marion, 81, 88
Tunisia: authoritarian regime in, 248–49; heritage development in, 17, 245–46, 249–53; post-revolution development, 254–55; tourism in, 243–44